T0162345

COLD WAR POETRY

COLD WAR POETRY

Edward Brunner

UNIVERSITY OF ILLINOIS PRESS

URBANA AND CHICAGO

Library of Congress Cataloging-in-Publication Data
Brunner, Edward, 1946–
Cold War poetry / Edward Brunner.
p. cm.
Includes bibliographical references (p.) and index.
ISBN 0-252-02592-X (alk. paper)
1. American poetry—20th century—History and criticism.
2. Cold War in literature. I. Title.
PS310.C6B78   2001
811'.5409358—dc21   00-008405

C 5 4 3 2 1

To Jane and Anna

Contents

Preface

The majority of poems written in America in the 1950s have long been deemed inconsequential. At the end of the decade, Robert Lowell produced *Life Studies* (1959), but that publication broke an eight-year silence during which he had published only a handful of poems. To literary historians, Lowell's silence came to seem indicative of a turn in the postwar era defined by a quietism that had overtaken even him. For poetry that was seriously engaged with important issues, the times were just not congenial. Only poets who had been driven underground were capable of producing interesting work. It took a regional press (San Francisco's City Lights) to support Allen Ginsberg's "Howl" (1957); Charles Olson and Robert Creeley self-published in the *Black Mountain Review* or with Cid Corman's *Origin*. To New York publishers, these publications were simply invisible. Virtually all of the poets whom Mark Doty found worthy of discussion in his chapter on the 1950s in *A Profile of Twentieth Century American Poetry* (1990) were outsiders in their time, like John Ashbery and Frank O'Hara, who received support from nonliterary subcultures. For Doty, the melancholy verse of Weldon Kees ("Outside white houses yellow in the sunlight") perfectly represented this hollow decade; that Kees had vanished in 1955 seemed an appropriate, perhaps even inevitable, gesture.

What this has meant for poetry, however, is that while literary historians and scholars have told us a great deal about the mavericks and renegades, about Ginsberg and Olson, O'Hara and Ashbery, who defined themselves against the center, we know next to nothing about the poets who constituted that "center." Or more precisely, what little we know of that center we know through the eyes of its fiercest opponents. The mainstream poets who successfully survived in their own time, who achieved broad institutional support, who produced the verse that was being published in the *Kenyon Review* and the *Hudson Review,* in *Poetry* and the *Atlantic Monthly,* in the *New Yorker* and the *New Republic,* now circulate in literary histories—if indeed they circulate at all—as the very type of literary disvalue. Did mainstream poets typically arrive at their college offices by 8 A.M., men outfitted in white shirts and bow ties, women decked out in heels and hose, to type Petrarchan sonnets to Eisenhower? No one believes that, and yet the majority of poetry in this era has been regularly described in terms that are no less cartoonish.

While the view of the 1950s as a period of unprecedented placidity has long been contested by cultural historians, this study challenges that simplification on a series of related fronts that pertain to the mainstream poetry that was widely published in America from 1945 to 1960. A prologue considers the formal properties of the so-called fifties poem—verse that was metrically regular, organized by stanza, and usually in rhyme—as part of a poetic project to signal the competency of a profession newly awarded disciplinary status within the university. Charged with helping to quarantine a mass culture that other intellectuals viewed as out of control, poets found themselves situated between two contradictory roles. On the one hand, they were ready to professionalize themselves by producing work that illustrated the high standards of a venerable literary tradition; on the other hand, they were charged with luring members of an audience new to the university (and new to poetry) away from leisure topics that were no more than vapid distractions. This impossible set of demands begins to explain the aesthetics of the "fifties poem" not as a lapse from some high modernist standard of experimentalism but as a time-bound construction burdened with a complex agenda.

No one negotiated that poetry as gracefully as Richard Wilbur. His quintessential achievement chapter 1 considers as the ability to accommodate a new postwar audience that was male, newly educated, and upwardly mobile—an audience that expected poetry to entertain them, instruct them, and convince them of their importance. As newly arrived members to their social class, many in this audience also wanted assurance that they could master authentic high culture; a poem had to have an intellectual edge, a manner that was reassuringly "difficult" without losing its accessibility. The academic verse that Wilbur developed in response to these demands valued intelligence, presented itself in a compressed fashion that was both efficient and elegant (an aid to the consumer beleaguered by lack of time as well as a mark of the skilled performer's quality labor), and honored the value of observing everyday events.

The poet as professional was on grand display in the two most influential anthologies of the early 1950s, John Ciardi's *Mid-Century American Poets* (1950) and George P. Elliott's *Fifteen Modern American Poets* (1956). Anthologies so similar—ten of the fifteen poets in Ciardi make a repeat appearance in Elliott—but six years apart are invaluable as documents tracking subtle undercurrents of change. As chapter 2 attests, though both settings continued to promote a poetry marked by its air of professionalization, what appear to be virtually interchangeable representations of the "fifties poem" have in fact been modulated in significant ways. Elliott, assembling a classroom anthology for a younger generation more familiar with the Korean war than with World War II, discerned another set of positions within the works of virtually the same poets. Elliott's alternative texts eliminated the elegiac strain in postwar poetry that was so important to Ciardi's anthology and substituted texts that suggested that the condition of war was deeply enmeshed in American culture. World War II as a defining instance has been replaced by the cold war as a perpetual condition. For Elliott, poetry helps condition us to the notion of warfare as a chronic malady, a state not to be altered, only accepted. Elliott's poets have lost what Ciardi's poets glorified in: a conviction of their own capability as agents of change.

For some poets, though, it was unlikely they could participate as satisfactory players. Chapter 3 examines the book review process as a means for constructing a "neutral" poetic language that, while it may have been designed to establish clear-cut standards for writing as a citizen-poet, in practice exercised a domination that quelled the emergence of any dissenting style. Since even the hint of a poetry that suggested a gay male lifestyle was subject to abrupt dismissal, it was left for poetry by women to become that which was targeted in the book review process as the central example of how-not-to-write-a-poem. An ongoing but one-sided monologue developed in which book reviews of female poets by male poets sidelined the female poets as effective players. In effect, by perennially addressing the work of female poets in a set of approaches that were repeated from poet to poet, male reviewers virtually evoked a composite portrait of the woman poet. Though the portrait could be broadly applied to Jean Garrigue, regarded in the 1950s as a writer both scandalously improper and yet acceptably "feminine," it could not be construed as helpful when applied to others. Because poetry by women in the 1950s was widely dismissed as undisciplined, disorganized, and inconsequential, the existence of a body of work by women writing with an innovative intent, in politically engaged voices, as trenchant commentators on race, class, and gender relations, has been forgotten. With the poetry of Rosalie Moore, longtime member of the San Francisco-based "Activists," and V. R. Lang, avant-garde playwright and close friend of Frank O'Hara, tragically dead at thirty-two of Hodgkin's disease, and the once-acclaimed but now forgotten Katherine Hoskins, chapter 4 recovers some of the range and diversity of poetry that women wrote in the 1950s.

No poetry from the years of high modernism (1915–30) enjoyed greater prestige in the postwar period than the long poem—the symphonic epic, subject of dozens of analytic articles. The subversive potential of its experimental discourse required handling with care if updated versions of it were to succeed in the far more constrained atmosphere of the times. John Berryman's much-applauded variant on the high modernist long poem form, *Homage to Mistress Bradstreet* (1953), must be regarded as a period piece, for it depends on a concept of the feminine as undisciplined and "naturally" excessive. By the end of the poem, as Bradstreet gracefully retreated to her rightful role as a homemaker, Berryman's version of the long poem was also promulgating a much-narrowed version of public space. Chapter 5 offers for renewed inspection other poets whose sense of the public space of the long poem was at odds with Berryman's example, notably Melvin Tolson (*Libretto for the Republic of Liberia* [1953]) and Hyam Plutzik (*Horatio* [1961]). Though these long poems are remarkably different, both gain their meaning when considered as bodies of work that address a crisis involving the diminishment of public space. Tolson's scope is vast enough, since his *Libretto* takes as its area of interest all of the postwar world, reconstructed from a perspective in Africa. But the pressure on an undertaking of such sweep is measured in the ingenuity to which Tolson must resort by using footnotes to convey powerful aspects of his overall argument. The future of public discourse is in question with Tolson, just as it is the true subject of Hyam Plutzik's *Horatio,* a poem masquerading as a sequel to the events in *Hamlet* but in fact exploring the failure of an intellectual and ruling class to find the courage to guide controversial historical and cultural discussions.

If some kinds of poetry (work by women, long poems by African Americans) proved to be strangely invisible, other kinds were nearly inescapable—like the sestina, a form that proliferated at the midpoint of the decade. While the sheer intricacy of the sestina's rules may suggest that poets in the 1950s have begun to feel comfortable communicating within circumstances that would by any standard appear to be outrageous, even arcane, chapter 6 argues that a better understanding is that poets obtain from the sestina—once its punishing requirements have been complied with—the permission to use the interior space of the poem as their very own, even in deeply personal ways. That poets feel they can only speak intimately after going to such lengths reveals the fractures below the placid surface of the well-made poem, otherwise so reassuringly on display in examples like the sestina. But sestinas by a range of poets—from Sylvia Plath to Jane Cooper, from James Merrill to Isabella Gardner, from Weldon Kees to Donald Justice—register not the satisfaction of completing craftsmanship with pleasure but the need to surround the private voice with defenses that will fiercely guard it. The flourishing of the sestina in the mid- and late 1950s is by no means simply an affirmation of sophisticated poetic skill.

The crisis implicit in the sestina's popularity—a poem may need secret corridors before serious communication can take place—is developed further in the final two chapters which trace the poetry written about the Bomb through the postwar period. Initially poets writing in 1946 and 1947 addressed the Bomb without self-consciousness, categorizing it like an example of the outrages visited upon civilians in wartime. But chapter 7 shows that as the Bomb's destructive potential grew, especially after 1948 when the implications of radioactivity became known to a wide public, poets began to register a new sense of cosmic disorder in writings that themselves featured a radically distorted language. By the 1950s, however, sanctions levied against those questioning government policy drove poets to resort to subterfuge to continue their critique. The pages of the distinguished but short-lived *California Quarterly* (1951–54) find leftist poets such as Edwin Rolfe and Don Gordon borrowing devices from formula genres like *film noir* to organize a critique of public policy that was itself expressed in an undercover manner to which it simultaneously objected. As the Bomb pervaded public life, protest against it became more cryptic, until it was the silence of those who refused to speak against the Bomb that came under indictment.

Chapter 8 tracks the fading trail of the Bomb poem deep into the middle of the McCarthyized fifties where even vestiges of its existence escape sure confirmation. Here are poems which may or may not pertain to the Bomb, poems in which the Bomb's sudden appearance has a radically defamiliarizing effect, and poems in which the Bomb, mentioned obliquely, targets a child or children. The appearance of the child as representative victim, while hardly new to poetry of protest, suggests a link between the disappearance of Bomb poems and the frequency of a specific sort of domestic verse suddenly popular in the mid-1950s in which the child is at the center. None of these domestic poems mention the Bomb; all are apparently apolitical. But poetic discourse about the Bomb may face in a new direction as the decade passes its midpoint. To read this new variant of domestic verse as a depoliticized "reply" to the Bomb is to recognize how deep is the despair surrounding those who sense the futility of hoping to alter governmental policies. Here is a secret poetry of protest mixed with despair. Defying the political situation but refusing to bring direct politics into play, this is a poetry that is, below its amiable surface, a discourse of alienation, disgust, and sorrow that insists, helplessly, on the primacy of the individual and the family over the state.

Darkly recontextualized, the domestic verse of the 1950s suggests the beginning of a new discursive formation, one which rearticulates the position of the responsible citizen, as earlier developed by Wilbur and placed on display by Ciardi, by shifting the primary allegiance of the poet from the state to the family. While mainstream poetry of the late 1940s and early 1950s quickly envisioned the poem as a site from which messages of responsibility and social unity addressed to wide numbers could be launched in a commanding fashion, the poetry of the late 1950s and early 1960s has begun to conceive of the poem as a sheltering space, an area whose quality makes its widespread appeal unlikely, a place from which the voice that emerges will be intimate and familiar. Texts that identify the family as the most sensitive register of social change also display an affinity with the foundational precepts of confessional verse. When confessional verse appeared at the end of the decade it was widely regarded as a break from the academic verse of the 1950s, but if a domestic verse that envisions family members as under siege from the state vies with an academic verse that is intent upon affirming the social unity of the state, then confessional verse may be less a breakaway text than a focusing of concerns that the decade has been struggling to articulate.

Nostalgia for the 1950s seems perennially to return, based on the time as one of innocence and naiveté. It can be regarded as a toy decade, an era when fools were in charge, whether in politics or elsewhere, and when the only honorable response was to go underground. But these poets of survival suggest that a more conflicted response is appropriate for the era. By examining such phenomena of the period as the "popular" academic poet, the power of the anthology to direct canon formation, the one-sided authority of the book review process, the ostracizing of female and minority poets, the fad of the sestina, and the tactics employed to construct a political verse in an apolitical time, this study rediscovers the 1950s as a difficult transitional period between the self-consciously populist poetry of the 1930s and 1940s and the sophisticated breakthrough poetry of the 1960s. While no apology for the 1950s, it is designed to complicate any simplistic view of its mainstream poets as political *naifs,* conservative anticommunists, and elitists. Eliciting the interplay between a discourse of discipline and a counter-discourse of dissent, it unearths the social text in the "fifties poem."

Acknowledgments

Not everyone was quick to warm to the idea of a study on the fifties poem (one colleague, predicting ruin, urged me to write on anything *but* this topic). Some who were especially helpful both early and late were Carolyn Brown, Charles O. Hartman, Stephen Holmes, Cary Nelson, Sherman Paul, and Richard Peterson. I hope this study repays their interest.

The detailed examples in chapter 3 are due in part to the sharp eyes of Gaynell Gavin, my research assistant for three weeks in the summer of 1994, for which I thank the English Department at Southern Illinois University at Carbondale. Richard Wilbur graciously granted me permission to reprint both "Tears for the Rich" and "We" in their entirety, two poems that I hope he will include in an expanded Collected Works. For allowing me to reprint in its entirety Jean Garrigue's "Setpiece for Albany," I am grateful to Aileen Ward, literary executor of Ms. Garrigue's estate. I am pleased that Rosalie Moore extended permission to reprint two of her poems in their entirety, and I am grateful to John Hart for providing me with invaluable information about the Activists. Jack Grant loaned me his copy of the privately printed 1959 edition of Alison Lurie's memoir of V. R. Lang and provided incomparable insights into the milieu of the Cambridge Poets' Theater. In a telephone conversation and in correspondence, Peter Davison offered similar glimpses. My gratitude is extended to Sayre Sheldon for allowing me to reprint examples of the poetry of her sister-in-law, V. R. Lang, and my thanks go to Alison Lurie for her helpful advice. I am pleased that Tanya Plutzik offered permission to quote so extensively from the writings of her husband, Hyam Plutzik. I am indebted to Jane Cooper for the interest she took in arranging the reprinting of the full text of

"Morning on the St. John's." Fred Whitehead's unpublished introduction to the collected poems of Don Gordon helped direct my understanding of what Gordon hoped to accomplish. Cary Nelson's suggestion that I annotate a long poem by Melvin B. Tolson led to a fuller understanding of the role of the long poem in the postwar years.

I am grateful to Robert McCown of the Special Collections of the University of Iowa library for answering questions about the papers there on the Writers' Workshop and the poetry of Paul Engle, and I owe thanks to Huah-ling Engle for permitting me to reprint a poem by Paul Engle in its entirety. Steven Huff of BOA editions helpfully extended permission to reprint a poem by Isabella Gardner in its entirety. For information about Robert Shelley, I am grateful to Ed Folsom for obtaining a copy of Shelley's application to the University of Iowa, to the late Carl Hartman for recalling Shelley's work as an editorial assistant on the *Western Review,* and to Robert Dana and Donald Justice for their memories of the early years of the Writers' Workshop. Iris Snyder of Special Collections in the University of Delaware was one of a number of librarians who gave precise and thorough answers to my questions; I would also extend thanks for similar services to Donna Anstey and Richard Miller of the Yale University Press.

I've come to understand a great deal about how poets reconceive a form like the sestina by listening to the conversations of Lucia Maria Perillo, Allison Joseph, Jon Tribble, and Rodney Jones. Paula Bennett encouraged the readings of poetry by women in chapter 4, by example and by precept. For innumerable useful suggestions, for shrewd counsel about organizational matters, for all-around general support, and for aid in identifying the proliferation of *noir* well beyond the cinematic, I am deeply indebted to Paula Geyh. Elizabeth Klaver, Clem Hawes, Robert Fox, and John Howell have helped answer questions I put before them; some of the good ideas in this study bear the mark of their intelligence, for which I am thankful indeed. My understanding of what is at stake in poetry was enhanced by working alongside Donna M. Allego, whose high standards for scholarly research were models for me to follow. The illuminating differences between the discipline of poetry and the art of scholarship have been brought home to me quite sharply on those occasions when I had to referee discussions and disagreements over the use and value of poetry as perceived by young writers and scholars; let me mention in particular the acuity of Paul Guest, Steve Long, Harry Newburn, Terry Oleson, and Bryan Salmons.

Ann Lowry has once again made the arduous task of shepherding a book from manuscript through typescript to published volume into a painless one, at least from my point of view; I also want to thank Terry Sears for her infallible guidance. Pat Hollahan's careful, detailed copyediting improved every page. Walter Kalaidjian offered shrewd commentary that I was grateful to receive. The contributions of Jane Cogie, along with the omnipresence of Anna Brunner, are embedded indelibly in every page; I could begin the delightful task of acknowledging them, but I don't know how or when I could leave off.

❖❖❖

Excerpts from "The Dispossessed," "Sonnets to Chris," *Homage to Mistress Bradstreet,* and "A Sympathy, A Welcome" from *Collected Poems, 1937–1971* by John Berryman. Copyright © 1989 by Kate Donahue Berryman. Reprinted by permission of Farrar, Straus & Giroux LLC and Faber & Faber.

"Morning on the St. John's," copyright © 1969 by Jane Cooper, from *The Flashboat: Poems Collected and Reclaimed* by Jane Cooper. Reprinted by permission of W. W. Norton & Company, Inc.

"Sonnet IX" from *American Child,* copyright 1956 by Paul Engle and reprinted by permission of Huah-ling Neih Engle.

"Children Are Game" and excerpts from "The Music Room," copyright © 1990 by The Estate of Isabella Gardner. Reprinted from *Isabella Gardner: The Collected Poems* with the permission of BOA Editions, Ltd.

"Setpiece for Albany," copyright 1953 by Jean Garrigue and reprinted by permission of Aileen Ward, Executrix of the Estate of Jean Garrigue.

"Understanding," "After the Late Lynching," "Guilt," and excerpts from "An Evening of Death," "Temple," "How Generous!" and "A Way of Being" reprinted with the permission of Scribners, a Division of Simon & Schuster Inc., from *Excursions: New and Selected Poems* by Katherine Hoskins. Copyright © 1966 Katherine Hoskins.

Excerpts from *Montage of a Dream Deferred,* from *Collected Poems* by Langston Hughes, copyright © 1994 by the Estate of Langston Hughes. Reprinted by permission of Alfred A. Knopf, Inc., and Harold Ober Associates.

"Tears for the Rich," "We," copyright 1948 by Richard Wilbur and reprinted with the permission of Richard Wilbur. Excerpts from "First Snow in Alsace" in *The Beautiful Changes and Other Poems,* copyright 1947 and renewed 1975 by Richard Wilbur, reprinted by permission of Harcourt, Inc. Excerpts from "A World without Objects Is a Sensible Emptiness" and "The Death of a Toad" in *Ceremony and Other Poems* copyright 1950 and renewed 1978 by Richard Wilbur, reprinted by permission of Harcourt, Inc. Excerpts from "At Year's End" in *Ceremony and Other Poems,* copyright 1949 and renewed 1977 by Richard Wilbur, reprinted by permission of Harcourt, Inc. Excerpts from "Mind," "Statues," and "Love Calls Us to the Things of This World" in *Things of This World,* copyright © 1956 and renewed 1984 by Richard Wilbur, reprinted by permission of Harcourt, Inc.

Excerpts from "Mutterings over the Crib of a Deaf Child" from *Collected Poems,* copyright © 1971 by James Wright, Wesleyan University Press by permission of University Press of New England.

COLD WAR POETRY

Prologue: A Cultural Horizon for the "Fifties Poem"

> Yet high culture, which in the civilized past has always functioned on the basis of sharp class distinctions, is endangered—at least for the time being—by this sweeping process which, by wiping out social distinctions between the more or less cultivated, renders standards of art and thought provisional. . . . It becomes increasingly difficult to tell who is serious and who is not.
>
> —Clement Greenberg, "Present Prospects"

No other crisis so thoroughly engaged intellectuals in the years immediately following World War II as the unprecedented growth of mass culture. So timely was this issue, as Robert von Hallberg among others has recognized, that it seemed "as if the fate of western civilization were hanging in the balance" (194).[1] The quarantining of mass culture, while it engaged the attention of all intellectuals, was especially important for poets, who were among the newest members to achieve disciplinary status within the university. While a handful of extremely well known writers had served in unofficial or adjunct positions in major Ivy League universities beginning in the 1920s (and while no college or university too actively discouraged its faculty from publishing fiction or verse), the existence of the "creative writer" in the university as a professional class was a postwar phenomena, fostered by the proliferation of graduates from new "writing workshops" at such state institutions as the University of Iowa and the University of Washington. These new young poet-professors, with their anomalous backgrounds, whose teaching schedules would almost certainly include courses in the literature of modernism—Eliot, Pound, Joyce, Faulkner—

were as controversial as the New Criticism that was at the height of its powerful battle with the forces of traditional scholarship.[2] The mass culture crisis was, for such poet-professors, a rite of passage. Would they rise to the occasion and function as serious members of the intellectual community, bringing standards of discipline to bear? Or would they revert to the posturing of bohemia, turning their back on responsibility? While no one who was watching the crisis and wondering about the outcome went so far as to demand that these new poet-professors must win over large audiences, the expectation was that their poetry must help posit decisive alternatives. Rewards were high for success. Poets would not only attain a broader audience, they would also allay the doubts of those who were still questioning whether the poet had a place within the university.

As defined in the postwar years, mass culture was different from the innocence of an older "folk culture" that was venerated in the 1930s and the brashness of the "popular culture" of jazz and comic strips that was celebrated in the 1920s: it was construed as a domestic counterpart to the totalitarianism that needed to be kept outside national borders. "At its worse, mass culture threatens not merely to cretinize our taste, but to brutalize our senses while paving the way to totalitarianism" (9), wrote Bernard Rosenberg, coeditor with David Manning White of a 1957 anthology of essays entitled *Mass Culture: The Popular Arts in America*. The threat was figured in two decidedly contradictory ways that together only increased its mystery and its danger. On the one hand, mass culture was held in disdain, as beneath anyone's interest and negligible in every way, with a content that was childish and trivial. On the other hand, it was regarded with alarm, as possessing an ability to insinuate itself into the mind, as though it could operate under a number of beguiling disguises. These contradictory views of mass culture only served to promote a sense of crisis, a vision of the popular arts extending far beyond previous boundaries, embarked upon unbridled expansion.[3] If the content remained childlike or "feminine," violent or dreamy, it was marketed now by a shrewd and conniving masculine mind. Murray Hausknaucht, in an essay commissioned for Rosenberg and White's anthology, began by presenting "a symbol of the main drift of contemporary society": the "technician whose job it is to hide a small microphone in the bosoms of women who appear on the [*Person to Person* TV] show so that they may be heard without the technical apparatus being visible" (375). This wonderful example manages to present itself as an instance of the invasive and the secretive at the same time, and to complain that TV is both too assertive and too submissive. Though it invades—the technician who plants the microphone has been permitted extraordinary access to an area of the female body that the 1950s found especially erotic—it situates nothing and brings back no information from that private spot or privileged site. Like TV, this microphone goes far into territory that had once been sheltered, yet it introduces (and brings back) only emptiness. This meaningless amplification is demonized as both voyeuristic *and* alienating.

What helped escalate crisis into panic was the growing conviction that the thirty-hour workweek would soon be available to all. At the Center for Leisure Studies at the University of Chicago, David Riesman and his colleagues pondered in *The Lonely Crowd* (1950) how citizens from all walks of life in unprecedented numbers who were newly gifted with time would react to their freedom. Commenting on the ubiquity of the mass media in *Small Town and Mass Society* (1958), a sociological profile of a village in upper New York State, Arthur Vidich and Joseph Bensman reported that "Television, particularly, is significant in its impact because for the first time the higher art forms such as ballet, opera, and plays are visible to a broad rural audience" (84). But these scholars wondered not who but if anyone was watching these "higher art forms." "Wrestling, Arthur Godfrey and Howdy Doody are common symbols of entertainment," the authors observed, crisply placing each example with a telling equivalent: "Equally available and pervasive among the classes and individuals to whom they appeal are pocket books, comic books, and horror and sex stories" (84–85).

The Intellectual as Pivotal

If intellectuals seemed especially eager to sound an alarm over the encroachment of mass culture it was because they believed it was a crisis that lent itself to management by them. Academics in the humanities saw themselves as professionals whose attainments involved instilling critical thinking skills in communities. Riesman was pleased to report on some of these communities (he called them "taste-exchangers") in *The Lonely Crowd*. One centered on hot rods, another on jazz:

> These people found in jazz, as others have found in the movies or comic strips, an art form not previously classified by the connoisseurs, the school system, or the official culture. They resisted, often violently, and occasionally with success, the effort of the popular-music industry itself to ticket its products: in the very form of their choices—preferences for combos over star soloists, preference for improvisation, distrust of

smooth arrangers—they set up their own standards in opposition to
standardization. . . . They developed their own language and culture to
go with their new skill. (340)

Here was a portrait of a model postwar audience: affluent, independent,
expressive. Riesman and his co-authors had little to say about how one
went about training others to be members of similarly responsible audiences, but he was one of a number of intellectuals who regularly defended
the mass culture environment by recasting its invasiveness as benign: "we
have today a situation in which it is economically possible for the first time
in history to distribute first-class novels and nonfiction, paintings, music
and movies to audiences that can fit them into patterns of great individuality" (341).

Complicating widespread anxiety about mass culture, then, was the
view that something like a mass market existed—or with the help of intellectuals could be made to exist—for quality materials. Although efforts to
market high culture were apt to be targets of parody, the conviction existed
that within the (American) masses themselves there existed an antidote to
the poison of (un-American) totalitarian manipulation. Edward Shils
sketched that scenario in an essay-review of the Rosenberg and White anthology that was featured prominently in a 1957 *Sewanee Review*. Though
he doubted that a majority of persons would ever be able to develop "taste
and judgment," he thought it was "quite possible that a substantial minority, after several generations, will be assimilated as producers or consum-
ers into one of the various traditions of high culture, and that they will
serve as a leaven among their fellows" (608). Shils's scenario depicted members of a settled middle class peacefully and naturally initiating those whom
postwar prosperity had thrust upward from their origins in the next lower
class. His vision acknowledges the social mobility of the time, as well as the
understanding that social stability in the 1950s was thought to rest in part
upon the successful transmission to newly arrived members of the middle
class of some of the rules and conventions for valuing cultural goods.[4]

Was there any way to accelerate that assimilation and, coincidentally,
tap into a new and rapidly growing market? Shrewd marketers put themselves in the service of higher values. Right from the start, *New World Writing,* New American Library's twice-a-year "Mentor Book" paperback that
was first issued in April 1952, presented itself in terms that hobnobbed
brashly with elite or intellectual culture. The outgoing blurb on the back
of the fifth selection (published in April 1954) affirms in a bold headline:
"Avant Garde means you!" The text continues by explaining: "Avant Garde

may sound stuffy—but it only means a reconnaissance party—adventurous people who willingly enter uncharted territory." With spellbinding rapidity, "Avant Garde," while still bearing artistic and intellectual reverberations, becomes hearty, male, and military (a "reconnaissance party") that sheds its association with violence by turning into a quest for the unknown, a voyage into "uncharted territory." To this deft repositioning, rival publishers paid attention. When Pocket Books, Inc., underwrote six issues of *discovery* (in a format identical to the Mentor book), it too appealed to a readership that, its copywriters maintained, had been tapped by "paperbound reprint publishers" who had sold "millions of copies of first-rate books to newsstand buyers, without censorship or abridgement."[5]

Statements like this, bordering on flattery, suggested uncertainty about the staying power of this audience, however. Each number of *New World Writing* was prefaced with a curious address, "A Note from the Publishers," in which the fate of the very publication once again seemed to hang in the balance. Apprehensively, these opening statements defined this issue's offerings in terms that wobbled defensively, uncertainly. They ended, as a rule, with a last paragraph proclaiming that there would be another issue: "The editors, with their group endeavor coordinated by Arabel J. Porter, are already deeply engaged with the sixth Mentor selection of *New World Writing* as this fifth volume is published." "The editors—with Arabel J. Porter, senior editor, coordinating their efforts—are already working on *New World Writing #9* as this 8th Mentor Selection comes before your discriminating eyes." By the eighth selection (October 1955) the editors had recognized an effective ploy. They continued to maintain that their publication differed markedly from mass culture at the same time as claiming it was acting upon mass culture to improve it: "We like to think that by its example *New World Writing* has contributed something, too, to the liberation of kindred arts, notably the cinema and even TV, from the grip of the rigid, banal and censorious elements—their new phases of integrity led by a new generation of talent which includes many of our contributors." At the same time, these unnamed editors (and Arabel J. Porter) were quick to add: "To be sure, there need be nothing revolutionary about good writing."

Such anxious positioning suggests that New York publishers thought of their target audience as one whose attention had always to be won again. It might be more carefully described as an audience that was eager to learn but not entirely in command of its abilities—an audience willing to take instruction but hesitant about how best to proceed. When viewed alongside such an audience, the traits of the "fifties poem" begin to lose their cartoonish attributes and take on life-size proportions. Formalist poetry—verse that was metrically regular, often rhymed, and arranged in stanzas (if not in some more traditional format like the sonnet, the villanelle, or the sestina)—would exude an appeal for a number of reasons.[6] If audiences now included the new, untutored, and weak, then the literary works before them became powerful and explosive forces that needed strong and elaborate containment. The marks of verse formalism conveyed the necessary strength of the containing mechanisms, and these would not only attest to the energy within the poem but also send notice that it would be safe to approach a work that was operating under a system of powerfully constraining laws. That system would also assure the reader that these rules of form have a directive purpose. Formal poetry lent itself to presentation as an array of professional devices each of which was designed to foster communication. The packaging of formalist devices openly displayed the poem as labor-intensive, an exquisitely balanced verbal machine crafted by specialists in the language arts. As an artifact, the poem was clearly distinct from TV show or comic book, because the formal attributes that have been carefully worked into the very texture of the poem (those rhymes, those balanced rhythms, those fourteen lines) testify to the excellence of its workmanship, assuring readers that any time they invest in reading and rereading will be repaid by an encounter with quality.

Populist Formalism

Acknowledging the existence of a fresh new audience that wants to learn how to act around art grounds the aesthetics of the "fifties poem" as nothing else can. The existence of such an audience has been widely remarked in recent explanations of the postwar triumph of the New Criticism which turn on its ability to provide an upwardly mobile audience an entranceway to the world of literature without requiring extensive preparation and without insisting on longtime intimacy with other elite cultural material. "By making literary study an encounter between a student and a text," Jonathan Culler points out, the New Criticism "offered an approach particularly suitable to the post-war university, which took in students from increasingly diverse social and educational backgrounds, who had little knowledge in common" (14).[7] To read New Critically, nothing intertextual was required. By insisting on the autonomy of the artwork, the New Criticism democratized the reading site. At the same time, the New Criticism succeeded in professionalizing that reading site by claiming a distinct set of interpretive procedures that would do justice to the literary text. Once the merit of a work of art was dependent upon its accessibility, then obscurity in poetry was no longer a virtue but a symptom of a particular failure: a mark of the incomplete work of the poet whose poems had not been suitably revised and polished. In the properly completed poem, all the elements had been placed in the service of communicating to the reader, who would be continually reassured that this work was ready for the reading and rereading that was necessary for it and which it deserved. All the parts were packed in place, all the material was properly assembled; everything was awaiting the attentive reader.

"When reading a book of poems you must be prepared to linger," John Ciardi advised in his introduction to his anthology *Mid-Century American Poets* (1950). "That thin volume will take at least as much reading as a detective story" ("Foreword" xviii). Ciardi wants to reassure his reader that a book of poetry is an attractive alternative to a detective novel, that it need not be forbidding, that unpacking its author's impressions can be entertaining, and that by following the contractual obligations of the poetic conventions, the reader will be led securely from one point to the next. In this poetry, as in the elaborate plot that unfolds in the course of the mystery novel, the work of integrating the disparate pieces has already been done by the author, and the reader can proceed confidently, knowing the way has been prepared. So carefully has the work been assembled, so elaborately yet professionally, that rereading will only deepen appreciation. At the same time, the poem is also distinguished from the detective story, a consumable that was essentially valueless as an artifact once its plot had been followed to a conclusion. The poem's clues chart a pathway that can be followed with deepening understanding and pleasure.

Formalism in this regard does not offer itself as a set of intimidating gestures that are tokens of elitism but as an assemblage of useful techniques that guarantee consumer usability. The new poem of the 1950s comes to the reader as helpfully pre-interpreted. Writing in 1955 in *New World Writing No. 7*, Donald Hall praised Richard Wilbur for pre-interpreting his material for the reader: "When suffering is a subject in a Wilbur poem, it is understood and discussed, not presented in the act. . . . Wilbur's poems present us with the picture of the poet meditating on a problem; and the finished thought, formed so that it affirms its shape as a necessary part of its meaning, is the finished poem" ("New Poetry" 242). Wilbur's poem is not just an orderly sequence of words: it "affirms its shape," becoming a physical presence that is a "necessary part of the meaning." That shape was constitutive even as it serves to guard against its own misconstruing. As Murray Krieger explained in his 1956 study of the New Criticism, *The New Apologists for Poetry,* the successful poem "is contained by verbal complexities. . . . It is these complexities which prevent the alert reader from 'using' the poem crudely, from treating it as a mere sign" (188). In a less-friendly variant, Cleanth Brooks in the lead essay of the Winter 1951 *Sewanee Review* deployed Donne as a touchstone for Milton and argued that Donne's "complexity" had a "very important practical consequence: it effectively locks us out of the poem until we have actually mastered the poem. The metaphorical complexities stand guard over the inner meanings" (21). By contrast, Milton's poetry, Brooks warned, was trickier to handle because of its lack of "metaphorical complexity": that lack "does not make Milton a less profound poet than Donne, but it does make him a poet easier to *misread*" (21, italics his). These remarks define a moment when misreading was an anxiety that critics hoped to allay. Acting on a similar set of premises, James G. Southworth, in one of the few books of criticism in the 1950s that directly dealt with contemporary poets, *More Modern American Poets* (1954), confidently predicted that William Carlos Williams was unlikely ever to be a popular poet. "The reason is obvious. He taxes the general reader more than the general reader wishes to be taxed. . . . He has eschewed the traditional aids of rhyme, regularly recurring rhythms, traditional stanza forms and a music arising from the felicitous juxtaposition of words" (1). Formal characteristics are aids to understanding; without them, the reader's course is uncertain. "[W]hen as much responsibility rests on the reader as Dr. Williams places there, the chances of failure of response on the part of the reader are greater than if the poet had made use of the traditional tools for controlling that response" (5).

When Southworth calls prosodic features "traditional tools" he is acknowledging poetry's extensive heritage while invoking a new spirit of accessibility. A generation of students, upwardly mobile and new to the university, could only appreciate such a program. Highly intellectualized poetry had been written by vanguard groups in the 1920s with the evident idea of establishing standards for readerly comprehension that were exceptional. When Eliot footnoted *The Waste Land,* for example, he was not attempting to widen his audience base; his formidable annotations firmly demonstrated that this modern poetry was not for everyone. (Early reviewers caught this but, misunderstanding Eliot's elitist gesture, complained that the notes were bogus because they weren't elucidative; for some years, then, and in some high intellectual quarters, the poem had to shake off its reputation as a hoax.) But in the postwar years, such barriers as had once been erected were falling, yielding to the pressure of young instructors priming undergraduates as well as graduate students in the techniques of reading. To the new generation of poets in the 1940s and 1950s it could only have been thrilling to appropriate the traditions of verse-making as though a group of newcomers never before invited within the walls of the university were now engaged in retooling the operation, using technique not to inhibit but to enhance understanding, to return poetry to the hands of first-time readers.

The New Look, Googies, Cool Jazz, and the Fifties Poem

When the formalist "fifties poem" is returned to its cultural context, it takes on features that are shared by other postwar phenomena, especially those that deliberately blurred lines which had previously guaranteed a rigid separation of classes. For women's fashion, for example, such a repositioning occurred when mass-market designers co-opted stylistic devices that had been formerly restricted to the wealthy. Angela Partington has pointed out that the New Look of 1950s fashion was not interested in "expressing the dominant ideological values of the 1950s, such as those upholding traditional femininity and domesticity" (147). She describes it instead as a "site of conflicted meanings": "As mass-market systems developed, working-class women were able to engage in forms of consumption to satisfy needs not anticipated by the professionals and therefore 'improper.'" (153). Postwar abundance fostered mobility, moving high-status markers within the reach of those who wanted them, who were able to recognize them. And the postwar environment placed at the disposal of the majority materials that had been formerly deemed completely exclusive.[8]

In a different domain, Alan Hess has argued that the 1950s coffee shop—the vernacular architecture familiarly known as the Googie (as first named by Douglas Haskell in a 1952 *House and Home* article)—introduced principles of modernist architecture to a wide populace: "The coffee shop version of [Frank Lloyd] Wright's Modernism . . . brought the spaces, imagery, materials and ideas of Modernism to a broad audience that would never have experienced them otherwise" (77). Just as the "fifties poem" employed formalistic prosodic devices to bring an art form closer to a wide audience at the same time as it sought to retain as many of its upscale elements as it could, so the Googie invited its numerous users to find pleasure in unfettered spaces, in sweeping lines: "The coffee shops are Gropius's dream come true—a new architecture used and appreciated by the masses, expressing the high standard of living brought by an advancing technology—except the forms were not what Gropius had anticipated" (95). Hess even defends the Googie in terms that recall the demonization of the "fifties poem": "Most assessments of Coffee Shop Modern are the product of high art critics' low opinion of the fifties: coffee shops are corruptions of the original, pure high art versions of the modern style. In the rush to establish a single reigning modern style, Googie became a dropped thread in the fabric of Modernism. Rediscovered it shows that Modernism has always been wider than the academies acknowledged, that its roots went deeper into the culture than has been admitted since" (119).

As suggestive as these parallel examples are, none is as strikingly apt as the similarities between the mainstream formalist verse of the 1950s and the "cool jazz" that originated sometime in the late 1940s and remained a powerful current in improvisational options well into the late 1950s. Miles Davis's 1948 sessions with a ten-piece group whose arrangements were orchestrated by Gil Evans and Gerry Mulligan among others (and known as "The Birth of the Cool") originated a style that would reach an apogee in 1957, when Davis would collaborate with Evans to produce the *Miles Ahead* recordings—a period that correlates with the development, ascendancy, and maturity of the "fifties poem." Like the "fifties poem" or academic verse, cool jazz (or "West Coast jazz") was consumed most enthusiastically by a university community that was eager to see itself as marked by a savvy professionalism that smartly identified superior trends. Academic verse, as pre-interpreted, would be more intellectual than emotional, more articulate than impassioned, and in this it resembled the air of detachment that André Hodeir, writing in 1956, noted as "a kind of modesty in musical expression not to be found in jazz before" (118). But Hodeir also understood that this modesty had an ambitious program behind it: "Even when the performer seems to be letting himself go completely (and cool musicians, as we shall see, cultivate relaxation), a sort of reserve, by which we do not mean constraint, marks his creative flight, channeling it within certain limits that constitute its charm. It may be said that the cool musicians have brought a new feeling to jazz. With them, jazz becomes an intimate act, rather like chamber music is by comparison with symphonies" (118). In promoting this comparison with chamber music, Hodeir was pointing out the way that cool jazz functioned as one more postwar example that actively blurred lines that had once drawn boundaries between low and high. When cool jazz modeled itself on chamber music, taking pride in its intricate orchestrations in small groups—from the nine-piece band of the Davis-Evans-Mulligan collaboration to Mulligan's pianoless quartets of 1952–54, to the Dave Brubeck Quartet (and an earlier octet of 1948), as well as to other small orchestras that featured trumpeters such as Clifford Brown and Shorty Rogers (and to large orchestras like Stan Kenton's that transformed themselves into small groups for certain featured arrangements)—it resembled that commitment to the short lyric form that dominated academic verse.

All these postwar developments generated anxiety among those who recognized that a transfer of power from one class to another might be well under way. The Googie horrified Alfred Barr, who snorted: "We are asked to take seriously the architectural taste of real estate speculators, renting agents and mortgage brokers!" (Hess 14). Hodeir could envision cool jazz as a falling-away from high standards: "Ignoring what bebop had achieved, the cool musicians generally adopted outmoded melodic and rhythmic conceptions . . . result[ing] in a kind of backtracking that may be only temporary but is nonetheless one of the most disquieting signs in the history of jazz" (121). He even warned that "music so intimate and excessively polished may lose some of jazz's essential characteristics and cease to be anything but a devitalized successor" (136). And in similar words, William Barrett, writing in 1957 after a stint as a *Partisan Review* editor, was provoked into dismissing contemporary poetry by invoking this modernist heritage: "If one considers the bulk of poetry that appears issue by issue in the little magazines, not merely alighting on a few favored names here and there, then one is bound to draw some dismal conclusions about the general atmosphere for poetry now prevailing. The bulk of this poetry is, to be perfectly blunt, bad, and not merely indifferently bad but bad in a way that suggests perversion of some kind. The perversion in this case is that it is a caricature of modern poetry in its bleakness, intellectualization, and remoteness of feeling" (145). Elsewhere in his essay, Barrett traces the flaw back to "Eliot's revolution in poetry" which made "irony and intellectual toughness . . . the great virtues of the day." Barrett also recalls John Crowe Ransom rebuking "an elder scholar for having said that behind Donne's conceits there was any *passion*." If passion had been declared off-limits by Ransom and if intellect had been championed by Eliot, then it seemed to Barrett that new poets were narrowly boxed in, with no incentive except to promote watered-down versions of their immediate poetic ancestors.

"Midcult" was the term that Dwight MacDonald introduced to define the art that began to prevail in the postwar years—an art that was neither popular (emerging spontaneously from the untutored) nor avant-garde (constructed by an elite with oppositional intent) but, in his mind, disturbingly produced by a middle class for widespread consumption. Like *Partisan Review* contributor Clement Greenberg, who imported the term *kitsch* to demonize artworks that aimed primarily to bring experiences ordinarily reserved for the wealthy and the educated within the reach of everyone else, MacDonald deplored the loss of influence that intellectuals like himself had once enjoyed as taste-makers and as gatekeepers. For them, the most disturbing aspect of phenomena as otherwise disparate as the New Look, the Googie, cool jazz, and the fifties poem would have been that all these productions not only emerge without the particular sanction of any specialist, without the necessary papers of introduction that the intellectual might have been asked to produce, but also that they actively embed within themselves their inclination to remain independent from any such interventionary figure. Not only can the New Look be worn by everyone from Mamie Eisenhower to her secretary, it can even be manufactured at home by anyone who is a patient seamstress. Some Googies were designed by architects, but most were improvised by contractors to fit their location, using materials that had been popularized in the public buildings of Frank Lloyd Wright. The young men who specialized in cool jazz emerged from no particular setting, out of the conservatory as well as the ghetto (or both—Davis grew up in East St. Louis but his studies led him to a scholarship at Julliard). And of course the fifties poem was designed to make its way without requiring interpretive aid from anyone outside it, whether scholar, literary historian, or New Critic.

These genuinely popular modifications of high culture artifacts were probably not what was envisioned in the postwar years when there was a call to quarantine mass culture. While that call could be understood most clearly as a domestic parallel to hysterical anti-Communism, it more subtly registers a widespread anxiety about the kinds of pressures that will be exerted when so many become upwardly mobile. The "quarantine" is thus at work in these modifications, restricting access to those who are able to see themselves in the distanced, "professional" terms that serve in part to define the liberal subject. But one consequence—perhaps inevitable, always unintended—is that the compromise site will be defined as much by pressures from below as pressures from above. Cool jazz is indebted to the concentration and intensity that accompanies European chamber music, which is admired for the attentiveness it demands from its participants, but no less committed to a display of stylistic individuality and self-dramatization that is quintessentially African American jazz. The fifties poem, in similar ways, was linguistically sophisticated even as it offered accessibility; it was also open to recognizing social practices and the need to be historically engaged, though it may have presented itself as operating from a position of professionalized detachment. But above all, it promoted a redistribution of power. Not only did it invite a new audience to read poetry, and equip that audience with the tools to comprehend it, it also took significant steps to guarantee that the audience could proceed in the future, on its own, with confidence in a relationship that had no need for the expert as mediator. This bold a project would need, if it was to be successful, to unfold in a time when social mobility pointed upward, when prospects of abundance were increasingly available, and when confidence in the authority of the state was high. In the postwar years, those combinations were remarkably in place, at least for a while, and for a long moment it would be possible to consider poetry as comparable in important ways to modes of fashion, styles of vernacular architecture, and schools of jazz— as an art that served to define a particular audience and helped to shape a postwar culture.

1

THE NOTORIOUS EXAMPLE
OF RICHARD WILBUR

Literal politics are not the concern of poetry. . . . The poet as the
sentimental professional rebel vanished; in his place was the young
instructor of English in privately endowed colleges wearing a
Brooks Brothers uniform.

—Horace Gregory (1935)

In Daniel Curley's "The Appointed Hour," one of the many fic-
tional renditions of the lives of college faculty that the *Kenyon Review* featured in the 1950s,[1] a well-known poet ("Robert Hatcher") was recalling an
incident at Upstate University. Hatcher described Upstate not as a university so much as a "small college with a lot of students." "Each time I spoke
there I got the feeling that every GI who ever wanted to go to college was
on that campus. That isn't strictly true, of course, but there were thirteen
or fourteen thousand of them at the peak" (546). Recalling campuses overwhelmed with numbers that they were ill-equipped to process, Hatcher
depicts a new set of students who were not only numerous but homoge-
neous. Upstate's student body is predominantly male, it is ex-GI, it is not
young. Hatcher wonders if these men know why they are on campus. Perhaps they are there because others like them are. And the fact that someone like Robert Hatcher, a poet, is invited to deliver a "talk" (the subject will
be "an open letter to a young man who wants to write") rests precisely upon
this new and large group that requires advice, that needs a letter from its
elders and is ready to listen to it. The poet is one of the catalysts which that
crowd needs to turn it into educated and culturally alert citizens.

That poet would do best in the postwar years who would be able to write for such a crowd.[2] And that poet would do spectacularly well who would write not only for that crowd but also for the more confident traditional audience that modern poetry had cultivated. Of all poets in the 1950s no one succeeded in pleasing so many serious readers as Richard Wilbur. Robert Lowell's work received a proportionate share of praise, but as the decade unfolded Lowell, at least as a publishing poet, remained at its periphery. After releasing his controversial second book in 1951, *The Mills of the Kavanaughs,* Lowell lived abroad for several years, writing little. The last year in which he had been an active presence as a poet was 1953, publishing a group of seven sonnets in the *Kenyon Review* and three other poems in various issues of *Partisan Review.* As a prose writer he was represented with "91 Revere Street" when it appeared in *Partisan Review* in 1956. Up until 1958, when sections of his new autobiographical poetry began to appear, Lowell was at best a shadowy presence. His remoteness, to be sure, may only have enhanced his reputation: the great modern poets of the past, still living though greatly aged—Eliot, Pound, Williams, and up until 1955, Stevens— circled in faraway orbits. Lowell would have sought comparison with them.

Lowell's contrast with Wilbur is most telling. Wilbur's engagement and enthusiasm were a reminder that there was a role for the poet other than the aloof dignitary or the elderly wise man: Marianne Moore, for example, who wrote poems about the Brooklyn Dodgers, who translated the fables of La Fontaine, and who, in an exchange of letters that the *New Yorker* had printed in 1957, was asked by the Ford Motor Company to help name its newest car (she proposed, among others, "Turcotingo" and "Pluma Piluma" and responded graciously when told its name would be Edsel: "You have certainly the ideal thing—with the Ford identity indigenously symbolized" [224]). Wilbur, like Moore in the 1950s, circulated freely in a variety of settings, publishing poetry in the *Atlantic* as well as *Botteghe Oscure,* reviewing contemporaries in academic quarterlies like *Furioso* as well as producing a coffee-table book with Alexander Calder (*A Bestiary,* 1955). Wilbur's activities in 1956 alone, as Peter Davison enumerates them in *The Fading Smile* (1995), his valuable memoir of Boston in the 1950s, indicate the sweep of his interests: "In that year he published his most acclaimed book of verse, *Things of This World;* he absented himself from Wellesley College to collaborate with Leonard Bernstein and Lillian Hellman on the musical version of *Candide;* and his first major verse translation, Molière's *The Misanthrope,* after its 1955 publication by Harcourt, Brace and its simultaneous production by the Poets' Theater, went into its first New York production"

(69). Wilbur published whole collections at the rate Lowell published sets of poems. His third collection in less than ten years (predecessors appeared in 1947 and 1950), *Things of This World* was awarded the Pulitzer Prize and the National Book Award. *Advice to a Prophet* in 1961 collected work from the second half of the decade. Of his contemporaries, both John Ciardi and Howard Nemerov were no less prolific, but the work of neither was so highly regarded.

Yet Wilbur's poetry has not retained the value it accrued over those years. Although a number of poets from the same generation enjoyed considerable success in the 1950s, no poet has continued to be so rigidly identified with that era nor has anyone paid more dearly for it. Today the "Wilbur poem" and the "fifties poem" have converged. In a 1982 anthology of essays on the work of James Wright, when contributors found themselves obliged to note that Wright broke from the "fifties poems" that he composed in his early years, the name regularly invoked as a foil was that of Wilbur.[3] "More often than not, when one thinks of the poetry of the fifties," wrote Donald B. Stauffer in *A Short History of American Poetry* (1974), "one thinks of Wilbur as a typical poet of those years" (385). Twenty years later, that opinion remains firm. "Wilbur is still admired," Robert von Hallberg notes in his contribution to the *Cambridge History of American Literature* (1996), "but really as the best poet of the 1950s" (58). Even though he is an outstanding example, he excels in a debased category. Among minor poets he is allowed to be most major, but among major poets he is not even considered the most minor.[4]

Earlier, such dismissals were unthinkable. Wilbur and Lowell were considered in 1962 by Donald Hall as equals, the two poets "who form the real beginning of post-war American poetry" ("Introduction" 20). Randall Jarrell agreed. In his 1962 address, "Fifty Years of American Poetry," he was particularly careful to single out Wilbur from the "academic, tea-party, creative-writing-class poets" whose work "rather tamely satisfies the rules or standards for technique implicit in what they consider the 'best modern practice'" (329). For Jarrell Wilbur was a demonstration that poetry could attract and hold a relatively wide audience. Robert Frost, himself an adept at holding a crowd, was remembered by Henry Taylor as saying, in the spring of 1961, that "Wilbur, because of the natural beauty of his language and craft, was one of the younger poets who, without any conscious effort to 'write down,' could reach the wider audience which poets (and audiences too) have dreamed of for a long time" (88). Wilbur represented proof, in short, that what Andrew Ross has described as the "Gresham's

Law" attitude toward mass culture in the 1950s appeared to be valid: "if we had a cultural diet that was good for people then the popular hunger for trash would disappear" ("New Age" 554).

Wilbur's achievement, in his own time, was to inhabit a ground midway between Wallace Stevens and Anne Morrow Lindbergh (whose savaging in a review by John Ciardi when he took over as poetry editor of the *Saturday Review* in 1956 provoked an outcry). He was not quite a challenging practitioner with a readership limited to the university community, nor was he conversely a popular poet with a truly large following. Jarrell's climactic tag line in his "Fifty Years" speech summarizing Wilbur was that his "lyric calling-to-life of the things of this world—the things, rather than the processes or people—specializes in both true and false happy endings, not by choice but by necessity; he obsessively sees, and shows, the bright underside of every dark thing" (331–32). Jarrell's formulation places Wilbur midway between the challenging intellectual positions of high modernism (which specialize in confronting many a "dark thing") and the reassuring platitudes that were a staple of much mass culture in the 1950s (which locate the "bright underside"). For Jarrell, this was only praise of a sort. The role to which Wilbur has since been consigned by literary history, however, depends upon a characterization of this middle ground not as an area that is difficult to access but as a simple place of blurry compromise. For James E. B. Breslin, arguing the case forcefully against the 1950s poetry of formalism, Wilbur inherits the techniques of the modernists but instead of deploying them to initiate radical shifts in sensibility, he "adapts these procedures to traditional verse forms" (30). The result is deplorable because Wilbur dilutes the modernist project of encouraging confident and assertive individualists. For David Perkins, Wilbur's work "followed currently favored modes but generally revised them toward perspicuity and charm" (*Modern Poetry* 383). Both Breslin and Perkins characterize Wilbur by explicitly referring to his predecessors, to the modernists whose techniques he adapts or revises, and that is how they account for his popularity. They assume that it is those predecessors who are the poets that Wilbur's followers would *really* want to read if only they had the cultural competence to do so. Wilbur is at best a helpful figure in an intermediate stage, a guide whose usefulness is that he can begin to train a neophyte sensibility.

New understandings about the popular text question such a reductive portrayal. Rather than being a placid area of easy compromise, the middle ground Wilbur inhabits, as even Jarrell hints, is a turbulent one. Wilbur regularly mixes together two texts that are widely regarded as opposites simply because their relationships with their audiences are so different—the aesthetic text and the popular text. John Fiske has sharply differentiated them:

> The reader of the aesthetic text attempts to read it on *its* terms, to subjugate him- or herself to its aesthetic discipline. The reader reveres the text. The popular reader, on the other hand, holds no such reverence for the text but views it as a resource to be used at will. Aesthetic appreciation of a text requires the understanding of how its elements relate and contribute to its overall unity, and an appreciation of the final, completed unity is its ultimate goal. Popular readers, on the other hand, are concerned less with the final unity of the text than with the pleasures and meanings that its elements can provoke. They are undisciplined, dipping into and out of a text at will. (106–7)

With Wilbur in the late 1940s and 1950s, however, there is an audience to account for which brings to a poem mixed motives and varying reading skills. Though it may wish to revere the text, that audience is also more easily distracted than it perhaps should be, and it finds pleasures that, strictly speaking, would not be encouraged by a disciplined reading. That the audience so strays from its proper task is nevertheless not surprising because Wilbur's poetry not only permits it but covertly encourages it. Wilbur's poems encourage both "distracted" readings that allow for strong audience engagement and "disciplined" readings that train an audience to respect the strengths of the author.

Postwar Sensitivity to Issues of Class

What would it mean to read Wilbur's popularity as an ability to sustain a mix of opposing textual types? Such an approach would have little in common with Bruce Michelson's searching examination that, by scrutinizing those poems often passed over, locates in Wilbur a darker aspect than has been previously noticed. Michelson's Wilbur is the *un*popular Wilbur, a figure little in evidence in the 1950s. (More accurately, Michelson curiously miscasts Wilbur in the role actually played by Howard Nemerov as the dark and skeptical counterpart to Wilbur's bright and airy temperament.) Beginning to think how Wilbur managed to be so popular a poet is long overdue. An understanding of Wilbur as a popular poet would help account for one of the puzzling aspects of his reputation: why critics both in the 1950s and after the 1950s have found his poetry so elusive. The source of a popular writer's power will always be elusive. Richard Ohmann has argued that a reading that is sensitive to the bases of a writer's popularity "does not look *behind* or *through* the text to 'background' conditions but reconstructs meanings that were 'there' in the text for properly schooled contemporaries" (38). Popular texts so reconstructed can display an intricate dynamics, but an "interpretive strategy not grounded in such knowledge and in such habits of decoding would have given the reader an experience of the story almost drained of tension, affect, and satisfaction" (38–39). In the 1950s, Wilbur's work impressed readers as beautifully lucid because it provided resolutions to issues impossible to consider directly; dealing with issues his audience might sense but not articulate, Wilbur's poetry would seem uncannily "natural," deserving the critic's helpless praise. After the 1950s, when matters once timely had succumbed to time, these same works would lose their edge, striking later readers as oddly insubstantial now that the issues that had helped animate them had fallen away.

Access to Wilbur's poetry, whether popular or unpopular, is in any case frequently blocked by critics who misappropriate it for instructional purposes. The negative category of the "Wilbur poem" is maintained by criticism like Charles Altieri's 1970 study *Enlarging the Temple,* which includes a reading of Wilbur's "'A World without Objects Is a Sensible Emptiness'" (from *Ceremony,* 1950) in which the poem exists only as a helpless foil to Robert Lowell's "Colloquy in Black Rock." Altieri admits that his "aim in dealing with both [Wilbur and Lowell] shall be less to give an impartial analysis of their work than to recover the way many younger poets come to view them" (53). Since Altieri's impression of "younger poets" concludes they followed Lowell and not Wilbur, he plans a reading of Wilbur designed to show why poets might react against him. This "historical perspective," as Altieri calls it, is actually the winner's perspective or Lowell's perspective. Under these terms, Wilbur's poem is overwhelmed by standards alien to it. Not surprisingly, then, it emerges as diluted modernism, as a "weakening and simplification" of its distinguished predecessors, as Altieri stage-manages a negativized reading in which Wilbur's words are, he says, "statements *about* experience" (58). Complaining that the contrast between the "tall camels of the spirit" (that stand for the arid intellect) and the "light incarnate" (that embodies a blend of intellect with sensation) is too contrived, Altieri asserts this isn't a dialectic, just "verbal artifice" (59). "Its metaphors are neither dramatic nor perceptual, but meditative" (59). What is the poem's organization, then, but "an example of New Critical doctrines of irony and paradox"? "Now, however, irony and paradox are no longer metaphors for an essentially tragic context in which man must play out his fate and learn humility and sympathy; rather, they are simply the conditions of human discourse to be accepted and enjoyed" (59). Altieri acknowledges the poem's careful construction but ends by pronouncing it a shell—a conclusion that was, of course, foreordained from the start.

What would make it not a shell, what might it have embodied for earlier readers, for those who eagerly anthologized it and cited it favorably in reviews? Clearly, the poem's stand is against intellects that are "too arid." But how could Wilbur, or anyone for that matter, be engaged by such a nonissue? The active life of the poem must lie elsewhere, and it only begins to emerge in the stanzas that negotiate in the opening and the closing of the poem where Wilbur pauses to reconstruct the crudely painted saints of Renaissance paintings "capped by the early masters, / With bright, jauntily-worn // Aureate pates, or even / Merry-go-round rings" (*New* 283). The pictures recall a time of innocence, a time when painters, still "early masters," were grappling with how to present the sacred. More important, Wilbur's defense of the clumsy yet well-meant reproductions of these painters displays his sympathies for the difficulties faced by those who are "early masters," those attempting a responsible role for the first time—like those numbers of students who, in this period, are first in their family to attend college. The poem is, on the one hand, a virtuoso demonstration of a work that is constructed by employing irony and paradox, and Altieri is correct in identifying Wilbur's enjoyment of his feat. But on the other hand, it also extends sympathy to those who must grow to accept the realization that "all shinings need to be shaped and borne." Within the dazzle of his framework, Wilbur constructs a sheltering space in which, not coincidentally, he addresses a wider audience in the vocative case ("Think" and "Turn, O turn"). For that audience of neophytes the emblem of the camels receives its significance. Part of the hesitancy of the neophytes may stem from an anxiety that with their new background, their new skills, their new prosperity they will drift away from their family and friends. They will move off to that land that Traherne described in the quote Wilbur chose for his title and be lost in a world of "pure mirages." The poem not only addresses their anxiety but even suggests a resolution by portraying at its close the attractiveness of the "Lampshine blurred in the steam of beasts, the spirit's right / Oasis, light incarnate." Like early masters, these first-generation *arrivistes* may express themselves clumsily, but they are down-to-earth enough not to fall into that "stilted stride" that leads to "the land of sheer horizon." Or so the poem could be made to assure those readers who, uncertain, are looking for signs of such assurance.[5]

What appears to later readers like Altieri as a poem that verges on the abstract, a neo-metaphysical poem that wittily regains its balance after tumbling through a set of arcane arguments (beginning with the marginal Traherne but ending with the centralizing Christian iconography of starlight over a barn) may have been to an earlier generation a text that acts with sensitivity toward their movement out of their old social class. Moreover, the dialectic unfolding that Altieri found all too obvious and thus contrived may have served this same audience by creating an alternative space that does not deny the rarefied world of the spirit, of the pure intellect, but simply recognizes that it may be taken too far:

> Wisely watch for the sight
> Of the supernova burgeoning over the barn,
> Lampshine blurred in the steam of beasts, the spirit's right
> Oasis, light incarnate. (*New* 284)

The poem signals that it is giving counseling, then, as it tells us to "Wisely watch." Wisdom is now that which the audience has a hold over, and the poem is designed to impart a confidence that was at one time in short supply. This low-key conclusion, by drawing on familiar depictions with links to the nativity scene, adroitly skirts the Christmas card setting to which it might succumb. It is the very recognizability of such a scene that sets it apart from anything arcane, including any association with the pure intellect; even as it retains an air of civilized deliberation it rejects the elitism that might display the poem as a place of privilege. Yet just as clearly is it set against the blandishments of mass culture. When Wilbur needs an example of a popular art he thinks of the anonymous painters of the Renaissance, not Walt Disney's animators. And he depicts them in terms that recall their anonymity and recognize their labor. Moreover, he is careful to underscore their skill, recalling their artfulness in the way he sees light playing off water, in the "halo-dialing run / Of the country creeks" (*New* 283) later in the poem. The effect is not flattery, however, but merely an observation. Wilbur is uninterested in suggesting handicaps of any kind: when "simple" laborers are presented with the opportunity to labor at making art, they produce detailed masterpieces. The poem partakes of these other worlds just enough to take its bearings as a work that is wonderfully effective in speaking to a range of quite different audiences.

To the generation that first read this poem, the text is doing its cultural work so well, working on so oblique a level, that it could only be recognized, not understood. And one sure indication that the poem participated successfully in the symbolic order of its time is that it was hailed as being virtually transparent. Reviewing *Ceremony*, Babette Deutsch offered a "tribute" to several poems (including "the memorable poem on a phrase of Traherne's"), insisting "they should not be paraphrased" ("Scenes" 37). A no less enthusiastic Reed Whittemore, in his review, nonetheless paraphrased the poem effortlessly: "The world of the mind or spirit is opposed to the material world, the former being like a desert and therefore full of heavenly mirages, the latter being no cheat but heaven indeed, 'the spirit's right oasis'" ("Verse" 43). One thing the poem would not be reviewed as, however, would be as a text about the uncertainties that accompanied social mobility. It cannot be *Marty*, the 1953 TV drama (and 1955 award-winning movie) that details through the eyes of a mother the trauma of her son's marriage and shift from his ethnic neighborhood to the bland suburbs. And yet the poem inhabited, at one time, a similar universe. The very success of Wilbur's poem depends on its ability to evoke and address an anxiety without directly naming it.

In some circumstances, Wilbur was less cautious in recording clashes between different social worlds. "Tears for the Rich" was published in the premier issue (December 1948) of the short-lived but impressive journal *American Letters* alongside contributions from John Berryman and others, but never collected in a volume:

Tears for the Rich

O sacrificial beauty of the rich:
We see them in the glare beneath marquees,
The straight old men with scalloped skulls who bear
The Atlas weight of eighty years of ease,
And freighted ladies palely bending there,
Bejeweled as with flies a Libyan lich.

The middle-aged are seen in galleries
Completing their collections, as they should,
Or waving for the films before they go
Alas again from shores not understood
To winter in a land they'll never know,
With twenty trunks, across undangerous seas.

The young, who dread to die in granny's bed,
Or softly after brandy in a chair,
Are thrown from thoroughbreds, or run away
As missing heiresses, to anywhere,
Or crashing in a custom-built coupé
Are pyred in frying metal, wealthy dead.

Pale porters of our wealth, who may not see
The least magnificence with grateful eye,
O takers of our ease, sad spenders whom
The world can tease but never satisfy,
I wish you other lives beyond the tomb
Of hunger, loss, and sweet anxiety. (12)

The privileged classes, as Wilbur glimpses them, hardly prove endearing.[6] Although the poem could be mistaken for an exercise in irony and paradox—an exploration of the idea that want begets appreciation—the tone of the work, curdling with contempt, yields Wilbur's assessment. The air of innocence with which each stanza begins has been sucked of all oxygen by the last lines as the sharply malevolent voice metes out Wilbur's disdain. Jewels, in line six, become as loathsome as flies. In line twelve, the vapid journeys of the rich cross empty seas, bereft of all danger. And in lines seventeen and eighteen, alliteration that borders on excess ("crashing in a custom-built coupé") and diction that is perversely inappropriate ("pyred in frying metal") convey a palpable relish at such deaths. His wish at the end, for those "other lives beyond the tomb" is impeccably correct as a metaphysical twist to embellish the poem even as Wilbur knows that lives of "hunger, loss, and sweet anxiety" are just the lives that the very wealthy would dread most of all. In later poems, Wilbur will manage to write endings that delicately blur their contradictory meanings, but here he only gestures in that direction.

Healing Trauma

If Wilbur's poetry is an art of negotiating among divergent perspectives, then it is even capable of playing within a range of expectations to signal awareness of traumatic situations whose outlines would have been most evident to those who had been in warfare. Randall Jarrell, whose World War II was spent in Illinois and Arizona instructing Army Air Force pilots and navigators, thought that "The Death of a Toad" veered into empty rhetoric:

> When you read "The Death of a Toad," a poem that begins *A toad the power mower caught, / Chewed and clipped of a leg, with a hobbling hop has got / To the garden verge,* you stop to shudder at the raw being of the world, at all that *a hobbling hop* has brought to life—*that* toad is real, all right. But when you read on, when Mr. Wilbur says that the toad *dies / Toward some deep monotone, / Toward misted and ebullient seas / And cooling shores, toward lost Amphibia's reveries,* you think with a surge of irritation and dismay, "So it was only an excuse for some Poetry." ("Three Books" 228)

Jarrell is thinking of Marianne Moore's "imaginary gardens with real toads in them" when he praises the realness of Wilbur's toad, but he dismisses as excessive what can only be called the elegiac music of the closing lines. Jarrell is most comfortable with the Wilbur who is seeing with a sharp, descriptive eye that presents the world in fresh new ways, but when Wilbur's writing turns effusive, when it reacts to matters with emotion and sympathy, then Jarrell draws back. This first way of writing Jarrell identifies with the project of other modernists while the second way is "only an excuse for some Poetry," just an attempt to manipulate our emotions and not worth the bother of serious readers. If the first way of writing is masculine like the hard edge of modernism itself, then for Jarrell the second way may be too feminized, like the soft lures of mass culture. But it is precisely just Wilbur's ability to deliver us from one extreme to another that makes his poetry particularly valuable. Insofar as the poem commemorates the last moments of a creature who is dying in isolation and unexpectedly, as the result of an accident over which it had no control, it could easily evoke a different response from someone with experience of the random reversals of combat. For anyone with friends who must have died in combat (crawling to shelter, accepting the place of the moment as their last place on earth)—and who must have himself at some time contemplated that he might die in just this way—Wilbur's sympathetic projection is not the overwrought gesture that Jarrell brands it to be but a return, almost a helpless return, to a moment of genuine emotion, intrusively appearing at an unlikely moment and in an unexpected setting. The albeit-excessive rhetoric with which Wilbur lavishly surrounds this creature who might otherwise be viewed as insignificant is, then, deliberately outsize. It must be, for it stands for all those other occasions when one had farewell words to say to another who was dying unexpectedly but had no opportunity to do so.

Jarrell's cumbersome reaction to "The Death of a Toad" suggests how latent in Wilbur's poetry are those designs available for one audience to appreciate and another audience to miss entirely. On the other hand, such designs must be latent if Wilbur is to acknowledge that the very audience that would sense a link between the death of a garden toad and of a friend fallen in battle is also an audience that is disinclined to mourn openly. This elegiac moment, fleeting as it is, is distinctly private. It allows for an expression of strong feeling without particularly admitting that strong feelings are being expressed. Within a situation that is heavily gendered as male—the lawn-mowing poet is manipulating a machine, the creature injured by the machine is not known for its grace or beauty—Wilbur discovers there is a need for sensitivity, for emotional release. There are pitfalls that exist for the veteran even within the sheltering blandness of the suburban environment, and even a harmless weekend undertaking can turn traumatic. At the same time, however, the poem escapes its own darkness by serving as an emotional release, demonstrating that such an emotional response is not inappropriate.

Among Wilbur's critics, British poet Clive James thought that Wilbur's approach to his writing had a healing function, that it unfolded against a background of trauma never articulated but implicitly negated by the moves of the poet: "Wilbur's intricately coherent art is suited to the long allaying of an old mental wound. . . . [H]e was able to employ the decade or so after the war as a time of tranquility in which his experience of wartime Europe could be assimilated and in a way given back: his images of order, his virtuosities of symmetry, are particularly orderly and symmetrical when he is dealing with Italy and France, the two countries in which he served" (108). It is not often remarked that Wilbur opened his first book with a set of a dozen or so poems set in the European war zone where he saw combat as an infantryman. (Wilbur's continuing decision to organize his collected poems in reverse chronological order guarantees our attention will be distracted from these poems, which the reader comes to, in the 1988 *New and Selected Poems,* on page 337.) That group portrays a Wilbur distinctly aware of the need for healing and restoration. In "First Snow in Alsace" newfallen snow softly but thoroughly obliterates scars of war, lying "rumpled on / What shellbursts scattered and deranged" (*New* 347), remaking the world from an innocent perspective: "At children's windows, heaped, benign, / As always, winter chines the most, / And frost makes marvelous designs." Nurturing is much in evidence. Snow "smoothly clasps" roofs that have been "trustless and estranged." To describe "the ration stacks" as "milky domes" is to turn an institutional larder into motherly breasts. The poem ends with the night guard, coming off duty, warming himself "with a boyish boast: // He was the first to see the snow" (*New* 347).

On the one hand, "First Snow in Alsace" is unquestionably a triumph of the aesthetic. It reclaims the land ravaged by war in the name of a series of elegant descriptions that distract from the reality beneath. But the poem has other work to accomplish as well. It is also a record of war and an act of healing. Wilbur presents that war precisely so it will pass away and be forgotten. First, by rendering everything upon which the snow has fallen as amorphous, it invites the poet to let his thoughts play across it, like a blank Rorschach test. That allows him to insist on good will and to recover noble sentiments from the gouged landscape. Just as healing, however, is the recognition that this snow will melt and pass away. Snow acknowledges its own impermanence, and what it sets in motion is not just a new and intricately constituted landscape that admits care—it also sets time moving, unfreezing the inert devastation by inviting others to think back on their past. The night guard walks slow because he is "Ten first-snows back in thought." Lost in the past he finds within himself the memory that he can place against the surrounding devastation. Everything in the poem contributes to the curative.

Encompassing Opposing Perspectives

One reason these poems resemble healing processes is that in the world that Wilbur constructs, abundance is endless. His poems never contract to a distinct point; they always expand to include additional meanings—a characteristic easiest to see in his briefest poems such as the eight-line "Mind" (from *Things of This World*, 1956). Wilbur compares the mind "in its purest play" to a bat moving with perfect ease through an unlighted cave whose edges it realizes at once and so avoids. But in its conclusion (or better yet, in order for it to conclude), the poem turns upon itself expansively: "The mind is like a bat. Precisely. Save / That in the very happiest intellection / A graceful error may correct the cave" (*New* 240). The poem ends here with an expansion so complete that beyond it there is nowhere to go. The poem must end with this correction of the cave, this modification of the simile which, of course, wins consent by enacting the very exception it proposes. Limits are always pushed and overturned by thought, as in this poem.

The pleasure in this turn-of-the-wrist transformation depends upon recognizing the infinity into which this small poem has just expanded. But the process is singular enough to be misunderstood. In a 1980 critical essay, Jonathan Holden considered "Mind" as demonstrating the New Critical commitment to the autotelic poem, a work that was an "elaborate contraption" designed to "assume significance independent of the life or sensibility of its author" (9). For Holden, the ending of the poem is a give-away, inadvertently revealing Wilbur's cavalier ability to adjust the poem in any way he wishes. In Holden's accusatory reading, the bat is unable to imagine a world outside the cave—it is boxed in, like the reader held captive in a formalist text. Holden wants Wilbur to see the error of his ways and change. He wants him to write a poem with a bat-breakthrough in which an escape is permitted from the cave's tight constrictions. That such a poem never occurred to Wilbur speaks volumes. No Wilbur poem arcs toward a "breakthrough." A Wilbur poem is not only satisfied with the tight spaces in which it finds itself—it revels in them, flourishing there, delighting in close quarters. For the Wilbur poem wants to be packed with a surfeit of meaning. It yearns to brim over with significance. What the poems are about is how much there is to appreciate. Tightness in a Wilbur poem, that sense of being full-to-bursting, is not a product of restraint but the result of abundance. There is always, in Wilbur's universe, more. Some short poems in which two voices speak ("Exeunt," "Two Voices in a Meadow," "Gemini," or "The Aspen and the Stream") are essentialized versions that demonstrate that one fullness leads to another fullness that surpasses even the first. It is never variety that Wilbur celebrates with these diadic constructs but rather the sense of richness that exists within even examples that appear to be radically circumscribed (that is why only two voices or views are entertained). Wilbur's expansions, then, are never permanent displacements since no one set of terms is exposed as dominant over the other. Instead, a new perspective reveals how one set encapsulates the other, incorporating it even while going beyond it.

Wilbur's poetry blocks our attempt to assign priorities. In the pleasure it takes in its own abundance, it fundamentally mystifies. In a poem first published in 1948, "Weather-Bird," he subjects the wind vane on his roof to some metaphysical ponderings that characteristically fail to encompass it. Wilbur wonders whether the iron swallow on its pole is constrained by "a leash he ever strains to break" or if, just the opposite, the swallow is saved from being torn away into the air at the last moment as though the house has "Cast him a line." How to resolve these antipodes?

> Both would be best. Contention magnifies,
> And this discarnate swallow is the crown
> Of all that pulls him down,
> Since as a schoolboy's kite he tries to rise,
> And must be held-to tight
> For fear the house will lose its touch with height. (130)

To choose is odious. Wilbur's poems refuse, generating a sequence of new perspectives that shift the grounds of the issue. Suddenly it is not the swallow but, in Wilbur's last line, the *house* that is the determining feature. Wilbur always embraces all.[7]

Wilbur is able to move with suppleness because he is careful not to restrict his presence in the poem to a specific point of origin. Who speaks a Wilbur poem? Whose voice do we hear and whose perspective do we look out from? In performance, a poem by Wilbur erases the social classes that it may otherwise lightly distinguish. There is no single center in a Wilbur poem, no one origin, in order for there to be many. "Year's End" begins:

> Now winter downs the dying of the year,
> And night is all a settlement of snow;
> From the soft street the rooms of houses show
> A gathered light, a shapen atmosphere,
> Like frozen-over lakes whose ice is thin
> And still allows some stirring down within. (*New* 302)

In a 1950 review, John Ciardi set out to demonstrate that Wilbur was a "master of subtle, urbane and self-convincing diction that was peculiarly his own," and he commented on the opening two lines of "Year's End." "'Settlement' is the fascinating word here," Ciardi proposed, noting that its several meanings—among which he singles out "descent," "colonizing or taking possession of" and "resolution of a dispute"—all combine to advance the poem. "It would be simple to show in a detailed analysis of the poem," he writes confidently, "that all of these happily concurring ambiguities are not only clearly intended but that they establish the very structure and development of the poem" ("Most" 53). Yet Wilbur has a proclivity for finding the word that introduces not just pertinent material but also impertinent. His words can wander from their duties, though attention must be called to them to make them obtrude quite distinctly. "Downs," in Wilbur's first line, is such a word. Like "settlement" several of its meanings can be made to harmonize: it indicates an end as the year comes to a close, and as snow falls it is memorialized by a gesture that is a falling. Yet one meaning is notably dissonant: "downs" also irreverently suggests the white feathers that stuff pillows. Linkage here depends on a visual reporting: white snowflakes resemble soft feathers in their whiteness. In the slowness with which they descend, and in the smoothness and softness they bring to edges of a landscape. As accurate as that meaning is, though, it is entirely at odds with those meanings which center upon the year's end and associate it with mortality, completion, fulfillment. This aberrant meaning turns year's end into a pleasant sleep, a dreamy drifting away. Even the cold of the snow, which serves as a direct connection with the dark meanings of mortality and ending, is erased with the featheriness of the pillow stuffing that is the color and softness of snow.

Both the opposed meanings of "downs," however, underscore the sense in which this poem establishes itself around two conflicting but related themes: the theme of apocalypse, of a final day, of a literal end to the world (so that the title "Year's End" means the end of all years, of all human time), and the theme of the human avoidance or disavowal of such a possibility (so that the title "Year's End" stands for a ritual or convention that, by marking the turn of the year, offers assurances that the passage of time will continue to flow). What is striking about the poem is Wilbur's insistence on sustaining both perspectives simultaneously. For Bruce Michelson, the poem is no more than a dexterous game with language, an exemplary updating of a metaphysical mode: "Every bit of wordplay in this poem has a complex job to do, for each pun must suggest both temporality and eternity, finished and unfinished thought, serene and anxious meditations" (49). But these comments reveal him to be a perfect reader for this poem, or more accurately, the very type of the person whose ability to overlook significant meanings Wilbur both encourages and exposes in the course of the poem. He is the reader unwilling to be engaged by the suggestive edge of the words, the reader who is content with an idea of poetic language as wordplay or punning, the reader whose very denial of the possibilities of poetry is addressed, cultivated, and subtly exposed. Still, it is difficult to imagine how anyone could hear the words in the concluding stanza and keep refusing to see how Wilbur has written a poem with a double edge, a poem that is on the one hand, and for a certain type of reader, a harmless meditation, while on the other hand, for another kind of reader, a dazzling exposition of the mind in the act of evading forbidden and terrifying thoughts, the mind just barely touching upon fear and doubt—and then refusing to acknowledge them:

> And at Pompeii
>
> The little dog lay curled and did not rise
> But slept the deeper as the ashes rose
> And found the people incomplete, and froze
> The random hands, the loose unready eyes
> Of men expecting yet another sun
> To do the shapely thing they had not done.

These sudden ends of time must give us pause.
We fray into the future, rarely wrought
Save in the tapestries of afterthought.
More time, more time. Barrages of applause
Come muffled from a buried radio.
The New-year bells are wrangling with the snow. (*New* 302)

Up to these fourth and fifth (and final) stanzas, it may be possible to feel
comfortable with the idea that "Year's End" is primarily a meditation in the
metaphysical mode on the wintry landscapes of late December. Wilbur
describes "frozen-over" lakes and recalls seeing leaves in ice, "frozen as they
fell." This he further associates with the imprint of delicate ferns in fossils
and, in turn, "Great mammoths overthrown" from their "gray / And
changeless lands of ice." Up to this point, the emphasis on flora and fauna
has kept the focus apart from humans. The end of time affects leaves, ferns,
and mammoths. But with the turn to "Pompeii," to a "little dog" to "people
incomplete," the poem moves into another key. Here is an apocalypse that
destroyed a civilization. Nonetheless, if the poem has now slipped into
disturbing territory, we should recognize that similar disturbances had
been at work in earlier passages. We can look back to the frozen-over lake
and see that the "ice is thin" and another glance at the second stanza reveals that the leaves that fell were "held as dancers in a spell." Those ferns
in the third stanzas "laid their fragile cheeks against the stone," in a trope
that in retrospect seems truly peculiar. Does a fern have a "cheek"? We accept it because Wilbur invites us to let "fragile" be the governing descriptive term. But why then are we so eager to accept that invitation to deny
this anthropomorphosis? The actuality, of course, is that Wilbur is playing
within and around our all-too-eager willingness to dissociate ourselves
from the notion of a civilization's demise. When he writes: "Great mammoths overthrown / Composedly have made their long sojourns, / Like
palaces of patience, in the gray / And changeless lands of ice," his description of the mammoths as creatures "overthrown" like "palaces of patience,"
even as it affords a link with dynasties and great civilizations, also occurs
in an adjectival phrase and a prepositional phrase that place such affiliation
deeply (and "safely") in the background. But Wilbur's deployment of syntax is no accident, and certainly not simply not a demonstration of an elegant hypotactic style: it is central to the hide-and-seek, evasion-with-
drawal that he sets in motion throughout the poem. Sharp seeing is
precisely what the poem does *not* enable—or more accurately, what the
poem helps enable us to grasp is how easily we lapse into a strategy in which

we prefer not to see sharply. Like the inhabitants of Pompeii who refused to believe in the extent to which they were threatened, such readers are "people incomplete" with their "loose unready eyes." It is indeed possible to get all the way through the poem, as Michelson demonstrates, with one's innocence intact, with eyes unfocused. But the reader Wilbur hopes for is the one who recognizes how the very language of the poem prompts a choice to be taken. And of course readers of the poem at its time of publication (1950) and for some years thereafter would be citizens of a country that was, on the one hand, nearly frozen with fear at the prospect of the A-bomb and then the H-bomb and, on the other hand, determined to proceed as if there was nothing anyone could do about the threat of imminent disaster.[8] It seems especially pointed that the cry for "More time, more time" in the last stanza is punctuated in such a way as to enervate it of any urgency.

Protocols for Appreciation

Although Wilbur has never returned to the scenes of combat that were so prominent in his first book, the movements of repossessing and renewing that are strategies for healing in a poem like "First Snow in Alsace" are perfected in his poetry of the mid-1950s. "Statues" (which the *Paris Review* published in 1953 and which was collected in *Things of This World* in 1956) uses a different setting (a public park), new protagonists (children playing, not snow), and other beneficiaries (not soldiers but pedestrians strolling), but it performs in the same way. Children who are playing at "statues"— they hurl themselves, then freeze in outrageous postures—delight bystanders who are charmed and refreshed:

> Two nuns regard it with habitual love,
> Moving along a path as mountains move
> Or seem to move when traversed by a cloud;
>
> The soldier breaks his iron pace;
> Linked lovers pause to gaze; and every role
> Relents,—until the feet begin to stroll
> Or stride again. (*New* 251)

Just as snow alters the war-torn landscape, so children playing eliminate hard edges and open possibilities. The multiplicity of options is stressed in Wilbur's description of maple trees that extravagantly reverse figure and ground: "Their shadows all a brilliant disrepair," Wilbur writes in one line, then in the next: "A wash of dodging stars." In "First Snow in Alsace" Wilbur carefully enumerated the possibilities that became available once snow took definition away from the landscape; in "Statues" he depicts those multiplying possibilities through the viewpoints of others who each respond from their own perspective. But Wilbur is staging it so that rewards fall to those who allow room for their daily pattern to be interrupted by this exceptional event.

Wilbur is also staging another aspect of "Statues": he is instructing his readers in how best to use his own work. To readers who follow Wilbur's promptings for the usage of the poem, his work aims to present itself as an exceptional event that ushers in a refreshing plenitude. It is not, however, a disruption: if anything, it reconfirms what most audience members would be likely to bring to the poem since the poem is organized to be capacious enough to include readings that even contradict each other. Wilbur's representative audience is not one but many. To the nuns, the children are one thing, to the soldier another, to the lovers a third. To emphasize the ability of the poem to represent so expansive a space Wilbur spikes "Statues" at the end with a reader who gets it wrong, who is unable to deal with the exceptional quality of the children playing. This is an "aging bum, / Brought by his long evasion and distress / Into an adamantine shapelessness," who doesn't belong to the community of strollers because he has lost his ability to play appreciatively in a game-like spirit. As a result, when he looks he "Stares at the image of his kingdom come." He responds to the children not playfully but by rigidly taking them as moralists commenting upon him. Of course we know at once why he is quick to extract such a message: he is too close to the reality of being found one morning frozen on his bench to take pleasure in children's games of "freeze" (one source of this pleasure is the distance that stands between the children at play and anything like mortality). But it is not quite accurate to say that the bum reads incorrectly. Rather, because of his fallen condition he is incapable of responding except in this moralistic way, extracting a message from the poem. That the richness of this experience exists for him only as a pointed moral is a symptom of his deep abjection. By contrast, the strollers (the surrogates for most readers) act in ways that are independent, and they respond to the children with freedom and with pleasure, appreciating lavish detail and accurate description. The last thing they expect to extract is a moral, and it is the last thing we should expect from poetry, too.

Wilbur produces poem after poem that eludes efforts to conscript it to some limited field of meaning. On more than one occasion, he is a deft practitioner who anticipates the charge that his poetry—or more broadly, the kind of experience in which his poetry specializes—might be inconsequential by displaying within the poem that the marginal events that his very poem is best at reporting do have a use when taken up by others and entertained. "Statues" helps direct us in how its events should be appreciated. Wilbur processes its reception by presenting a representative audience that demonstrates the appropriate range of responses. The pleasure and delight they take become a model for how a reader should appreciate the poetic moment and even accept that it may not be immediately useful. Wilbur allays the anxieties of new readers who hesitate before the poem, expecting it to be more of a meaningful than a pleasurable experience. With Wilbur's help, they have a chance to accept the pleasure of the moment without expecting it to be more, even as their possible fears about how the pleasurable is to be used are set to rest by the way the poem demonstrates its pleasures being used.

This ability to conflate both pleasure and usefulness is at the center of the work that was not only the most widely admired of all Wilbur's poems but one of the most highly regarded poems of its time. "Love Calls Us to the Things of This World" has been described by Peter Stitt as "Wilbur's best-known, most-admired poem" (35). Peter Davison quoted it in its entirety as a prelude to the memoir of Wilbur in his reconstruction of the daily lives of poets writing in Boston in the 1950s (58–59). Anthony Ostroff used it to inaugurate his series in which contemporary poets commented on distinguished works by their peers (and in which Robert Horan, May Swenson, and Richard Eberhart admired it). One cannot, however, call its success enduring. It has not fared well in recent major anthologies: neither the fourth edition of the Norton anthology of American literature (1997) nor the third edition of the Heath anthology (1997) nor the Oxford anthology of modern American poetry (2000) include it among their selections. What was there about this poem that once made it so authoritative and what has changed to make it fall from favor?

A poem so wildly popular might presumably divulge the secret of its popularity through its structure, but the situation of this poem, when paraphrased, only emphasizes its oddity. The poem begins as its third-person speaker wakens in a bright morning suddenly to believe that the air is "awash with angels." This is not a fleeting impression: it continues to be pursued and elaborated over two of the five-line stanzas that make up the poem. When the wind suddenly dies, it is revealed that the angels are merely laundry lent temporary animation by the wind, and the illusion is broken. A sense of loss, regret, and anger spills into the fourth stanza in which the poet yearns for there to be "nothing on earth but laundry . . . clear dances done in the sight of heaven." But as the sun rises and the poet more fully awakens, "in a changed voice" he brings the poem to a close by distributing advice that is suffused with a sense of largesse. The idea of angel-laundry is no longer held tightly, as if one must no longer cling to the remnants of a lovely but fading dream: it is imaginatively distributed to all in a celebratory spirit in which Wilbur is nonetheless poking fun at himself or at the need to furnish a "climactic" ending to his poem. His seriocomic pronouncements mix wryness with pomposity:

> "Let there be clean linen for the backs of thieves;
> Let lovers go fresh and sweet to be undone,
> And the heaviest nuns walk in a pure floating
> Of dark habits,
> > keeping their difficult balance." (*New* 234)

The poem may be said to move "dialectically" with this final statement presenting itself as the earned resolution, the harmonious product of the process unfolding as the work moved from idealism to realism to this pragmatic compromise in which real bodies wear real clothes. But the poem's charm lies in the half-smile Wilbur wears throughout the performance. As correct as the poem is, there is something slightly foolish and even trivial about it—laundry as angels? The rising sun solving all? Then the closing benediction and the zany distribution of the laundry—clothes for the backs of thieves who should be punished on their backs, sweet clothes for lovers who will just take them off right away, and dark habits for nuns who should not find their balance difficult to keep?

The idea of such a silly poem has provoked Marjorie Perloff. In a debunking mood, she is quick to question, in a 1998 essay, the whiteness of the sheets glimpsed in the cityscape in which Wilbur (once in a descriptive comment) placed the opening scene, insisting that they would "probably be covered with specks of dust, grit, and maybe even a trace or two of bird droppings" ("1956" 86) At the very least they "would surely be a bit on the grungy side" (85). Moreover, Wilbur's lack of realism extends even to the real (and hidden) agent in the poem, the woman whose work is indispensable if the laundry is to be done. Where is she in the poem, as a matter of fact? And where indeed are the "things of the world," Perloff asks, when so many of the aspects of the poem that deal with things and worldliness seem studiously avoided?[9] Everything, not just the sheets and clothes and towels, has, she hints, been "laundered," and she would expose Wilbur as the behind-the-scenes manipulator who has steadily presented a scene that is suspiciously neat, free of discord—in short, a false balance, not "difficult" at all: "it is the poet as producer, not the poet inside the poem who is in control, and thus there is no room for deviance, no message from one person to another" ("1956" 87).

It is notable, as Perloff observes so sharply, that the laundry-experience is blissfully intangible. Richard Eberhart, one of the poets commenting on the poem for Ostroff's 1957 symposium, nearly undoes the whole poem with a single down-to-earth remark: "I ought to add that it is a man's poem. Certainly not all women would like a laundry poem which pays no heed to hard work and coarsened hands. They might say, poet, have your ruddy dream, but give us better detergents" ("On 'Love'" 5). Yet it seems essential for the opening vision to be as remote and unreal and otherworldly as possible. It opens with a fantasy that is rich with an unvoiced guiltiness—a longing to be free of the messy individuality of persons, to be the single subject in a world of things in which all the objects are graceful and dance in the light. The poem's first half performs its freshening, illuminating false-dawn recovery of the world of the angelically unreal in order that we may turn out from it to accept the chastening discovery of the "truth" of the morning world in which clothes are worn by humans, not inspirited by angels. The essence of this poetic is to offer first refreshment, then reality. The artist's world is here linked to the ephemeral, the marginal, to the world of women's work and children's games. When that world is withdrawn, the effect is shattering: there is a sense of emptiness that overwhelms, and there is rage in the heart. "Blessed rape" resembles a curse that the disgruntled figure hurls at the world. It is what happens next, however, that is the central point of the poem. The poet does not remain cast down, for the reality is that this is not just a dream or a daydream in which the loss of a moment of supernal loveliness is truly shattering, even embittering. It is, instead, a poem that is very much staged: Wilbur as (in Perloff's words) "producer" now goes on to demonstrate the advantage of the poetic turn, which is that it *is* possible to take up that pure moment of origin with which the poem opened, even to lose it for a moment or to find that it has become utterly intangible, but then to invoke that opening instant, in a new way and on a new level, wherein what is lost is recovered and what had been overturned as empty is now understood as filled.

The ending, of course, is not supposed to be the least bit sober. Thieves, lovers, nuns are thrown together quirkily, as if they all might find things to say to each other—and from Augustine's view (as a onetime libertine whose writings were foundational for the Catholic church) they surely do. If Perloff is in some way right, then, to accuse Wilbur of silliness, and even unreality, why then was the work so welcome in its time? While Perloff's theory that the poem exemplifies an interest in "equipoise" and "universality" goes along with a dismissive narrative that paints Wilbur as a bland craftsman in an era committed to deliberate acts of forgetfulness, it is unlikely that so abstract a project would have the deep appeal of this poem.[10] In its time, the poem accomplished a task more arduous and more pointed, nicely demonstrating the distinction between the world of dreams like daydreams (which is also the world of mass culture), and the world of dreams which is the world of poetry (if not also Augustinian idealism). When a daydream-like dream is over, the resulting plunge back into reality resembles the collapse in which angels are exposed as just a mistake: emptied out, the spirit is downcast, the absence of its once-glittering vision disorienting and dismaying. As daydream, the vision cannot be reconstituted. And were Wilbur not producing a poem, the experience would end in the darkness of this plea that also resembles a curse: "Oh let there be nothing on earth but laundry." But the turn that Wilbur makes transforms his experience into poetry—it is that displacement and repossession of the vision by conceiving its local application. Poetry's real dreams downsize deep dreams and accommodate them to actuality. Of course the possibility that the turn cannot be taken is also explored in the poem, long enough for us to recognize those feelings of loss and disorientation that accompany the recognition that something wonderful which we had thought to have made our own turned out to have been just as impossible as it had seemed. That moment of despair and loss is what the poem plays off and moves against. What is most "real," then, in the poem is just that sensation of having been cheated or left behind: not the wild belief that the air is filled with angels, which of course must be proven to be a fantasy, but rather that sharp pang of loss in which the fantastic turns out to be merely what it was—the fantastic. That is not a moment that is particularly limited to the 1950s, though the sense that abundance is not enough, that the combination of wealth and free time did not necessarily deliver happiness, was an important discovery that seems to have been made over and over in the course of the postwar years. When Wilbur demonstrates how to recoil from that keen disappointment, how to recover by inventively assuming the role of someone who drolly distributes feelings of largesse and pleasure, then he is not only modeling how to act but he is also acknowledging the negatives and positives of a world in which the abundant is continually presenting us with moments of intense pleasure that may just as abruptly turn fleeting.

Here as in other poems, Wilbur continues in his role as the postwar poet whose sense of audience encompasses those still new to poetry. He can recognize and address the experience of feeling aesthetically cheated by a vision too impossibly alluring, but what is more, he can responsibly point a way beyond the moments of dislocation and anger. Perloff's claim that "the actual 'things of this world,' in 1956, are studiously avoided" is only true if those "things" are limited to "the real hands of laundresses, hands that Eliot," Perloff adds, "half a century earlier, had envisioned as 'lifting dingy shades in a thousand furnished rooms'" ("1956" 86). But Wilbur has long advanced past that half century, and when he sighs over "Rosy hands in the rising steam" he is mocking himself and his longing for an unreal perfection. Remarkably suited to the limits of a culture of abundance, few poems dealt more smartly with worldly things circa 1956.

2 ANTHOLOGY WARS

The "Chicago School" has been known to readers of the quarterlies until now for its commando raids: essays on critical theory and aesthetics. . . . With this book they are making a landing in force.
—Eliseo Vivas, "Neo-Aristotelians" (1953)

What no one should have doubted is becoming more and more glaringly obvious: that A Portrait of the Artist as a Young Man *and* Ulysses *constitute question and answer, fortress and siege-gun: an indivisible aesthetic whole.*
—Hugh Kenner, "*Portrait* in Perspective" (1948)

Here and there, however, the intrepid dilettante has seized a beach-head and refuses to be thrown off, and nowhere is he more sternly ensconced that on that peninsula of biology called "natural history."
—Edward Philip Sheridan, "Review: Handbook" (1953)

Military phrases, martial turns of speech, and metaphors drawn from war appear throughout the 1950s in even the most unlikely places. All military talk is, of course, a pointedly masculine discourse, and its omnipresence may confirm the existence of a new social class in the university, one familiar with the front lines of war. But that the discourse flourished suggests that martial tropes lent themselves easily to a variety of situations. One of the most visible battlegrounds as different groups sought to define the era in terms that suited themselves was the poetry anthology, although these skirmishes were often mounted as guerrilla actions, and not all conquests were evident.

Of course the very idea of assembling a definitive anthology of *contem-*

porary poetry was already an aggressive action. Prior to this, poetry anthologies either prudently reduced their holdings as they approached the present (Louis Untermeyer, Oscar Williams) or served as special-interest compilations for poets actively campaigning for recognition (the Georgians, *des Imagistes*). But the 1950s saw one anthologist after another stepping forward to define a new generation of contemporary poets, packaging that poetry and certifying its freshness. By 1965, George Garrett could reasonably complain that "these days new literary generations appear, announce themselves, are evaluated, question that evaluation, then by inevitable compromise find a niche, and vanish with a frequency which would baffle even the most subtle demographer" (222). Why the frequency? One answer is that the poetry anthology of the 1950s was typically edited by a poet or by poets, not a scholar or an academic. What David Perkins in *Is Literary History Possible?* has called the "inertia of cultural transmission" (76)—that reluctance by scholars to modify too extensively the findings of their predecessors—applied less to poets who were not so much interested in maintaining historical continuity as in arranging a center-stage setting for their own work and the work of friends. As a result, these postwar anthologies offered surprisingly bold repositionings that affected even poets with reputations that might have been thought to be secure.

Some of the brashness of these poet-anthologists may have been inherited from their immediate precursor, Selden Rodman, whose 1949 anthology, *One Hundred Modern Poems,* went on to enjoy a prolonged life as one of the earliest New American Library "Mentor" series of softcovers (reprinted in 1951, in 1952, twice in 1953, in 1956, and in 1958). In this anthology as in others, Rodman was an effective spokesperson for the Left.[1] The one hundred modern poems of his title are spread evenly over four sections with twenty-five works in each, not all of which are in verse. Kafka, Joyce, Hemingway, Faulkner, Agee, and even Norman Mailer can represent "the modern poem" in prose excerpts because what characterizes the modern poem is its unstable blend of experimental language and social activism. What is most interesting in Rodman's organization is that it effectively minimizes any rupture between the experimental 1920s and the political 1930s. Part 1, "Beyond Frontiers," uses writers such as Rimbaud, Blok, Rilke, Michaux, Pasternak, and Seferis to establish a foundation for modern poetry that is international. Part 2, "Forerunners," depicts a specifically Anglo-American modernism in which works by Yeats, Eliot, and Auden, as well as Hart Crane and William Carlos Williams, form British and American counterparts to the European texts of part 1. Part 3, "The Age of Satire," continues to feature British and American poets in the Anglo-American tradition. And part 4, "The 'Forties," introduces works by Dylan Thomas, Robert Lowell, and Richard Wilbur along with poems by lesser-known names—Adam Drinan, Fleming MacLiesh, and Myron O'Higgins.

Rodman's juxtapositions are designed to be provocative and insightful. For example, he will follow an excerpt from Gertrude Stein's "Four Saints in Three Acts" with an excerpt from Kenneth Fearing. Stein's language play—her extreme attentiveness to the "interval" between words that, as Karen Ford explains, "mediates their meanings both by bringing them together and keeping them apart" (77)—brings out the density of the verbal surface in Fearing's colloquial line, while Fearing's dramatizations of the way in which, in Walter Kalaidjian's words, "one's full social being is constantly deferred and dispersed across a network of alienating subject positions" (204) are matched by the linguistic roles that Stein effortlessly and playfully slips in and out of. Nor did Rodman limit his bold repositionings to poets like Stein and Fearing whose reputations were not yet settled. Consider the role in which he cast Eliot—a role it is possible to describe as piquant. Of the one hundred modern poems, Eliot is credited with just two. As a "Forerunner" in part 2, and a proponent of Anglo-American modernism, he was represented by an excerpt (the first thirty-seven lines) from the first chorus in his verse-play *The Rock*, "The Eagle Soars in the Summit of Heaven." Here Eliot frets, in flat and prosaic lines, about the marginalization of the church in England. The excerpt concludes:

> In the pleasant countryside, there it seemed
> That the country now is only fit for picnics.
> And the Church does not seem to be wanted
> In country or in suburb, and in the town
> Only for important weddings. (91)

By publishing the Eliot who laments the loss of the institutional role of the Christian church, Rodman foregrounds Eliot's activist strain. But Rodman also sets Eliot's tendentiousness in a wider frame, placing him alongside and in dialogue with European counterparts like Paul Claudel, from whose "Five Grand Odes" Rodman extracts a passage that includes these lines: "But after the abundance of April and the superabundance of spring, / Here is the work of August, here is the extermination of noon, / Here are the broken seals of God that are come to try the earth by fire!" (64). In Rodman's arrangement, both Eliot and Claudel are experimentalists who blur, each in their own way, distinctions between prose and verse, even as they both take on the role of apologists for Christianity—a Christianity divided into differing sects of Anglican and Catholic.

Eliot's second appearance occurs in part 3, as a player in "The Age of Satire," where he is represented by "Mr. Appolinax." To select from Eliot's poems of the 1920s only this one (Eliot did not include it in his own 1950 paperback *Selected Poems*) may be an aberrant choice but perhaps an inspired one. As a portrait of a type from a social class, the poem lends impetus to Rodman's claim that the 1920s and the 1930s could be linked together as one age of satire. "Mr. Appolinax," after all, looks ahead to Auden, one of whose selections is "Herod," a prose passage from *For the Time Being* (1944) that, insofar as it depicts a type, echoes "Mr. Appolinax" even as it looks back to the Christianity of *The Rock*.

Rodman's anthology shrewdly purveys an identity for the modern poem, circa 1880–1950, as a work that partakes of both the experimental and the activist. If that poem's language is a powerful new instrument that acknowledges a linguistic revolution, that instrument is in the service of issues that have social consequence. None of this work is experimental for its own sake, nor is any committed to directly delivering a social message. Works engage readers, in Rodman's presentation, to upset conventional expectations *and* to launch thoughtful social critique. The figures that he pairs are not Eliot and Pound, not twin figures of high modernist experimentalism, but rather Eliot and Auden, older- and younger-generation representatives of poets who, as a group, are embarked on a program to revitalize the tradition of verse-writing while working through a sustained critique of current social beliefs.[2]

A Poetry for a "New Class"

Although *One Hundred Modern Poems* included a small selection of contemporary American poets, defining a new poetic generation was not its primary goal. That task fell to John Ciardi's *Mid-Century American Poets,* published in 1950, the first anthology to propound a concise aesthetic for postwar poetry. Yet Ciardi's anthology was by no means in disagreement with the presumptions that underlay Rodman's version of literary history. The worth of American poetry at mid-century, Ciardi wrote in his "Foreword," is that it has "captured the American voice-box" (xiii) by smoothly enlisting the services of previous technical advances by forerunners like Eliot and Pound. This new generation of poets has drawn upon, Ciardi explains, "continental *avant garde* experiments" to endow itself with a "stock of techniques richer and more varied than any that has been available to American writers" (xiii). Here poetry is not so much individual self-expression as it is intelligent conversation, "a poetry of individual appraisal, tentative, self-questioning, introspective, socially involved, and always reserving for itself the right to meet experience in its humanistic environment" (xxx). Open to worldly activities, it promotes thoughtful discussion.

Ciardi's view of the postwar generation presents poetry as a highly socialized text that is the product of a community of writers whose interests converge with those of informed citizens. "This is a generation not of Bohemian extravagance," he maintained, "but of self-conscious sanity in an urbane and cultivated poetry that is the antithesis of the Bohemian spirit" (xxix). And to emphasize that poets had become active members of a responsible community, he invited the fifteen poets he had solicited for inclusion in the anthology to select their own works. Those fifteen writers included two women (Muriel Rukeyser and Elizabeth Bishop) and thirteen men (Richard Wilbur, Peter Viereck, Theodore Roethke, Karl Shapiro, Winfield Townley Scott, John Frederick Nims, E. L. Mayo, Robert Lowell, Randall Jarrell, John Holmes, Richard Eberhart, Delmore Schwartz, and Ciardi himself).[3] In addition, he asked each one to write a brief "prose foreword" that would introduce their work, some indication of their "personal writing principle or rejection of principle" (xxvii). (Ciardi furnished a prompt in the form of twelve "suggested questions for the statement of writing principles" which he also placed on display in his overall introduction.) These decisions demonstrated not only Ciardi's trust in the community of poets but also his commitment to an audience that might benefit from commentary that would smooth their way as they read. For Ciardi, the anthology hinged on just such an awareness of audience, as he explained in a 1949 letter to Karl Shapiro, soliciting him as a contributor: "My special concern is for the reader of poetry. I cannot escape a feeling that the poets must face the responsibility of providing themselves with a wider audience. That does not mean an all inclusive audience" (*Letters* 56).

Not everyone in these same years, it is worth mentioning, was eager to open doors widely to a new audience for poetry. Remarks by Allen Tate should remind us that, however effectively the New Criticism was disseminated by second- and third-generation followers in the postwar classroom, some first-generation New Critics would have been the last to conceive their work as a democratizing social movement. Tate continued to elevate reading as an arduous and scrupulous practice, one that deserved comparison with the sciences at their most theoretical. To dilute that practice was, to Tate's way of thinking, a threat to the future of poetry. In his introduction to the American poets in the anthology he coedited with David Cecil, *Modern Verse in English, 1900–1950* (showcased as an article in a 1956 *Sewanee Review*), modern poetry was marked by flashes of highly individualized genius that, precisely because they were idiosyncratic and unpredictable, would remain forever apart from ordinary usage. A poetry that was "difficult," not "accessible," had value: it "resisted the strong political pressures which ask the poet to 'communicate' to passively conditioned persons what a service society expects them to feel" ("Introduction" 45). Tate endorsed Stephen Spender's observation that "a modern American poem is frequently a 'cultural act,' a conscious affirmation of an international culture above the commercialized mass culture of the United States at large" (47). But he had no interest in attempting to lure a new audience away from that "commercialized mass culture." The poems chosen for Tate's anthology might go unread, Tate conceded, but wasn't that symptomatic of this dark time? Rather than play down to an audience that could never appreciate them, poets were better off writing for each other. In a passage that he thought important enough to italicize, Tate summarized his sense of the relation between poet and audience: *"My neighbor cannot understand or even try to read my poems, but I am expressing something about him that he himself doesn't know"* (47).

For Ciardi, that neighbor was the very person who should not be left behind. In the introduction to his own group of poems in his anthology, entitled "To a Reader of (Some) General Culture," he resorted to italics for his first principle— *"Poetry should be understandable"*—and his third— *"Poetry should be about the lives of people"* (248–49). Ciardi's "people" is already nomenclature different from Tate's "neighbor," which bears within it a hint of condescension. Tate's neighbor is someone next door with really no attributes. By contrast, Ciardi has such a vivid impression of his audience that he begins the introduction to his poems by describing not his poetry but the audience for whom he wrote that poetry. "Who is the reader of general culture?" he asked:

> I am willing to apply the term to any man [*sic*] who meets most of the following specifications. He goes to symphony. He likes to spend an afternoon at the museums and galleries and he has some notion of what he looks at there. He knows part of the difference between the Ballet Russe and a chorus line. He has read enough psychology to know that

only an expert should tamper with Freud. He is aware that ideas have histories, and that the ideas held by the people about him are usually retrograde in the best history of things. He has browsed through philosophy in a general way. He knows other societies have come before his, and that others will come after his, and that none have been absolute and that none will be, but that some common dynamics of the human spirit has shone through them all, and that the best name anyone has found to give that dynamics is Art. He entertains ideas and seeks to place them in perspective. He tries, as best the world and his checkbook will let him, to keep up with the best prose available, and he does not confuse the best prose with the book club selections. He knows some of the poetry of the past and values it, and would like to know more about the poetry of his own times, but has found over and over that the books he picks up to read simply baffle him. (244)

There are a great many things to be said about this profile, not the least of which is its portrayal of the audience as patently male, but perhaps the most salient point is that it so clearly epitomizes the individual who has recently entered what Jackson Lears has described as that "'new class' of salaried managers, administrators, academics, technicians and journalists—people who manipulated symbols rather than made things, whose stock in trade consisted of their organizational, technical, conceptual or verbal skills" (50). If Ciardi's depiction of the ideal reader produces a figure who is conspicuously masculine—a middle-management professional who values confidence and mobility—that portrait further translates into social terms what Ciardi envisions for poetry. Portrayed as if it could easily cross between high and low culture, this poetry will be urbane, floating free of parochial considerations, mobile, operating within spaces notable for their breadth and scope. (It will not be sentimental, overly passionate, obsessively committed, nor will it display any form of excess; it will not depend upon or call forth exquisitely delicate responses.) With this kind of writing, the poet bids to enter the public domain as a player with serious and smart (not solemn and pious) attitudes.

Ciardi was not alone in envisioning such possibilities. His poets inherit a mantle Louise Bogan was defining in *Achievement in American Poetry* (1951): "The poet of the future need waste little time and energy in establishing the fact that his art has importance. Neither will he be forced to uncover for himself the scope and difficulty of that art" (108). As serious undertakings, poems are thought-provoking observations of a citizen whose attention has been engaged by matters in the surrounding world.

Bogan also believed poetry was poised to address a new and ready audience. She listed the opportunities that awaited the poet:

> In America, a great many of the cultural advantages asked for by Pound in *Patria Mia* (essays on American culture written prior to 1913, but only recently rediscovered and published), have come to pass. Foundations devoted to the subsidy of creative talent generously function. Libraries and museums have opened out and become usable institutions. Certain universities have come to include "creative" courses in their curricula. And, in spite of all evidence to the contrary, as opportunity for the training of talent has broadened, a growing audience has, at the same time, come to appreciate sincere and original work in all fields of the arts. (108)

Bogan pronounces an end to the poetry of modernist exile. Today's poets attract a "growing audience" because their originality is balanced with a sincerity that wins them respect. Both audience and poet have matured.

The poets that Ciardi sponsors keep true to this vision of civic responsibility. They present themselves as trustworthy guides, individuals of evident character. When they stand outdoors at night, below the stars, it is not to admire the delicacy of their light:

> Huge as the night with stars above your house
> These patterns laid on emptiness revolve
> Beyond all searching.
> (E. L. Mayo, "In the Web" 152)

> The brittle night sky sparkled like a tune
> Tapped and tinkled upon the xylophone:
> Empty and vain, a glittering dune . . .
> (Delmore Schwartz, "Starlight" 298)

> From the grove under the spire
> Stars shine, and a wandering light
> Is kindled for the mourner, man.
> (Randall Jarrell, "Country Life" 198)

> . . . I one fleck on the numbered face
> one dot on the star-swarming heaven
> stand here in this street of all our streets . . .
> (John Frederick Nims, "New Year's Eve" 126)

These poets know that present-day stars wheel in a void. To have the strength of character to endure an indifferent universe is one measure of the poet's integrity. These poets accept their role as responsible witnesses. When they speak in the first person singular, the "I" who is observing is careful and thoughtful—a figure always more representative than particular. Yet masks are never welcome. No "persona" stands between Richard Eberhart and the example of death that he confronts in "The Groundhog": "In June, amid the golden fields, / I saw a groundhog lying dead" (234). The flat straightforwardness of this poetry testifies to its honesty, its decision not to lay claim to any of the special pleadings of rhetoric. Elizabeth Bishop's hesitations and corrections testify to the effort with which she pursues accuracy, getting the detail fixed right:

> and then I saw
> that from his lower lip
> —if you could call it a lip—
> grim, wet, and weapon-like,
> hung five old pieces of fish-line,
> or four and wire leader
> with the swivel still attached . . .
>   ("The Fish" 277)

Bishop's painstaking sense of precision had special value for a generation that had experienced the rhetorical excess of wartime. These poets sought a writing that moved with directness but retained its intimacy:

> The world is full of loss; bring, wind, my love,
> My home is where we make our meeting-place,
> And love whatever I shall touch and read
> Within that face.
>   (Muriel Rukeyser, "Song" 66)

Yet these poets also recognize the intricate new world that surrounds them. No down-home colloquial style can put things over. Their language remains dry, spare, verging on the epigrammatic. Delmore Schwartz excelled at that:

> You cannot sit on bayonets,
> Nor can you eat among the dead.
> When all are killed, you are alone,
> A vacuum comes where hate has fed.
>   ("For the One" 288)

But so, in this collection, did Theodore Roethke:

> The wasp waits.
>> The edge cannot eat the centre.
> The grape glistens.
>> The path tells little to the serpent.
> An eye comes out of the wave.
>> The journey from flesh is longest.
> A rose sways least.
>> The redeemer comes a dark way. ("Shape" 80)

There may be irony in some of these poems but few ironic stances. A stance would be too protective, but a touch of irony is necessary to register the painfulness that resides in real-world events. Winfield Townley Scott describes how a sailor who had beheaded a Japanese soldier cleaned his "souvenir" by dragging it aft in a net on his homeward-bound ship:

>   the cold bone tumbling
> Beneath the foaming wake, weed-worn and salt-cut
> Rolling safe among fish and washed with Pacific . . .
>> ("U.S. Sailor" 112)

The ironic note introduced by "Rolling *safe* among fish" is no more than a detail, unnerving though it may be. It occurs in passing as a dry, knowing, worldly touch—the bit of cynicism worn lightly.

The Predominance of the Elegiac

The poets that Ciardi selected generally agree on the virtue of what has been sometimes called a "middle style"—a style that is adjectivally unadorned, restricted to a diction of familiar words, and straightforward in its syntax. But there was one area in which these rules of conduct were suspended: in writing elegies to those whose deaths were directly associated with World War II. In these elegies language regularly fails at containing its topic. The surface of the poem is disrupted, and words are dislodged from regular syntactic formations. Nims's "Trainwrecked Soldiers," for example, reports on the irony of an event in which soldiers far away from battlefield perils meet the death they had otherwise avoided. The choked anger with which it ends expresses itself in a verbal stutter:

But we who walk this track, who read, or see
In a dark room the shaggy films of wreck—
What do the carrion bent like letters spell
More than the old *sententiae* of chance?—
Greek easier (*alinon, alinon*) than this fact.
You lie wry X, poor men, or empty O,
Crux in a savage tongue none of us know. (133)

Although the page begins in Nims's characteristic style, it ends by insisting that the enormity of this death has disrupted the poet's ability to continue in the customary manner. A similar breakdown is marked in Peter Viereck's elegy to a shipmate killed in combat. "*Vale* from Carthage (Spring 1944)" recalls a promise to meet in Times Square at war's end. It concludes:

I saw an ancient Roman's tomb and read
"*Vale*" in stone. Here two wars mix their dead:
    Roman, my shipmate's dream walks hand in hand
    With yours tonight ("New York again" and "Rome"),
    Like widowed sisters bearing home
    On tired heads through hot Tunisian sand
    In good cool urns, and says, "I understand."
Roman, you'll see your Forum Square no more;
What's left but this to say of any war? (33)

These various elegies reveal themselves to be impressively adaptive to different maneuverings. Lowell's elegy rather quickly spills over into (among other things) a critique of the Protestant Ethic:

I see the Quakers drown and hear their cry:
"If God himself had not been on our side,
If God himself had not been on our side,
When the Atlantic rose against us, why,
Then it had swallowed us quick." ("Quaker" 171)

Lowell spends little time brooding as he openly bends the occasion to his own agenda. By contrast, Muriel Rukeyser had begun a series of elegies after the Spanish Civil War had claimed dear friends. She chose to print the tenth, "Elegy in Joy," that concludes the series, and its passages of ecstasy affirm "the expiation journey / toward peace which is many wishes flaming together":

Now there are no maps and no magicians.
No prophets but the young prophet, the sense of the world.
The gift of our time, the world to be discovered.
All the continents giving off their several lights,
the one sea, and the air. And all things glow.
　　　("Tenth Elegy" 64)

Rukeyser's expansiveness contrasts with the lightly worn irony of Ciardi's "Elegy Just in Case," a self-commissioned wake that articulates the helplessness of the modern soldier. Its military jargon is one index of war's anonymity. What except bitter humor protects the soldier? (And bitter humor is no protection at all.)

File the pages, pack the clothes,
Send the coded word through air:
"We regret and no one knows
Where the sgt. goes from here."

"Missing as of inst. oblige,
Deepest sorrow and remain . . ."
Shall I grin at persiflage?
Could I have my skin again

Would I choose a business form
Stilted mute as a giraffe,
Or a pinstripe unicorn
On a cashier's epigraph? (253)

Jarrell, by contrast, spoke in the voice of the wife of a pilot killed in the Pacific whose death years later she was still mourning:

　　　　　The sea is empty,
As I am empty, stirring the charred and answered
Questions about your home, your wife, your cat
That stayed at home with me—that died at home
Gray with the years that gleam above you there
In the great green wave where you are young
And unaccepting still . . . ("Burning" 195–96)

Jarrell writes from the noncombatant's perspective, as the onlooker or marginal figure caught and pressed beyond themselves to find words to ease their pain. But in Karl Shapiro's "Elegy for a Dead Soldier" the circumstance of dying is horrifyingly inconsequential:

The end was sudden, like a foolish play,
A stupid fool slamming a foolish door,
The absurd catastrophe, half-prearranged,
And all the decisive things still left to say. (94)

It is worth remembering that the poets themselves chose these works to represent them. That almost all included an elegy among their work is, of course, a testament to their proximity to the war, but it should also remind us how firmly this group of poets could lay claim to an identity as a generation. Brought together by historical forces—depression, war—and educated in the same schools (eight of the fifteen had studied or taught at Harvard), these poets shared a commitment to the language of poetry as a fine-tuned instrument. Having survived the war, they were eager to take up the living that they had postponed—to shape a career, to begin a family, to travel with friends—but they had no intention of trying to escape from the shadows of those who were no longer with them. Moreover, the centrality they bestowed upon their elegies suggested that the intensity with which they took up their citizen-like roles as poets stemmed from the solemnity of their brush with history. Certainly for these poets, Bogan's sober admonition to write a poetry that demonstrates "art has importance" need hardly be said.

Ciardi's Second String

Like any anthologist, Ciardi was not entirely free to pick and choose his representative writers. Some poets would have been unthinkable to omit: Karl Shapiro, Randall Jarrell, Delmore Schwartz, and Robert Lowell had all been featured in Rodman's 1946 update and expansion of the 1937 Modern Library *Anthology of American Poetry* and F. O. Matthiessen's 1950 update of the *Oxford Anthology of American Poetry*. At least two others, Richard Wilbur and Theodore Roethke, were on the verge of joining this select group by virtue of rapidly growing reputations based on newly acclaimed collections. Practical editorial decisions further bracketed Ciardi's options. Excluding all poetry by women would have been injudicious. Muriel Rukeyser was a figure impossible to ignore. She had, by 1948, five collections of poetry to her name. Elizabeth Bishop was at the same point in her career as Wilbur and Roethke. Though she had published only a single collection it was one that had been much heralded. Beyond this core of eight, however, Ciardi had an open field from which to choose. No single other young poet in 1949 had a reputation so powerful that it virtually dictated inclusion.

The seven young poets that Ciardi introduced to round out his group then become surprisingly crucial to his project. While a handful of major figures sketch a literary generation it is the addition of minor figures who bring details that block in a portrait. Who were these others? One, of course, was Ciardi himself; he could only think it proper to present his own work. Yet to a significant degree, Ciardi's own verse anchors the poets he is newly introducing. The poetry of Peter Viereck, Winfield Townley Scott, John Frederick Nims, E. L. Mayo, John Holmes, and Richard Eberhart was essentially interchangeable with Ciardi's own. Together, they represented an extreme—if that is the appropriate word—of the "middle style" on display in the anthology. Whole lines, entire stanzas, could be removed from the poem of one of these and comfortably inserted into the poem of another. All of these poets preferred that instrument of prosody that goes the farthest to ease communication, the familiar iambic pentameter line. They always sought to communicate with prose directness. They were inhospitable to the blandishments of intricate form, though all submitted to the requirements of rhyme. The workmanlike sonnet was a tool that all appreciated. And the subjects of their poems appeared close to home. They wrote about events that seemed actually to have happened to them. No grand imaginative projections liven their writing. Poetry for them was an art of the telling detail, admirable as an efficient communicating tool which operates by effective compression.

Finding a group of poets with like-minded artistry meant avoiding others who were equally available. Surely Ciardi was aware, for example, of Robert Lowell's fellow student at Harvard, Harry Brown. Ciardi was at Harvard himself as a Briggs-Copeland lecturer in from the late 1940s to 1953. Brown had published a narrative poem, *Poem of Bunker Hill* in 1941 at a precocious twenty-four, then followed that with a selection of poems with New Directions and then a larger collection in 1943, *The Violent.* In 1949, when Ciardi was making his selections, a third collection, *The Beast in His Hunger,* was released by Knopf. He had also written a well-received war novel, *A Walk in the Sun* (1943), and a play, *A Sound of Hunting* (1946), that had been produced on Broadway. Brown's verse was clearly affiliated with Lowell's. Not only did they share certain themes, including a long-standing interest in comparing America to the Roman empire, but Brown also wrote a densely compacted, sinewy, and intellectual poetic line. The remorselessly grinding brainwork of Lowell's earliest poetry, like the ten-part sonnet sequence "Caron, Non Ti Crucciare" that Rodman had published in his 1946 Modern Library anthology (and that Lowell left out of *Lord Weary's Castle*), was an unpolished version of what Brown attained in his verse. Young Lowell could write (in lines he left uncollected):

> Virgil, who heralded this golden age,
> Unctuous with olives of perpetual peace,
> Had heard the cackle of the Capitol Geese,
> And Caesar toss the sponge and patronage
> Of Empire to his prostituted page.
> The gold is tarnished and the geese and grease,
> Jason has stripped the sheep for golden fleece,
> The last brass hat has banged about the stage. ("Caron" 416)

Brown's variation on a similar theme was less intense but equally trenchant in its display of confidence and learning in this excerpt from one of the four elegies that open *The Beast in His Hunger,* "Fourth Elegy: The Poet Compared to an Unsuccessful General" (the poem had been printed in *Poetry* in 1947):

> Not that bald Caesar, all the world's right arm,
> Who, carried from the mountain of his pride,
> Sprawled as a delta for his russet blood,
> His soul shucked like an oyster—not that late
> King's darling, by an embassy of knives done
> To Stateless death beneath the marble wreath
> That curled so cold on Pompey's murdered brow,
> Is the sought man, the poet's looking-glass,
> Wherein, grown vast, he sees his variant face
> Reflected like a comet in a lens. (10)

Brown returned from war (where he had been a *Yank* correspondent) with a sharp sense that his learning had, in one sense, not been in vain. His poetry bristles with the sense that the tales from mythology, events from ancient history, and their blending in the narratives of the Latin and Greek poets—with all their primitive barbarism still intact—were lenses that delivered an appropriately harsh focus to the experience of war and the dishevelment of the postwar moment.

No other poet who had been in the war was so readily willing to dwell upon the futility of war and its eroding effects. "Where are the living?" he asks, in "The Flotsam Man":

Dead, dead; dead like the stones; like the still stones dead,
And I gnaw their bones at night and I sift their dust at noonday,
Poor messenger, survivor, poet vivid with wounds. (*Beast* 30)

Brown's poetry obsessively returns to situations of intense trauma: "Bitter beneath / The hero's wreath / Words unspoken / Have hearts broken / Their sly wound / Makes no sound / Yet is found / In the crowned" ("Finger Exercises," *Beast* 57). At the end of "The Outlet," the poem closes:

At least we each come
To the grove and the voices and the unrehearsed decision:
To flee, or to remain where
Monsters move through heat, towards the end of heat. (*Beast* 47)

The poem's task is not to make a decision but to leave us acutely aware that an insurmountable crisis exists.

Not to reprint Brown's work suggests how dearly Ciardi valued the importance of poetry that explicitly moved beyond wartime trauma. Not surprisingly, then, poets like Weldon Kees (who had published his second book, *The Fall of the Magicians,* in 1948) or Edwin Rolfe (who had appeared in both Rodman's 1937 and 1946 Modern Library collections and whose second book had been submitted to the Twayne series but rejected by Ciardi) also went unrepresented. They believed, like Brown, that the war was not so easily shaken off, that it had left an indelible mark. They would have agreed that poetry was just the site where the effects of the trauma of war could be worked through; they would certainly have insisted that any poetry which failed to register the sense in which a generation had been seriously and complexly wounded would risk becoming a poetry of trivia. In Kees's "Crime Club" (collected in *The Fall of the Magicians,* 1948), the poem ends with the case unsolved, with its sleuth "incurably insane": "Screaming that all the world is mad, that clues / Lead nowhere, or to walls so high their tops cannot be seen; / Screaming all day of war, screaming that nothing can be solved" (*Collected* 75). In other poems, Kees sketches Robinson, a figure whom the occasion always assimilates, as the modern city-dweller is virtually erased by proceeding from one trivial event to the next:

Robinson walking in the Park, admiring the elephant.
Robinson buying the *Tribune,* Robinson buying the *Times.* Robinson
Saying, "Hello. Yes, this is Robinson. Sunday
At five? I'd love to. Pretty well. And you?"
Robinson alone at Longchamps, staring at the wall. (*Collected* 129)

Participial phrases are both intensely localized even as they drift in a nebulous universalized space.

While Kees particularized the disastrous aftermath of war, Rolfe insisted on carefully discriminating among the wars fought from the 1930s onward. *First Love and Other Poems* (1951), which circulated unsuccessfully among different publishers before Rolfe self-published it in a tiny edition of 375 copies, had since 1944 carried the working title *Two Wars:* its verse set out to contrast the difference between the Spanish Civil War with its volunteers from all countries and World War II with its conscripts arrayed against nation-states. "We must remember cleanly how we fought," he began one poem. In "Elegia," his homage to Madrid and the international spirit, Rolfe made it clear that he would be drawing precise lessons from history, distinguishing between just and unjust wars. The poem ends with an unabashed vow not to forget the extraordinary communal moment of the Spanish Civil War:

> And if I die before I can return to you,
> or you, in fullest freedom, are restored to us,
> my sons will love you as their father did
> Madrid   Madrid   Madrid (*Collected* 189)

Rolfe can legitimately address a city as if it were a person because the idea of "Madrid" as realized in the Spanish Civil War resulted in the astonishing (but temporary) personalizing of the inhabitants of an entire city.

If Ciardi had wished to extend himself even further, to consider representing more than just two female poets, he could have found work by Winthrop Palmer (just on the verge of collecting her second volume, *The New Barbarian,* in 1951) that registered itself in the strong, clear voice that he admired in his other poets. Observing from her privileged position among the wealthy cultural elite of Chicago and New York City (her connections helped support *Poetry London-New York* when it was edited by the flamboyant Thurairajah Tambimuttu in the later 1950s), Palmer wants us to recognize that we are all just about to become the new barbarians. Her poems of urban life begin by observing incidents with a bleak eye that further unsettles them: "The old woman in a wig, / (She's a lady in waiting for the queen) / Teeters between taxis and trucks / To the corner where the gutter's a latrine" ("Ante Urbem," *New* 17). Where others in the postwar years found promise in the renewed activity of city life, Palmer glimpsed an incipient totalitarianism. Her icy tone is all that stands between the harshness that threatens both her and us. How easily, now, the city and the military exchange places. "Evensong" is a lullaby:

Hush-a-bye baby, the street is marching,
Eagles fly and the bridges sway,
Where the sky grows light, ships are lurching,
And beaks of brass have cleaned the sea. (*New* 19)

Her verses are brief because she finds so little to say, living in what may be our last days. "Make way for imperial armies and the tribute of corn. / Barbarians enter the city. Be afraid, / Roman, at the long cry of the hunting horn" ("Barbarians," *New* 35). Of course Palmer also represents a poet whose pessimistic view of the postwar moment would have clashed with Ciardi's. She does not even write a wartime elegy that calls out for its own surpassing. And elegies, it would seem that Ciardi believed, existed to be surpassed. No poet in Ciardi's selection carried elegiac feelings forward into an anguished present, as Brown did. Nor did any poet continue to dwell upon the political significance of warfare, as Rolfe did, nor did any find that the aftermath of war could be traced in innumerable haunting fragments, as Kees did.

Ciardi's decision not to sponsor any of these other poets effectively withheld them from a public arena that would have advanced their careers. Their current obscurity has a basis in 1950 when Ciardi passed them by. And their absence from the anthology removes strong voices resistant to the idea that beginning with a fresh start was possible or even prudent. Consider for a moment how the inclusion of Harry Brown's powerful elegies would have had an interesting dislocating effect on other poets. Alongside Brown's work, Lowell's poems would have seemed less the rare products of a precocious youth than texts that emerged from a conservative tradition that invoked the collapse of the Roman empire as a stern warning against the excesses of modern democracies. With Brown's work at hand, the poetry of Delmore Schwartz would have been subtly repositioned as an effort to bring the intellect to bear in poetry to identify and work through intractable contradictions. And the astringency in Rukeyser's lines might have seemed less a reflection of an aesthetic interest in the vernacular and more of an engagement with intellectual dilemmas. (And incorporating Kees or Rolfe or Palmer would have registered an even more far-reaching ripple effect: their quite different fascinations with the urban site, with New York or Madrid, would have emphasized that aspect in Lowell's work and revealed its absence in Wilbur's poems.) But Ciardi's choice of back-up poets like Mayo and Viereck guaranteed that there would be no restless turning back to subjects whose obsessive hold on the poet determines the course of the poem. Instead, the new poets that Ciardi introduced will serve to demonstrate their mastery over such compulsions. The new poets get on with the work of daily business. For Ciardi, the social value of much of this poetry—especially that work by poets he was newly introducing—was that it touched upon the trauma of the war just enough to propose that it was important as a past event that had to be superseded.

A Cold War Teaching Anthology

Though Ciardi's anthology did not enjoy the numerous editions and the resurrection in paperback that guaranteed the wide circulation of Rodman's *One Hundred Modern Poems,* in one sense it had a life that seemed to stretch beyond its postwar moment: so many of its poets made a return engagement in a 1956 anthology by George P. Elliott, *Fifteen Modern American Poets,* that Elliott's text had all the earmarks of a sequel. These two collections possess a continuity not typical of most anthologies with different editors and publishers. Consider their numerous resemblances. Ciardi had gathered work by thirteen men and two women born between 1904 and 1921 who were at the time of publication between twenty-nine and forty-six years old. Six years later, Elliott's anthology reprinted ten out of those fifteen poets. A third women, Josephine Miles, joined Bishop and Rukeyser. Also continuing on were Eberhart, Jarrell, Lowell, Roethke, Schwartz, Scott, Shapiro, and Wilbur. Five males dropped out—Ciardi, Holmes, Mayo, Nims, and Viereck—and four checked in: Howard Nemerov, Hyam Plutzik, James Schevill, and Robert Penn Warren. And yet despite this shuffling, the demographics of Elliott's poets conformed exactly to Ciardi's: these poets too were born between 1904 and 1921—though Elliott gave them the formal title that Ciardi had refused to produce: "the middle generation." They were, of course, an older group at the time they appeared in the 1956 anthology, ranging in age from thirty-five to fifty-one. In both anthologies the median birthdate was 1913 but in Elliott's the median age had increased from thirty-seven to forty-two.

Such agreement with Ciardi suggests that Elliott introduced new players not to contest the outline of a specific postwar generation but only to make small adjustments in the roll call of its participants. Yet Elliott's adjustments are, on closer inspection, subtle but significant changes, beginning with diverging assumptions about audience. While Ciardi still dreamed of capturing the attention of the general reader, Elliott was targeting the college student. If Ciardi's audience had to be wooed, Elliott's audience was already captured. Ciardi's anthology was a hardback volume designed to compete for shelf space in bookstores nationwide. It performed respectably enough to warrant a second printing in January 1952, and Ciardi had the highest expectations for it. On January 22, 1953, he reported to Theodore Roethke that unsold copies were being returned and confessed his dismay: "Mid-Century Poets has more or less petered out, and I don't know what the exact figures are, but they're not nearly what I had hoped for. . . . The salesmen got enthusiastic about arguing bookstores into advance sales and it looked as if we were really hot until the returns began to come in" (*Letters* 84). By contrast, Elliott's *Fifteen Modern American Poets* was never designed to catch anyone's eye. Issued as a paperback in the generic, salmon-colored cover that identified it as "No. 79" of the "Rinehart Editions" (its companions on either side were No. 78, Jonathan Swift, *Shorter Prose and Poetry,* and No. 80, Jack London, *Martin Eden*), it was engineered exclusively for the college classroom. In his brief preface, Elliott chatted amicably about his procedure, explaining that simple mathematics and the realities of the college classroom dictated he arrived at poets in the number of fifteen: "Each poet has been allotted about twenty pages . . . on the hypothesis that college courses in the study of modern poetry for the most part benefit more from a sizable representation from several poets than from a smattering from fifty or a hundred" (xi).

From these different assumptions about audience, other distinctions followed. All Ciardi's poets wrote introductory explanations to their work except Lowell, who was (as Ciardi confided to Roethke) "suffering a breakdown" (*Letters* 57). Not all, it is true, were happy about their role; Bishop's replies were decidedly sullen. (Perhaps this was an offshoot of her wish to guard her privacy. She too was hospitalized, and as she wrote in a letter to Lloyd Frankenberg in May or June 1949, was "still trying to get out of writing Ciardi a 5,000 word essay on my innermost thoughts" [*One Art* 186].) Her statement, entitled "It All Depends," ended with her insisting that she was not opposed "to all close analysis and criticism": "But I am opposed to making poetry monstrous or boring and proceeding to talk the very life out of it" (*Mid-Century* 267). When contributors hesitated, if that is the word for Bishop's response, it was Ciardi's job to prompt them with a list of twelve questions that, as he explained to them, "may be considered in any order." Question number four asked: "The function of overtone?" and question six wondered: "Subject matter? (Any predilections? Restrictions?)" To these Bishop replied with special testiness: "I do not understand the question about the function of overtone, and to the question on subject matter (any predilections? Any restrictions?) I shall reply that there are no restrictions. There *are,* of course, but they are not consciously restrictions" (267). Ciardi's questions could seem invasive were they not jotted down in such an evident shorthand. Clearly, his aim was not to valorize the concept of an authoritative poet-critic but quite the opposite: to demystify, to invite the actual poet to guide us around her or his own workshop. Karl Shapiro's offering, entitled "The Case History of *The Minute,*" was unlike anyone else's but in the right spirit. It conducted the reader through the various drafts of a poem. Rukeyser's was nearly as estimable: she untangled, with impressive clarity, the threads of thought that had come together in a recent poem, "Orpheus" (unfortunately not included in the anthology). Writing is work, hard work, as Shapiro illustrated, and poems don't appear from the sky, as Rukeyser attested. But the writer's craft need not be mystifying. The poem is as approachable as any made thing. It is not the product of superhuman intuition. The result is to boost the confidence of the audience in its ability to determine meaning.

When the site for reading poetry shifts from the living room to the classroom, one consequence is that trust is less likely to be offered to neophytes who might abuse it. Elliott's presentation of his poets bluntly promoted their authority. Not once does he elicit any helpful commentary from them; they remain lordly, aloof figures whose lives are encapsulated in brief biographies that emphasize their exceptional education, national awards, and admirable skills. Hyam Plutzik, for example, appears in this formidable guise: "Reared in the country in Connecticut. Educated in Trinity College and Yale. Worked on newspapers during the Depression; has taught English at University of Rochester since World War II. Received awards from the National Institute of Arts and Letters and shared Poetry Awards Prize with Rolfe Humphries one year" (*Fifteen* 310). Ciardi's sketch of the General Reader seems positively congenial compared to this icy recital of a dim figure who has a career but no life, no family, and no apparent interests outside of his poetry.

Elliott's reluctance to provide his poets with a particularizing history is in accord with his practice for distributing footnotes which grudgingly contribute minimal background information for the poems. Only Robert Lowell is an exception: commentary on his work is not only extensive but gathered through an exertion of effort—Elliott cites from remarks Lowell made in a "reading at the Paul Shuster Art Gallery in Cambridge in July 1955." This glimpse of a life beyond the page, however, shuts down almost as soon as it opens. For all other poets, notes were kept to a minimum and sharply abridged: the entire comment on Wilbur's "'A World Without Objects Is a Sensible Emptiness,'" whose title rephrases a sentence from one of the religious meditations in prose of Thomas Traherne, is to say unhelpfully, perhaps even misleadingly: "Traherne was a 17th century English poet" (*Fifteen* 315). Information so reluctantly deposed would be less noteworthy had not Elliott spent fully one-third of his two-page preface developing a classificatory system in regard to his footnoting. Notes are useful, he explained, when they "give aid with facts not readily come by but of some importance to understanding the poems" (xii). But if some poems require a footnote, other poems include information that is just a matter of the poet's personal knowledge, such as the fact that Private John Hogg in "Codicil for Pvt. John Hogg's Will" was the grandfather of Winfield Townley Scott. That kind of information, Elliott proposes, can be recognized as personal because it will not be accompanied by a footnote. But still a third category is that of "learned reference," a category straddling the first two in that it includes information that is both factual and personal, the result of poets who are "great and curious readers." Whether *that* information deserves a footnote is a judgment call. For Elliott, annotating poems, as such an extended and convoluted defense suggests, may be a matter of some anxiety. That it must be so is symptomatic of the position Elliott holds toward poetry: beholden to the New Critical taboo against importing information into the poem (so that work that had been buttressed by numerous annotations would be open to suspicion as a failed text) at the same time as committed to a poetry that unfolds almost exclusively within the classroom setting where it exists as an object of discussion. Elliott cannot call for extensive outside support, for that would effectively rule against a poem's aesthetic achievement, but neither can he assume that an audience prepared to subject a poem to lengthy analysis will situate the work in a context that will grant it a suitable complexity. (For Ciardi footnotes were never an issue: only two appeared, and these were asides that poets themselves deemed necessary—Bishop's remark that "Man-month" was a misprint for "mammoth" and Wilbur's translation of a French term.)

By eliminating all but the sketchiest of backgrounds for a poem, Elliott necessarily prompted readings that turn on appreciating the poetry's communicative skills. This aestheticizing effect has a depoliticizing component, displacing intellectual discussion away from even those poems that skillfully engage their readers in social and political issues. It is especially instructive to chart the alterations in the profile of Richard Wilbur that occur in the very different selections in Ciardi and Elliott. Ciardi's Wilbur, of course, is actually Wilbur's Wilbur, since Wilbur selected the ten poems that he offered, among them "At Year's End," a work that depends upon a subtle interplay between attention and lack of attention, between an alert skepticism and a servile willingness to be distracted. This is the poem that questions the extent to which denial of nuclear annihilation has now permeated our consciousness, and it turns on the strategy of offering, within the poem itself, various opportunities for the reader to choose to swerve away, to shift the subject from one that is disturbing to one that is simply neutral. At the same time, the reader can also become alert to this propensity in his or her reading practice, at which point the ground of the entire poem undergoes a massive shift. With this possibility in mind, the other poems that Wilbur selected lend themselves to against-the-grain readings which might prompt a clued-in approach to "At Year's End." One of these, "Still, Citizen Sparrow," cautions against a too-rapid dismissal of the vulture, saluted here as one who "mocks mutability," in a poem that unexpectedly ends with the example of Noah. "Museum Piece," which closes with Degas purchasing an El Greco upon which he hung his pants while he slept, discourages an attitude toward art that is excessively reverential. "The Terrace" reveals the human propensity for self-delusion and shows how easily poetic descriptions can both exaggerate the reality they appear to reproduce and become convincing depictions. From these poems, we can conclude that Wilbur's Wilbur is an urbane practitioner whose skillful scene-shifting alters the poem's prospects and encourages its audience to pursue various lines of response. This Wilbur moves easily within several different artistic and political discourses; his poetry is clearly situated in the world. The careful reader of these selections would find it scarcely credible that "At Year's End" is a mere scrapbook of end-of-the-year ruminations.

Elliott's Wilbur, however, is very different indeed: this Wilbur is a master of descriptions so vibrantly lifelike that his virtuoso exactitude is designed to rivet the reader's gaze. This Wilbur is a naturalist of the exquisite, especially good with small creatures, like insects and birds. Of the twenty poems representing this Wilbur, one-quarter center on birds ("In a Bird Sanctuary," "Lightness," "Marché aux Oiseaux," "All These Birds," and "A Black November Turkey"), and two revolve around insects (the cricket in "Exeunt," the cicada in "Cicadas"). As celebratory poetry, this work is supposed to take delight in its elegant recovery of items that the rest of us lack the fine eyes to see. Marvelously, the relics in "Driftwood" are "cast here like slag of the old / Engine of grief" (*Fifteen* 288) and the beauty that Elliott's Wilbur finds in them bears a particular message: "They are fit to be taken for signs, these emblems / Royally sane" (289). Here is a poet who is teaching us that with proper seeing we can obtain not just "sane" directions from the world around us but directions that are "Royally sane": that presumably elevate us into an aristocracy of perception, which is of course the realm occupied by the poet. Elliott's Wilbur values virtuoso skill above all—a skill on display as he juggles words in "Juggler": "the broom's / Balancing up on his nose, and the plate whirls / On the tip of the broom! Damn, what a show, we cry" (291). Such a word-juggler intends to reduce his audience to the status of delighted observers, of goggle-eyed infants. It is not surprising that such a poet would have affection for this childish audience, because he apparently longs for the defenseless innocence of the creature, whom he places, in "Beasts," at the opposite end of the moral spectrum from the human, whose aspirations are intertwined with forces that can only destroy. Elliott's Wilbur, then, is an Ivy League crew-cut version of a Robinson Jeffers who has been deprogrammed from his misanthropy and undergone a radical conversion to formalist principles. When this bright-eyed, healthy aesthete writes about leaves that have "frozen where they fell / And held in ice as dancers in a spell" so "Graved on the dark in gestures of descent, / They seemed their own most perfect monument" (292), there is not the slightest trace of a disturbing referent in this description. It firmly sets out to celebrate one more instant of overlooked beauty, here rescued for our delectation in "At Year's End." By surrounding Wilbur's poem of nuclear disavowal with verses that indeed sport numerous remarkably dazzling portrayals, Elliott sensitizes us to a Wilbur whose aesthetic marvels overwhelm and distract from anything but their own momentary unfolding.

Within the valence of Elliott's selections, Wilbur is remarkably transformed. Other poems than "At Year's End" have been affected. One has only to shift any of the poems from Elliott's selection into the group of poems that Wilbur selected for himself to see what has been added and subtracted. "Beasts," for example, if placed in the Ciardi anthology, moves strongly toward a close that now seems disturbing, for the events that the "suitors of excellence" set in motion essentially create history, but the events of history—the founding of civilizations, the commemoration of the hero, and the prosecution of wars—are brutally, even dismissively portrayed, in the last lines of the poem: they are the events that will be bringing "Monsters into the city, crows on the public statues, / Navies fed to the fish in the dark / Unbridled waters" (*Fifteen* 264). The creatures who are here associated with human markers of history serve to level out any attainments. Wilbur's remarkably jaundiced view of history leaves not an inch of room for glory. Indeed, by quite carefully distinguishing between the "suitors of excellence" who are at "high windows" and the men whose dreams the suitors are "Making" and which they know will "break their hearts," Wilbur produces an example of the hierarchical relationship that distinguishes humans, which of course makes them disturbingly different from the innocence of the beasts that slumber "in peace tonight." But the same poem, surrounded in Elliott's anthology with examples of Wilbur's detailed description of creatures, can be mistaken for a miniature bestiary with a virtuoso passage that celebrates the werewolf. Wilbur's prowess is in truth such that it is possible to let the music of his verse carry us away. But it would be a reaction to only a segment of the poem—and a reaction that, insofar as it downplays Wilbur's engagement with troubling issues, tends to infantilize the poet and our experience of reading his poetry.[4]

Erasing History, Routinizing Warfare

Elliott's anthology only looks like an affable sequel to Ciardi's. The more closely the two are compared, the more radically they diverge. Although Elliott carried over a majority of Ciardi's poets, of the *poems* that Ciardi collected he retained only a handful. Only nineteen of the 235 poems that Elliott printed had previously appeared in Ciardi. Of those nineteen, moreover, three were crucial sequences so highly regarded that no anthology of the time could reasonably neglect them: Lowell's "Quaker Graveyard at Nantucket," Roethke's "The Lost Son," and Rukeyser's "Ajanta." Some of the others were already well-known favorites—signature texts like Bishop's "The Fish," Schwartz's "The Heavy Bear," and Wilbur's "Ceremony." What this meant, of course, was that Elliott, choosing texts not merely on his own but in opposition to selections that the poets themselves had previously made, was establishing a profile of mid-century poetry that deliberately omitted many of the works that its poets had most valued.

Out of the notable omissions, it is the lack of the wartime elegies that most severely wrenches Elliott's anthology away from Ciardi's. Not only were numerous elegies absent but so too were the poets who had written most intensely about the war: Ciardi, Viereck, Nims, and Holmes. And of the poets who remained, Elliott further downplayed their engagement with the war. Eberhart's "Fury of Aerial Bombardment" was quietly dropped, as was Shapiro's "Elegy for a Dead Soldier." (Shapiro's "V-Letter" remained, however: its status as a war poem was uncertain and perhaps overridden by its mode of address, which laid claim to the conventions of love poetry.) Jarrell's work survived the purge, but then again if the war were placed entirely off-limits it would have been difficult to represent Jarrell at all. He becomes, by default, *the* war poet of Elliott's collection. Of course as a war poet Jarrell's status as a noncombatant places him at an oblique angle to experiencing war. But Elliott's project is not, it should be stressed, to efface warfare from our immediate history. What he succeeds in doing is not untypical of a certain type of cold war attitude: he produces example after example to imply that warfare has become deeply embedded in the texture of daily life. Jarrell, then, with his civilian perspective gives us a viewpoint by which we can grasp our distance from war even as we experience it as ongoing. Poems that further appreciate that perspective by taking up the issue of adjustment to war's aftermath are also included by Elliott, such as Scott's "The U.S. Sailor with the Japanese Skull." One of the new poems that acknowledge the omnipresence of war is Schevill's "The Coastguardsmen in the Fog," which focuses attention on the effort of a sensitive civilian to adjust to witnessing the death of a pilot whose plane has crashed in fog.

Ciardi's poets selected work that sketched a similar trajectory over and over, an implicit narrative in which their civic-minded and responsible poetry emerged from the sobering experience of their brush with history. Elliott's selections scramble any such narrative, merging as they do aspects of warfare with civilian circumstances. A poem like Scott's "Three American Women and a German Bayonet"—not chosen by Scott to represent his work in Ciardi's anthology but now selected by Elliott—unfolds against this newly domesticated background of war for which Elliott serves as sponsor. Though this poem is clearly centered on World War II, its meaning undergoes a subtle shift in Elliott's anthology. In the poem, three American women unpack a German bayonet from a "souvenir bundle." The women are mother, sister, and spouse of the soldier whose souvenir bundle this is. Each one has a different response to the "great knife," the "hard tool of death" that is unpacked to sit on the kitchen table. The mother is appalled, stating over and over: "I do not like it. Put it down." The sister plays with it as a child would, holding it as an "awkward toy." The wife, however, when the mother and the sister leave, takes on the job of repossessing it. Half the poem is devoted to her as she circles around the object to comprehend it entirely. The poem concludes:

Like a live thing in not-to-be-trusted stillness,
Like a kind of engine so foreign and self-possessed
As to chill her momently between worship and terror
It lies there waiting alone in the room with her,
Oddly familiar without ever losing strangeness.
Slowly she moves along it a tentative finger
As though to measure and remember its massive, potent length:
Deep-death, tall as life,
For here prized from the enemy, wrenched away captive, his
dangerous escape and hers.
Mary his wife
Lifts it heavy and wonderful in her hands and with triumphant
     tenderness. (*Fifteen* 232–33)

Scott's poem is divided against itself. On the one hand, this poem about three American women viewing a German bayonet on a kitchen table transforms the war into a foreign intrusion, something remote and slightly unreal as this bayonet is, "Its gun-body lost . . . here exposed on the American kitchen table." So the memory of war is unbearable, and we want to dismember it as quickly as these three render the bayonet into everything except what it was designed to be, a tool that would ruthlessly kill. Thus feminine community triumphs, emasculating the phallic that had been misdirected away from the procreative. On the other hand, the bayonet, as "socketed in its worn wood handle," makes the war into a presence that permeates even a kitchen. In this alternate reading, war will never go away, and we must accustom ourselves to it. Its avatars are everywhere, and a man will no longer be able to be simply a son or a brother or a husband—the three relationships each of the women activate—but he must always also be a soldier.

Scott might have helped resolve these opposed readings if he had offered stronger clues about the fate of the American soldier. If the soldier had returned alive from the war, then the harm of the bayonet would be distanced, and it would be a souvenir of the past, brought vividly to life for a moment but almost instantly dispersed by the differing attitudes of the three women. Mary's lifting of the heavy blade would be, then, a reenactment of her husband's return, echoing the "triumphant tenderness" with which she greets him, extended here to an artifact only remotely associated with him. But the absence of the man most strongly suggests a death in combat, and in that most likely scenario, the bayonet becomes an emblem of the menace of war, its insistent presence on the kitchen table a measure of the war's penetrating power. Mary's lifting of the heavy blade would then figure the sorrow she now has to bear. The "triumphant tenderness" a mark of the fondness with which she would have greeted her husband but which she must now transfer to this blade, absolving a world of violence that robbed her of her companion.

That no vivid clue exists within the poem to resolve the status of the man as living or dead indicates Scott's tact in composing a work for persons to use as they needed. Selden Rodman included "Three American Women and a German Bayonet" in *One Hundred Modern Poems* (one of two Scott poems he anthologized, providing him with a stature identical to Eliot's), but its appearance in Elliott's anthology, surrounded by other poetry that integrates the war into the fabric of everyday life, suggests that its usefulness in 1956 was to support an understanding that domesticates the war mentality. Elliott prints another poem by Scott, "Codicil for Pvt. John Hogg's War," a poem whose Civil War setting underlies war's American roots. From Robert Penn Warren's "Mexico Is a Foreign Country," the poem he chooses to reprint is section 4, "Small Soldiers with Drums in Large Country," a poem that distances war and normalizes soldierly activity by depicting warriors as being like children at play. But it is the work of Jarrell that serves Elliott most effectively in his proceedings to routinize war, for Jarrell frequently approaches war as that which must be reduced to some acceptable dimension in order for the persons involved in it to be able to endure it.

Jarrell's most disturbing poems from this civilian perspective are not, of course, what Elliott includes. Those are works in which individuals struggle to encompass what cannot be understood, what lies beyond the frame of their thought. In "Protocols" (certainly not unfamiliar to Elliott because just reprinted in Jarrell's 1955 *Selected Poems*) children react to their arrival at a death camp with eagerness, like the adventure it seems to them to be. Up to their ending, Jarrell alternates their voices as though their excitement cannot be contained:

> They had hot water in a pipe—like rain, but hot:
> *The water there is deeper than the world*
>
> *And I was tired and fell in my sleep*
> *And the water drank me. That is what I think.*
> And I said to my mother, "Now I'm washed and dried,"
> My mother hugged me, and it smelled like hay
> *And that is how you die.* And that is how you die. (*Complete* 193)

With a directness that risks sentimentality, Jarrell focuses our attention on basic human traits—the child's imagination and love of explanation, the parent's care—and with a rage and fury at their betrayal that his words barely contain, he reminds us of how utterly war shreds these. The monstrousness of war looms just beyond these scraps of dialogue. War occurs on an unimaginable scale, and finally it is absolutely remote from the details through which lives gain meaning.

Poems like "Protocols," however, it bears repeating, Elliott did *not* reprint. Instead, he chose other works in which Jarrell's war lends itself to repositioning within the scheme of things as a fate that can only be borne—such as "2nd Air Force" which is spoken by a mother visiting her son at the base where he has been trained as a bomber pilot. Her struggle to recast the situation in terms that diminish its violence gives the poem its pathos, as in this passage:

> She saves from the twilight that takes everything
> A squadron shipping, in its last parade—
> Its dogs run by it, barking at the band—
> A gunner walking to his barracks, half-asleep,
> Starting at something, stumbling (above, invisible,
> The crews in the steady winter of the sky
> Tremble in their wired fur); and feels for them
> The love of life for life. (*Fifteen* 59)

Jarrell is no apologist for war, that much is certain. He identifies as thoroughly as he can with the mother's perspective and emphasizes her helplessness. But within the setting of Elliott's anthology, his sympathetic portrayals of noncombatants struggling to "understand" war by acknowledging its disruptions can represent an attitude toward combat that authorizes its continuation as well as lays out a position for the civilian in which the tacit acceptance of war is appropriate.

"It is through modes of display," as Peter Wollen has said, echoing Guy Debord, "that regimes of all sorts reveal the truths they mean to conceal" (10). The literary anthology, of course, is the literary culture's version of a New York department store window at Christmas. What Elliott's anthology erases through its small but pertinent adjustments is the brutality and horror of warfare, the turmoil and destruction that are so clearly inscribed within the elegies that virtually all of Ciardi's poets insisted upon placing on the record. And not only is warfare minimized, it is subtly domesticated. War is no longer an exception, a breakdown, and a catastrophe but that whose inevitability requires us to prepare ourselves psychologically for it. One intent of the elegies by Ciardi's poets was to make the horror of war beyond forgetting. But for Elliott, poetry serves as a philosophizing buffer that makes the unbearable acceptable. In Ciardi, history is a moment in the present which invites change. The poetic generation he champions has just paid an enormous price for its right to be players whose actions have consequence. They believe that their intervention should matter. In Elliott, such intervention has been replaced by a polite acquiescence.

Elliott's classroom-oriented anthology helps establish a university setting that is conspicuously apolitical even as it subtextually promotes a form of quietist politics. It is even more striking to find how it transformed and repositioned a group of poets who wrote works that supported a view of art as responsible and civic. New selections as well as subtle presentational adjustments (biographies, footnotes, introductory comments) had a severing effect: Elliott's anthology was less likely to be perceived as a sequel to Ciardi's and more likely to be considered a major upgrade, a superseding of what had once been current. Perhaps most disturbing, however, is the tendency in Elliott's presentation to infantilize the poet. Ciardi prodded his poets to speak for themselves and to select their own work because he understood that the active, engaged, and thoughtful role they took on within their work was transferable to a more public setting. Elliott sequesters his poets. Why is it, we may wonder, that their personal lives unfold at such a vast distance, in the notes at the back of the book? And why, when we have a biographical note, is it so generic? It is an impersonal list of their credentials from college and publisher. Kept deeply in the background, poets begin to take on outlines of mystery, as if they were only capable of functioning within the small space of the poem, which in turn, through Elliott's selections, dwindles even further into the tight space of the lyric.

When poets seem to lack any voice to speak outside their own poem, outside a site that has been marked by its singularity and intensity, then poetry begins to seem just one more specialty, that which is practiced by those who are inclined to be "poetic," self-expressive, absorbed in language. Poetry becomes that which is discussed and debated in a classroom, not that which is pondered and internalized as one takes it into the home. Poets begin to lose their credibility as insightful observers or, for that matter, even trustworthy participants in the cultural and social life around them. Elliott's decisions, then, not only serve to routinize a situation in which a cold war becomes a practice that we can only accustom ourselves to but they sharply diminish the role that might be played by the poetry of those, like these very poets, who would have been quick to resist such a change.

3 POLICING THE MAINSTREAM/CURTAILING FEMININE EXCESS

PRISCILLA HEATH is the wife of a Professor at Kenyon College and one of her first published stories appears here.
—"Contributors," *Kenyon Review* (Summer 1952)

This is JEAN WYLDER's first published story. Her husband is in the English Department at Bradley University.
—"Contributor's Note," *Western Review* (Spring 1952)

RUTH STONE, Our Fellow in Poetry this year, lives at Vassar, where her husband teaches English.
—"Contributors," *Kenyon Review* (Autumn 1956)

The mainstream verse of the 1950s was underwritten in several ways, one of which was a simplified version of the New Criticism, a "Glossary of Terms to the New Criticism," that the editors of *Poetry: A Magazine of Verse* sponsored and published in ten-page segments over the course of three issues in 1948 and 1949. So popular was this compilation of the latest in critical theory that it was separately reprinted and bound and made available to readers for seventy-five cents. It soon reached a fifth printing and remained available (and presumably in demand) up through 1953, at which point it devolved into a bonus that new subscribers received with their first issue. Along with the 1950 edition of Brooks and Warren's *Understanding Poetry* (1938) and Stanley Edgar Hyman's 1948 assemblage of semi-scholarly sketches of the careers of several new critics (fashionably titled *The Armed Vision*), this "Glossary," directly commissioned from Brown University professor William Elton, encouraged a generation of influential readers of contemporary poetry to read (and when appropriate, write) in accordance with a specific set of expectations. That this information appeared in *Poetry* signaled that the principles of New Criticism had truly arrived. The practicing poets and apprentice poets who were a significant portion of the audience for *Poetry* were being addressed with the assumption that these were the sets of readerly expectations that would have to be mastered for success in the coming years.

Miniaturized for portability, how did the New Criticism appear, and more important, what directions for the writing of poetry could be deduced from it? A spatialized sketch that accompanied the glossary bravely traced a skein of pathways through a thicket of terms, but the arrows that flew from name to name, sometimes zooming across the page in a sweeping diagonal, sometimes taking the smallest of steps, never quite attained the organizational chart clarity to which they aspired. More than one oddity results when the helter-skelter practice-oriented commentary of individual poet-critics as diverse as Blackmur, Burke, Empson, Tate, Richards, and Winters was boiled down into a system, especially one organized around (in the glossary's prefatory remarks) "more than one hundred of the terms in what might be called the basic vocabulary of the New Criticism" (Elton 153). That "basic vocabulary" was, to be sure, a construct, as was made clear from the start; the "resulting compilation" was accurately described by associate editor Hayden Carruth in an introductory note as "partly a glossary, partly a concordance, and partly a work in speculative aesthetics" (152). Elton was not naïve, but neither was he easily daunted. He worked to define terms that were functional for each critic and establish if not links at least points of comparison among them. Inevitably distortion occurred. For 1950s verse, the most pertinent twist involved the role that language should play—or in this case, not play.

From this glossary, a reader could conclude that one mark of the modern literary work was that it successfully dissolved the material aspects of its own language. Authentic poems engender in their readers a kind of pure thought without the distractions of words or even that which might be deemed a style. More particularly, a poem transforms the dross of mere wordage into the gold of the Hegelian "concrete universal" which fuses the general with the particular. Language becomes transparent, superseded as it is by this most precise form of knowledge—poetic understanding.[1] At no point is any of this openly prescribed, but it is presented at more than one turn. Under "Knowledge, Poetry as," for example, the entry begins: "The belief that poetry affords a special kind of knowledge, distinct from scientific knowledge, is central among the New Critics. Poetry provides 'realistic cognitions,' the universal being represented through the particular" (Elton 238). Look up "Tension" and find that in Allen Tate's view a poem is "a configuration of meanings, both abstract and concrete" (304). If you turn to "Sensibility" you read that in R. P. Blackmur's terms, "value" associates with the "experiencing of abstract concepts in sensory terms" (209). Do not, however, bother to look under "Language": there is no entry. The deft balancing of thought and feeling is appreciated above all. What remains questionable is anything that resembles a style that is overt or individualizing. If style does not melt seamlessly into subject, the poem is less than literary.

Elton's glossary accurately reflects a New Critical concern that the true poem should leave no impression of superfluity. No ornamental embellishments, to be enjoyed in themselves and for themselves, should distract from the serious business of delivering poetic knowledge. Of course Elton never intended as prescriptive this sense that the materiality of language is left behind the moment understanding occurs. For the New Critics themselves, their admiration was won by poetry by Donne whose difficulty stemmed proportionately from the struggle to strike a balance between deep-felt emotion and intricate intellectualizing. But Elton's readers were precisely those who were unlikely to peruse the arguments unfolding in the pages of *The Well-Wrought Urn* (1947) or *The Verbal Icon* (1954). They wanted answers they could use and positions they could, as poets, inhabit. They would have been drawn to the possibility that the moment of understanding so prized by New Critics could be facilitated by a poetic language that was easy to leave behind—a language, that is, streamlined rather than multivalent, which never strayed far from clear prose. To such an audience the Eltonian New Critical ideal encouraged a style in which the discursive trappings of language would recede into the background. In short, in the process of describing the concrete universal, Elton also promoted a version of the poem that esteemed a language marked by austerity and restraint.

With its endorsement by *Poetry* and its availability to those who would be producing the poetry of the upcoming years, Elton's glossary exerted an influence far beyond its five printings. But it was not the only source lending support to a "transparent form." Critics and poets had been remarking on the stripped-down quality of the postwar poem, a work designed to be more sober than alluring, more serious than attractive. In 1949, Robert

Fitzgerald, reporting on Peter Viereck's success as winner of the 1948 Pulitzer Prize for *Terror and Decorum,* noted that several of its "lively" poems with their "neat, coarse clarity" give evidence of a shift "from visionary concentration in poetry—from the high styles of Yeats or Crane or [Allen] Tate or [Dylan] Thomas—to a drier and airier attitude, a more epigrammatic vein" (17). Viereck himself, writing in a 1951 essay for *Atlantic Monthly,* proposed stripping poetry completely of anything that drew attention away from what the poet intended to state. Content should dominate form in the work of the "new generation, writing in 1950," he argued, because this generation had been "forced—in fact, thrown—by war service into a willy-nilly preoccupation with the content of the realities around them. No wonder then that we of this generation, while returning to form, use it not for its own sake but as a means to enhance the content, including the intellectual and moral values implied by the content and the lucid communication of those values" ("Education" 77).

The anthology that demonstrated the eagerness with which the new poetry set about to communicate itself lucidly was, of course, Ciardi's *Mid-Century American Poets* of 1950. Of the fifteen poets Ciardi selected, only a handful stray from a poetic language that is straightforward, grammatically proper, "clean," and generally free of expressive emotion. John Holmes had the style mastered, as this stanza attests, one of six from "Metaphor for My Son" (as included in Ciardi's anthology):

> Angry as I am when the tough, the rare, the tall
> Fliers with all their wisdom burn and fall,
> I hope you'll live to learn to rage at their death
> Too young by unnatural causes away from the field.
> I want you to measure as I have measured breath
> Then, and to keep the deep wells of grief sealed. (*Mid-Century* 218)

Holmes's lines carefully husband their prose sense. Word order is disrupted just slightly, and usually over a line break where the disruption will be less of a strain. Typically, adjectives have been chosen for their modesty as qualifiers. To write of "unnatural causes" or "deep wells" is to use the adjective to confirm the expected. The effect of the poem turns on the weight of its inevitability. It aspires to a sense of sober truth; as such, it need not insist or make a special plea. But, as the passage itself maintains, withholding emotion is in general perceived as a virtue equal to that of being able to experience emotion. The language is not to call attention to itself; it is self-denying, standing aside in order to let its message predominate. As it downplays expressiveness, it suggests not the absence of strong passion but the likelihood that strong passion has been met, checked, and adroitly refocused—its energies channeled in a new direction. The poem, then, instructs us in our civic responsibilities, though with sensitivity to just how difficult an instruction that can be. Holmes's balance is not easily obtained. It is a matter of discipline. Indeed, an element of discipline—discipline that is itself judiciously balanced—is itself most to be desired. It is what Holmes displays (or more accurately, what he permits us to deduce from his tight-lipped speech). And such a gift is precisely what he wishes for his son.

The Feminine Baroque and Sexual Politics

For there to be a mainstream style on the order of magnitude that existed in the 1950s, the circulation of poetry had to be policed. Such policing would not mean banishing alternatives to the commonly accepted style. Rather, effective policing would instructively retrace just where the borders of the acceptable began by regularly publicizing examples of poetry that had tried to attain yet clearly failed to emulate the appropriate style. Negative examples would serve not only as a reminder of the vast territory that was occupied by the mainstream but also as a friendly warning to those who might consider settling elsewhere. No other site offered itself so readily to this as the book review, a traditional locus for monitoring poetic change. But in this postwar era, with its strong emphasis on social unity and professionalization, the book review too frequently became the site of a monologue. Those who were most often targeted in this process were precisely the writers who deviated just enough from a mainstream style to serve as useful objects of instruction. (Those deviating more completely were just ignored.) And with so many players in this period committed to defining verse-writing as an activity that warranted discipline, that demanded the rigor of a professional outlook, and that required a check on one's emotions, what was regularly portrayed as an instructionally useful example of deviance was poetry by women.

Contemporary poetry by women in the postwar period was thus endowed with a distinctly irregular status that would, in fact, complicate its reception for years thereafter. Indeed, we remain shockingly unaware of the strong and effective poetry written by women in the postwar era largely because we remain within the influence of valuations of their writing produced by contemporaries—valuations that were, in the 1950s, deeply flawed, implicated as they were in issues of gender and sexual politics. Yet from one perspective, the postwar era appears to be a golden age for women poets whose work can be found everywhere. *Poetry* regularly allotted its prestigious lead-off position to women, and volumes of poetry by women were consistently appearing from university and East Coast publishers. But when this same poetry that had once been featured in the opening pages of a journal was up for judgment in the back pages of the book reviews—in a review that was most likely not written by another woman—then what had been acceptable as a general cross-section of current poetry lost its allure when it came under surveillance for canonical inclusion. When it came time to match women's poetry against a standard of decorum, then problems suddenly loomed, significant problems. Virtually all the poetry by women that was surveyed by men in book reviews in one way or another was reported upon as simply unable to meet basic norms of acceptability.

Reviewers spelled out this failure indirectly, by employing elliptical phrases that were nonetheless clearly coded. Women were widely regarded as heiresses of a poetic tradition often given the name of "baroque." "Rosalie Moore," Henry Rago proclaimed in the opening sentence of a 1949 review, "writes good strong baroque" (99). But anything baroque was, by the standard of transparent form, excessive. Descriptions of the feminine baroque of the 1950s uncannily evoke a dark, demonized version of the *écriture feminine* developed by Hélène Cixous, Julia Kristeva, and Luce Irigaray. Needless to say, at the time the feminine baroque was not acknowledged as an oppositional discourse but stigmatized as a series of missteps that seemed, to reviewers who were largely male, to demonstrate a fatal inability by the female to attain the arduous balancing act out of which emerged the powerful achievement of the concrete universal. As these reviewers described it, in the feminine baroque feeling overwhelmed thought. Disruptive word-clusters signaled a disequilibrium, an intensity that should have been contained, shaped in some way, *disciplined.* Instead, it was as though emotions had broken through a wall usually maintained to keep words in proper and separate spheres. The feminine baroque was, to be sure, a resounding success when it came to expressing large gusty emotions, but that was also its weakness and of course its danger. Its ready alliance with powerful emotions produced a heteroglossic language that was a threat to the precision and discipline of the responsible poem of the mainstream.

One reason why the feminine baroque as produced by women poets may have been so quickly seized upon as an example of that-which-was-marginal-yet-still-acceptable was that just beyond it loomed that which was not merely different but, to the 1950s sensibility, thoroughly unacceptable—not just "minor" but wrong, profoundly troubling and nearly unmentionable: the disruptive, chaotic, playful, and more or less heteroglossic (and perhaps overwhelmingly "feminized") writings of a male homosexual subculture. This verse would receive a name of sorts in 1960 ("the New York poets") in the pages of Donald M. Allen's *New American Poetry* anthology, where this poetry would be associated not with the visual arts but with experimental theater, yet it was hardly unfamiliar: work by John Ashbery and Frank O'Hara had been appearing with regularity in *Poetry,* which numbered the two among its frequent contributors, as well as in the *Quarterly Review of Literature,* in the *Kenyon Review,* which printed "Two Scenes," the opening poem in Ashbery's *Some Trees,* and in occasional issues of *New World Writing,* whose first number included a poem by O'Hara and whose later numbers published Ashbery. However, as was the case for women's poetry, it was one thing to print this poetry, and another to single it out for serious discussion, where it could be granted legitimacy. The homosexual text was not a subject that invited calm discussion. It was bold of *New World Writing No. 4* (October 1953) to publish an essay, whose author was identified only by the pseudonym "Libra," in which a number of postwar writers who were homosexual or wrote about homosexuality were singled out for praise: "Carson McCullers, Paul Bowles, Tennessee Williams are, at this moment at least, the three most important creative writers in the United States" (311). At no point, however, was homosexuality named. The author defended what was called their interest in "sexuality" by claiming that the "concern with sexuality which informs most contemporary writing is . . . the reflection of a serious battle between the society man has constructed so illogically and confusedly and the nature of the human being which needs a considerably fuller expression sexually and emotionally than either the economics or morality of the time will permit" (312). This was a pioneering bit of cultural criticism that proposed that a culturally constructed sexual identity failed to account for the diversity of human sexuality. And yet as bland as this and other pronouncements in the essay were, the essayist nonetheless declined to be identified. And within the year, as if to confirm the wisdom behind the author's decision to appear anonymously, Hilton Kramer arose to savage the essay in a point-by-point "refutation" in *The Avon Book of Modern Writing No. 2* (1954).[2]

Homosexuality as such could hardly be called a condition alien to the lifestyle of the poet. Apart from the overall social conservatism of the era, why was it such a vexing topic? The homosexual text threatened to import a world of disruptive and feminized sexuality into the professionalized discourse of intellectual discipline that mainstream poets were trying to construct. Judson Jerome, reviewing James Merrill's *The Country of a Thousand Years of Peace* (1959), found it too distasteful to speak directly about the poetry, but believed it to be important to signal to others just what kind of contamination it represented. After quoting the opening stanza of "Thistledown," a poem in which Merrill describes a thistle ball, he comments: "The grammar is diffuse, the touch so delicate as to be (for me) indiscernible. 'Aspin'"—this is a word that Merrill uses in the poem as a variant on "Aspen"—"isn't in my dictionary—but I don't sense any message I care much to decode. Something about a few of the poems"—he names three—"came through to me, but the chief effect was of beautiful limp words seen underwater, transmitted by a quiver of a brow, on a wave length I am not equipped to receive" (424). Jerome's own "unspecialized" equipment saves him, but he must urgently convey to others the peril of this menace which transmits its charge on secret wavelengths.[3]

The gender and sexual politics of the book review process, as well as the employment of a coded vocabulary in a discussion that justified dismissal, is particularly evident in the reviews surrounding John Ashbery's first book, *Some Trees* (1956), a volume whose features underwent remarkable alterations as commentators pro and con locked in battle over it. From the start, the existence of the book had been problematic. Eliminated early in the competition for the Yale Younger Poets series by a reader screening entries, the manuscript was brought to the attention of series editor W. H. Auden just as he was prepared to announce no volume would be published that year. Auden allowed the publication of Ashbery's manuscript to go forward even as he dissociated himself from it. "Remarkably disaffected" (22) is how Richard Howard has described Auden's five-page foreword to the collection. There, Auden spent one-third of his time recollecting a now-lost golden age in which poetry defined reality by performing ritual functions. While those days, Auden notes, are long gone, ever since Rimbaud some poets have insisted that "in childhood largely, in dreams and daydreams entirely, the imaginative life of the human individual stubbornly continues to live by the old magical notions" (*Some Trees* 13). Ashbery is thus introduced as belonging to a secondary tradition linked with childhood and with daydreaming. Indeed, aberrations are very much at the center of these poems, according to Auden. The woman who speaks in Ashbery's "Illustration," Auden maintains, "denies the reality of anything outside herself; that is to say, she is insane" (14). An even stronger objection Auden reserves for his ending sentence, though it so elaborately traverses a syntactical maze that it appears calculated not to do harm: "If in the eighteenth century, with its interest in the general and the universal, the danger for poets was a neglect of the singular, the danger for a poet working with the subjective life is the reverse; i. e. realizing that, if he is to be true to nature in this world, he must accept strange juxtapositions of imagery, singular associations of ideas, he is tempted to manufacture calculated oddities as if the subjectively sacred were necessarily and on all occasions odd" (16). Auden was not a happy reader of Ashbery. His telling summary of "The Instruction Manual" (certainly the clearest as well as the funniest piece in the collection) humorlessly presented it as a somber contrast between a "profane situation" and the "sacred memories of a Mexican town" (13).

Some Trees, in fact, was to receive only one favorable review, and that was written by Ashbery's friend Frank O'Hara. He undertook damage control in a 1957 issue of *Poetry* by attempting to portray Auden's negative commentary as remarks on just "one aspect of the poems": "their relation to the dream-impulse in French Surrealism." Quoting the same lines from "Illustration" that Auden had singled out as exemplifying insanity, O'Hara proposed they revealed Ashbery's sympathy with a suicide who "feels she is performing a saintly act of imitating nature" (311). O'Hara's sharpest defense was to contend that the poems deliberately avoided an interpreting frame "which might only be a comfortable way of looking away" (311). Other reviewers, however, were not moved to venture outside their own interpretive frames. Donald Hall's comments were wedged in a two-paragraph piece in the *Saturday Review* that was not so much a review as an extended notice. He announced that Ashbery's poems "contain faults which may be mentioned before we consider his substantial virtues" ("Oddities" 26). Enumerating those faults occupied three-fifths of the review, entitled "Oddities and Sestinas," which also included a quote from one of Auden's most negative summaries. When the "substantial virtues" finally arrive in the second paragraph they are not enough to offset the previous damage: "Mr. Ashbery has a fine ear and an honest eccentricity of diction which, used properly, excites the attention and speaks with oblique precision" (26).

While Hall's brief remarks could be read in several different ways, William Arrowsmith's comments in the *Hudson Review* withhold sympathy as unconditionally as he could without accusing Ashbery of deviance. Arrowsmith takes every measure he can to quarantine Ashbery's influence, opening his review with some bluntness: "I could make very little headway in understanding Mr. John Ashbery's *Some Trees,* and I take some comfort from what I take to be Auden's similar difficulties in the Introduction" (294). Only four lines from Ashbery are quoted, and they appear parenthetically, at the end of a passage in which Arrowsmith's distaste for Ashbery's writing is strong enough to appear as a half-disguised warning about its homosexuality: "What does come through is an impression of an impossibly fractured brittle world, depersonalized and discontinuous, whose characteristic emotional gesture is an effete and cerebral whimsy. ('He is sherrier / and sherriest. / A tall thermometer / Reflects him best')" (294). Whatever one might think of Ashbery's early work, it would be impossible to regard these four lines as representative of it. Their quality as doggerel makes them an outrageous, even a malicious choice.

Fairfield Porter thought so. Arrowsmith's review provoked a letter from him, then better known as an art critic than a painter but also familiar as a poet who had appeared in *Poetry* (he was also a close friend of Ashbery). But Porter's letter of July 23, 1956, submitted to Arrowsmith at the *Hudson Review* for publication, went unprinted at the time. After some judicious opening remarks ("I think Auden, in his introduction to the volume, though he writes interestingly, does somewhat miss the point of the poems. . . . You say it seems to you that he had similar difficulties to your own" ["To William Arrowsmith" 32]), Porter seeks to shift the grounds for judgment away from whether Ashbery is intelligible to whether his work is likable. The opening lines of "Two Scenes" carried "surprise in the sequence of words—there is, as it were, space enough between the nouns, modifiers, and verbs" (35). Porter gamely defends Ashbery's opacity, but a defense of words that have "space enough" between them is a losing argument. "Ashbery's verbal phrases are to me ideas in the way that musical phrases may be so considered" (36). No argument was more likely to fall on deaf ears, given the period taste for "transparent form." Exactly what seemed to Porter to be words of praise would have been taken by Arrowsmith as further evidence of Ashbery's unsuitability.[4]

In these negative evaluations of Merrill and Ashbery, the homosexual lifestyle is assumed to be an undercover agent of infection that must be quarantined. The narcissism ascribed to the language of the homosexual poet is itself the very sign of excess. It undermines all attempts to discipline it, and it boldly displays its failure to attain even the minimal balance of thought-with-feeling that would qualify it as reasonable poetic discourse. The homosexual text is drenched in helpless desire, every word tainted with the poet's dark personal affect. Out of control, never truly in touch with the intellect, all mysterious passion, it represented all that mainstream poets dreaded.

Jean Garrigue and the Limits of Appropriate Behavior

The "surprise," the "space," and the "music" that Porter hoped Arrowsmith would acknowledge as worthy features of Ashbery's work are characteristics of the feminine baroque. But reviewers who were on guard against a display of the material signifier of language, that metonym for bodiliness (and ultimately sexuality) that the homosexual text was supposed to flaunt, were able to pose a direct question to women poets: were they disciplined enough to write the poem that negotiated the difficult balance between the emotions and the intellect? The question was never asked of gay poets because the answer was foreordained: it was clear they were beyond controlling themselves—if they could control themselves they would not be gay. The feminine baroque thus defined a *legitimate* borderline area. It was not a symptom of an ingrained perversity but an example of excess, and as such it was susceptible to discipline. It was no threat to the social order because of the way it so neatly contrasted with the reigning style. It even served to help demarcate the lines between majority and minority discourse, dominant and subordinate. As much as it was targeted for negative criticism, it was also supposed to circulate; its instructional disvalue was immense.

The very model of the woman poet of the 1950s whose reputation was inseparable from her excess was Jean Garrigue. When she needed a metonym for her poetry she chose the architecturally baroque setting of the Villa d'Este in Rome. In her "For the Fountains and Fountaineers of the Villa d'Este" fountains "play by light on the water, making arcs / Of a spectrum in the din and bafflement / Of that most muffled watery bell beat, pell mell and lulled stampede" ("Fountains" 64). Both she and Anthony Hecht happened to write long descriptive poems about the same place at the same time, but Hecht's quintessential academic verse (his poem on the Villa d'Este, "La Condition Botanique," originally appeared in the Spring 1953 *Kenyon Review*) is all balance. When it entertains the possibility of excess, it is only to demonstrate the urgency of controlling it. "For thus it was designed: / Controlled disorder at the heart / Of everything" he writes, in elegant eight-line stanzas:

> . . . and tension lectures
> Us on our mortal state, and by controlled
> Disorder, labels to keep art
> From being too refined. ("Condition" 95)

Hecht is a model of propriety and reserve. In 1989, Ashley Brown pinpointed the verse exactly when he described it as "a *jeu d'esprit* of the New Criticism (Brook's paradox, Tate's tension, Warren's pure and impure poetry, and so forth)" (14). By demonstrating a poetry complicitous with the New Criticism, Hecht's work exemplified that moment of high civilization of which the Villa d'Este is a supreme example. By contrast, when Garrigue is taken with the fountains of the Villa d'Este, she is drawn to the least stable aspect in the estate. Those powerful jets of water, pushing upward in dramatic spumes, are like impulses to which she must respond. She digresses freely, taking off in unexpected directions, just as likely to ramble excitedly as lavish her attention on one tight spot:

> Fountains, our volatile kin,
> Coursing as courses the blood,
> For we are more water than earth
> And less of flesh than a flame
> Bedded in air and run by the wind—
> Bequeath me, be with me, endow my hunger
> With sweet animal nature ("Fountains" 69–70)

This it was possible to categorize as "erotic." Unlike the homosexual text which seemed to be invasively attempting to feminize the world, Garrigue's eyes fell primly on those powerful objects to which she was drawn for their ability to support the "feminine." There was an orderliness under her excess in which the rules still retained their authority. In many of her passages, she turns toward a companion and asks for help in controlling an intensity that is about to overflow. It is as if her work allegorizes itself as a contest between a balance of thought and feeling and emotional imbalance that is then translated into masculine and feminine positions.

Garrigue's work (coincidentally) sanctions itself as a counterposition to Hecht. Had Hecht not existed, Garrigue would have wanted to summon him or at least his work into existence. What is "wrong" with her poetic scenes is their linguistic eventfulness; what is "right" about them is that they unfold within a controlled set of circumstances in which flirtatious interchanges between men and women (or more broadly between male and female principles) become possible, often on a grand scale. "Setpiece for Albany," published first in the *Quarterly Review of Literature* in 1951 and then collected in Garrigue's third volume *The Monument Rose* (1953), demonstrates not simply her willingness to stray far from the requirements of transparent form but also the alternate plea-

sures that she substitutes—pleasures that are grounded in feminine/mas-
culine differentials:

Setpiece for Albany

From the station at Albany
Drafty like tunnels but domed
And round as a drum and as drum-dark
Where the stranded passengers snored
Or with mallets and pickax old workmen
Started games with blue-bonneted railmen.
Others, rattling black chains, started and started,
Humped on the benches, dead between trains—
I emerged, after two hours of waiting
Into the seven o'clock of the virginals, sun.
Two statuesque columns meeting
In a robust marrying of clouds under clouds
Rose from the equal stacks of chugged engines
One fire-eaten, a pearl-mothered grey,
The other, ebullience untempered.
Both hissing wound and unwound
Or hissing and mixing fumed
Round rays of the stately clear gold
Their untoppling pillars straight to the sun!
And pigeons from the green pediments
Of an absurd center place for much changing
Dirty from so much expulsion and clanging
Flung down and strove through the white
Into grey—their flashed feathers charging—
Till into the clear aerations,
Genius-released condensations
Of the pure unperplexed vapors of snow
Or, more extreme in its volatilizations,
The white exhalations of flowers on clear banners,
Came the slant massy ray and, unfolding,
The down-pouring light-bearing rose.
And the delicate rime of hoar
Frost, shedding its spines and scales
And bringing on the small points of spears
So much christened paleness of dew!
Fresh as diamonds—
I got from this glittering scene into the train
With its low modest cars and green chairs

Whose landmen with lunch pails and railmen addressed
With just as much massy hellos! and hurrahs!
The several first trumpets of morning. (51–52)

We are, to be sure, a long way from Elton's "concrete universal." Always moving unpredictably, Garrigue refuses to stay in one place. Much of her pleasure lies in reproducing the moment in its vivaciousness. A certain level of confusion is not only acceptable but regarded as winsome—a challenge to be handled. But Garrigue also forms alliances as she moves through her poem, though they are unexpected ones indeed: The poet and the laborers cohabit similar space because of the inordinate delight they take in where they are at that moment that is the poem. Garrigue excels because of the comradeliness that passes between her and the "landmen with lunch pails and railmen" who are buoyant, untroubled and self-delighting. A keen sense of the improvisational enables Garrigue to detect games while other passengers "snored" and some employees were "dead between trains." She is primed for the morning journey, and in the long passage that is midway between a promenade and a strut, when she emerges from the confines of the station to mount her coach, she is ready to comprehend all she sees as if the world were nothing but unexpected alliances. Thus one observation is set against another to mix them. Passing the two steam locomotives on either side of the platform, she sees that "Two statuesque columns meeting / In a robust marrying of clouds under clouds / Rose from the equal stacks of chugged engines." While the passage conceives of a unity—"meeting," "robust marrying," "clouds under clouds," and "equal stacks"—the passage that follows delights in distinguishing one engine from the other: "One fire-eaten, a pearl-mothered grey, / The other, ebullience untempered." To try to resolve such shiftings would be to lose their active spirit. Even an obvious proposal, that the erotic fully governs the scene—that the mingling columns of smoke are sexual and the engines are differentiated as if they might be gendered—tempers the circumstance too neatly. Mixing contrary discourses is her delight: she portrays clouds of steam with an eye to their fragility, as though horticultural metaphors were appropriate ("the white exhalations of flowers on clear banners"), then turns toward the crystals that form as the condensing steam makes "the delicate rime of hoar / Frost," even as she ends in a further turn with a "dew" that is equivalent to "diamonds." Garrigue plays with deviations that are temporary, like smoke, and certainly not serious. After all, her title announces a "setpiece." That declaration, by framing the poem as gamelike, anticipates and blunts possible objections. It also sanctions a display of obvious exuberance.

To contemporary reviewers of her work, Garrigue was a source of scandal, a mixture of right and wrong. If charming, she was also in need of a good talking-to, which reviewers were not shy about administering. W. D. Snodgrass in the *Hudson Review* sighed. "So much elegance, so much eloquence, so much polish," he continues. "Soon the lines stop making sense, one is carried away much as he might be with Poe" ("Four" 128–29). Concluding that "Miss Garrigue's eloquence seems an end in itself," he warns that "all objects and meanings may evaporate" and the only subject of her poetry "will come to be the virtuoso performance of the poet herself" (129). Theodore Holmes in *Poetry* discerns a similar flaw. "Each of her poems seems to me over-expanded, to contain in places a use of language considerably in excess of what it says. . . . At times she loves the antiquated, unusual word almost for its own sake—often when the simpler word would have been more to the purpose" (121). Thom Gunn in the *Yale Review* simply loses patience with her. What, he wants to know after citing a passage in which appear the compound words "wind-eagling" and "earth-castling," "can conceivably be the meaning of the two pairs of hyphenated words, which grow considerably more obscure the more one looks at them? This is an all too typical example of the blurring approximation in Miss Garrigue's use of language" ("Voices" 594). Describing a "most typical" poem, he asserts that "she works at her attractiveness so hard that most of the poem gives no impression at all beside manner" (593). For Gunn "writing like this can only be enjoyed by an audience which wants from poetry an opportunity to bask lazily in genteel sensationalism" (594).[5]

Disciplining Bad Girls

If these reviewers had singled out Garrigue as a target for their diagnostics, their corrections might retain some credibility. Clearly Garrigue is uninterested in the tidy poem that is representationally realistic. Defending Dylan Thomas, Garrigue wrote that he alone in an "age of relativity, pessimism and skepticism . . . wrote of the exuberant powers of the natural world and its capacities to nourish and sustain" ("Dark" 113). Her own poetry overtly engages in lavish displays, and she makes no secret of her inclinations, as her titles openly announce: "A Setpiece for Albany," "The Opera of the Heart: Overture," "The Maimed Grasshopper Speaks Up," "Invocation to Old Windylocks," "For Anybody's Martyr's Song," "Address to the Migrations," "One for the Roses," "A Figure for J. V. Meer," "Dialogue in the Dark Tower," "A Fable of Berries," "Incantatory Poem." Such titles, with their emphasis on performativity, signal her disinterest in analytic speculation. But the negative comments that male reviewers proffered are not so much local instances generated by a specific response to Garrigue as they are typical reactions that take over the book review in order to stage the difference that is perceived between men and women, between responsibility and excess, between a thought-and-feeling balance and an emotional imbalance. The 1950s book review, in fact, dramatizes almost as stylized an encounter between male and female as the most trivial bit of pulp fiction. Female poets are perceived as bad girls—bad because they act upon their transgressive desire to be poets, a role that males best fill because of their ability to exert control over their emotions. And just as these bad girls become bad by failing to resist their urge to invade male territory, so their writing displays a similar lack of control. While male poets rebuff this invasion of unfettered emotionality most importantly in their own work, where passions are held in check, they also use the occasion of the book review as an opportunity to chastise openly their unruly charges, subjecting them to a display of public humiliation by posting their failures of excess for all to see.

Because bad girls lack organizational skills, book reviewers must patiently explain to them their faults. Of Naomi Replansky's *Ring Song* (1952), M. L. Rosenthal writes in the *New Republic:* "her poems give the effect of having been set down with not quite enough revision, or with less than full development" ("Lucidity" 29). Rolfe Humphries, reviewing Dilys Bennett Laing's *Walk through Two Landscapes* (1949) in the *Nation,* questions even her ability to comprehend the relationship between the title poem and the title of her book. After describing her themes, he writes: "These are not exactly what she means by the two landscapes described in her title poem; I do not think she realizes, in that poem, exactly what she does mean, but she seems to me to be telling the truth there when she says she is uneasy in her abstract world" (235). No wonder, then, that Reed Whittemore in the *Sewanee Review* can react with such pleased surprise when he finds two poems in Emma Swan's *The Lion and the Lady* (1950) in which "she demonstrates as much control of her medium as any disciplinarian could desire" ("Four" 725). But his ardor soon cools, and he illustrates her failings in three lengthy quotations; he must report that "she is all too ready to sacrifice sense and substance to sound and pattern, all too ready not to make sense at all" (725). Too attached to the emotional, it seems, to be able to present matters with clarity, these poets are always swept away with excitement. Reviewing Rosalie Moore's *The Grasshopper's Man* (1949) for *Poetry,* Henry Rago states that "the poet's best moments are in her triumphs over her own virtuosity, when she can keep the poem from splintering into too-bright images and instead make lines and phrases humble before the complete task" (99). That is the job these reviewers accept: to humble women poets when they forget to write clearly.

When women attempt to objectify their emotion, and to strike a balance between intellect and feeling, they demonstrate instead only their inability to think. In the *Kenyon Review,* A. Alvarez, reviewing Elizabeth Bishop's *Poems* (the title under which *A Cold Spring* appeared along with a reissue of *North and South*) in 1957, invokes a touchstone line from Richard Eberhart to try to explain how it's done:

> Eberhart's language has a kind of physical complexity which Miss Bishop can never reach. When, for example, he writes of:
>
> > The abrupt essence and the final shield
>
> the difficulty is peculiarly unintellectual; it lies in his attempt to fix in words an obstinate desire for the metaphysical. The difficulty, in short, is in the nature of the poet's experience. On the other hand, when Miss Bishop writes:
>
> > . . . each riser distinguished from the next
> > by an irregular sawtooth edge,
> > alike, but certain as a stereoscopic view,
>
> or when she goes off into one of her many geometric excursions, she seems only to be trying to force a hard intellectual manner upon the otherwise soft and easy flow of her verse. (325)

Bishop is being given contradictory advice. She is mistaken if she tries too hard, for the "soft and easy flow of her verse" is going to be damaged in some unspecified way if it is not left untouched by "hard" intellect that isn't within her province. But that "soft and easy flow" is precisely what Alvarez characterizes as second-rate. There is no way, then, for her to reach the effects that Eberhart obtains. If those effects are "in the nature of the poet's experience" then Bishop can only aspire to be a poet.

More accurately, she is typecast as a perpetual minor poet.[6] Alvarez opens his essay with an overview of the rise of Imagism, a movement that he argues "coincided with the enfranchisement of women" (321). Before Imagism, a woman had to be "very exceptional indeed to be recognized. . . . But to be a good Imagist all that was necessary was a feeling for detail, as in arranging a drawing-room, and sufficient good manners to keep it up" (321). To this dainty nook Alvarez consigns not just Bishop but most other women poets: "Though Imagism, *tout court,* has faded quietly away, its influence still remains in the well-bred fastidiousness of many of the contemporary women poets" (322).

There is a tradition of women's poetry, then—but one that is explicitly subordinate to the tradition that defines the mainstream. Other reviewers evoked that alternate tradition as a way of acknowledging women's difference without crediting any value. Mulling over Garrigue's work in *The Monument Rose* (1953), Howard Nemerov concludes: "In general her idea of meter goes back to a time when the English line was a lighter or slighter thing than the dramatists made it, with more hesitations, charming uncertainties of stress, the time of Wyatt" ("Seven" 317). Garrigue's peculiar writing style (its "uncertainties" are in some way "charming") can be traced back to a poetic tradition whose inadequacies others have long know about. "Wyatt" here may also serve as a code name for a secondary and debased tradition since the metrics of his poetic line are notoriously unstable. Hayden Carruth was struggling to pinpoint Babette Deutsch's effects when he reviewed *Coming of Age: New and Selected Poems* in 1959 for *Poetry:* He cites five lines in which "Miss Deutsch has not succeeded" then he produces "a workable example"—which turns out to be not her original work but four lines from her translation of a Pasternak poem. Only at last does he reproduce a whole poem by Deutsch, after which he sums up: "Miss Deutsch has ventured courageously on a kind of writing that is difficult and very rarely accomplished well. We think of the rich locus of the eighteenth century, yet we retain very few examples in our anthologies" ("Three" 118). Why so few examples? Because anthologies only retain important texts in the primary tradition. Whether the tradition of women writers is identified with the Imagist movement or with poets like Wyatt who were superseded by Shakespeare or with minor verse from the eighteenth century, it is figured as a subordinate tradition.

These book reviews have the outward appearance of respectable proceedings, and they can be reconstructed as a running set of lecture-notes on the precepts of academic verse. But that fails to register the human cost involved in reviews that are not just negative but designed to damage. In the *Nation* in 1954, John Ciardi, assigned a number of poets to cover, mentions two books that "deserve enthusiastic notice," Babette Deutsch's *Animal Vegetable Mineral* (1954) and Howard Moss's *The Toy Fair* (1954). But he handles these works in rather different ways:

> Babette Deutsch's sixth book of poems is a strangely uneven book, but one that will reward the reader's patience with at least two memorable poems. Having been traduced by my family into paying advanced prices to see "The Robe," I can insist that anyone can afford $2.75 to have in his head such poems as "Homage to John Skelton" and "Afternoon with an Infant."
>
> We can let Howard Moss speak for himself. Here is his summary of Venice: "The swank and stink of the imagination / Beautifully gone bad." And this: "A mountain is an opera for the eye." Howard Moss has not only a fine ear but a mind in which the word feels like a thing, a poet's mind. ("Recent" 184)

Both poets are introduced as equals, but Deutsch's work is surrounded by gestures that downgrade its value. Just what are those two "memorable" poems in her volume worth? Well, more than the cost of a high-priced movie ticket—a commodity that links women's work to sentimental products of mass culture such as movies based on Bible stories. Howard Moss, citizen of the world and aphorist, gets to be heard. Just as Moss sums up Venice, so Ciardi finds himself summing up the virtues of a well-balanced poetic language when he praises Moss's ability to write so that "the word feels like a thing." Deutsch is represented by two titles, one paying homage to a minor poet, the other delimiting an area associated with woman as caregiver. Even Ciardi's locutions are telling. It is possible to "let Howard Moss speak for himself." Deutsch is yet to earn the status of one who is quotable.

Ciardi's withholding from Deutsch the opportunity to be heard, to speak in her own words, is not an exception in 1950s book-reviewing practice of women. A particularly disturbing feature of many reviews, this silencing is not simply the omission of examples from the review: at times the reviewer speaks over the voice of the poet entirely, substituting words as parodic equivalents. Though the woman appears in the review, she lacks representation within it; she has become that which is subject to the reviewer's fantasizing. Harry Roskolenko, reviewing Lillian Rockwell's *Impatient Lover* (1952) along with books by W. S. Merwin and Robert Hillyer, quotes not a word from Rockwell in a review that otherwise finds space to cite three stanzas from a long poem by Merwin and one poem in its entirety by Hillyer.

Roskolenko instead quotes from Rockwell's dust jacket. "In this first book she has, to repeat a blurb statement, devoted herself 'almost excessively to a poetry of delight—a concentrated theater of the senses.' . . . After considering the merits of this candid statement regarding her special concentrations, one is forced to be just as candid in defining her range, as well as her specialized relationship to the sensuality so generously implied in her blurb" (35). He produces, in the next two paragraphs, a paraphrase that is a lexicon of degrading allusions. "It is a lively tune she sings," he begins, diminishing her writing into a vocal performance. "Photographically, her images bed down with ease," he explains. But lest we think all who read between these pages will succumb to fantasy, he also warns that "You are constantly being shrieked at, which hardly prepares one for erotic overtures" (35). Substituting the dust jacket quotation for Rockwell's own words (there is no evidence she is responsible for the blurb), then brutalizing Rockwell herself in a sexual caricature, Roskolenko subjugates her completely. And in all this, we never once hear a line of Rockwell's poetry for ourselves.

Roskolenko's performance, if extreme, is not unique. Men reviewing poetry by women have a hard time keeping their eyes off their book dust jackets. The body of the book, when it belongs to a woman, is apparently more than just an outside wrapper; it can be a whole collection of other features, each of which can be a potential distraction. Of course in an era when the New Criticism marked biographical information off-limits, the inclusion of background material in a review was already a signal that the work did not merit serious consideration. To quote from a dust jacket without conveying an insult required genuine tact. Richard Wilbur opened a 1955 review of Robert Graves's *Collected Poems* with the words "As Graves himself says on the jacket, 'the mainly negative work begun by the "modernists" of the Twenties in exploring the limits of technical experiment is finished and done with'" ("Graves's New Volume" 175). But Wilbur had been careful to make the apparatus subordinate to the strong poet's presence. The dust jacket has been taken back from the marketers and transformed into a forum for the writer. But the female poet was rarely perceived as strong in this way; indeed, she was presented as demonstrating her weakness in other ways—using the dust jacket to appeal to an audience for special favors. When Thom Gunn shifts his attention to the dust jacket in his review of Pauline Hanson for *Poetry* in 1958, he is ready to pounce: "Most of her book is taken up with the poem from which it gets its title, *The Forever Young*. The dust jacket tells us that this was published in 1948 in a different form and has since 'without tremendously wide circulation or "popular" comment, won a very avid and significant audience as one of the truly valued longish poems of the times.' I cannot say that I feel very avid or significant about it" ("Calm" 383). Why should a voice that is not Hanson's be identified with her and then accorded such weight? Is even an anonymous blurb-writer less negligible as a "voice" than the speech of a woman poet? But Gunn wants to deliver a warning about a poet who, in his opinion, quite mistakenly pursues wide popularity. Such a pursuit is already a mark of limitation, and here it is associated as a mark of the feminine.

Dust jacket copy, even when clumsily written and obviously bad, need not be applied against a poet. Julia Randall, reviewing volumes by Dilys Bennett Laing and Selwyn S. Schwartz in *Poetry* in 1950, finds little to admire in either poet, but when she reproduces dust jacket copy she specifies that her target is not the poets but their publisher, the Twayne Library of Modern Poetry. Her review extends sympathy to poets whose work has been inadequately described in fashionable but empty critical jargon, and she mocks not the poets, who are victims of crude marketing procedures, but the blurb-writers for their "wonderfully vague and pretentious language" (231). By contrast, male reviewers are apt to confuse the dust jacket's ornamental material with the poet, as if the poets had chosen it for their own adornment. Reviewing May Swenson's *Another Animal* in *Poetry* in 1956, John Berryman explains that Swenson is "described on the jacket as having come from Utah 'to New York City where she holds an active job.' One looks to the next sentence to hear what this may be. No: 'Her poems have appeared' etc. It is hard to know whether to be pleased that she holds an active job, or sorry, for an inactive job is surely better for a poet" ("Long Way" 53). Berryman perhaps means only to tease, but his whimsy plays with notions that diminish Swenson's stature. He has her coming to the East as an outsider from a remote western region, arriving not to be educated but to support herself—a decision that, he also manages to suggest, may interfere with the dedication serious poetry demands. If she is insufficiently serious, it may explain why Berryman opens his review with this droll recounting of her background. In any case, the number of words he cites from her dust jacket (fourteen) is eight more than the number of words he quotes from her poetry which consists in one line: "Yield to the wizard's piercing kiss." This quote stands out so peculiarly at the tail end of a 600-word review that it seems to be a personal message that Berryman wants to deliver to Swenson. Nonetheless, this is an improvement over his presentation of P. K. Page, whom he discusses just before Swenson. Although he pulls words from her dust jacket—"She is a lady (in private life, says the jacket, Mrs. Irwin, the wife of the Canadian High Commissioner in Australia)" (53)—he nowhere cites a word of her poetry.

In the rare instance when the women poets were to be admired, they often had to undergo a period of humiliation. In the *Yale Review* Thom Gunn begins a review with a move that is negative enough to discourage most readers from continuing:

> Louise Bogan is quoted on the back of *Light and Dark* as saying that its author, Barbara Howes, has among other things "found her own voice." Yes, I thought, glancing through the book for the first time, but isn't that voice a trifle affected? Why, for example, does she say Cocorico rather than Cockledoodledoo? And don't the following lines
>
> > Cicadas at their pastime, drilling
> > Eyelets of sound, so many midget Singer
> > Sewing machines
>
> impress one only with their eccentric ingenuity? ("Excellence" 299–300)

Surprisingly (in the light of this overture), Gunn then reverses himself, writing that his own "first glance is misleading however, and I now find Miss Howes a very exciting writer." But his initial depiction, though conceded to be an error, nonetheless retains its prominent position at the beginning of the review. Feminine "failure" seems to remain firmly on the record at the moment when it is supposed to have been erased; it is complicated further by his reproduction of Louise Bogan's voice, which he then takes issue with. Even when women were allocated space within a review for their own words, then, the correctness of their speech is placed in question. Indeed, what was sometimes quoted in a review were not strong lines but samples of their weakest. Reviewing two first books, *The Catch* (1952) by T. Weiss and *Immediate Sun* (1953) by Rosemary Thomas, E. L. Mayo in *Poetry* quotes four times from Weiss, each time choosing passages that demonstrate Weiss's "reticence and strenuousness, his refusal of easy melodies and affirmations, his delicate ear for the cross-grained, snag-fingernailed speech texture of our time" ("Two" 325). Mayo also quotes four passages from Thomas, but two of these illustrate weakness. "Sometimes we revert to the prop room," Mayo explains, introducing lines he believes flawed. Why cite lines that fail? Mayo does it again, even less explicably, as he cites only the three lines that he considers "threadbare" from a work that is "an otherwise brilliant poem" (327). The brilliant lines he never quotes. In a similar vein, Kathleen Raine wins Dudley Fitts's approval in 1952, when he is reviewing her work in the *New Republic,* because "Miss Raine has wisely chosen to limit herself—wisely, as though realizing that the lyric sweep, the sustained figure, are not for her—and the result is a contemplation of the great basic themes in miniature" (27). Of course this offers with one hand only to take back with the other. Raine has limited herself before someone else could urge her to do so; appropriately, she lowers her sights and turns away from the great tradition. And her art is inevitably a miniature one. Yet Fitts rewards her prudence by sprinkling his review with several quotations that he lauds—only to turn at his conclusion and dwell at length on what he deems to be her lapses, reproducing two passages in which "things have got out of hand." Though he closes on a gracious note ("Let us admit the strangeness, then, for certainly there is much excellent beauty"), he has nonetheless recorded his doubts in a strong, detailed manner. When Raine moves away from the miniaturized, when she begins to turn toward large-scale forms that are the mainstay of the primary poetic tradition, then she indulges in a "putting on of the singing robe, and Miss Raine cannot sing in this way without appearing self-conscious" (28).

Lecturing the poet, as in Fitts's remarks to "Miss Raine," is a regular occurrence in these reviews. As Theodore Holmes explains patiently in his review of Jean Garrigue: "Poetry demands more of us than a way of getting along with life; it requires a degree of consciously achieved mastery over our existence" (119). This need by reviewers to return to basics, to explain the zero-degree tolerance level for writing, stems in part from the business of the review as an occasion for defining fundamental values that have been threatened by an alien incursion. But the effect of such a lecture is to project into the review a subjectivity for the woman poet as a feckless sort incapable of understanding even the simplest obligations. Reed Whittemore is even driven to segregation in his lecturing in a 1950 *Sewanee Review* essay. Dividing his review (entitled "Four Men and Three Women") along gender lines, in its second section—headed up, for maximum clarity, "II. Women"—he opens with a lecture that is prominently placed because his audience of women poets is so derelict that, without this special arranging, they are likely never to find it:

> "Constant revision" is a phrase that has come to be a bad joke in this particular cranny of the literary world. We use it with bright ironic overtones to indicate to exasperated freshmen, overworked English majors,

and tired poets that although the work (poem, theme, essay) they turn
in to us is not, as one might say, right, and although a great deal of back-
breaking labor has yet to be put in on it to make it even partly right, still
we recognize that revision is a boring as well as an endless task, and we
sympathize wholeheartedly (though not actively) with their disappointment in discovering that revision is necessary. ("Four" 722–23)

Whittemore's tone, though patient, is weary. He must spell out hard truths
for the ladies. (Actually, he has a rather complicated argument to unfold:
he must indict Ann Stanford for having an excess of—well, *discipline*.) But
the counterpart section of this review ("I. Men") begins in a brisk and
hearty fashion: "John Frederick Nims is a good poet" ("Four" 718). It is
wonderful to be able to speak directly and trust that one's words will be
heard. By contrast, the "we" who are invoked in the opening paragraph in
"II. Women" are clearly not women. "We" demand from others the "back-
breaking labor" to "make it even partly right," trying against all odds to
convince women (whose coequals are the beginning student, the English
major, and the poet who is "tired") that they must revise. Defined by contrast, then, "We" represents the calm mentor, the successful critic, and the
bright and alert poet. To have an author, or whole set of authors, addressed
in a simple terms tinged with exasperation cannot but diminish confidence
in the alertness of those being addressed.

As infuriating as such lectures must have been for the women supposed
to hear them, consider the further damage caused by certain momentary
asides in which the reviewer reaches for a metaphor or a figure of speech
or a point of comparison that suggests that communication with the
woman poet can only be effected through a highly specialized "feminine"
allusion. These moves are not quite the same as the gender-based ridicule
that Randall Jarrell regularly heaped on his victims as he exercised his famous wit. "One feels about most of her poems," Jarrell writes in the *Nation*,
questioning whether Muriel Rukeyser's work was too devoted to political
causes, "pretty much as one feels about the girl on last year's calendar"
("Verse" 512). So outrageous was Jarrell when bent upon needling the object of his attention that he could almost be ignored as someone who had
his own particular problem. About Constance Carrier he wrote in 1955 in
the *Yale Review:* "what she says is earnest and reasonable and commonplace
enough to make you feel that the norm or mean or median of all members
of the PTA, of the AAUW, of the League of Women Voters is there before
you, scanned and scrubbed and shining" ("Recent" 225). Jarrell, of course,
turned vicious in the company of all writing that fell short of his standards,

but his reviews were lengthy enough that he could counter his most flamboyant remarks with passages of thoughtful interpretation. Other reviewers had far less space, and were even less inclined to be interpretive, but wanted to imitate his flash. "Compared to much modern poetry," wrote John Ciardi, reviewing Leonie Adams's *Poems: A Selection* (1954) for the *Nation*, "Miss Adams's gold stain shines like a splendor. Yet, touch it against a poem like [Dylan] Thomas's 'Refusal to Mourn'—to cite only one—and the gold stain seems dimmer. It remains to be sure, a thing of the spirit, but more nearly of the spirit's jewelry than of its ray and center" ("Two Nuns" 445). Would Ciardi have drawn on images from gold and jewelry—ornamental designs—to explain his own verse? Jean Garrigue especially provoked reviewers into finding words that they thought to be appropriately feminine. Hayden Carruth described her poems as "often maimed by the ravels and snarls of her argument" ("Poetry Chronicle" 578), as though they were constructed from yarn and twine. Geoffrey H. Hartman, acknowledging the appeal of Garrigue but unwilling to encourage her, thought it effective to call her someone who "throws herself somewhat too willingly on the mercy of the court" (695). W. D. Snodgrass preferred to fantasize in more domestic terms: "Miss Garrigue appears to have learned from Milton much of how to maintain a long sentence, spun out and strung to dry over the line endings" ("Four" 129). Garrigue's words, like an array of wash-time garments, are confused with things worn around the body. In each case, these formations portray the reviewer as bending down to find words that the woman poet can hear, as if she dwells in some alien yet oddly parallel dimension.

Garrigue especially is in the unfortunate position of inadvertently exemplifying in her poetry the very features that would match a composite "portrait" of the woman poet as it might be assembled from a sampling of these reviews. In their view, that poet is predominantly a spontaneous creature, too entranced by the activity of the moment to entertain analytical thoughts. Feckless, this poet limits herself to a vocabulary that is simple, in which phrases are repeated for emphasis. The woman poet's lack of interest in the intellect is signaled by a correlative attentiveness to the body. Appearance matters, not the depth that exists below an attractive surface; that surface is never pierced. And finally, the woman poet communes best with herself, or with other women, as she occupies an alternate and subordinate tradition that has, for generations, shadowed the mainstream and dominant tradition of the western male. Each of these attributes is not simply identified but virtually evoked by the tactics of male reviewing, from the breezy manner in which the woman poet is discussed to the undue interest on the material of her dust jacket to the speed with which the reviewer's words are allowed to substitute for the poet's. And Garrigue's considerable strengths as a poet—her ability to enter a scene and transform it with her positive vision, her interest in descriptive play (reproducing in detail minute activities, many of which revolve about a surface), her commitment to a voice that is unreservedly animated and that delights in its volubility—also lend themselves to supporting roles in a prejudicial encounter.

A wide range of different circumstances made issues of discipline important in the 1950s, including the new and still somewhat uncertain alliance between the university and the practicing poet (what would be the grounds for winning tenure?); the increased social mobility that brought to the campus large numbers of first-generation college students unclear about the protocols of the educational establishment; and for male poets, a nagging defensiveness that emerged when the vocation of writing poetry, which was widely associated with emotional expressiveness, was extended professional status. With no particular outlet for these anxieties in the actual writing of poetry itself, it is not surprising that struggles to deal with them might surface elsewhere. Like most issues that cause anxiety, these did not lend themselves to frank discussion, and it is perhaps not surprising that the book review site, a quintessentially anomalous location, would find itself under invasion from them. While the gatekeeping function of the review-by-a-peer conferred a degree of importance upon the process (here was a rare opportunity for direct feedback in a public realm), the stringent limitations of the endeavor (the review had to be brief and to the point; several volumes could be assigned willy-nilly) withheld complete seriousness from the occasion. As a result, the review was, on the one hand, negligible—it was not a poem and merely prose, and prose of a journalistic stripe—even as it was, on the other hand, highly public, a place where issues of legitimacy were in a spotlight. The practical effect of these pressures was to invite widescale abuse. Rather than judiciously policing poetry in the 1950s, book reviews by male poets often became the literary version of a police riot in which reviewers, provoked by the threat of genuinely different alternatives, ran amok, disrupting the protocol of the review process to berate, ridicule, humiliate, and ultimately suppress the voices of difference.

4 VERSIONS OF THE FEMININE BAROQUE

My writing makes me what, in old rural terms, was known as egg money.

—Katherine Hoskins, "Conversation Pieces"
(excerpts from a journal, ca. 1959)

Women poets looking back on the 1950s typically remember it as a time when the poetry they wrote was not what they wanted to write—when they were able to write at all. Adrienne Rich in 1971 wrote about her second collection, *The Diamond Cutters,* published in 1955: "I was already dissatisfied with those poems, which seemed to me mere exercises for poems I hadn't written" ("Introduction" 42). Rich has been acknowledged, with Jane Cooper, as a rare survivor of a bad time. Cooper recalled that from 1949 to 1953 "I worked strenuously and perfectly seriously on a book of poems (a *book,* not just poems), then 'gave up poetry' and never tried to publish one of them" ("Nothing" 48). At the University of Iowa Writer's Workshop, she remembers being told that "to be a woman poet was a contradiction in terms" (43). By pairing the experience of Rich and Cooper in *Stealing the Language* (1986), Alicia Ostriker could sum up the 1950s as a period in which the voice of the strong women poet had been effectively silenced.

Largely because of Ostriker and Tillie Olsen's *Silences,* which reprinted Cooper's anecdotes, we know a great deal about the women's poetry that was *not* written in the 1950s, but we know next to nothing about poetry by women that did appear in that decade. David Perkins has sensibly remarked that where a literary historian decides to begin a narrative has a powerful determining effect on what will be said: "Events subsequent to the inaugural moment . . . are narrated at length, and hence their diversity can be recorded. . . . Thus it often happens that a phase of relative synthesis or homogeneity is said to have preceded the period that is the subject of the book" (*Literary History* 36). Using 1960 as a pivotal date for the renascence of women's poetry necessarily downplays women who attained partial success in the previous decade. Until important postwar poetry by women from the 1950s is restored to prominence, it will not be possible for the 1950s to be understood as an incubator for the 1960s.

From that collective portrait of the woman poet that can be coaxed from the pages of their male reviewers—a portrait that is a summary of recurring strategies that reviewers assumed were appropriate to address the woman poet—it is possible to see that several of the women poets of the postwar period actually wrote the works that questioned, if not directly undermined, key elements of that composite sketch. California-based Rosalie Moore, for example, specialized in a poetic line whose idiosyncratic diction expressed her conviction that realms of feeling—realms that escape the hold of the intellect—can nonetheless be depicted, in an analytic fashion, through a judicious use of highly precise phrasing. Violet Lang's exaggerated ventriloquizings of the lover's voice or the tourist's voice or the showgirl's voice is her distanced inhabitation of social roles whose limitations she knowingly sounds out. And Katherine Hoskins's poetry frequently begins in mid-dialogue, almost in mid-sentence, insisting on participating in a conversation from which she will not be excluded—a conversation that pointedly associates gender and race. If the woman poet as assembled in composite is undisciplined, utterly immersed in the moment, and essentially silenced, then these three poets each in her own way resist being so addressed by male reviewers. At the same time, of course, it is open to question whether their tendencies to speak back so clearly may explain why their reputations have not prospered.

Rosalie Moore, "Activist"

Perhaps no poet whose reputation was high as the 1950s began has suffered a reversal more complete than Rosalie Moore, a writer linked with one of the rare organized schools of poetry to appear in the postwar years, the San Francisco-based "Activists" driven by the theorizing and instruction of UCLA professor Lawrence Hart. The Activists were remarkably strong as the decade opened. W. H. Auden singled out the works of not one but two for inclusion in the Yale Series of Younger Poets, Robert Horan in 1948 and Moore in 1949. A portion of a 1947 issue of the *Quarterly Review of Literature* featured the Activists, with an introductory essay by Hart, and the entire May 1951 issue of *Poetry* was edited by Hart and devoted to them.

William Carlos Williams, invited to comment (and perhaps nostalgically appreciative of any group activity now that the days of "movements" seemed so far away), offered some not-unfriendly but no doubt impertinent advice, suggesting the Activists could be put to work translating Gongora (the very type of the poet of excess). Moore was the bright star of the Activists, always the lead-off poet in these magazine selections. She was the object of an essay of appreciation in the May 1951 *Poetry,* recipient of Guggenheims in 1951 and 1952, lead-off poet again in a January 1957 *Poetry,* and an essay-writer herself when in 1958 *Poetry* yet again set aside space for Activists (though this time only a portion of an issue for an "update"). In the yearlong experiment when *Poetry* ran snapshots of selected contributors her photo was one of those included in 1948.[1]

Activists sought to convey immediacy through compression and word-association, the aim being to avoid what Hart called "the conventionalizing, labeling elements of language" that "function also as a mental mechanism for holding off experience at arm's length" ("About" 104). "Moving, by Roads Moved . . . ," with its play on being "moved" emotionally as well as physically, expressed this shifting scale in its title. It was the poem by Moore which introduced the Activists in the 1947 *QRL* (reprinted in *The Grasshopper's Man* in 1948):

Moving, by roads moved—
Will, like a shunted horse.
Nowhere before been, but get
The meticulous present of strangeness.

Place is of all things vaguest,
Terrifying to haul,
No load so heavy before mention,
Or a smile—its vine-thin history.

Place, place—ornamental deceiver.
Be the location constant, its
Circuit of moles or hills—
An illusion finer than eyes is,
Invites you to come not in.

One rather remembers
How, in the child's dust,
He took up a fine handful
And heard, through the thews and wheels,
The voice of the horse auctioneer.
(*Grasshopper's Man* 29)

Activists made few concessions to their audience. Moore's poem is typically dense and characteristically self-descriptive. That is, her reference in line 4 to "The meticulous present of strangeness" is a reference to the very moment in the poem that we are in. Moore wants to take us to a place "No-where before been" (line 3) even as she hopes to depict that sense of its strangeness meticulously. The diffuse syntax of the opening line, which sets movement in motion only to interrupt it in line 2, prepares us for the crisis of line 3. There we discover we are three lines deep in a poem and still have no comprehensible context for the work—but this is exactly where Moore hoped to deliver us. All of stanza 2 then comments upon the white light of the presentness into which the poem has thrust us and which it now sustains. This curious space exists "before mention," as if prior to language, in a "vine-thin history" in which nothing has a stable past, or in which all placement is under erasure. The third stanza continues to sustain the sensation of being in a place that is summoned within language even as that place exists apart from language. The ending, then, by thrusting us into the realm of memory, offers the only closure possible for this poem: it positions us in an instant that is "frozen" because it is long passed. The sense of dwelling in an immediate present is thus interrupted. Yet the final impression, the moment of memory, is, in its emphasis on attentiveness to detail and acute listening, most appropriate, for this is the sharp sensibility that we have been cultivating. Is it possible to look and listen so keenly as to conceive the past that is implicit in an event? Moore suggests it might be, in poetry.

More important, perhaps, is Moore's startling ability to convey the virtual sensation of the moment in language that is descriptively apt, with a playful music, a wayward syntax, and a word choice driven by considerations of sound. "Summer Camp: Wane" led off the May 1951 issue of *Poetry*:

> The peripatetic stars without any longer
> Their easeful hair;
> The steppers over
> The pepperwood.
>
> Oh the people all are sleeping
> Together as in a waltz.
> Under the trees in cots
> They idle their engines.

Away to the Hayward Hills the cars in pairs
Rise to a roar, wail—
Loose the wild country gone through:
Western billboard and buffalo
Leave to its fences.

And all night long without motor
The stars on the move:
Calypso, Juno, Gemini,
The former tenants, gone and handless—
Moved by the scenery movers and unvaulted
As seed out of a new summer.

That tired priest who comes out of
Anything tearing its autumn up,
Wreaking its colors,
Is shaking his sleeves, is here.
        (*Of Singles* 63–64)

Full of delightfully unexpected turns, the poem is also convincingly observed. How to convey this skeptical secular generation's sensation of looking up to stars and perceiving not just their dazzle and brilliance but the emptiness among them? At one time constellations were personified and nightwatchers could envision "easeful hair" as they wheeled through the night sky, as if the stars were "peripatetic," as if so close to us they could be "steppers over / The pepperwood" (an affectionate phrase that has not a whit of glory attached to it). Moore's universe isn't empty. But the grandiose schematics of the past are gently displaced by her easygoing theatrics. As she exclaims (and her "Oh" is a somewhat un-Activist-like construction), her summer camp outside sleepers, turning about, "waltz" together; snoring, they idle their engines. Motors are softened in this poem (cars are "in pairs" and their roar gives way to a "wail") just as the gulf between the stars yawns less forbiddingly. The slack syntax of the last stanza conveys the mood at summer's end, when the seasons are beginning to turn in a different rhythm.

Like Jean Garrigue, Moore employs a poetic discourse far from the mainstream, but where Garrigue is sexual, provocative, and bodily, Moore is cosmological, exploratory, and liberating. Auden had no problem (in his foreword to *The Grasshopper's Man*) defending Moore's work for its denial of "the conception of poetry as the defender of the humanist values of intelligence and order against irrationalism" (8) as well as for its denial of "poetry as an instrument for arousing public emotions about political and social issues" (8–9). "It is a good thing," Auden wrote, "that we should be reminded that a poem is not, like a teacher, a bridge between the truth and the ignorant reader, which becomes superfluous once the relation between the latter two has been established, but is itself the terminus of a relation" (9). Auden was able to see that the Activist approach, especially in Moore's hands, was oriented toward the poem as an experience. Moore writes in a poetic language that is predominantly phrasal: the governing unit in her poetry is not the line so much as the phrase—the line quite often waxes or wanes to accommodate the phrase. That emphasis allows her to construct a poetry that is both ruminative and immediate, a poetry in which a moment can be summed up in a phrase, as if the poem proceeds by such a series of summations, each one a dazzling pause, an incisive summation, that urges us on to the next. The poetry, in one sense, is surprisingly intellectualized: the phrases lend themselves to analysis. But in another sense, the poetry moves in spontaneous leaps, establishing a distinctive pace in which one moment may unfold rapidly and then another with infinite slowness. The pacing, perhaps, is the most idiosyncratic feature of a Moore poem, for the text seems to operate outside any laws that might be suggested by the stanza structure or the length of the line (the rhythm in a Moore poem is entirely subordinated to phrasing). Yet finally, everything about the work seems judicious and apt and measured; it could not have unfolded any other way.

Moore's aesthetic may be seen as deeply rooted in the work of West Coast artists and poets, and that explains in part how she was apt to fall into obscurity. Her poems originated in a workshop setting. When Moore's project is repositioned within the group of artists and poets that Richard Cándida Smith in his 1995 study loosely identified as "postsurrealists," her verse fits clearly within the parameters of the California post–World War II avant-garde. In Smith's words, this aesthetic was intent upon valuing the sacred over the profane, preferring the "cosmological-theological over psychological-sociological understandings," privileging the "individual choice" over "social unity," and depicting conformity as "an unnatural attempt to repress what lay inside each individual's soul" (141). As alien as Moore's poetry may have been by mainstream standards, by regional standards it was not strange at all. Working within a region (Berkeley and San Francisco) that could offer such support to its poets and artists—consider, for example, the (albeit somewhat different) community nurturing Robert Duncan and Jack Spicer—sustained Moore in her experimental play. But the drive underlying so much academic verse in the 1950s was to erect widely acknowledged standards that could establish contemporary poetry as a discourse with clear professional aims. The very idea of a regionalist aesthetic was at odds with that vision. And the model for the author-audience relation in academic poetry was based on that very interchange between student and teacher that Auden evoked as contrary to Moore. Her writing, when set against academic verse, was especially disquieting: mainstream verse's emphasis on character type, fundamental situation, and "common sense" language seemed by contrast to be burdened with the fictions that the social world hopes to live by. Moore's achievement is to remind us that experience cannot be subsumed under some authority but must remain contradictory and ambiguous. That was not a message many were eager to pursue in the 1950s—even as her appearance in the by-invitation-only fortieth anniversary issue of *Poetry* indicates the esteem in which her work was held.[2]

V. R. Lang and the Poetry of Termless Play

Moore's work had a bent that was deliberately idiosyncratic and simultaneously intellectualized *and* emotionalized. What individualized it had been thoughtfully considered. As Auden's comments underscore, the Activist poetic discourse that she practiced anticipated the conscious and calculated oppositions to patriarchy that would develop in the 1960s. By contrast, the poetry of V. R. Lang (Violet Lang, known to her friends as "Bunny"), eccentric and original, was inescapably stamped with her particular personality. Until her untimely death from Hodgkin's Disease in 1956, at the age of thirty-two, Lang's work appeared with gratifying regularity in the pages of *Poetry* (May 1949, November 1949, June 1950, November 1952, December 1953, May 1954, and April 1955). She was one of the guiding forces behind the Cambridge Poet's Theatre, actress as well as author/director of two plays, and in the words of Peter Davison (who shared the stage with her in John Ashbery's 1956 production *The Compromise; or, The Queen of Cariboo*): "youngest of many daughters of an organist at King's Chapel, once a Boston debutante, later a member of the Canadian Women's Army Corps, an editor of the *Chicago Review,* and a quondam showgirl at the Old Howard Burlesque House" (25). All memoirs of Lang—there are two others: a superb and lengthy piece by Alison Lurie (1959, revised 1975) and a brief and witty comment by Nora Sayre (1995)—at some point recite a similar list of unlikely and contradictory combinations. Lang is someone who labors over her poems, rewriting some forty times, but she is also some-one who decides almost on a whim to sponsor Gregory Corso, whom she invites to Harvard and hires for the Poets' Theatre. She is someone who submits her work to the most prestigious and competitive journals, *Poetry* and the *Quarterly Review of Literature,* yet in the photo she submits to *Poetry,* her hand reaches up to frame her hair in a sensual gesture, and the trenchcoat and severe makeup she wears suggest adventure. She is some-one who runs up enormous bills on shopping sprees in fashionable stores, then earns the money to pay off her debts by dancing in the Old Howard chorus line, an experience that reappears in *Fire Exit* (1953), her verse drama retelling the Orpheus myth and situating Eurydice not in hell but in a bur-lesque house in Union City, New Jersey.

Lang's poetic voice was close enough to her friend Frank O'Hara's that when one of her poems, "To Frank's Guardian Angel," was found among his papers, it was attributed to him and published in O'Hara's *Collected Poems.*[3] (It is when O'Hara recalls her death, in "A Step Away from Them," that his own voice breaks.) Like O'Hara, Lang excelled when she worked the edge of wherever her writing assignment was taking her, as if her fascina-tion was held by the poem as an environment that was being constructed by an interplay among words to which she was as much spectator as par-ticipant. Her texts can drift in an exquisite daze. In "A Lovely Song for Jack-son" (Roger Jackson who, as Jack Rogers, performed in several Poets' The-atre productions), it is as though the motive force behind the poem is finding new couplets that rhyme:

> If I were a seaweed at the bottom of the sea,
> I'd find you, you'd find me.
> Fishes would see us and shake their heads
> Approvingly from their submarine beds.
> Crabs and sea horses would bid us glad cry,
> And sea anemone smile us by. . . .
>
> If I were an angel, and lost in the sun,
> You would be there, and you would be one.
> Birds that flew high enough would find us and sing,
> Gladder to find us than for anything,
> And clouds would be proud of us, light everywhere
> Would clothe us gold gaily, for dear and for fair.
> Trees stretching skywards would see us and smile,
> And all over heaven we'd laugh for a while,
> Only the fishes would search and make moan,
> Wondering, wondering, where we had gone. (107)

Just as Lang believes Jackson will find her, so the poem seems to step off into space with confidence that some rhyme will appear. A couplet in the first stanza of this two-stanza poem reads: "Fishes would see us and shake their heads / Approvingly from their submarine beds." The lines are, in one sense, awful. The concluding phrase of "their submarine beds" seems to be there only to suffice as a rhyme for "heads." But in another sense, it is sublimely right, its last-minute appearance to clinch the rhyme a magical intercession, like Jackson finding her at the bottom of the sea even in the guise of seaweed. Poems, for Lang, are where everything is always something else. The slightly chaotic swarm of impressions this promotes she greets with simple pleasure.

"Already Ripening Barberries Are Red," a four-part sequence in which the poet is on vacation near a beach, begins with an epigraph from Rilke's *Book of Hours* (from which her title takes one line) that includes these words: "Who is not rich, with summer nearly done, / Will never have a self that is his own." Lang hears a bullying tone behind this high-culture advice. Her poem exposes the summer vacation spot, so remote from metropolitan diversions, not as a setting of placidity but as a fearful melange of Rilke-like examples that implicitly instruct. She always refuses to see value in "nature":

> Yesterday I drove four miles to get the mail,
> Today I lie here going bad, you know I can.
>
> The sun leaves the beach like the tide itself,
> Washed out like water, soda-bright and mineral—
> Sinks to the sand grass, then breaks fall
> To sit above me on the dunes. I lay awake all day.
> I stared at a burnt match six feet away
> Stiff at my feet like a scarecrow's spine.
>   So by a buried animal
> Sometimes a stick will stand, without his name. (86)

The melodrama of this lies halfway between O'Hara's exaggerated self-mockery and Sylvia Plath's high-pitched dramatizations of deep melancholy. Lang is as likely to come across in metrics that comically thump ("On Pentecost, I think it was, / A dog I patted bit me on the leg") as she is to evoke moments of genuine distress in off-rhymes that grate like nails on slate ("Heard at the P.O.: Hate. Nobody likes his mail. / Even the mothers of sons grow weak and spoil. / 'I wanted a dog—' one wept, I heard her cry. / Or a white hawk, or a shark. That was July"). The seriousness behind such dis-

affection is Lang's resistance to the claim that poetry should encourage one
to locate, in Rilke's words, "a self that is his own." Selves, for Lang, depend
on settings, and when her settings are constricted, as in this seashore context, then "Our selves are done and known" (88). Poetry for Rilke is a means
to perfect the self; for Lang, poetry is a place to try on the selves one should,
as a lifelong project, always be trying on one after the other.

Lang in a poem is, in some sense, Lang on stage, and the works that she
writes express themselves as roles that are self-consciously played, acted
out. Since she always writes from the point of view of a woman, she thus
insists that we understand how self-consciously, how dramatically, the role
of the feminine is a virtuoso performance that women do particularly well.
The monologue of "Anne, a Chorus Girl Quitting the Line, to Society" ends:

> Say that I'm yours! (I am)
> Our Waltz Clog and our Elevées
> Were ways like any ways to please
> But never face to face You must
> Not love me any longer just because I'm One
> Out front (with you) alone   I know
>
> I'm one of you   I know
> That everywhere I'll go
> I'll have to tell my proper name   I'll sign
> I LOVE YOU   and I'll always want You   A*N*N*E (96)

The ending flourish is impeccably gaudy, a delightful affront to decorum.
How to believe in the sincerity of a signature that is, typographically speaking, up in lights? But Lang insinuates that such role-playing is what, in fact,
determines much social practice. When Lang presents the glittering surface, then, it is self-consciously and skeptically surrounded by quotation
marks if not blazing asterisks. Like O'Hara, Lang could simulate casual
speech, but such speech seemed to be utterly scripted. The cadences that
she shared with Ashbery, by contrast, were, if more lilting, no less enacted.
Compare the sarabande-like off-rhymes of Lang's "They praised a polished
purity / Which calculated rarity" or "They agreed instead to honor the
merry convention / That desire presupposes fruition" (from "The Elizabethans and Illusion" as first published in *Poetry,* June 1950) with Ashbery's
"This is perhaps a day of general honesty / Without example in the world's
history" (from "Two Scenes" as first published in the *Kenyon Review,* Spring
1956). Like Ashbery, Lang can turn on a dime. What Lang cannot do well
is Ashbery's shrug-it-off scuttling motion; his selves he can don with an

effortlessness she can never quite muster. Her lines, even when most feigning, retain their gravity (just as there is a dark Plath-like side to the whimsy of her beachside scenes). It is as if her playacting is too deeply embedded in actual social practice to be ever entirely effortless. In so many respects her work is so fine that the true scandal of the 1950s may not be that *Some Trees* had to be shepherded through the selection process at Yale by Ashbery's friends but that Lang was never encouraged even to assemble a manuscript for the competition.

Katherine Hoskins's "Arresting Sentences"

Not all female poets have been forgotten who spoke back in a distinctive voice in this era, who talked in such a way as to shatter the complacency of the composite portrait. While Rich was noteworthy for ability to blend in with the crowd who were defining the mainstream (only a poetic dialogue by Frost himself could compete with Rich's "Autumn Equinox" from her 1955 *The Diamond Cutters*), that was hardly the case with Mona Van Duyn, Ruth Stone, May Swenson, or Barbara Howes—though their origins in the 1950s are not generally stressed because their careers have continued well beyond that decade. Nonetheless, they wrote the outstanding poems of that decade: Van Duyn's "Toward a Definition of Marriage" (published in 1953 and collected in *Valentines to the Wide World* in 1959) was a reply from the front lines to a Marianne Moore well entrenched in the rear, and it virtually redefined the grounds upon which domestic verse was to be understood. Stone's lyrically wondrous "In an Iridescent Time" (from the 1959 volume of the same name) was a poem both elegantly simple and ravishingly musical, which also effortlessly celebrated the profound dimensions of matriarchal understanding. One poet, however, who had been widely recognized as a major figure in the postwar years has now vanished entirely from literary history. Her reputation has been so thoroughly erased that it stands as a vivid demonstration of the speed with which even a poet—and perhaps especially a woman poet—with a significant purchase on a degree of fame can plunge into obscurity.

From the mid-1940s well into the 1960s, the name of Katherine Hoskins circulated in the best intellectual circles and literary quarters. Indeed, its currency was so strong that when poet and editor Cecil Hemley, while reviewing Donald Allen's 1960 anthology *The New American Poetry,* was reaching for a way to describe the poetry of then-unknown Barbara Guest, he thought it helpful to explain that Guest "is modern in much the same way as is a poet like Katherine Hoskins" (628). Her reputation in these years was supported by three books of poetry, all under the imprint of publishers of consequence. The first, *A Penitential Primer,* was published in 1945 in a limited edition by the prestigious Cummington Press. Hemley's own Noonday Press published her second collection, *Villa Narcisse,* in 1956 (for which, *Poetry* reported in its April 1957 "News Notes," the forty-five-year-old Hoskins was awarded a Brandeis Creative Artists Award as a "younger artist of great potential"). In 1959, a third collection, *Out in the Open,* which also reprinted the full text of *A Penitential Primer,* was selected for the Macmillan Poets series that M. L. Rosenthal edited. (Ultimately, there was a fourth and final volume which Harry Ford at Atheneum presided over: *Excursions: New and Selected Poems,* released in 1967.) As substantial as these publications were, Hoskins's reputation was not based entirely on her poetry. Pieces of short fiction appeared at various times in the 1950s in the *Western Review,* the *Hudson Review,* and the *Sewanee Review.* The *New Republic* in 1952 printed "A Field of Vision," Hoskins's thoughts on the current state of poetry, and in 1959 the *Hudson Review* printed "Conversation Pieces," brief observations, sometimes a sentence long, sometimes a paragraph that might have originated in a commonplace book or working journal. In 1957 and 1958 she regularly contributed reviews to the *Nation.* Hoskins was not just a poet but a commentator whose speculative abilities warranted attention.[4]

That her prose observations were regarded well enough to be published is a mark of the admiration her poetry commanded—though she was also a figure around whom controversy could rage. Among her detractors, none was more vocal than Louise Bogan, who viewed her increasing stature with alarm. For Bogan, Hoskins violated every precept of good writing. "The term 'baroque,'" Bogan wrote from her influential position as longtime poetry critic for the *New Yorker,* "which in our day has crept over from critical discussions of art and architecture into discussions of music and literature, surely applies to Miss Hoskins' verse" ("Verse" 239). But Bogan deplored this mongrelization of cultural discourses just as she deplored Hoskins's linguistic profligacy. She was not at all hesitant to draw a fiery cordon around her work: "As for style, she dispenses at will with that accepted rule of modern prosody—natural words in the natural order. Syntactical inversions abound; impenetrable and peculiar modifiers accompany equally odd nouns and verbs. And strain is present in experience as well as in description: people walk through block marble, and one senses the ocean in the rufflings of a cat's fur" (239). To counter such a powerful adversary, Hoskins had in her corner an equally formidable defender in Randall Jarrell. Reviewing the "year in poetry" for *Harper's* in 1955, Jarrell noted the appearance of new books by Stephen Spender, Isabella Gardner, and Louis Simpson, but added in a separate paragraph: "None of these three poets, however, seems to me as original and as highly developed a poet as Katherine Hoskins, an extraordinary writer whose work still hasn't been published in a regular book" ("Year" 247). (Jarrell apparently discounted the Cummington Press edition of 1945, perhaps because it was a limited edition and a noncommercial venture.) In 1956, with the publication of *Villa Narcisse,* he no longer had grounds for complaint. He could place her book as the climactic moment in a review published in the *Yale Review* which opened: "When I first read *Villa Narcisse* I was so delighted with the good lines and poems, the existence of a new and individual poet, that I hardly cared about anything else" ("Five Poets" 269). Jarrell's praise was almost unstinting. Even when he circled toward a complaint, he pressed himself back from it: "Sometimes the poems are a size too small; yet they are always part of a most private life, are never mere social behavior" ("Five Poets" 271). But perhaps Jarrell's most complimentary acknowledgment of Hoskins came when he dropped her name among those whom he wished he had more time to mention when he was summoning up fifty years of American poetry in his 1963 address to fellow poets at the Library of Congress.[5]

Jarrell was not the only poet-critic to meet Bogan's opposition. "I am happy to register my pleasure in discovering the poems of Katherine Hoskins" ("Poetry Chronicle" 450), wrote Anthony Hecht in the *Hudson Review* in 1956. A measure of Hecht's admiration is that he not only singled out several poems for praise but printed one in its entirety. In the *Sewanee Review,* James Dickey noted that "while there are a great many difficulties" in *Villa Narcisse* "even the least of her poems are so full of invention and sharp, quirky aptness that there is not much point in dwelling on her faults, which the virtues seem quite naturally to harbor or display in the bad poems and suppress or make inspired use of in the good ones" ("Babel" 527). Although Dickey could not resist speaking over and against her voice by quoting from a poem he deemed inferior, he ended his review with a long quote from "one of the good ones" and a list of poems that he further endorsed. Of course not all reviews of Hoskins's work escaped the charges routinely filed against women poets. "Mrs. Hoskins is less rigorous with herself than she should be" ("Ladies' Day" 239), grumbled M. L. Rosenthal in the *Nation* in 1957—even as he would shortly choose her next manuscript for the Macmillan paperback series that he was editing. But to an unusual extent, her work extracted admiring glances from powerful reviewers. Even Robert Lowell, in a slash-and-burn omnibus review in the *Sewanee Review* in 1946 which opened by dismissing one-fourth of the poets under consideration ("The hopelessly bad books," he proclaimed, "need not be analyzed" ["Current" 145]), while noting that Hoskins's first book was "marred by coyness, eccentric language, and idiosyncratic symbols," also conceded that "nevertheless, arresting sentences are to be found in almost every poem; and the close reader will doubt not either the freshness nor the sincerity of her experience" (148). (Lowell would also contribute one of his rare dust jacket blurbs to Hoskins's last collection in 1967.)

What was Hoskins's secret? Why did she win the accolades that were withheld from other women poets? It was not, it seems to me, her rebel spirit that was being appreciated, though she was pointedly rebellious by the standards of the time. Rather, a large part of her success stemmed from the fact that her work lent itself to being understood within the terms by which male reviewers had often judged women poets as wanting. Even though her poetry resembled the feminine baroque, differing both lexically and syntactically from the transparent academic style (as Bogan accurately charged) by entertaining a vocabulary that went well beyond ordinary usage and nestled within intricacies of syntax that were unapologetically dense, Hoskins also signaled how strongly her intensities were to be contained by developing notably elaborate verse forms of her own invention. Her verse demonstrated that insofar as excess exists, it can be responsibly self-curtailed. As this excerpt from a poem entitled "How Generous!" indicates, her verse can visibly appear to be squeezed into a stanzaic pattern that values precision:

> How generous are the poor
> In things!
> Their sagging door
> 's a-swing—
> Shove in, Son—to any poorer yet.
> "So may children knock-
> ing find
> A door unlocked
> and kind-
> ness when they wander through the world alone." (*Villa* 88)

Hoskins's self-invented forms superficially resemble Marianne Moore's. However, Moore's eccentric line breaks force pauses that prescribe a lingering over instants, while Hoskins's poetry displays a strong forward momentum that overrides the line break and propels the work along. As a result, when Hoskins's oddly patterned forms call attention to themselves it is not to signal their innate delicacy but to vaunt the extent to which they are strong and bold and distinctive. These line breaks register an attempt to slow or give pause which the syntax refuses to acknowledge as it defiantly unfolds. The poet's desire to express feelings that are powerful is thereby enacted. James Dickey perhaps overstated when he wrote that "the main mission Hoskins has given herself" is to "compress until the poem chokes and quivers with its own held-down violence" ("Babel" 527). But his remarks convey admiration for her formal control. He added: "One can feel the strain: one reads these poems with tight jaws and the beginnings of sweat on the forehead" (527). Clearly Hoskins was one woman who was able to discipline herself.

Signs of Dickey's admiration—tight jaws and sweaty forehead—suggest that as he read Hoskins he was caught up in a dramatic tale, and that is one other source of Hoskins's power in her time: her poems are laced with devices that suggest the material of prose fiction. Not that her own writing is prosaic—its display of intricate syntactical construction and a rarefied vocabulary moots that—but it frequently unfolds in an exchange of speech, through characters who speak in dialogue. This is different from Garrigue's titles that announce and underscore the expressive nature of the poem about to unfold. Hoskins's poems frequently open with a fragment of ongoing dialogue that stands as a momentary puzzle we are about to be equipped to understand. Her poems can be set in motion by someone saying something to another, as in these first lines from a handful of her works, all from *Out in the Open*: "Renoir once said, if women hadn't breasts / He wouldn't paint" (8); "'What does she do?' I cried, /'In that desolate countryside?'" (49); "My life, this man once said, / Is like a book" (57); "So here it is, he said, and left / his bride and beauty free of the castle's / beds of flowers" (93). In their to-and-fro interchange, these poems resemble extracts from a larger narrative.

More important, talk does not simply enter the Hoskins poem, it is pivotal to the poem. Without overly emphasizing the point, Hoskins presents herself as someone who will not be silenced and who will not allow another to speak for her. The exchange may be elliptical, it may even be trivial. But that matters less than the fact that it is taking place. In the meditative journal fragments that were published in 1959 under the indicative title "Conversation Pieces," Hoskins opened with this observation: "Perhaps the most terrifying of Freud's dicta is his denial of communication between people except by sound or sight," a perception that, she felt, reduced personal exchange to "a wooden loneliness of marionettes" ("Conversation" 82). Poetry can surmount this limitation. A Hoskins poem is likely to shift its way through a range of varying registers, as if the different voices within it are speaking across the lines to one another, as in this poem, entitled "Understanding," one of a series of twenty-six on states of sensibility whose presentation in alphabetical order constitutes *A Penitential Primer*:

When the vacuum filled the rooftree
like a smogless powder factory
exploding, I choked on my throat
while the child sat still between afraid or not.
So, swallowing, That old Mr. Thunder
certainly is bustling his furniture
around, I said,
and almost added,
Honey. I spoke authentically
in the voice of an early
nurse of my own, of the good
nurse of all times, everywhere,
of the kind person, the interpreter. (*Out* 93)

From its opening line's technical description her terminology shifts into a militarized (and masculinized) reference before it takes up the problem of how to speak before the present audience of the child. How to converse is foregrounded, too, in that Hoskins herself is temporarily choked, as if overwhelmed by the variety of ways she has to explain the thunderclap. None of those explanations serve the present situation, and she must swallow them, then find from within herself, from within another conversation from her past, words that are pertinent. That the remembered voice of her own good nurse—the one she suddenly hears herself carrying forward as if in a quote—is so intimately a part of her attests to the residing power of the "kind person." Gentle language that explains, whether in speech to a child or in technical terms, counters violence. For Hoskins, what is most attractive in such speech lies in the restorative power of the conversational. Extending oneself in a caring gesture to another turns out to be an act that is continuous with other events in one's past life, so that this conversation is as much internal as external. It recognizes the social community one carries within oneself, composed of other caregivers.

Hoskins's talk, then, does not simply register linguistic shifts. Its abrupt changes of register can also recognize social boundaries that pertain to race, class, and gender. In a handful of poems that seem to draw on autobiographical incidents, Hoskins recalls a childhood that unfolded among markedly different social spheres. "At Night All Cats Are Grey" recalls her running to her mother after failing to dissuade the gardener from drowning a rat. What complicates the somewhat traditional report of a child's first awareness of death is that the gardener is African American. The poem contrasts caretakers (gardener and mother) who are black and white, servant and "master," and masculine and feminine. But Hoskins sees the child as mediating between these binaries so none is ever privileged. She is "small pink" to the gardener's "large black" in a relationship that extends authority to him. As a child she remained innocent of these matters; as an adult, Hoskins announces these differences through an intricate description of the play of light and shadow with which the poem opens—a move that keeps neutralizing the differences between the dichotomies. As shadows "trail the regal suns like veins / And longer, longer grow until they merge" (*Villa* 44), their interplay acknowledges but also unsettles the social hierarchies that might otherwise predominate.

In a far more disturbing poem, "An Evening of Death," the opening lines frame a situation from which a conversation emerges:

> One stone in the boundless ennui of the always
> Poor, he drops on the bed, rippling ennui
> Over the stove, the chair and Rose his wife,
> The starveling oaks beyond the sagging door,
> > Over his every day, his life.
> > > I came for the kitten Jerdan,
> > > That you promised me, the white child says;
> > > The pink and gold and white, the beauti-
> > > ful angel-child from the mansion house.
>
> He turns away. He has been kind all day,
> His work a center for her lonely play.
> He has no more to give, he'd like to get
> And curses Rose whose kindness knows no time,
> > Who scoops the litter up and says,
> > > Sit on the steps, chile, and choose your kitty.
> > > Jerdan tahd, he don' want no play. (*Villa* 23)

In seven more stanzas Hoskins shows the child's desire to continue her "lonely play" by choosing a pet disturbingly coincides with the violence that surrounds the lives of the poor. Someone appears from the shadows with a present of gin—for Rose? Jerdan assumes the worst and gives chase to the intruder, a chase that quickly turns tragic: his throat is sliced just after his feet have crushed the very kitten the child has chosen. It is left to Rose, on the day of the funeral, to comfort the child, who is old enough to mourn for her kitten but unable to recognize Rose's grief. "Is Jerdan dead, Rose?" asks the child as the poem ends:

> He daid, chile, like you say. Jerdan is daid.
> (So's my kitty, and weeping winds her in the empty
> Arms.) He tahd after that 'ere race,
> Daid tahd. And so is Rose. Rose feels it's late.
>   Choose you a cat and scamper home.
>   But I have chose. I chose
>   Poor Blackie there and now he's dead.
>
>   Bright angel, keep right on your singing,
>   Jerdan and Rose are listening. (*Villa* 25)

This poem that so carefully records black voices in and out of dialect is not, needless to say, a frequent device in 1950s verse. By its close, the voice of Rose and the child have not only become the poem—the poet who at the outset used a word like "ennui" or could describe oaks as "starveling" has retreated entirely—but we have come somewhat closer in learning how to hear the voice (or voices) in which Rose speaks. From the weariness in her response to the child we understand that the child's inability to comprehend Rose's position is not new but all too typical of what Rose must deal with. In this respect, Rose echoes "Race." Hoskins reproduces the voice of a race that is once again being subordinated, asked to be patient and accepting and understanding—as in the concluding lines where the assumption is that the racial role is to be accommodating, to reassure and comfort, to operate as the protector whose presence can guarantee that the child can "scamper home" in safety, as though her kittenlike frailty will always be sequestered from harm. (The poem's narrative, of course, argues the impossibility of that.) Jerdan's presence is invoked in the last lines as if he were still alive, even though the child knows he is dead. But on some level, Hoskins angrily insists, the child does not know Jerdan is dead. On some level the white child functions as a disembodied figure like an angel who is kept thoroughly separate from others who have been turned into beasts who hunt and kill each other out of their misery and exhaustion. How much longer can Rose, or the race she represents, go on listening? Or more pointedly, how much longer can one group be entitled to make its requests while the other is compelled to fulfill them?

Conversational Poetics

In the 1950s, readers who were inclined to ponder the contradictions that Hoskins had assembled in this conclusion to her poem would have had little within the current poetic discourse to draw upon as a framework. Not only was the notion of working through divergent voices alien to the norm of transparent style but particularly out of bounds were voices in black dialect. That went beyond "the baroque." Yet as alien as Hoskins's work was from the mainstream, it quietly overlapped with other writings by southern women who were redefining the prose tradition of the short story. Like Eudora Welty, Flannery O'Connor, and Carson McCullers (all of whom were rising stars in the postwar era), Hoskins set in motion a dialogue between members of different races. When asked to contribute to her entry in a collection of biographical sketches, Hoskins mildly remarked that "My themes appear to consist of Nature and People wherever I happen to be— often, in thought at least, south of the Mason-Dixon line" ("Hoskins" 742–43). Still, Hoskins's southernness manifests itself in ways that were, at least for poets, outsized in the 1950s. Virtually alone among white poets, she set works in an environment that naturalized African American participation. By contrast, one would look in vain for traces of an African American presence in other white poets of her generation who were southern, including James Dickey in his first book, the 1960 collection *Into the Stone.* (One exception would be Robert Penn Warren, in his 1953 verse-play *Brother to Dragons,* where the plot was at least motivated by the scandal of a slave's brutal murder.) For Hoskins, this sometimes means no more than a background detail whose offhandedness indicates the ease with which she alludes to the material: "Virginia Negroes used to say / You never see the Jaybird Friday / because he's then in hell among the damned" (*Out* 24). For Hoskins it is clear that African American speech is just as suitable for starting a poem as any other kind of speech. Other poems reflect her own southern upbringing. "For Moses" explains that those who mother come in many different guises, and it concludes as an homage to the black man who cared for her as a child, "him whom no birth // of any sort ennobled / but for whom care ennobled" (*Villa* 43). But relationships between black and white in the South Hoskins also understands for their complications. Is it Moses whom Hoskins is revisiting in one of the stanzas directed against herself in a passage from a poem entitled "Guilt"?

> An old black nurse took ferry, trolley, bus
> To call on his beautiful child, now grown-up:
> Grown-up too vain to doff her busyness
>   Before his tiredness. (*Out* 13)

Our small crimes perhaps most truly define us; the victims of our timidity, arrogance, aloofness are those whose injuries seem most wounding because they could have been avoided so easily. What is especially striking is the low-key manner with which she can recognize the imprint of race. This is not a poem about a black-white relationship, but a poem in which blackness figures no less than differences based on age and class.

A more fully orchestrated poem is "After the Late Lynching," which powerfully employs the Hoskinian device of numerous shifting registers, of beginning in one voice only to slide into another. The poem leads out of a linguistic situation nearly claustrophobic in its intensity, where nearly every line might commandeer an explanatory footnote, into a situation quite the opposite, where there can be no mistaking the speaker's meaning. That clear voice at the end, though, reveals suffering and violence on such a scale that it makes the evasive, muffled tones of its opening somewhat understandable. From the start Hoskins must fight her way toward a position that newly clarifies a woman's perspective. In this respect, the conversation which sets this poem in motion is especially pertinent. Few of her poems, indeed, are so directly intertextual. She begins with a "No" that disagrees firmly with this passage in John Crowe Ransom's "Philomela" (a passage that Hoskins might wisely have offered as a clarifying epigraph):

> Procne, Philomela, and Itylus,
> Your names are liquid, your improbable tale
> Is recited in the classic numbers of the nightingale.
> Ah, but our numbers are not felicitous,
> It goes not liquidly for us (*Selected* 38)

Ransom's readiness to extract from the names of the suffering primarily their "liquid" sounds is countered by Hoskins even as she calls up her own list of names of those who have suffered:

No,
It goes not liquidly for any of us.
            Yseult
            's as hard as Troilus.
        Heloise is far away and
                Difficult.
            Nor's death felicitous.
Not princes' proud defiant trumpets,
        Not good men's easyness
            With Death is ours yet

Whose lives construe so little of what is brave.
            Grace notes
        Should not be asked of slaves.
    Slaves' is, lunk-dumb and mutinous,
            At whipping posts
        To crouch and whine till they've
Spelled out the primitive construction—
            So plain, so difficult—
        Of a death and a woman.

Nor not from whitest light of foreign poems
            Hope help;
        But from her native woe
    Who took that black head in her hands
            And felt
        "A sack of little bones";
Whose arms for the last time round him knew,
        "All down one side no ribs
        But broken things that moved" (*Villa* 55)

Even by the time we are halfway through it, a poem so riddled with digressions seems scarcely underway. Indeed, at its center a line juts with syntax that is virtually opaque: "Slaves' is, lunk-dumb and mutinous . . ." Do the words compress a sentence construction such as: "Slaves' [lot] is [to be], lunk-dumb"? But the difficulty of speaking is central to Hoskins's concern, which is to spell out "the primitive construction— / So plain, so difficult— / Of a death and a woman." To ask for help from European literature as she does at the opening is, she understands, to doom herself to rummage through a dusty attic. (Her quarrel with Ransom is that he does not understand this.) To compose a modern *pietà,* one that is relevant to circumstances today, she needs an American image, one whose power rests on its ability to uncover a link between race and gender. For Hoskins to move beyond high cultural bric-a-brac into poetic breakthrough she must find a voice that she can engage as a conversation. Nonetheless, the woman who gives her voice to the last lines, describing the shattered body that her arms surround, reports violence so extreme no words are left to describe the structure of the body, only "broken things that moved." But wordlessness is widely inscribed over the closing of the poem. When an arena is cleared in which women are finally allowed to speak, it is at a moment of suffering so intense that nothing is left about which they can speak. Yet the triumph of the poem is that that sense of the unspeakable does enter the poem. And it is not simply that a voice that might otherwise be lost actually speaks, it is also the case that the voice is set over and against a range of other voices, voices representing a tradition of European literature within which this new voice—the voice of a woman (and a voice that by no means excludes being that of an African American)—now takes its place.

"After the Late Lynching" was the poem that so impressed Hecht he printed it in its entirety in his 1956 review. At its largest, Hoskins's project uses poetry as a site for an exchange of voices that the larger culture implicitly discourages. At its most subtle, it sets out to record not merely that voice as it is speaking but that voice as it is frustrated, left unheard by others who refuse any claim it might have upon them. Since her poems of race and class also acknowledge gender (it is Rose who is finally left to comfort the child; it is acceptable for a black man to be a nurse), it is a short step to take toward poems that center on the status of women. In these her task is to show both the centrality of the position of women as well as its invisibility and inaudibility. The poem entitled "Temple" probably refers to the New Hampshire town where Hoskins spent her summers (it figures by name in some of her "Conversation Pieces"), but it also identifies a sacred site, though one rarely acknowledged as such:

> The place is of women, the long haired women
> Of family who make bread and sew,
>> Who roses tend and throw
>>> Doors open
>>> For the children:

> And gossip at dusk with their murdered men-folks
> Gathered beneath the great-boled ash (*Villa* 51)

Nothing here accomplished is conspicuous. It is that perennial daily work of caregiving that never ends. But Hoskins is always suggestive in her positionings. Doors held open for children, which seem neutral enough in their own stanza (one more task), actually open onto the communing at dusk, as though the continuity among generations depends upon these evening narratives in which stories of the dead are retold. The absence of men suggests the length cast by the shadow of war, another aspect of the contemporary rarely discussed openly in the 1950s. Nothing is dramatic here (an earlier stanza explains that "The Gaudy song-birds do not venture / So far North"), but everything is rendered with quiet drama. "Its charm is delicate and seeps / In a mild radiance through the mind" (*Villa* 51) the poem begins; Hoskins pledges herself to reproducing that mildness—the world circumscribed by women in its inaudibility, its invisibility.

"Where a woman asks for understanding," Hoskins writes in one of the shortest entries in "Conversation Pieces," "a man is usually content with forgiveness" (89). It is a remark crafted to indicate the limits of exchange between male and female. By asking for understanding, the woman places herself within a social relationship. But the man with whom she would speak is disinclined: the forgiveness he requests is designed to put matters behind him so he can move on, not talk more about them. Furthermore, if Hoskins's remark pertains on a wider scale to infidelity ("understanding" and "forgiveness" imply a response to a betrayal), then her larger subject is the disagreements of men and women in maintaining a long-term relationship like a marriage. Hoskins takes up this subject in a selection of twelve poems in *Out in the Open* under the title "'A Factious and Elvish Hearte.'" Openly written from a woman's point of view, these poems trace the inequalities between husband and wife that the institution of marriage only magnifies. The simplest of these poems assert (with a pointed directness) that a strong-voiced woman has no occasion upon which her voice can be heard. One poem is particularly lucid on this topic:

The Young Wife's Song

What is this man,
My gaoler or my friend?
Old wives say both.
They say some day I'll understand.

Who curses me, next moment brings
A flower for my hair.
But is his hatred true
Or that half-arrogant, half-begging

> Love he also knows? The old wives say,
> You will get used to him,
> Your feelings will grow dim,
> Curses and love will be alike the day
>
> That you're old. But I a new wife
> Am and wonder
> At this monster
> That one day will have been my life. (*Out* 50)

This poem's tone deepens inwardly until its final line. Though the poem is about talk, and though it reports on conversation, it is equally about what cannot pass between wife and husband. The poem reveals that wives talk among themselves, but (so old wives report) husbands and wives do not. Husbands employ speech ritually as a curse, or deliver "gifts" voicelessly. But they do not speak to their wives. And the talk that wives share among themselves, which is about husbands, is also unsatisfactory. That talk lacks the inward-musing tone that the poem carries forward, that sense of someone mulling this over deeply within herself. Despite her chat with older wives this woman has no one with whom to talk. By her last line, Hoskins has made it clear what will be the explicit cost of continuing such deep and inward musing—an entire life.

Hoskins's most ambitious attempt to depict the confusions and misalignments of a lengthy marriage occurs in "The Journey," the longest poem in the group (and later promoted to end-of-collection status in the 1967 selection of poems). Seven sections, varying from sixteen to twenty-eight lines in length, describe the stages in a single day's journey across an alien landscape. At the same time, the poet is narrating the stages in a decades-long marriage that unfolds experientially across the male body. It opens:

> Threat, he smiles. And big with the lordly strength
> Of passiveness, he stretches him full length;
>   A Country
>   For her discovery.
>
> While she, his blue-eyed—faithful immigrant
> Or facile tourist—dallies hesitant
>   Before happiness,
>   So much like holiness.

Mists of dawn en-island tops of trees.
Black pines striate the pallid hills that seas
    Or serpents seem, or lariats—
    Now undulant, now flat. (*Out* 59)

"Exploring," of course, is usually a trope recognizably set over against the "domestic." By reconfiguring the wife's role not as caretaker but as explorer, Hoskins proposes a display of marriage from an unconventional perspective, a view that will highlight the problematic. Can one happily be *both* immigrant and tourist? What is to be explored stretches out full length not with a sense of its own capability but of indolence. The land as male body lacks a structure of the cooperative. It pronounces ("Thereat") and that is supposed to be final. Its overlooks never turn out to reveal a mountain pass, only more barriers. Hoskins's verse form lends itself to such formulations:

Sick, scared, infatuate, she may guess
Into this coldly guarded privateness
    Of a man's estate
    But never penetrate (*Out* 60–61)

Continuing to borrow from masculine tropes ("penetrate" is not usually a feminine ambition), Hoskins nonetheless registers her discomfort in a stanza form that begins expansively in its first two lines then quickly closes down in its last two. What starts out as sweeping grandeur cannot be sustained. It ends in severe contraction. The long journey initially planned for is always truncated. In all but a few stanzas the motion of thought is syntactically complete, with a full stop closing down each stanza.

Even when men and women do talk, they are unable to converse. What is more, they may not even know they are unable to converse. "A Way of Being" opens with someone speaking:

My life, this man once said,
Is like a book. The wife I had
And the other one, a girl
In summered Maryland, my captain
At the war, the war, the crows
My boyhood spent shooting. Paris
In miserable August. I sometimes look
Them over but can never
Wish them back, continuing or different:
For they are stories. (*Out* 57)

Hoskins's nemesis is the man for whom speaking is never an occasion that might prompt a reply but an announcement that extinguishes further speech. Here, this speaker's sentimentalized narratives fix events, even as they are only preserved in a hopeless jumble, with the important and the mundane mixed. When a countering voice responds, in a follow-up stanza later in the poem, it debates him point by point: "So we, then, are but fictions," this other voice begins: "What we have been or done's / Imagining. Paris / Is brown." The poem can only end in anger, after several lines that surge with contempt ("Stay for a long moment with the page thus / Poised—*maître*"):

> While we, illiterately transcribed page
> Or half-remembered phrase
> Will blow down dirty streets
> As from a golden age. (*Out* 58)

Most poets grow animated when they discover the perfect auditor for their work. Hoskins becomes animated when she incorporates into her text that other whose hearing is distinctly blurred, imperfect, lacking—who fails to listen apart from his own needs and, if he hears at all, is apt to misunderstand.

Hoskins comes closest to being the single poet of her own time most capable of conceiving a way of talking that male reviewers might have heard. Working with careful versification, usually in rhyme and in stanza structures of her own invention, Hoskins wrote not about the intensity and passion of sexual love but with curiosity and uncertainty about the misapprehensions of married love. Although she honored the site of the domestic—the nurse was invaluable, an interpreter—she was unhesitant about opening it to speculation. She ventured into territory untrodden in the 1950s, such as black-white relations. She responded to male taciturnity with anger and despair; she knew when she was not being listened to, and she refused not to beard. Her opening lines as well as her shifts in register virtually require both an intellectual and emotional investment to follow them. Insistently discursive, her poems insist that we join her in an ongoing conversation. And her sliding registers shift us from one angle of vision to another, the Hoskinsesque poem a pell-mell assemblage, driven by a singular momentum. Its idiosyncrasy is never in the service of mere display. It commands attention on its own ground. It is part of an insistence on social interchange. But this is also carefully reconfigured as a species of interpretive skill. When she considered the roles that were open to women she sought to bolster them. Yet her poems maintained their quirky edge. In the gender-divided 1950s, Hoskins was perhaps writing the only poetry that could establish a temporary bridgehead between the voices of men and the voices of women—so profoundly constructed by postwar social circumstances to be different that the basis for an understanding would go unmeasured for nearly another decade.

5 EPICS TRUE AND FALSE

*[D]efenders of Poetry magazine . . . would do poetry and the
magazine a lot more service, it seems to me, if they would stop
all this "great heritage" talk. Not only is it false; it produces, when
it has any effect at all, poets who are inordinately sensitive to the
vast cultural burden they carry and who are therefore very self-
conscious, very much aware of their role as producers of things
monumental. There's got to be a better reason for writing
than some vague impulse to produce monuments.*
— Reed Whittemore ("Modern Idiom" [1957])

Whittemore's impatience with "monuments," which I take to be
those pieces of writing that exercise the poet's ambition to its fullest—
elaborate, multilevel, idiosyncratically organized exploratory texts that
develop in public space, that unfold on the streets of a city like London or
New York and that take up, albeit indirectly, issues of civic welfare—is
widely shared in the postwar years. Why did long poems grow scarce in the
1950s? Lynn Keller notes that the "only major group of poets whose members eschew the long poem are the Southern Agrarians and the other practitioners of tightly crafted lyric popularized by Eliot and the New Critics"
whose "standards dominated American poetry during the forties and the
fifties" (548). These Agrarians, too, were careful to conduct their discussions
about public matters in prose, whether taking a stand in 1930 or defining
the precepts of a New Criticism; in their poetry, they remained within a
private world of the lyric, and several of them (notably Allen Tate) openly
doubted whether the lyric could ever include public concerns.

Examples of the lyric that did include public matters were, it is true, available in the 1940s, but for the most part they were the products of an earlier generation and lent themselves for viewing as a continuation of a previous project. Pound went on with his *Cantos,* and beginning in 1948 Williams began to publish *Paterson,* while Stevens added to his long meditative excursions with "An Ordinary Evening in New Haven" and the title poem of *The Auroras of Autumn* (1948). And in these poems, it is true that the "public" exists as a trace only. New Haven is a challenge for Stevens to incorporate poetically, to transform imaginatively, much as Pound's public self in *The Pisan Cantos* is identified with the cage into which he has been thrust and from which he must rhetorically escape into such fantasies as the approach of the lynx-goddess in Canto LXXIX. The conversational gems in Canto LXXX ("'Beauty is difficult, Yeats' said Aubrey Beardsley / when Yeats asked why he drew horrors") are all that glimmer, in Pound's view, from the murk of history. Although Williams's *Paterson* was quite different from Pound's work—it is, in effect, a restless search for a viable public space, since those that it finds always prove wanting: susceptible to co-opting by commercial interests or the indifference of misguided masses—it suffers from its ambitions as a belated attempt to join the line of great modernist poems. In one sense, the lyrical epic or symphonic epic which formed the matrix of high modernism at the very center of the 1920s was that which had already been done. Charles Olson's *Maximus Poems* attracted little interest when they began to be collected in 1953 and again in 1956 (as *Letters 11/22*) because they seemed to play out a modernist vein that had been exhaustively explored by an earlier generation whose aged members were even now producing esteemed variations. Robert Lowell's 1971 description of the Black Mountain poets as the "journeymen" of Pound and Williams (both of whom he admired as "spirits" who were both "freer" and "more cultured") was at once a summary and a dismissal: "Olson's *Maximus* is *Paterson* and the *Cantos,* though woodier" ("Conversation" 273). What remained invisible to Lowell was Olson's innovative return to a bounded geography, for that in turn forced a recovery of the issue of civic welfare (the problem of the "polis") as it was powerfully dramatized in the first three books: an interest in working-class values and history from down under, a no-nonsense revisionist approach to the founding of Massachusetts as a business venture, and a deromanticized portrait of the sea as the ultimate dangerous working condition.

But Olson's poetry met with dismissal, its originality mistaken for timid imitation. From its example, it is clear that the ambitious extended work of the 1950s had to distinguish itself sharply from its precursors as Olson had seemingly failed to do even as it needed cautiously to acknowledge a debt to them. While amalgamating aspects of the symphonic epic, it also would need to remain firmly committed to the single-voice analytic lyric that was so prevalent in influential anthologies by Ciardi and Elliott. No one succeeded in achieving that mix as completely as John Berryman in his *Homage to Mistress Bradstreet,* whose appearance in 1953 in an issue of the prestigious *Partisan Review* was an index of its acceptance. On the surface, the fifty-seven eight-line stanzas of the poem seemed a worthy successor to the long poems of a previous generation. Berryman, as a poet-protagonist, positioned himself as restlessly moving between past and present, measuring each in terms of the other. His precisely convoluted syntax—sentences unfolding in a meaningful rather than a straightforward sequence, with hesitations and digressions borne within them—gestured broadly toward both Hopkins and Dylan Thomas. To Thomas's mellifluous lyricism, Berryman brought a knife-edge idiomatic phrasing wrapped in a syntax tensed to spring ("white air lashing high thro' the virgin stands / foxes down foxholes sigh" [2:2–3]) that was for him a breakthrough style, hardly in evidence in the humdrum Audenesque notations of his 1948 collection, *The Dispossessed.* The poem clinched Berryman's reputation. When it was published in a distinguished coffee-table edition in 1956 with woodcuts by Ben Shahn, it was hailed on the dust jacket by Conrad Aiken as "a classic right on our doorstep."

Yet to succeed in these cold war years, Berryman's poem had to be no less effective in its ability to distinguish itself from the high ambitions and extensive reach of the earlier cultural epic of high modernism. Unlike those precursors, Berryman chose to remain within one poetic style. Even if that style was, in best high modern fashion, engineered to maximize the drama of a divided mind in the process of discovering a way to act, it was nonetheless a decision that was pointedly restrictive. Eliot, Williams, Crane, Pound were always being thrust into radically different styles of writing because epic ambitions required them to constitute a variety of circumstances. When Berryman conjured up the spirit and voice of Anne Bradstreet from his scholarly research, he provided at best only glimpses of New England Puritan life; what was more, those glances made it seem remarkably similar to the domestic rounds of a housewife in the postwar suburbs. Yet this radical constriction, this intense sharpening of focus, was itself a primary signal of poetic competence in the 1950s. It was staged elsewhere in texts that prescriptively followed formalist procedures—the sonnet, of which Berryman's own sonnet sequence of 1948 was itself an example, and later the sestina. But the concept of "containment" had still wider implications:

not only registering the value of disciplinary thinking and promoting the authority of professionalism but also restricting elements that otherwise inclined toward the disorderly. To set limits to that which seemed unduly excessive was central to the "plot" of Berryman's long poem—the dangerous task of conjuring from the past a woman who was a poet.

Scholarly Research as Office Romance

What made Berryman's poem an undertaking with larger cultural resonance was that as it evoked the spirit of Anne Bradstreet, it assured its readers it was delivering a portrait that was both accurate and vivid by showing how often Bradstreet lapsed from control of herself. Lacking the discipline of other poets—of other *male* poets—she will be unable to balance head and heart, thought and feeling. Berryman's poem is about, first, recording just how this disorderliness wells up from Bradstreet, and, second, demonstrating that he can take the measures necessary to restrain or curtail her. While the poem thus allows its explosive moments to happen, there is the promise that all order will be restored at the end. Needless to say, this was not the promise delivered at the end of *The Waste Land, The Bridge,* or other cultural epics which deliver us precisely into an instant in which we are poised for a new world to unfold—in which, in an even more radical reading (that is yet in keeping with the poems themselves), it is now up to us the readers to continue, in the world, the work of the poem.

More accurately, Berryman plays variations on the need to restore control, a problem he recasts by deciding how an "artistry" that is female (that is emotional, excessive) should be channeled, curtailed, and contained. Andreas Huyssen's insight linking mass culture with the female helps explain how a poem about a colonial American poet might wind up in the pages of *Partisan Review,* the very pages in which Clement Greenberg had, in 1939, published his influential essay warning against the encroachment of mass culture. It is not simply the figure of Anne Bradstreet, then, that Berryman is recognizing as lacking in discipline, too emotional, and in need of a strong male presence as a guide. When Berryman takes charge, demonstrating that the analytic male can fulfill the needs of the emotional female and eventually place her with firmness in the minor but useful role of the obedient servant, he is simultaneously demonstrating how successfully savvy intellectuals could guide and direct a culture dangerously drifting away from strong values.

"Bradstreet," then, is less a historical figure than a loose collection of features that can be attributed to the "feminine." Above all, the task for which

Bradstreet is most ill-equipped calls upon a discipline that she lacks. Even at moments when she herself recognizes a need to exert control, she is presented as unable to manage. Early on in the poem, she says: "I must be disciplined, / in arms, against that one, and our dissidents, and myself" (11:7–8). But events that follow quickly dramatize her failure. She pledges to guard against the temptations of "a barbarous place" (12:4) that presents itself to her eyes as highly eroticized—"by the day Spring's strong winds swelled, / Jack's pulpits arched, more glad" (11:1–2). Her desires spill over and make their claims felt upon others—most particularly, of course, the Berryman-figure in the poem. If he is her opposite, the representative of organizational skill who commands enough knowledge of poetic craft to construct a complex eight-line stanza that can accurately report scenes from her life from three hundred years earlier, he is also prone to be distracted by her charms and, at the midpoint of his poem, to yield and comply with her "demands," and to enjoy tangled moments of intimacy before he regains the composure necessary to restore focus and return to his role as overseer.

How is it that his own discipline is temporarily compromised? The answer rides on the idea of the identity, so important to the 1950s, of the poet as professional. The affair between Berryman and Bradstreet starts as the scholarly *and* poetic equivalent of an office romance, with two persons who share a professional interest being thrown together until they agree that they have enough points in common that they begin to act "unprofessionally." It is not as a potential lover but as a fellow poet that Berryman speaks when, in a key instant, he breaks from his role as impersonal chronicler and blurts out a negative assessment of her poetry: "all this bald / didactic rime I read appalled" (12:5–6). Isn't she just writing that way, he asks, to please her father? It is a question in which the psychoanalytic commonplaces of the twentieth century suddenly play back over the customs and habits of the seventeenth century, and for a moment the gap between the two eras is bridged. But the important shift underlies the similarity of interests the two share. Prior to this moment of badinage, Berryman had behaved himself impeccably. After some Whitman-like fretting at the opening ("I come to check, / I come to stay with you" [4:6–7]), he withdrew into the background, dexterous administrator of rhymes and off-rhymes in the rhythms of the eight-line stanza that constructed a space from which Bradstreet could speak as if from her own perspective.

The first move, then, is (according to Berryman's presentation) not Berryman's but Bradstreet's: she is the (undisciplined) seducer who turns his initial professional interest into something different. It is her voice that takes on a new modulation, after Berryman's outburst, when the focus narrows again on the seventeenth-century Bradstreet. Her voice becomes now sharply autobiographical, increasingly intimate. Now she broods on her past adolescence ("at fourteen / I found my heart more carnal and sitting loose from God" [13:7-8]), and on her courting by Simon (who "burned" for her [14:4]), and on the hardships of life in a wilderness far from "Boston's cage" (16:8) where her husband is "much away" (17:5). Although childbirth and raising children provide other activities distinct from those in the stanzas in which she ponders what might be called her "carnality," these events serve to bring her even closer to our present. The rigid gap of three hundred years that separates Bradstreet and Berryman has grown increasingly flexible. Thus when her friend Anne Hutchinson has been "exiled" (25:1), in an event that reminds her own her own exile, and she is on the verge of a breakdown herself, it is then that she finds herself suddenly able to speak back to Berryman. When she cries out to the absent Anne Hutchinson, "Bitter sister, victim! I miss you!" Berryman answers:

> —I miss you, Anne.
> Day or night, weak as a child,
> tender & empty, doomed, quick to no tryst.
> —I hear you. Be kind, you who leaguer
> my image in the mist.
> —Be kind you, to one unchained eager far & wild . . . (25:2-8)

If Berryman initiates this dialogue by speaking words that could be voiced by Hutchinson in a reply to Bradstreet ("I miss you, Anne"), the issue of a tryst between lovers is rapidly introduced as Bradstreet gives to her remarks an inflection that is not entirely innocent. When Berryman speaks to her, he does so descriptively, in the voice of the professional—"Deep / in Time's grave, Love's, you lie still" (26:2-4). But when he repeats his last two words ("Lie still"), she responds by describing her "most long, rare, / ravendark, hidden, soft bodiless hair" (26:5-6). From then on, discussion between the two never strays far from intimate murmuring. Turning now to the landscape, the poem finds it steeped in the erotic:

> —It is Spring's New England. Pussy willows wedge
> up in the wet. Milky crestings, fringed
> yellow, in heaven, eyed
> by the melting hand-in-hand or mere
> desirers single, heavy-footed rapt,
> make surge poor human hearts. Venus is trapt—
> the hefty pike, sheer—
> in Orion blazing. (31:1-8)

Though it is Berryman who speaks these words, he clearly speaks them to Anne and for Anne, recording details of the New England setting that they both share.

In Berryman's work as a whole, the text which most resembles *Homage* is the sonnet sequence that just preceded it, completed in 1947. Berryman properly believed that the poems in that sequence, which described in revealing detail an adulterous love affair, were too candid to be published in the 1940s (though they would appear as early as 1967, collected as *Berryman's Sonnets* and later collected as *Sonnets to Chris* in the 1989 *Collected Poems*). The fantasized *Homage* provides satisfactions that are absent from the autobiographical *Sonnets*. The 117 sonnets that unfold the narrative of an illicit affair most often lament the withdrawal of the erotic from the landscape. There is much anxious looking, many hurried glances, but never a moment of lovely balancing, such as there is in stanza 31 of *Homage*, where the world seems momentarily to be at one with lovers. In those sonnets of illicit love, Berryman is either looking forward to a tryst or lamenting the withdrawal of his lover and depicting the world as suffused by her absence: "The ghosts of breezes widowy small paths wander, / A fruitless bird pipes its surprising sorrow" (*Sonnets to Chris,* sonnet 59:10–11). Of course the sonnets aim to be a chronicle, seeking to preserve a record of what was occurring as it was unfolding, and they include the frustrations and doubts that complicated an actual relationship, while in his *Homage*, Berryman has stepped into a realm where it becomes possible for anything to happen that he wishes. Not surprisingly perhaps, some of the sorrows as recorded in the illicit sonnets are recuperated in *Homage* as the pleasures of intense conversation between male and female. What once had been uncertainty has now become perfectly managed, including the central moments in the poem where control is permitted to lapse.

Yet in another sense the *Homage* merely restages on a larger scale the masqueradings in the sonnets. The sonnets elaborately encoded names, places, and times under a facade that half-hid, half-recorded events. The orange-and-black school colors of Princeton, where the affair began, appear in "The Old Boys' blazers like a Mardi-Gras / Burn orange, border black" (*Sonnets to Chris,* sonnet 17:1–2), but they designate a setting only to those adept at converting active verbs ("burn," "border") into exact details. *Homage* continues this masquerade: its tryst with a ghostly Bradstreet acknowledges (and indirectly legitimates) Berryman's actual affair with "Lise." Details from the *Sonnets to Chris* appear in *Homage:* a climactic interchange in which Anne speaks: "I *want* to take you for my lover" and

Berryman replies "—Do" (32:5) was taken over from a remark duly recorded in one sonnet as spoken by the woman: "'I *want* to take you for my lover' just / You vowed when on the way I met you: must / Then that be all (*Do*) the shorn time we share?" (sonnet 42:12–14). *Mistress* Bradstreet was, of course, seventeenth-century protocol for addressing a married woman, but it also serves, for Berryman, as an added nudge-and-a-wink in the direction of his past affair.[1]

That the figure of Anne Bradstreet is largely a male fantasy has not escaped the notice of critics like Alicia Ostriker, quick to point out that "Berryman created, out of his own yearning, a lover-anima-muse figure who could never be seen as a colleague, collaborator, or equal" (27). The appeal of the *Homage* in the 1950s, however, would have rested less on the kind of personality that Berryman lent to Bradstreet than on Berryman's prowess in coping with an individual who would have been typified as interesting but "difficult." Yet Berryman's skill in managing this relationship is not so much demonstrated as it is assumed, especially in one of the central transitional passages, where abandonment seems the only word to describe what happens between the two. In fact, Berryman simply leaves Bradstreet behind after a certain point in the poem, and the two go separate ways, she back to the seventeenth century and he back to chronicling her life. That so crucial a dramatic moment can occur without apparent disruption is itself a testimony to the authority that Berryman could assume was his as well as the invisible aura of rightness that apparently surrounded women when they were deposited back within scenes of domesticity. It takes only one stanza—indeed, a few lines within it—for Berryman to slip Bradstreet back into the role of mom:

> Faces half-fanged, Christ drives abroad,
> and though the crop hopes, Jane is so slipshod
> I cry. Evil dissolves, & love, like foam;
> that love. Prattle of children powers me home,
> my heart claps like the swan's
> under a frenzy of who love me & who shine. (39:4–9)

So much for "that love": it dissolves "like foam," like soap washing away down the drain. (In case there is any question that an important shift is occurring here, Berryman draws attention to it in his notes to the poem, indicating its odd status as a nine-line stanza in a poem of eight-line stanzas and linking it to an earlier exception: "The stanza is unsettled, like 24, by a middle line, signaling a broad transition.") Bradstreet is made to redis-

cover that the "powers" of children's "prattle" are what her heart desires—
not the ambition of greatness, whether great poetry or a love affair that
shatters conventions. From here to the close, Bradstreet is the impeccable
family woman, cooking for her kids ("I pare / an apple for pipsqueak Mercy
and / she runs and all need naked apples" [40:4–6]), calming their fears
("Our friend the owl / vanishes, darling, but your homing soul / retires on
heaven" [41:5–7]), and boasting of their first achievements ("Sam's to be /
a doctor in Boston" [45:5–6]). For this new suburbanized Bradstreet, these
are the important incidents in her life. And in fact these stanzas move with
a luminous ease that is unlike anything else in the poem, and virtually
unique in Berryman's own writing.[2] The signal that Bradstreet is now prepared to acknowledge her authentic social role as mother, as cook and nurse
and caretaker, is evident in the vagueness with which she now alludes to
her poems. "How they loft, how their sizes delight and grate" (42:5), she
says of her children; of her poems, she is almost indifferent: "The propor-
tioned, spiritless poems accumulate. / And they publish them / away in
brutish London, for a hollow crown" (42:6–8). This rather surprising restoration of proportion to Bradstreet's life is registered with approval in the
(perhaps now-misnamed) *Homage.* Her name will not live in poetry, it
seems, except of course in this poem in which she is identified as *Mistress*
Bradstreet, fixed in a double role as both domestic and erotic. Yet the trajectory of the poem makes it clear that the erotic must ultimately be subjugated by the domestic. Berryman restores order to his poetic world by
withdrawing from Bradstreet, which in turn allows her to slip into humdrum satisfactions in which she is overshadowed by her children, her parents, her husband.

Alan Golding has contended that the *Homage* deployed its resources to
depict Bradstreet as a "poet-rebel in conflict with her culture's dogma"—a
deliberate strategy by Berryman, who then used his alliance with her to
attest that he was identified with "the role of the cultural outsider" (63). But
how far "outside" is Berryman in his long poem? The powerful long poems
of the 1920s, in which the poet-protagonists proudly developed their positions as outsiders, often proceeded by summoning up the past. But the
past or pasts they summoned always depicted a reality so substantively
different from the present that it served to undermine the validity of the
present. Is that Berryman's role? It was his insistence, in fact, to oppose
Homage to *The Waste Land.* His poem, as he said, had "personality and
plot—no anthropology, no Tarot pack, no Wagner."[3] What it also had was
a sense of the past that was *not* viewed with an eye toward presenting its

difference from the present in order to initiate a perspective from which change might occur but quite the opposite: that some aspects of human relations would never change. The woman of 1648 had needs remarkably similar to the woman of 1948. That an intimate exchange over three hundred years could happen so effortlessly was an assertion, first, about the bonds that existed between poets but, second (and especially as the poem continued), about a certain universal nature in women. *Homage to Mistress Bradstreet* offered reassurance in the rightness of the way things were in virtually every one of its aspects, whether in its commitment to a rigorous stanzaic form, or in the assurance with which it presented the psychology of the woman poet who had to divide her allegiances between her art and her family, or in the confidence with which order was restored, after a tumultuous but distinctly demarcated emotional interlude.

If *Homage to Mistress Bradstreet* is, then, arguably the most prestigious long poem to emerge in the 1950s—a poem that seemed to influential people at the time to be, unlike Olson's *Maximus,* a genuine advance over its precursors—it at best only mimicked aspects of the early modernist lyrical epic. Its interplay between past and present, its convoluted style, were airy gestures toward the symphonic epic of high modernism. But on a deeper level, the poem dissolved the difference between past and present and affirmed that for the American woman the "new world" involved lovemaking, child-rearing, and caring for the elderly. Most notably, it insisted that the woman herself was not just incomplete but lost, profoundly confused, out of control—until partnered with a man.

Mapping a Devastated Geography

When poetry is in the process of redefining itself, as it was after World War I, the long poem is invaluable for the invitations it offers to enter new linguistic and semantic territory. Its open expanse encourages the development of multiple viewpoints that will newly comprehend a subject in its variety and without the layers of convention that customarily surround it. Post–World War II American poetry, however, as Ciardi noted in his introductory remarks to *Mid-Century American Poets,* was most interested in consolidating the gains of the past. Thus when Randall Jarrell wrote his rave review of the first book of Williams's *Paterson* in 1949 he was careful to emphasize its achievement as an organizational not an exploratory feat. *Paterson* was not, in Jarrell's presentation, a text like Eliot's or Crane's that was clearly engaged in risky maneuvers, in passages that daringly swerved in disarming directions, but a work that was preeminently orchestrated, to be appreciated precisely for the mastery it displays: "Dr. Williams introduces a theme that stands for an idea, repeats it over and over in varied forms, develops it side by side with two or three more themes that are being developed, recurs to it time and again throughout the poem, and echoes it for ironic or grotesque effects in thoroughly incongruous contexts" ("Poets" 206). *Paterson*, of course, set out to map a devastated geography—a highly localized and actual "place" defined in a variety of poems as both interesting in and for itself and as dramatically representative insofar as that which had been neglected in it suggested a range of related contemporary issues. (In this sense, Olson's early letters on Gloucester in *Maximus* trace a direct lineage to it.) But it won accolades from Jarrell for placing its readers in an intimate relation with a landscape they might otherwise never see, never experience. While Jarrell asserts that Williams's overall interest lies in his language, in attempting to find a nonpoetic way of poetically incorporating the real, a language that is "so close to the world that the world can be represented and understood in it" (207), the challenge of such a project rests precisely in a willingness to deal with material that is intractable, with the littered and disheveled and overlooked landscape of industrial New Jersey, layered in a history that is itself contradictory and bewildering. What compels interest, according to Jarrell, is the knowledge Williams brings back from this remote area, knowledge about, for example, the "speech of sexual understanding, of natural love" (209), as well as the actuality of "obstinate and thwarted lives, the lifeless perversions of the industrial city" (210), along with the mysterious survival skills of an area that resists attacks from all sides, including an earthquake. Jarrell exclaimed: "how wonderful and unlikely that this extraordinary mixture of the most delicate lyricism of perfection and feeling with the hardest and homeliest actuality should ever come into being!" and he predicted that if the next three books were as fine as the first "the whole poem will be the best very long poem that any American has written" (212).

Since Jarrell's enthusiasm was not sustained by the next three books that Williams published, which in fact turned increasingly improvisational and which led Jarrell to eventually withdraw much of the praise he had been so lavish with, he may have been unwilling to agree with the suggestion that the words he used to single out *Paterson* were just as deserved for Langston Hughes's *Montage of a Dream Deferred* (1951)—a sequence that has suffered for not being discussed as an extended work that is centered on a specific region and that employs experimental techniques, like those of

Williams's *Paterson,* that register the ways in which gaps between the personal and the social, the private and the political, can be startlingly bridged. Moreover, Jarrell's central claim that "the organization of *Paterson* is musical to an almost unprecedented degree" ("Poets" 206) can be met and topped at any point in *Montage.* "This poem on contemporary Harlem," Hughes announces in a prefatory note, "like be-bop, is marked by conflicting changes, sudden nuances, sharp and impudent interjections, broken rhythms, and passages sometimes in the manner of the jam session, sometimes the popular song, punctuated by the riffs, runs, breaks, and disctortions [*sic*] of the music of a community in transition" (387). Hughes's Harlem opens out from street life, its social gatherings, its public ceremonies—a world defined by its peppery rhythms: speech rhythms that arise in relation to musical rhythms, which together construct a discursive environment that shifts from speaker to speaker and even within the talk of a single speaker.

That the variety in the talk that Hughes presented went unrecognized when *Montage* was first published established a critical approach that withheld from this work the status of long poem. Berryman in a 1972 interview recalled how his own long poem had set out to imitate Eliot but had taken a different turn: "In *Homage to Mistress Bradstreet* my model was *The Waste Land,* and *Homage to Mistress Bradstreet* is as unlike *The Waste Land* as it is possible for me to be" ("Art of Poetry" 29). Berryman's positioning himself in relation to Eliot discloses how important it seemed for his long poem to be in dialogue with this central poem and then, however obscurely, to supersede it. Marring the reception of Hughes's poem was the assertion by Babette Deutsch, inscribed in the title of her review from the 1951 *New York Times Book Review* ("Waste Land of Harlem"), that made Hughes's relation to Eliot a dysfunctional one: "The title of this book of verse tells a good deal about it. The language is that of the work-a-day urban world whose pleasures are sometimes drearier than its pains. The scene is the particular part of the Waste Land that belongs to Harlem. The singer is steeped in the bitter knowledge that fills the blues. Sometimes his verse invites approval, but again it lapses into a facile sentimentality that stifles real feeling as with cheap scent" (32). If Eliot absorbed urban voices into a more expansive cultural setting that explained and even dignified their despair, then in Deutsch's formulation Hughes's "montage" merely reproduced urban voices in helpless fragments that indicated his inability to provide a perspective ample enough to be transformational. She suggests that the "bitter knowledge that fills the blues" is insufficient and probably an impediment to effect a transformation. And by invoking as a symbolizing frame-work the blues—a notably small-scale form with obvious associations to popular culture—Deutsch further disconnects Hughes from the tradition of the experimental long poem, one of whose alternate labels was "sym-phonic epic." Deutsch suggests that the successful long poem is a highly orchestrated arrangement—Eliot harmonizes the voices within his work—while Hughes's "montage" is a random collection of isolated voices, some-times inviting our approval but more often lapsing into sentimentality.

To atomize the voices that Hughes has carefully assembled is to under-mine the authority of a long poem that aims to enact a moment and a place in African American history that is "in transition." Although its conformity to geographical unification raises a question about its status as a modern-ist long poem (the "London" of Eliot's *Waste Land* is always bisected by material from other times and other places, just as Crane's *Bridge,* though intricately engaged with the New York cityscape, dutifully ranges across the American continent and moves backward in time to its past), the territory that Hughes defines could not have borders more crisscrossed with com-plexity. As a successful playwright Hughes presents voices in monologue and in dialogue with each other that an audience can engage with to dra-matize and define urban space as a "stage" with conflicts that are being held up for inspection and, when possible, resolution. Brief verses crackle with one-liners. The speaker in "Motto" ("I play it cool / And dig all jive. / That's the reason / I stay alive" [*Collected* 398]) offers a contradictory creed that both embraces and withdraws, its last two lines then suggesting that this is a minimal survival strategy, this ability to cultivate inwardness while displaying an outgoing manner. But here as elsewhere, the meanings of each line remain open to a variety of inflections, such as how nuanced "jive" might be, ranging all the way from a simple term for any music that is up-tempo ("jive" as moving rapidly) to its far more intricate formulation as a sign of excess and exaggerated artifice ("Don't jive me"). Pausing over lines for such questions to occur is crucial to the accurate and full recep-tion of this poem.

The daring of Hughes's project lies in the centrality of the role it de-mands from its listeners. By 1950s poetic standards, to cede so much con-trol to the audience was to court misunderstanding if not outright lack of comprehension. Traditional formal verse techniques were effective tools for guiding listeners toward docile receptivity. When Hughes dispenses with them, the danger is that listeners like Deutsch will refuse to ask the ques-tions that the texts engender: What might she have identified as the "bitter knowledge" in the poem "Hope"? "He rose up on his dying bed / and asked for fish. / His wife looked it up in her dream book / and played it" (425). To believe that this poem scandalously chronicles a breakdown in communication among family members is to refuse the poem its obvious mode of operation: to intrigue with anecdotes that necessitate the summoning of larger explanatory contexts—contexts in which, in this case, reveal how actions are dictated by poverty, in which dreams are always tinged with a sense of desperation, and in which the direct expression of signs of abiding affection may be an impossible luxury. One can choose to deny the artistry in such locutions, but the result is to perversely impoverish what is presented, after all, as a single long poem in several sections, not a scrapbook of incomplete jottings. To move through the contesting voices in *Montage*—to discover themes returning, transformed in newly inflected ways, so that the "boogie-woogie rumble of a dream deferred" and the numerous onomatopoetic reproductions of the phrases around bebop (a term still fluid enough that it is represented here in some of its earlier variants like "re-bop" and "re-dop")—is to find one's sensibility appropriated for this larger enterprise, this formation of a new Harlem, evolving who-knows-where in this postwar moment.

Montage is a work of monumental complexity and endless subtlety that, no less than other examples of the long poem in the twentieth century, depends heavily on the willingness of its readers to position themselves within it. It is helpful and perhaps even necessary to know that Hughes's distinction between boogie-woogie and bebop is substantial and marks a significant generational difference, though both are variants of tactics of musical improvisation that flourished in African American urban communities. Perhaps most important is the fact that both are musical styles that are transparently virtuosic and that proved resistant to transplanting by others outside of the African American community. The older of the two variants, boogie-woogie is heavily invested in chord sequences identified with so-called blues progressions (flatted thirds and sevenths) that are traditional bases for jazz. Associated first with keyboard instruments, boogie-woogie piano takes for its signature a left hand that establishes a running bass line of rapid-fire dotted eighths and sixteenths. Against that busy, constant, and fundamentally driving rhythm, the right hand finds melodic variations. As a development of ragtime and "barrel-house" piano, the boogie-woogie style evolved when 1930s pianists (notably Albert Ammons and Meade Lux Lewis) submitted standard songs or basic blues to fast-paced virtuoso performances, and when swingtime bands orchestrated the rapid-fire bass line as a background musical riff. Bebop, by contrast, courted harmonic complexity. Not only did it employ the full range of chord progression associated with commercial tunes but its hallmark was to destabilize the harmonic sequence of the musical line by substituting variants on the original chords or by privileging the upper intervals of the chord. In either case, drifting tantalizingly far from the root of the chord was encouraged. So, too, were rhythmic accents that displaced a regularizing beat. The powerful drive of the boogie-woogie bass was transformed into bebop's unanticipated swerving: what Eric Lott has recently described as an "aesthetic of speed and displacement—ostentatious virtuosity dedicated to reorienting perception even as it rocked the house" (460). Originating in the early 1940s, aspects of its development were lost by a wartime recording ban that, insofar as it freed musicians from commercial pressures, may have served to incubate so radically innovative a music. It had already penetrated black popular music by 1948, the year *Montage* was completed.[4]

By placing two musical styles that overlapped even as they conflicted in the same poem, Hughes not only acknowledges a pluralistic and multi-generational Harlem community but he indicates that the rapid evolving of one from the other signals the thrust and speed of the black community. With giant steps, one generation advances beyond the last. Bop is to boogie as Stravinsky is to Handel. With only twenty years separating them, these two styles indicate a startling advance in musical sophistication—an advance, it goes without saying, unmatched in the social realm. Indeed, the musical styles as Hughes employs them are encircled by different social attitudes. The two resound as a poetic shorthand for evoking attitude contrasts that audience members may or may not be acculturated enough to appreciate. The "Dream Boogie" with which *Montage* opens incorporates two broadly distinct kinds of rhythm in its lines:

> Good morning, daddy!
> Ain't you heard
> The boogie-woogie rumble
> Of a dream deferred?
>
> Listen closely:
> You'll hear their feet
> Beating out and beating out a—
>
> > *You think*
> > *It's a happy beat?*

Listen to it closely:
Ain't you heard
something underneath
like a—

> *What did I say?*

Sure,
I'm happy!
Take it away!

> *Hey, pop!*
> *Re-bop!*
> *Mop!*

> *Y-e-a-h!* (*Collected* 388)

The intrusive, italicized voice aligns itself with bebop since it closes the poem in a little flurry of onomatopoeia that suggest an origin for the term "bebop" (one of these terms, "*Re-bop!*" appears in a later poem, "Neon Signs," as a synonym for bebop: "Mirror-go-round / where a broken glass / in the early bright / smears re-bop / sound" [397]). Bebop in 1947 is still enough undetermined to be sometimes called re-bop—and it will entertain further transformations such as the "*De-dop!*" that brings closure to two poems (both in coda-like endings: the "Figurine" that ends "Question" and the "Figurette" that ends "What? So Soon!"). It will even, in "Flatted Fifths," drift off into nonsense syllables with a family resemblance such as "*oop pop-a-da.*" Just what these noises mean—obscure, probably irrational, but kinetic, vivid with energy, though with no channel for that power—is not developed; they represent a fracture in the present and a gesture toward a future as yet unknown. By contrast, the boogie-woogie musical style that dominates the opening is far less alarming; its pace is brisk and snappy. The notable difference in duration between the accented and unaccented metrics in "boogie-woogie rumble / Of a dream deferred" (where the accented syllables are hit smartly and the unaccented syllables pass at a speed made even faster by the alliteration and consonance in the line) even suggest the rapid-fire dotted eighths and sixteenths of the left-hand piano in boogie-woogie. Both of these musical styles are in the poem, however, as representative attitudes enacted through the dialogue. It is not the presence of a "dream deferred" that the first lines in the poem ask us to hear within "the boogie-woogie rumble" (and the shuffling feet that represent, within the dance step, humble obedience and display of unthreatening lassitude) so much as it is the interruption of that act of deferral by a new voice that arises from who knows where. It may be a voice internal to the speaker of the first lines; it may be the voice of an irreverent narrator, but without doubt it is the voice of the future. But Hughes's achievement here as elsewhere is not just to give voice to a contrast: it is to intervene most dramatically by addressing us in ways that require our interpolation. It is we who complete two lines in this dialogue by supplying the phrases "happy feet" and "dream deferred" to clinch a rhyme. And when the italicized bebop voice asks *"What did I say?"*—in a question phrased so as to refuse responsibility—we understand that the voice has both not "said" anything and said a great deal just by posing its interrupting question. To hear the first voice then shift so completely, as it leaves behind the driving rhythms that it had three times introduced to the poem, and drop down into a voice that might have seemed just neutral ("Sure, / I'm happy! / Take it away!") were it not for its resemblance, now, to the bebop voice, is to believe that a great deal of frustration is being expressed within a poem that it would be a grave error to accept as merely a fragmentary exchange. "Take it away!" signals a stylized ending of nonsense syllables that resembles bebop scat singing. In scat singing, the voice improvises a melodic jazz line using nonsense words in sound combinations. Such a nonlexical performance, in one sense, means nothing; in another sense, of course, it registers a protest against silencing of all kinds, against an inability to speak and be heard. (It also suggests that the bland phrasings that precede it, including "Sure, / I'm happy," are so much nonsense.) The *"Y-e-a-h!"* at the close, drawn out expressively, confirms the accuracy of the entire dialogue, validating it further with its sharp edge of irony: this is an affirmation only in the sense that it so effectively yet so secretively registers conditions that involve censorship, interrupted messages, and multiple voicings.

"Listen closely," Hughes says, then urges again: "Listen to it closely." Comprehending its many voices and internalizing them in their multiplicity, that listener then experiences the entire poem as circling about, as a viewer might experience a montage (without a single point of view exerting a protocol but numerous coexisting viewpoints). The frequently anthologized lines from "Theme for English B" (undoubtedly the most famous of the poems in *Montage*)—"As I learn from you, / I guess you learn from me / Though you're older—and white— / and somewhat more free" (450)—take a sharp and challenging turn if Hughes insists that if we are to "learn" we must place ourselves at the center of not only this poem but each poem. This, of course, is exactly what has never happened. "English B" has been canonized, its eminently polite voice preserved as exemplary, while the other poems in *Montage,* with which it is in active dialogue, remain obscure, the work of hearing them left undone. (It is as if we knew *The Waste Land* only in an excerpt that was section 4, the hauntingly beautiful lines about Phlebas the Phoenician.) These other voices are acutely discomfiting, for Hughes's refusal to promote an essentialized definition of blackness allows him to discuss issues of class as well as race: "How can you forget me?" a voice asks in "Low to High" (411). "But you do! / You said you was gonna take me / Up with you— / Now you've got your Cadillac / you done forgot that you are black." "Likewise" explicitly links prejudice not just to racial but ethnic origins: "sometimes I think / Jews must have heard / the music of a / dream deferred" (425). With his background in radical causes of the 1930s, Hughes renders the variety of Harlem in episodes that foreground positions that have been defined not just by race but by class, ethnicity, and even gender. When one or more of these collide, Hughes has a poem like "Question":

> Said the lady, *Can you do*
> *what my other man can't do—*
> *That is,*
> *love me daddy—*
> *and feed me, too?*
>
> > *Figurine*
>
> De-dop!

In such "throwaway" moments Hughes writes lyrically but not poetically, asserting the vernacular over the discursive, pushing his text directly toward the overheard fragment, even framing it with what he calls a "*figurine,*" a musical or rhythmic phrase of embellishment.[5] So minimal is the poem that its voice can easily go directly past us. Hughes demands a subtle acknowledgment. To be loved is not difficult; but to find the material basis for supporting another is, in Harlem, a problem. It is a familiar problem, and it is not one easy to resolve: the poem unfolds as a question, not a delighted cry of recognition. Moreover, it is spoken by a "lady": this is a serious, even a dignified request, though it comes from a woman who already is in a relationship with another. Underneath it is a question of family stability that also places a twist on the slang "daddy": if there is no economic basis for a family to survive, then the concept of patriarchy is diminished, and male pride is undermined. What answer emerges to this question? The laconic "De-dop!" registers that the question has been heard, but it also suggests that the question is rhetorical or has no answer; it can only be acknowledged. In half a dozen lines, Hughes treats matters that touch on the family, the economics of poverty, masculine pride, and feminine dignity.[6]

Just before the last lines in "Likewise," Hughes writes *"Hey! / Baba-re-bop! / Mop! / On a be-bop kick!"*—linking the "music of a / dream deferred" with these scat-singing syllables. Bop talk or scat singing, as musical as it may be, can also sound like nonsense or chaos. *Montage* directs us toward realizing how appropriate it is for Harlem in the late 1940s to conceive a nonce language that inserts itself at telling moments (often toward the end of the poem) and preserves an underlying rhythm of high-energy activity. The bop talk in *Montage* exists not to be decoded. With nothing to translate from the mysterious sounds, no "message" to be transmitted, what is registered is a cry on behalf of a dignity that will not be lost, that demands recognition of the subtlest kind. Its unintelligibility, however, is deliberate, not helpless: a gesture and a promise toward the future. To hear a dream, especially one that has been set aside, requires sensitivity to the moment of deferral—the swerving or digression that aims to draw attention away from itself. As instants of deferral dislocate the poem, then, they ask to be recuperated by the attentive listener who is now positioned to understand that the opening words are not so much overheard as they are directly addressed to whomever is listening: The "Good morning, daddy!" that promises a new beginning is now matched with the follow-up query: "Ain't you heard / the boogie-woogie rumble / of a dream deferred?" As variations on these opening lines recur, Hughes accustoms us to embellishments on the increasingly familiar theme of attentive listening. Thus there are the explicit requests in "Lady's Boogie" (412) that seem to sketch an upper-class audience that is white: "See that lady / Dressed so fine? / She ain't got boogie-woogie / On her mind—// But if she was to listen / I bet she'd hear / Way up in the treble / The tingle of a tear. // *Be-Bach!*" And there are examples of a white voice that resist some of the object lessons on display, as in "Comment on Curb": "You talk like / they don't kick / dreams around / downtown. // *I expect they do— / But I'm talking about / Harlem to you!*" (428). As the sequence unfolds, Hughes tests us to see whether we now understand lines that might have seemed negligible before his instruction:

Wonder

Early blue evening.
Lights ain't come on yet.
Looky yonder!
They come on now! (394)

By writing poems of implicit omissions that require our involvement, Hughes proposes that we rewrite the imagist fragment as social text. We hear now two voices, one urbane and the other provincial, in this sketch of a big-city moment that is presented as it occurs (the streetlights come on in the interval between the voices). And when they light up, they suddenly disclose how numerous they are and the depth of scale that they abruptly bring to the cityscape: *"Looky yonder!"* As delicate as such a moment is, it also rises out of a sharp awareness of a culture of poverty—this simple act constitutes a spectacle—at the same time as it reminds us that the desire for beauty, like other forms of desire, cuts across lines of class, gender, and race. To envision those rows of streetlights, transforming the evening as they abruptly appear, is a moment shared. Our perception blends with the voices of the speakers, which may be, as a matter of fact, not necessarily two separate individuals but one person, recalling in this particular moment an introduction to a new city life through the first moment of seeing the lights appear.

Neither glamorizing city life nor portraying Harlemites as passive victims, Hughes puts on stage the public life of street-corner exchanges, as he works within but also against that tradition in art that uses defamiliarization as an aesthetic criterion. Bop talk and street chatter comes at us as an estranged discourse, as African American voices, at least in this era, must always already be. The form of the imagist fragment—working with the line break to admit dramatic pauses, working with the line as a unit to suggest that phrasings are not isolated but may range from the parallel to the apposite—amplifies "voice" and evokes contexts that can be marshaled to explain the resonance that surrounds the lines. Against the atomization that is also powerfully registered in the *Montage,* Hughes attempts a recovery of street language and a placement of it within a set of social practices that redeems those who speak it and condemns the cultural politics whose presence is felt in its distortions. Dreams not just as expressed but also as *deferred*—as interrupted, postponed, even unstated—keep returning in a set of sharp moments whose serial and repetitive quality becomes a deliberate because necessary rejection of the very possibility of composing a text that would mount cumulatively toward a synthesizing climax. Affirming and denying the possibilities of the high modern long poem, or better yet, proposing and then withholding such possibilities, the voices in the *Montage* postpone the dismissal with which they would otherwise be greeted.

Pan-Racial, Multicultural, Utopian

Hughes was chided by Deutsch for writing that was too unlike the example of *The Waste Land;* for yielding to Eliot's example all too successfully, Melvin B. Tolson was faulted. Although the long poem that Tolson published in the same year (1953) as *Partisan Review* featured Berryman's *Homage* was, in the words of Michael Bérubé, a text of "staggering density and inaccessibility" (170), what was just as likely to doom it to obscurity was its Olson-like unabashed insistence on fulfilling a tradition of modernist experimental writing. No poet in the 1950s manipulated the conventions of the symphonic epic of high modernism as boldly, as shrewdly, and as exhaustively as Tolson in his *Libretto for the Republic of Liberia.* And not surprisingly, no other poem extended its subject into so vast a geography. At the same time as Tolson produced a poem that seemed so incontrovertible an example of high modernism as to win accolades from Allen Tate, he simultaneously unveiled a work that celebrated skills of endurance and resilience, that placed on record a neglected chapter in the history of American slavery, and that registered objections to the historical narrative that "explained" the cultural authority of Europe, even as the poem itself was composed in an idiom that combined the extravagant demands of European high modernism with the linguistic bravura of the African American tradition. Many of the issues that Tolson had structured in his poem were those that, as the success of Berryman's long poem suggested, the era was most heavily invested in *not* wanting to consider: the existence of a historical narrative that suggested there were alternate ways of reading the present, the possibility of a counterdiscourse not only equal to the current discourse but perhaps in its display of pleasure an improvement over it, and the value of ranging extensively across a series of cultural planes whose differences could not be quickly assimilated.

Since Tolson's poem so clearly did not resemble anything like Keller's "tightly crafted lyric," it could appear as strangely old-fashioned—about twenty-five years out of date, by Bérubé's reckoning in his extensive study of the reception of Tolson's work: "At the very moment of Tolson's 'conversion' to modernism, then, modernism's academic critics—themselves both agents and products of modernism's 'success'—are writing the epitaphs for what modernism was" (39). It is true: Tolson's long poem was a textbook example of the experimental extended epic of high modernism, a book-length poem 770 lines long, carrying a hefty seventeen pages of footnotes, and divided into eight separate pieces (each one titled according to the ascending notes of the diatonic scale: Do, Re, Mi . . .) that devised impressively original ways to describe the present-day African republic of Liberia as well as the historical events behind its founding.[7] Each poem, in good high-modernist fashion, devised its own individuating form. "Sol" unfolded in three-line stanzas, three or four beats to the line, in the free verse of a Williams:

> This is the Middle Passage: here
> Gehenna hatchways vomit up
> The debits of pounds of flesh.
>
> This is the Middle Passage: here
> The sharks wax fattest and the stench
> Goads God to hold His nose! (*"Harlem"* 164–65)

Its successor, "La," however, was in four-line iambic trimeter stanzas that rhyme as tightly as the quatrains in Pound's "Mauberly":

> Leopard, elephant, ape,
> Rhinoceros and giraffe
> Jostled in odysseys
> To Africa: siamang laugh
>
> And curse impaled the frost
> As Northmen brandished paws
> And shuffled Europe-ward,
> Gnashing Cerberean jaws. (*"Harlem"* 168)

The work's final two poems exceeded the scope and ambition of the six that preceded them. Each one alone accounted for one-third the length of the entire work. Moreover, the climactic poem, "Do [2]," after a virtuoso sixty-six lines in which phrases in a dozen languages swept past, like the flotsam and jetsam of a global culture now in ruins—

> lincoln walks the midnight epoch of the ant-hill
> and barbaric yawps shatter the shoulder-knots of white peace
> > *jai hind* (Dawn comes up like thunder) *pakistan zindabad*
> > britannia rules the waves *my pokazhem meeru*
> > > the world is my parish *muhammad rasulu 'llah*
> > > *hara go gette iru* oh yeah *hugashi no kazeame*[8]
> > > > (*"Harlem"* 179)

—closed with long sweeping lines designed to convey a futurist world of movement and speed, in which the geography of Africa, including its own sacred places to be named in honor of the African great, will be as familiar as that of western Europe:

> The Futurafrique, the accent on youth and speed
> > and beauty, escalades the
> > Mount Sinai of Tubman Uni-
> > versity, the vistas of which
> > bloom with co-eds from seven
> > times seven lands . . . (*"Harlem"* 182)

This panoramic poetry emerged from a series of poetic meditations that shuttle between descriptions of present-day Liberia and recollections of moments from its African past and its founding by Americans and African Americans. At the same time, its epic impulse flowed from its own historical moment: few works captured so fervently the global ambitions of the years just after World War II, the sense that a truly new beginning might be possible out of the ruins of Europe. Even so, it was a work also prepared to check that optimism by bringing to bear on it the full weight of a global history in which civilizations rise and fall. To cover so vast a project, with so extensive a timetable, required a poetic language that was able to be both elaborate and condensed, as in the spit-shine-polished strong stress of "Re" which relates the African civilization of Timbuktu, whose gold reserves and centers of knowledge made the Niger River a crossroads for late medieval civilization:

> In Milan and Mecca, in Balkh and Bombay,
> Sea lawyers in the eyeservice of sea kings
> Mixed liquors with hyperboles to cure deafness.
> Europe bartered Africa crucifixes for red ivory,
> Gewgaws for black pearls, *pierres d'aigris* for green gold:
> Soon the rivers and roads became clog almanacs:
>
> The Good Gray Bard in Timbuktu chanted:
> *Wanawake wanazaa ovyo! Kazi yenu wazungu!* (*"Harlem"* 161)

Passages were apt to shift, Pound-like, without warning from English to French or Spanish or German, as well as into transcriptions from Japanese or Arabic or Russian or African dialects. So erudite a performance lent itself, Eliot-like, to footnoting. The footnote to line 72 (the final line in the last quotation) helpfully translated the two exclamatory phrases as "The women keep having children right and left" and "It's the work of you white men." And a footnote to line 69 ("Gewgaws for black pearls, *pierre d'aigris* for green gold") suggested how carefully selective these notes will be: "Black pearls. V. Shakespeare, *Two Gentlemen of Verona*, V, ii. Also *Othello*, I, i: 'Well prais'd! How if she be black and witty?' Mr. J. A. Rogers treats the subject and time and place adequately in *Sex and Race*" (*"Harlem"* 192). The prim demeanor of these notes is usually misleading, especially when one follows the trail of their allusions. When one looks for a gloss for "black pearls" in act 5, scene 2 of *The Two Gentlemen,* what is discovered is the character of Proteus remarking: "The old saying is, / Black men are pearls in beauteous ladies' eyes" (lines 11–12)—which makes the follow-up line from *Othello* pertinent because it is a question that is asked by Desdemona. Here as in several other passages from Shakespeare to which Tolson's footnotes direct us, the poet who resides at the absolute center of English literature speaks openly of interracial desire (even noting it as an "old saying"), the topic under discussion in Rogers's 1942 study which is subtitled *A History of White, Negro and Indian Miscegenation in the Two Americas* and cited by W. E. B. Du Bois in *The World and Africa* (1946). Immensely complicating the brutally one-sided economics of the slave trade ("Gewgaws for black pearls"), Tolson suggests, is the attraction felt by one human for another, always playing havoc with the dominant culture's simple equations. And because "black pearls" are now revealed to be in fact human beings, the *"pierre d'aigris"* bartered for African gold seem to be "bitter stones" indeed, and certainly not just another example of the mercantilism by which a ruling country provides manufactured items to a colony in exchange for raw materials. This intricacy is typical of many footnotes; they are an impressive adjunct to the poem—nearly two hundred in number and spread over seventeen pages.

Tolson is not just imitating techniques that Pound and Eliot had developed. He also knows the radicalism at the heart of the modernist project as it was reconceived in America by William Carlos Williams and Hart Crane. On the one hand, then, the modernist epic is a familiar collection of linguistic strategies that, by the postwar era, have become so acceptable they are beginning to be recognized as objects of academic study—so fully acknowledged that they may be even adopted to ends that eschew controversy (Berryman). On the other hand, those strategies have been used, and can be used again, to mount a series of raids against various kinds of established authority. Since Tate's one foray into the cultural epic, his "Ode to the Confederate Dead" of 1928, scarcely deviated from a straight pentameter-line narrative that shunted back and forth from past to present, he himself was less prepared than he might have thought to appreciate the advantages that the modernist epic secures. To the extent that it commissions its own rules, the epic uses the always-multiplying "symphonic" forms of the individual poems as powerful delivery services that tantalizingly withhold their meaning, compelling repeat perusals, each one of which contributes to the subtle reprogramming of the reader's perceptual framework.

Admiring Tolson's opening stanza, Tate recalled its sudden effect, as electric as a religious conversion:

> On the first page I received a shock, in that region where bored skepticism awaits the new manuscript from a poet not clearly identified, when I saw Liberia invoked as

> > . . . the quicksilver sparrow that slips
> > The eagle's claw!

> From that passage to the end I read the poem with increasing attention and admiration. ("Preface" 216)

Tate's "increasing attention and admiration" was carefully orchestrated by the structure of feeling that Tolson set in his stanzas. The final lines of the first stanza *are* particularly deft at replicating the movement they describe:

> > Liberia?
> > No micro-footnote in a bunioned book
> > > Honed by a pedant
> > > with a gelded look:
> > > > You are
> > The ladder of survival dawn men saw
> > In the quicksilver sparrow that slips
> > > The eagle's claw! (*"Harlem"* 159)

Just as the sparrow is a "quicksilver" that darts rapidly and eludes the grasp of a larger predator, so the line itself surges out from under the steady propulsion of the iambic pentameter line. As the repeated "s" and "i" sounds accelerate the pace of the last two lines, their gracefully animated movement makes iambic pentameter sluggish by contrast. The achievement of the little escaping the large, the triumph of the smart over the powerful, is rendered at the prosodic level where its claim on our attention is irresistible. Given the eagle's associations with the United States of America, it is daring of Tolson—but utterly right—to arrange a perspective in which the eagle's loss is a gain. This is, after all, a poem about establishing a new republic outside the borders of the United States. But there are not many epics which twist national allegiance so thoroughly in their opening stanza.

That way of thinking differently, moreover, has the status not just of a counterdiscourse that is opposed to a mainstream way of thinking—not just a slippage out from the weight of iambic pentameter—but of a way of conceptualizing that has roots identified with the African American community. Widely expanded from the ad-lib insults that linguists associate with the term, "Signifyin(g)" has been associated by Henry Louis Gates with virtuoso improvisational and allusive speech that displays (in terms Gates cites from Claudia Mitchell-Kernan) "indirect intent" and "metaphorical reference" (85). In the seven stanzas of his opening poem, Tolson explicitly signifies on "Liberia" in a call-and-response format in which, answering the first call, the response is always that it is *not* this and *not* this and *not* this, but, in answer to the next call, the response is that it *is* this, it *is* this, it *is* this. Within this format, the reader is not required to have a referent for every phrase, because Tolson always supplies three negatives and three positives. The structure permits signifyin(g) to flourish, with attention shifted to the poet's improvising variations that are appositions of each other.

Customizing the Footnote

If one axis of Tolson's project is to introduce a print-dominated audience to the pleasures of oral literature, the other is to introduce an audience comfortable with oral traditions to the opportunities that print culture offers. Just as the pattern of repetition and return is associated with oral literature, so the footnote—the particular and detailed footnote that drives a point home—is central to written texts. Introducing an audience with a sharp ear for quick repartee to the footnote is no less challenging than teaching whites to hear bop prosody. Of course the first signal that the footnote in this poem will be more than just a fussy adjunct to the text is its appearance in the poem's second line, where Liberia is described as "No micro-footnote in a bunioned book / Honed by a pedant / with a gelded look." Can a footnote be other than "micro"? To those ready to dismiss the footnote as a distraction, Tolson is ready to show how much can happen within a compressed space. Dan McCall observed that Tolson's footnotes are never stable: they are "now-scholarly, now-sly" (538).[9] His footnotes are original enough, and provocative enough, and so essential a part of the entire poem that, like Eliot's, they represent a further extension of the forms available to the poet of the symphonic epic.

It was Karl Shapiro's idea, according to Tolson, to supplement his text with explanatory footnotes. But textual evidence suggests that Tolson's footnoting was not a neutral follow-up to his finished work but another stage in composition, a generative interplay in which footnoting became a process that gave rise to new lines that in turn required their own footnote. As published in *Poetry* in 1950, the last lines in the final stanza of "Ti" looked like this:

> between Yesterday's
> golden goblet and truckling trull
> and the ires
> of rivers red with the reflexes of fires,
> the ferris wheel
> of race, of caste, of class
> dumped and alped cadavers till the ground
> fogged the Pleiades with Gila rot: Today the mass,
> the Beast with a Maginot Line in its Brain,
> the Gravediggers' men of base alloy,
> the *canaglia—Gorii!—die Untertanen,*
> the *hoi barbaroi,*
> Il Duce's Whore, Vardaman's Hound,
> the *vsechelevek,* the people, Yes—
> the *hoi polloi*
> ride the merry-go-round!
> Selah!
>
> ("Ti [from *Libretto*]" 214–15)

When these same lines appear in 1953, collected in the final printing in volume form, they have been expanded (Tolson's additions or modifications are underlined):

> Between Yesterday's wills of Tanaka, between
> golden goblets and truckling trull
> and the ires
> of rivers red with the reflexes of fires,

the ferris wheel
of race, of caste, of class
dumped and alped cadavers till the ground
fogged the Pleiades with Gila rot: Today the mass,
the Beast with a Maginot Line in its Brain,
the staircase avengers of base alloy,
the ville canaille—Gorii!—the Bastard-Rasse,
the uomo qualyque, the hoi barbaroi,
the raya in the Oeil de Boeuf,
the vsechelovek, the descamisados, the hoi polloi,
the Raw from the Coliseum of the Cooked,
Il Duce's Whore, Vardaman's Hound—
unparadised nobodies with maps of Nowhere
ride the merry-go-round!
Selah!

(*"Harlem"* 177)[10]

Tolson's catalogue of the "unparadised nobodies" who are the second-class citizens of the world include the *"descamisados"* (which a footnote translates as "the shirtless ones") who are equivalent to the *hoi polloi* (ancient Greek for "the many" but not translated in a footnote). Their presence next to the Russian (a footnote translates it as "universal man," but then quibbles with this as inaccurate) is designed to emphasize that the masses have existed in every country and the names they have usually been given in their particular languages reveal their degraded status. When Tolson adds further names, he does so to swell the ranks but also because of the footnoting opportunities they provide. Adding the line "the *raya* in the *Oeil de Boeuf*" allowed Tolson to generate this aside: *"Raya.* In the Turkish conquest of the Southern Slavs, the maltreated people became *raya* or cattle. Conquest salves its conscience with contempt. Among the *raya* for five hundred years, the ballads of the wandering *guslars* kept freedom alive" (*"Harlem"* 200). No link with slavery in America is actually spelled out in this display of historical information. Yet Tolson's own observation about conquest and conscience brings a personal and disarming twist to the staid convention of the note. Further parallels become possible. Of special interest is the contribution made by wandering musicians who use a folk tradition to "keep freedom alive." Tolson's footnotes for the line continue: *"Oeil de Boeuf:* a waiting room at Versailles. Cf. Dobson, 'On a Fan That Belonged to the Marquise de Pompadour'" (*"Harlem"* 200). Tolson's new line brings the long-derided peasantry (using the name that their conquerors had forced upon them) inside the walls of a location exclusively reserved for the privileged, thus conceiving a revolutionary explosion, a collision between peasants derided as "cattle" and a drawing room with a window named "bull's eye" ("eye of the bull" in French). But the footnote cuts even deeper. The 1878 poem by Austin Dobson imagines a fan skillfully deployed as an erotic extension of its owner. In the passage that Tolson cites, it flutters in the hands of a courtesan, "Thronging the *Oeil de Boeuf* through" (line 10), and it thus influences history's course by scrambling great men's brains— a sharp contrast to the artistry of the wandering balladeers in the previous note whose songs kept the concept of freedom alive for five hundred years. In short, these are not footnotes that will cultivate a "gelded look": they are packed with dynamite information, and they unfold upon and within one another, developing their brief but devastating scenarios.

That Tolson is processing information through the footnotes, taking advantage of their "secondary" role to import disturbing material that has been kept out of the record, is signaled in—where else?—a footnote to a passage in "Sol." In his poetic text, Tolson is describing the first impressions of Elijah Johnson, a founder of Liberia in the nineteenth century, when the new colonists first glimpse the African shore: "hallelujahs quake the brig / From keel to crow's next and tomtoms gibber / In cosmic *deepi-talki*" (*"Harlem"* 165). The footnote text to line 163 explains *"deepi-talki"*: "Cf. LaVarre: 'My black companions had two languages: *deepi-talki,* a secret language no white man understands; and *talki-talki,* a concoction of many languages and idioms which I understood'" (*"Harlem"* 194). This double-tiered communication which exists in oral culture (with two languages, one of which is official, the other private) has a parallel in print literature in the two-tiered expressiveness of main text plus footnote. The talk-talk of the main text carries on its official discussion even as the deep-talk of the footnote moves below it in a variety of ways, lending further support to the main text, or digressing from it, or even undermining it by raising questions. Though the footnote is supposed to be a faithful servant, it can also perform acts of subversion and rebellion.[11]

Tolson's deep-talk footnotes volunteer information hard to find in the 1950s. Whether one thinks of the interchange that Tolson sets up as another form of Gates's signifyin(g) or a trace of the improvised call and response familiar from jazz, the effect is to set in motion a dialectic of disruption in which it is no longer possible to confidently assign what is primary and what is secondary. Some footnotes, then, by contesting for dominance with the main text provide an important disorienting function: they enact a relativization of cultures. "Sol" opens with this stanza:

White Pilgrims, turn your trumpets west!
Black Pilgrims, *shule, agrah,* nor tread
The Skull of another's stairs! (*"Harlem"* 164)

Both lines 141 and 142 have footnotes:

141. *Shule, agrah:* "Move, my heart." Cf. Sharp, *Shule, Shule, Shule, Agrah.* It is a refrain from old Gaelic ballads.
142. *Skull: "gulgoleth,"* a place of torment and martyrdom. *Another's stairs.* Cf. Rossetti, *Dante at Verona,* the epigraph from *Paradiso,* XVII:

> "Yea, thou shalt learn how salt his food fares
> Upon another's bread—how steep his path
> Who treadeth up and down another's stairs." (*"Harlem"* 193)

Here poetic text and footnote text mutually interact. Which is deep-talk and which is talk-talk is impossible to say. The poetic text, which is beginning to describe the return journey back across the Middle Passage of ex-slaves leaving America and seeking to found Liberia, distinguishes black pilgrims from white pilgrims. Whites turn westward, trumpeting their search, announcing their presence as loudly as possible. But blacks turn eastward in deep sorrow, as exiles in pain, moved by intense feeling ("Move, my heart") as exiles everywhere are. They are like Dante, living far from his beloved Florence. The footnote, then, presents the black experience as both particularized and universalized, different from the "White pilgrims" yet not unlike experience that anyone associated with outcast and exile would have and that has been canonized in the example of Dante.

Tolson is not simply demonstrating particular skill and competence in the juxtapositions that his footnotes promote: he is unveiling a web of connections that are pan-racial, multicultural, and utopian—in which there is a stronger connection between Dante Alighieri and displaced African slaves than there is between Dante Alighieri and Dante Gabriel Rossetti. He may begin by answering questions about the past of Liberia—an unfamiliar region that seems to merit no more attention than a micro-footnote in a book of world history that is already too large, swollen with too much information—but he ends with a global perspective set in the future. Tolson's visionary strain meets and exceeds his searing critique. His footnote, in one sense, is a mark of rebellion, as it demonstrates its lack of satisfaction with its role as a mere parenthesis in the text, obediently in thrall to the text itself. When the lowly footnote becomes an agent of change, pursuing its own strong agenda and even offering revolutionary insights, then a narrative in which the subordinate becomes the dominant is also embedded in Tolson's annotations. But at the same time his footnotes network a constructive set of new alliances with juxtapositions that reach across cultures, beyond customary borders. Out of the ruins of Europe, a new political geography will emerge. Tolson's extraordinarily ambitious epic not only responds to that possibility but enacts its occurrence by demonstrating constitutive powers that are equal to the most innovative works of its predecessors.

Escape from History: Diplomatic Distrust

The footnotes Tolson injected in the closing pages of his long poem represent one of the few moments in the 1950s when information appears that might provoke a discussion that centers not only on historical matters but on the question of what fails to get recorded in history. When Tolson's footnotes refer to such incidents as *"el grito de Yara,"* the declaration of Cuban independence by Carlos Manuel de Cespedes that launched the Ten Years' War in which Cuba first attempted to break from Spanish rule (and which would not be fulfilled until 1898), or when they quote not once but three times from Euclydes da Cunha's *Os Sertones* (1902) (translated by Samuel Putnam in 1944 as *Rebellion in the Outlands* and often called, though a work of history, the national epic of Brazil)—the astonishingly detailed historical study of the geography, ethnic groups, and social structure of the south of Brazil that attempts to explain why the state would perceive as a threat the peaceful settlement of a large mass of poor people who were the religious followers of a self-declared prophet—it is clear that these citations to historical incidents have razor sharp edges and that their emphasis on class and revolution raises questions that many Americans would have found especially awkward. At the same time, these footnotes are themselves in masquerade, appearing to be dry and diminished things that can be passed by if necessary. By placing so much within a form that is not exactly equipped to hold it, Tolson also registers the pressure to streamline if not eliminate some historical narratives, to forget vast areas of the past. The few historical incidents that George P. Elliott favors in his selections in *Fifteen Modern American Poets* get no further away from the United States than excerpts from Robert Penn Warren's "Mexico Is a Foreign Country" and Elizabeth Bishop's "Arrival at Santos."

If Elliott's anthology engendered a shift toward the kind of verse that could be safely discussed in the 1950s classroom, then it might seem that one of his most effective allies would have been Hyam Plutzik, especially in the two excerpts that Elliott printed from Plutzik's long poem that would be published in 1960 under the title *Horatio*. Plutzik was one of the five new poets that Elliott promoted when he omitted the work of Holmes, Mayo, Nims, Scott, and Viereck. The two extended segments which together account for almost half of Plutzik's twenty-page allotment introduce a long poem that promises to follow the twists in Horatio's life as it unfolds with Hamlet no longer living but very much a presence. In the two excerpts Elliott prints, misunderstandings abound, and the vein is comical. In the first, which takes place not long after Hamlet's demise, when Horatio stables his horse he gets an earful from the hostler, a quintessential representative of the working class, who has his own version of the Hamlet story, one rife with court intrigue and sexual hanky-panky. Horatio fails to convince him of the inaccuracy of these glamorized events, much as, in the second excerpt, he is unable to interrupt the monologue of his old tutor (who was also Hamlet's), Dr. Faustus, who elaborates his own theory of Hamlet's demise, which turns out to be a half-baked mix of the hottest buzzwords in medieval academe. Here, in short, is plenty of material to stoke the fires in half a dozen classroom discussions.

And yet even in these brief excerpts, Plutzik's poem suggests it might transform itself into something more disturbing than the high comedy that it first promises to be. It displays itself less as an academic text than as a learned one, though in a register entirely different from Tolson's—one that depends on Shakespeare's *Hamlet* as a pre-text, one that also draws upon other Elizabethan narratives like Marlowe's *Doctor Faustus*. Living by words and through interpretations is also the calling of the long poem's central consciousness, Horatio, who is a courtier and diplomat. And the entire poem features a middle section that depends directly on numerous literary references. In that section, an incognito Horatio infiltrates a shepherd camp that represents the underclass of his time, where an oral version of the Hamlet story circulates, a legend of "Ambleth" which can be recognized as a mythic narrative derived in part from the Oedipus story even as the names in this legendary version (Ambleth, Fang, Gertha) are versions of names from the twelfth-century *Historia Danica* of Saxo Grammaticus (Amlethus, Feng, Gerutha) that Shakespeare scholars recognize as a basis for a story retold in Belleforest's *Histoires Tragiques* (1576) that was the probable source of the lost play by Kyd from which Shakespeare borrowed. Plutzik's long poem, then, while amply packed with allusions and references, also centers attention on the issue of miscommunication, especially across lines of class and profession.

At its simplest, Horatio's project as conceived by Plutzik is to live up to the obligation with which Hamlet charged him in his last words ("Absent thee from felicity awhile, / And in this harsh world draw thy breath in pain, / To tell my story"). In one sense, Plutzik's long poem lends itself to a neat formulation in which explicitly literary communication becomes its central topic. But in another sense, just as forcefully the poem disinters issues that were, in the 1950s, awkward to confront. Because Plutzik worked for so many years on *Horatio*—it was begun in 1945 but not published until 1961, the year before his untimely death at the age of fifty-one—the span of its writing covers the entire postwar period.[12] Plutzik's own long-term commitment to writing *Horatio* parallels the fifty-six-year time span in the poem which takes Horatio from youth to old age and which delineates the changing significance that the figure known as "Hamlet" has to different social classes at different times and under different circumstances. It is never the case that this long poem alludes directly or even indirectly to particular events in the postwar years. Nevertheless, it is a work in which reputations are besmirched, often for reasons that are unscrupulous or that verge on personal vendettas; in which history is rewritten by combinations of events that lurch from the inadvertent to the manipulated and back again; in which diplomatic interventions are limited by the personality traits of those conducting negotiations; and in which those who live under premodern conditions, outside the amenities of a technologically advanced civilization, are second-class citizens who struggle with surviving on a day-by-day basis and whose propensity for violence always promises to be destabilizing. And in its final sections, it opens to question whether there has been progress over the last five decades, whether the vanity of the players on the field of diplomacy has disabled them from seeing with the clarity necessary for firm decisions. It continually implies that the historical fabric is almost unbearably complex, a labyrinth of tangled motives that resist penetration. If *Horatio* begins as if it will be written by a scholar-poet gazing admiringly at Shakespeare, it develops into the work of a subtle poet of politics and culture who ends by glaring darkly at despicable circumstances which have compromised public discourse.

The two excerpts that Elliott publishes are harmless fun. It is easy for a reading audience, especially those who are familiar with the Shakespearean "true facts," to feel superior to the ignorant stable worker with his scurrilous version of sexual intrigue and to the pompous academic who is blind to the egotism displayed in his own theories. But Plutzik's third poem in his opening group—a flirtatious interlude with a countess who, though "more than thirty years" have elapsed since Hamlet's death, is still drawn to the story, probably because of its aura of danger and youthful intrigue—is eerily akin to the version of court life for which the hostler had been earlier ridiculed by Horatio. And with the fourth poem, a confidential interview with a brutally realistic prime minister, the official version of Hamlet's death is recounted in language that not only carefully guards against deniability—

"No, the only man who 'heard' the ghostly palaver
Was he who stood, or hoped, to profit the most
By his capable uncle's death, which he therefore schemed:
Hamlet himself, a disgruntled, ambitious fellow,
Of mysterious, changing moods, so unreliable
That, luckily for Denmark, our Electors
(Against the weight of primogeniture)
Had cast their vote on the more solid Claudius
When the elder Hamlet died." (152–53)

—but clearly resembles the self-deceptive narration of Hamlet's professor, Dr. Faustus. What begins as farce ends as establishment discourse. The harmlessly deranged professor of the second poem has somehow mutated into the diabolical politician of the fourth poem.

Horatio is composed of three parts, each in turn made up of several poems. In the four poems in part 1, those who are educated circulate one type of story, those who are not, another. The three long poems of part 2 are reports from the underclass that, in the keen sympathy they reveal Plutzik extending to the poor, go unmatched by any other postwar poetry except perhaps that of Langston Hughes or Gwendolyn Brooks. Plutzik sees that lives of the poor are never simple and always too complex, and his genius is to imagine the stories they might tell as a mixture of efforts to allay their fears, to bolster their confidence, to complain of their powerlessness, to mock their enemies, and to parade their mastery of new interpretive frames like Christianity, even as they sturdily resist yielding their old pagan ways. Plutzik's achievement is stunning: seldom has folk art been reconceived in such a virtuoso fashion as a window into an underclass. As Plutzik presents these tales by simple shepherds, it is never certain whether the lies and betrayals and reversals that are being ascribed in them to the wealthy are genuine exposures of the corruption of an upper class or reflections of the disappointments and frustrations that the poor experience in their own lives. In the first poem, which is the telling of an ur-Ambleth tale (it will be followed by two poems that are sequels), Ambleth is the offspring of a secret affair between Queen Gertha and King Humble's brother and rival Fang. Fang, in conspiracy with Gertha, poisons Humble and ascends to the throne. Humble's ghost urges Ambleth to be his avenger, and Ambleth feigns madness as he plots revenge. His madness is put to a test by Fang, using Polonio's daughter Olivia. If he is sane, he will respond to her seductions; if he is mad, he will spurn her. But the plot goes awry when, in the dark of night, Queen Gertha is confused with Olivia. After unwittingly seducing his own mother, Ambleth then proceeds to kill Fang. When Gertha reveals what he has done, she kills herself and he goes insane.

This Ambleth version, a story of desperate love and dangerous living and ultimate disappointment, lies over and against *Hamlet* as a B movie might compare with a big-budget Hitchcock thriller. But in Plutzik's hands, that downtown version is never simply a sensation-driven, violence-prone, misunderstood version of a high culture story—to the contrary, it is the Shakespearean twist that appears as the whitewash and cover-up: the Ambleth version conveys an urgency and emotion that has lapsed from the effete Elizabethan update. What the poor especially understand is that when justice operates, it unfortunately works in tandem with irony, so that all events exact a cost that seems to have been precisely calibrated. The idea that no one ever comes out ahead registers belief in a cosmic justice that is one effort to withdraw authority from the privileged class. Nonetheless, the poor know all too well the wisdom of protecting themselves from every direction, and right in the middle of the ur-Ambleth tale, in a scene drawn from a pagan myth, Fang meets with four creatures to whom he has entrusted the divided body of Humble. At the same time as Plutzik has Fang charge these four with their mythic instructions, he also has Fang speak within the framework of the new Christianity:

> So I am safe, my sons,
> To empty this scabbard for building of the age
> (Already begun, foretold in the prophecies)
> Of whoredom, the axe and the sword, the wind and wolf.
> Keep well your charge; hell only knows what tricks
> He may try there in the dubious place where he thirsts
> For that sacrament, that holy water, to quench
> The heat that makes him unquiet, the little flame
> That keeps him from perfection . . . (168)

If Fang is a pagan tyrant, he also fits the image of the Christian devil. Powerless storytellers prudently cover all bases. Without power themselves, they know it is unwise to ignore the power that belongs to others.

In both of the sequels that Plutzik has his shepherd storytellers perform, though the tale of Ambleth grows tangled, it continues to offer cautious advice. In the first ("The Book of Metamorphoses"), Ambleth has magically divided himself into versions of the fox, the wolf, the weasel, and the fish and moves secretly among these animals in an effort to recover the lost body of Humble and restore proportion to the world. Ambleth must employ deceptive tactics:

> Wolf Ambleth mingles with the company.
> "You haven't seen me before? Through the indulgence
> Of your noble king, I joined you yesterday
> Before he struck at that herd of antelope.
> One licks his chops still over that feast.
> Nothing could be more sweet, except perhaps—"
> And he watches closely the expression of the other—
> "Some *humble* meat fit for a delicate *fang*." (176)

This tale, not surprisingly, shows how much it values skills of deception and admires animal cunning. When fox Ambleth's deceit is uncovered and other foxes chase him down, he skirts the edge of a farmyard and "He pants alarm to his ancient enemies / Whom he can outwit, he knows, as often before, / If they will but loosen the foul grip on his shadow" (177). In this world of unbridled chaos, enemies are in disguise and friends cannot be trusted. Riddles initiate this story, and the solutions to their questions are no more satisfying than the riddling questions. In the second sequel ("The Harrowing of the House of Eyes"), a now-insane Ambleth seeks refuge in "the mansion of the High God" where he looks into eyelike openings which replay events from his life (the murder of Humble, the struggle to kill Fang). Each image is another version of Ambleth, as the storyteller explains: "Brothers, in the crooked mirrors the eyes of God / Made to his mortal sight, he saw only / Himself in his damned disguises" (182). The new rules of Christianity, whose trappings this sequel displays (an archangel soberly oversees guards who eventually eject Ambleth and preserve order), are no better than the old rules at fulfilling expectations. Ambleth wanders away from the House of God and "toward the walls / Of the Holy City" (183), to become a permanent wanderer, haunted by moments that remain enigmatic:

> Once on the pavement before an archangel's house
> He found a small lark's feather, wet with blood.
> And once, at a palace window, there was a face
> Oddly like Polonio's. From the outer wall—
> The last challenge answered—he looks away
> Across an endless plain of flickering grass
> In which, to a faint moan on the wind, far distant
> A cloud of dust whirled, as if two armies
> Horse or foot, were locked in struggle, maneuvering. (184)

Ultimately, the tale undoes the possibility that wisdom can be accrued. What one's life moves toward in age are mysterious incidents that increase in number and perhaps deepen with intensity.

Like Hughes listening on the streets of Harlem, Plutzik portrays the disenfranchised not as victims but as inventive survivalists who ingeniously cobble together versions that work for them. If their versions reveal the limits of their understanding and the brutality of their lives, their ingenuity in coping with violence on so vast a scale earns them a respect that Plutzik withholds from those who need not be so inventive. With his skeptical edge sharpened after his encounter with the storytelling shepherds, Horatio cannot exempt himself from the harsh judgment he had once reserved for others. In the coruscating self-analysis that he subjects himself to, late in his life, as an elderly statesman of seventy-four, he comes to doubt even his understanding of Hamlet's final words, words that had been the foundation of his lifelong mission. Perhaps Hamlet was not commanding him to defend his reputation but distracting him from momentary despair, from drinking poison. There was

> an expression
> On that dying face I could not understand,
> So hid away, but know now that it spoke
> No more of Hamlet but of Horatio:
>
> . . .
> Hoping indeed the current of life would seize me
> And give me its own stronger reasons for breath;
> Meaning "Live!" when saying "Live for me!";
> Meaning "Horatio, live and be yourself!" (192).

But as with Henry James's Lambert Strether, whose epiphany in *The Ambassadors* this passage clearly echoes, this knowledge arrives too late. Horatio sees that his caution and prudence had been versions of timidity and evasion. His generation has failed to produce leaders of courage and strength. In the wake of the death of Hamlet, a man who had possessed the courage to doubt the rightness of things, who had plotted and schemed to save the nation from leaders with corrupt ties to ruling power, no one had come forward. (That Horatio would have been the fated choice to fill this power vacuum is left unstated.) With Hamlet's own reputation destroyed or beyond any defense that Horatio could conceive, there was no model for political action. The state began its years of ominous drifting, and the best of men, the best of those who might have intervened, had lost the force of their courage.

While it comports itself, at least in its opening movements, as if it might be no more than a curiosity, a fussy and mannered sequel to the Shakespeare play, *Horatio* is a text that foregrounds its period in history as intricate with a duplicity that ensnared even the best of individuals. Horatio's good-hearted decision to stand in the wings as a dedicated servant is presented as both understandable and utterly unforgivable. Unlike the storytelling shepherds who have to invent a way to survive, Plutzik's highborn Horatio is a model of attentiveness, patiently reading others, thoughtfully suspending judgment, a figure of courtly respect. At the end of life, however, the ashy taste that remains with him is a measure of the times and a mark of his failure. If Plutzik's text lends itself to classroom discussion, to fostering the rereading and interpreting that Horatio models, it also raises the question of just when interpretive skill turns into a mandarin occupation, when the fine art of precise communication becomes an escape from moral action. Hughes and Tolson, fighting to be heard, keeping alive the concept of high public communication in poetry, stand as the exceptions that illuminate just the concerns that Plutzik dramatizes with a circumspection that itself verges on the symptomatic.

6 THE LURE OF THE SESTINA

The poéme bien fait, *which filled the quarterlies of the fifties, was usually not that damned* bien fait. . . . *The experiments of 1927 became the clichés of 1952. American poetry, which has always been outrageous—consider Whitman and Dickinson—dwindled into long poems in iambics called "Herakles: A Double Sestina."*
—Donald Hall, "Introduction," *Contemporary American Poetry* (1962)

Why "Herakles: A Double Sestina" and not "Herakles: A Triple Sonnet" or "Herakles: A Cycle of Villanelles"? Neither would have been so barbed. Hall was targeting the devices 1950s poets fell back on when they needed to clinch their authority. To them, titles of poems with a subtitle acquired a dot-the-i scholarly air that fashionably blurred the lines between verse and essay in a time when the critical essay enjoyed a prestige that the poem did not. Herakles with a "k" displayed a Greek orthography that paraded a command of scholarly matters extending even to a mastery of traditional forms such as the sestina. Challenge enough to work with that most daunting of poetic structures—but how much better, then, a *double* sestina. (In an earlier version of his essay in 1959, Hall's hand was even heavier, invoking "Herakles: A Quadruple Sestina" ["Ah, Love" 317].)[1]

Not every poet in the postwar years self-commissioned a sestina. If James Wright, Adrienne Rich, or Louis Simpson tried, they left their results unpublished. Richard Wilbur went on record in a 1974 interview stating the form never held his interest ("Interview" 38). And James Merrill consistently downplayed his, either leaving them uncollected or reprinting them in collections destined for a limited circulation. On the other hand, Elizabeth Bishop wrote not one but two, "A Miracle for Breakfast" in *A Cold*

Spring (1947), which was reprinted in 1955 in *North and South,* and "Sestina," first published in the *New Yorker* in 1956 and eventually collected in *Questions of Travel* (1965). ("A Miracle for Breakfast" was one of the few poems to appear in both John Ciardi's *Mid-Century American Poets* anthology of 1950 *and* George P. Elliott's *Fifteen Modern American Poets* of 1956 where, incidentally, it could be in the company of Richard Eberhart's "Sestina.") Several years separate Bishop's two sestinas. Not so W. S. Merwin's two, "Sestina (for Robert Graves)" and "Variations on a Line by Emerson," both of which appear in his first book, *A Mask for Janus* (1952). In another first book, Howard Nemerov's *The Image and the Law* (1947), may be found "Sestina I" and "Sestina II." Two sestinas also appear in William Meredith's 1958 collection *The Open Sea and Other Poems* and in John Woods's second book, *On the Morning of Color* (1961). But two sestinas to a book was hardly exceptional. John Ashbery went for three in *Some Trees* (1956), and Donald Justice followed his two standard sestinas with two variant examples in *The Summer Anniversaries* (1959). Sestinas were commonplace in first books of poetry, especially award-winning books (Justice's won the Lamont Prize in 1959, and the volumes by Merwin and Ashbery were selected for the Yale Younger Poets series, then edited by W. H. Auden.) The 1958 and 1959 Yale Younger Poets selections, John Hollander's *A Crackling of Thorns* and William Dickey's *Of the Festivity,* each had its requisite sestina. Prize-winning or not, a book of poems in the 1950s must have seemed unfurnished without a sestina, or so perhaps believed Howard Moss in *The Toy Fair* (1954), Donald Hall in *The Dark Houses* (1958), David Galler in *Walls and Distances* (1959), Ronald Perry in *The Rock Harbor* (1959), Daryl Hine in *The Devil's Picture Book* (1960), Robert Francis in *The Orb Weaver* (1960), and Frederick Bock in *The Fountains of Regardlessness* (1961).

If collections seemed incomplete without a sestina, so did the pages of the most prominent intellectual journals, even though they set aside a fraction of their space for verse. Despite these restrictions, the *Kenyon Review* published in Autumn 1952 Isabella Gardner's "Sestina," a poem Gardner left uncollected, and Edgar Bogardus's "In This Hotel There Are No Rooms" in Winter 1955, a poem left unreprinted after Bogardus's untimely death precluded a second volume (his first, *Many Jangling Keys,* was the Yale Younger Poets series winner for 1955). David Galler also never collected "Appraisals at Quiet Beach," which appeared in the *Quarterly Review of Literature* in 1955. The *Sewanee Review* published Robert Pack's "Sestina in Sleep" in its Spring 1955 issue, G. Stanley Koehler's "A Winter Gardener" in Summer 1956, and Francis Golffing's "Ode to the Memory of Paul

Wightman Williams, Painter" in Spring 1958 (Golffing's sestina had previously appeared in the *Nation* in 1957). The *Hudson Review* was especially hospitable, welcoming William Meredith's "Trees in a Grove" (Winter 1949), E. Stambler's "Sestina Mezza Forte" (Autumn 1950), British poet John Holloway's "Sestina" (Winter 1955), Donald Justice's "Sestina on Six Words from Weldon Kees" (Spring 1957), and Ronald Perry's "Sestina for a Landscape" (Autumn 1959). In the monthly *Poetry,* sestinas appeared almost annually—Stanley Moss's "The Ships Go Nowhere" (July 1949), R. P. Blackmur's "Mr. Virtue and the Three Bears" (December 1951), Patrick Anderson's "Sestina in Time of Winter" (February 1953), and Harvey Gross's "Seven Views of the City" (October 1953)—until the tenure of Henry Rago began, after which not a year went by without the magazine publishing at least one and sometimes two: Fairfield Porter (who contributed two to the issue of March 1955), John Ashbery (December 1955), David Galler (January 1956), John Woods (January 1957), Robert Stock (April 1957), Samuel French Morse (July 1957), William Sylvester (September 1958), and Rosellen Brown (December 1959).

Unlike much else in the 1950s, the sestina was *not* gender-specific. May Sarton included "From All Our Journeys" in *The Land of Silence* (1953), and "Sestina for Warm Seasons" appeared in Mona Van Duyn's second book, *A Time of Bees* (1964). Leah Bodine Drake published "Drone" in the June 1953 *Atlantic.* Jane Cooper's "Morning on the St. John's" remains an impressive example of how extensively a text could circulate as long as it kept finding admirers: originally published in the *New Yorker* in 1956, it was selected for the Borestone Mountain annual anthology of the best poems of the year, then included in Paul Engle's Random House anthology of Iowa Writers' Workshop graduates, *Midland* (1961)—all before it was collected in a volume as the opening poem in Cooper's Florida sequence in *The Weather of Six Mornings* (1968). Sylvia Plath's sestina, by contrast, never circulated at all. Prompted by a 1958 solicitation in *ARTNews* for verse on paintings and painters, Plath wrote "Yadwigha, on a Red Couch, among Lilies," based on a Henri Rousseau painting, but failed to place it with any magazine or include it in any collection. (Her April 22, 1958, journal entry records a consolatory note from the *New Yorker* in which someone—"Howard Moss or 'They'"—liked her two submissions, including the "Rousseau sestina" [*Journals* 219], but not enough to publish them.)

The length of this list is remarkable. When practiced with fidelity—and few practitioners in the 1950s attempted to bend its formidable rules—the sestina must be counted as among the most unforgiving of verse forms. In

C. Hugh Holman's 1960 revision of William Flint Thrall and Addison Hubbard's *A Handbook to Literature,* it is helpfully described in the terms of a do-it-yourself kit that any hard-working poet could assemble:

> Sestina: One of the most difficult and complex of the various French lyrical forms. The *sestina* is a poem consisting of six six-line STANZAS and a three-line ENVOY. It makes no use of the REFRAIN. This form is usually unrimed, the effect of RIME being taken over by a fixed pattern of end-words which demands that these end-words in each STANZA be the same, though arranged in a different sequence each time. If we take 1–2–3–4–5–6 to represent the end-words of the first STANZA, then the first line of the second STANZA must end with 6 (the last end-word used in the preceding STANZA), and the second with 1, the third with 5, the fourth with 2, the fifth with 4, the sixth with 3—and so to the next STANZA. The order of the first three STANZAS, for instance, would be 1–2–3–4–5–6; 6–1–5–2–4–3; 3–6–4–1–2–5. The conclusion, or ENVOY, of three lines must use as end-words 5–3–1, these being the final end-words in the same sequence, of the sixth STANZA. But the poet must exercise even greater ingenuity than all this since buried in each line of the ENVOY must appear the other three end-words, 2–4–6. Thus so highly artificial a pattern affords a form which, for most poets, can never prove anything more than a poetic exercise. Yet it has been practiced with success in English by Swinburne, Kipling, and Auden. (452–53)

Virtually all 1950s sestinas honored these requirements, and when poets deviated from them, it was to submit to variations even more rigorous.[2] Such obedience was not the practice of previous generations of poets. To the first generation of modernists and their immediate successors, the sestina was one more convention that could only be improved with tinkering. Pound in 1908, Louis Zukofsky in 1938, Eliot and Jarrell in 1942, Auden in 1944, Nemerov in 1947, and Blackmur in 1951 all published poems that reworked the options of the sestina. Some adjustments were as small as Pound excluding two end-words from the envoy of "Sestina: Altaforte," others as large as the six-page verse interpretation that Zukofsky appended to "Mantis." But what these versions had in common was that none of these poets felt obligated to the form. Eliot's quasi-sestina in the second movement of "The Dry Salvages" uses a phoneme as an end-word. Presenting "-ailing" as one of its monorhymes roughens the form considerably, so that in this portion of *Four Quartets* when Eliot writes of the ocean what is heard is not an identifiable word so much as an elusive sound. Although Auden in the 1930s completed two sestinas that met all requirements, the sequence of four in *For the Time Being* (1944) use a novel word order that, in Harvey Gross's words, "mutes the insistence of the end-words and allows a greater syntactical freedom" (255). (Auden used a still different rotation of word order for Sebastien's speech, a sestina in his 1945 poem, *The Sea and the Mirror*.) Blackmur never rotated his six end-words in "Mr. Virtue and the Three Bears," and Nemerov's 1948 "Sestina II" deliberately omits its final half-strophe, truncating the ending at the moment the speaker of the poem threatens to disappear. Jarrell's dramatic monologue "The Refugees" (*Complete* 370–71) breaks off after only four stanzas, its life interrupted like that of its subjects. In fact, so extreme are some of these modifications (Eliot and Jarrell especially come to mind) that to label the final product a sestina may be a misnomer. But the point remains: for Eliot and company, some occasions called for a form *resembling* the sestina. However, for the majority of poets in the 1950s, the sestina was an occasion on its own. Its challenging rules were to be embraced, not evaded. James Merrill provides a striking example of how attitudes toward the form tightened in the 1950s. In Merrill's first published appearance in *Poetry* in 1946 (at a precocious nineteen) he led off with a sestina, "Perspectives of the Lonesome Eye," in which, in Audenesque fashion, the end-words cycled through an unconventional rotation. Honored then was the spirit not the letter of the law. But a few years later, when crafting his one-act play *The Bait* (first performed in May 1953), Merrill cast the words of his central character, when he appears on stage solo at a climactic moment, as a sestina. The speech stands out as the only formal device embedded within a play that is sometimes in prose, sometimes in blank verse. And here Merrill follows the rules of the form to a T.

The Sestina as Shop Talk

If sestinas in the 1950s were as common as UFOs, in the years to follow they vanished no less completely. What made them once so in vogue? The least controversial answer is that in an era of labor-intensive poetry, that form which requires a heavy investment in labor is bound to be in ascendance. Auden alluded to the form as a benchmark, explaining in his 1956 inaugural lecture as Oxford Professor of Poetry, that while he had no touchstone for judging poets, he had a number of them for gauging the aptitude of critics, and the third on the list of questions to which the good critic must unhesitantly answer "yes" was: "Do you like, and I mean really like . . . [c]omplicated verse forms of great difficulty, such as Englyns, Drott-Kvaetts,

Sestinas, even if their content is trivial?" ("Making" 40). On this occasion, Auden also suggested that recognizing "difficulty" in poetic forms was a way of acknowledging that poetry had a lengthy and distinguished lineage. Versifying is among the oldest of skills, and it has evolved over centuries, an ancient guild. In a time of professionalization, his remarks position the poet nicely: the poet that Auden will admire is not the short view specialist and certainly not an amateur who versifies on weekends. No breezy practitioner of free verse, Auden's poet displays poetry's deep heritage through a brisk familiarity with traditional verse forms.

Of course a form that lends itself so quickly to elaborate rhetorical strategies also threatens to collapse into a specialist's discourse, a matter of pleasing the guild's membership. James E. B. Breslin was objecting to that guild mentality when, writing in 1984, he proposed a modification in William Carlos Williams's observation that the 1950s was an "age of sonnets": "Williams might have been a little more accurate had he declared it the age of the sestina—and other such intricate forms that come to the reader marked as difficult and artificial" (38). For Breslin, "stable traditional forms" discourage individual initiative; their rules are shelters that trap. "Inherited forms," he maintains, "aligned beginning poets not with any specific and therefore threatening authority but with a diffused idea of authority" (26). But if the sestina's laws discourage deviation from them (and, in a somewhat simple sense, thereby render poets docile), those same laws can be seen to be erecting barriers behind which poets are able to converse freely about their art. Indeed, John Hollander in 1981 defined the sestina as "the ideal generic example of a scheme to be allegorized in the unfolding" (*Rhyme's* 108). Hollander limits himself to describing only those sestinas that, as they unfold, also describe (and in his examples actively deplore) the features of the form that is the sestina. His examples restrict the form to clever gestures, as in fact Hollander's own 1958 contribution did, a playful dirge in which the longevity of winter in Bloomington, Indiana, sanctions a text that also proceeds in extreme slow motion. The joke sestinas that Hollander cites (in fact, he does not cite his own) are instances in which the form is appropriated for behind-the-scenes shoptalk. Alan Ansen's 1961 "A Fit of Something against Something" is a tour de force in which the length of the lines in each stanza shrink as the poem grinds on, as if enacting the down-the-funnel inevitability of the form. But Ansen also wants to conceive of a curse that will banish the sestina, so this literal shrinkage is the sign of a task being accomplished. At the end, the half-strophe is down to only the six end-words, two to a line: Sestina, order, austere, master, be, gone (42). And Donald Hall's "Sestina" which begins "Hang it all, Ezra Pound, there is only the one sestina" (*Dark* 47) revisiting Pound's address in Canto II ("Hang it all, Robert Browning, / There can be but the one 'Sordello'"), in turn gave rise to Robert Vaughn's "A Sestina on Ezra Pound" in the Autumn 1958 *Western Review* which begins by misquoting Hall: "Hang it all, Ezra Pound, there is only one sestina" (62). All too often, it seems that one sestina is responsible for another, and poets are drawn in so deeply that they construct even more hermetic versions of the sestina, such as Robert Stock's, entitled "That the Sestina Is What It Is Despite What It Is Not."[3]

In Sylvia Plath's 1958 sestina, however, this shoptalk about the artist's role is undertaken, with the virtuoso ambition that is Plath's signature, through references to the visual arts. The poem takes off from Henri Rousseau's "The Dream," a painting that discovers the woman of the title, Yadwigha, on a red couch that is apparently located in the midst of an impossibly lush jungle. As Plath's individual stanzas force a return to the same setting, each explains this artwork from a new angle. First the painting is described in a manner that will please "literalists." In the next stanza the painting is described anew when "consistent critics" demand an explanation for a red couch. This leads to a third description with Rousseau himself offering an unconvincingly ordinary explanation (he says the woman in the painting, Yadwigha, fell asleep and dreamed the jungle) which in turn leads to a fourth description as critics gather to launch their own official explanation. Finally, in the last description Rousseau confides to a "friend, in private" that his eye was "so possessed by the glowing red" of the couch upon which Yadwigha sat that he was compelled to paint her there "To feed the eye with red: such red! Under the moon, / In the midst of all that green and those great lilies!" (*Collected* 85).

If the audience for art prods and pokes, intrusively and untrustworthily, peskily hankering after explanations, the artwork itself remains above the reductive narratives that swirl around it, an object endlessly manifold, unfathomable, provocative, as if the talk which it generates bears it along but never touches it. Explaining is at odds with the free spirit which the artist needs to make art. Flashes of the magisterial power of that art, as well as the artist's struggle to manage it, dart out in the recurrence of "red" in every stanza (and twice in the half-strophe). For Plath, "red" is an unofficial seventh word that not only circulates with and among the six end-words but actively pairs up against one of the official end-words in a passage that recalls Stevens:

> But the couch
> Stood stubborn in its jungle: red against green,
>
> Red against fifty variants of green,
> The couch glared out at the prosaic eye. (*Collected* 86)

The "prosaic eye" may be art's enemy, but it is too bland, too trivial to do any harm. What will prevail is the (irrational) passion that underlies art, the red that stands against green, "against fifty variants of green." Indeed, Yadwigha, the indirect subject of Rousseau's passion to make art—who was addressed at the beginning of the poem then set aside—is addressed again at the end. Her name in all its extravagant unpronounceability opens the half-strophe.

Throughout her sestina, Plath is half-concealing a theme that relates the irrational powers of art. Most people, the poem maintains, aren't ready for art, or at least are unprepared to entertain its uncertainties. People prefer explanations to questions, narratives to fragments. But even the artist himself is capable of forgetting just what it was all about. Outside of the actual moment of making of art, the artist is just an ordinary observer. But inside the moment of the making, the artist is powerful, extraordinary, superhuman. The sestina duplicates both ordinary and extraordinary as it modulates through its compartmentalized stanzas but then constantly unbalances each one with the intrusion of "red," a word both proper and improper (rather like the painting itself with its couch and jungle and very much like the art itself for which the painting is a metonym): a seventh word that recurs outside the official form. "Red" here, though, is signed as a trace of the abundance of something that is called, helplessly, the artist's spirit or the fount of creativity—a force that eludes a satisfactory label but that artists recognize as the power behind the making of the work of art. The insistent reappearance of "red" in its floating position asserts this artistic freedom that is always present but continually escapes explanation.

The Sestina as Intimate Message

Sestinas that are merely about the practice of writing the sestina are diminished things next to Plath's use of the rule-driven sestina to present a theory of art as rule-breaking. Few poets were capable of managing a compromise at Plath's level of elegance, a solution that complies with the form even as it overtops it. Not Plath's unpublished poem but Donald Justice's 1957 example, "Sestina on Six Words by Weldon Kees," better defends the sestina as serious talk between artists. Justice underscores the communal aspect of sestina-making, that it is an event first reserved for poets, whose ability to traverse this field qualifies as a rite of passage. As his title states, he will produce a sestina that, in its appropriations of the end-words from the sestina of another poet, will continue the tradition of sestina-making. But Justice further underscores the sheer difficulty of that tradition by accepting strictures that another poet has previously borne rather than selecting end-words that might be congenial to his own temperament. Finally, he both complicates and personalizes this gesture by writing a response to Kees's sestina that recognizes it as a cry for help that requires a sympathetic response. As Robert Stock has remarked, Kees's sestina "reads like program notes for a disappearance" (190). When read alongside Justice's response, it almost becomes that suicide note that Kees never did leave when he disappeared in 1955.[4] This is elaborate recasting indeed, and talk among poets of a high order, all the more extraordinary for the sensitivity with which a very youthful Justice (a recent graduate of the Iowa Writers' Workshop) works his multiple transformations.

To an extent startling even for Kees, his "Sestina: Travel Notes" (collected in *The Fall of the Magicians,* 1948) is sullen, reluctant, and withdrawn at its close. Justice, in his 1960 preface to Kees's *Collected Poems,* noted that Kees's quiet voice emanates from "one of the bitterest poets in history" (vii). Traveling only exacerbated that bitterness. His "Travels in North America" implacably reveals the dead ends from one end of the nation to the next: "The stars near Santa Fe are blurred and old, discolored / By a milky haze . . . Autumn light / Falls softly on a file of candy skulls" (115). The sensitive phrasing we begin by admiring peels back like a bandage covering a bruise and reveals itself as the soft spot of our decay. That we so often pretend otherwise is one source of Kees's smoldering mixture of rage and dismay. "Sestina: Travel Notes" explores once again our moral failure, a failure whose pervasiveness the sestina form helps make relentless.

Kees opens with an innocent sketch of people ritually bidding one another farewell, going off into the night as if at the close of a party. The facile aspect of this leave-taking becomes a target: "we all are harmed / By the indifference of others," he writes, adding later that "We are concerned with that destructive silence / Impending in the dark, that never harms / Us till it strikes" (63). This by way of analysis and right thoughts, but how to implement them? "We must chart routes that ease the voyage / Clear passageways and lift the burden. // But where are routes? Who names the burden? / The night is gifted with a devious silence" (63). As thoughts grow more tangled, the poem moves toward its dissatisfied ending:

You knew before the fear of the voyage,
You saw before the hands that warned away,
You heard before the voices trained to harm
Listeners grown weak through loss and burdens
Even in city streets at noon that silence
Waited for you, but not, you thought, for others.

Storms will break silence. Seize on harm,
Play idiot or seer to others, make the burden
Theirs, though no voyage is, no tunnel, door, nor way. (64)

Kees's voice, often tinged with anger or muted with despair, seems untypically distraught in these final lines. To make others aware of the "burden" that is carried will provide no relief to the "you" who is addressed so self-accusingly, nor will the assumption of responsibility either by others or by the speaker thereby create an opportunity or any passage to a future. The list that brokenly closes the poem ("You knew . . . You saw . . . You heard") represents one outlet after another implacably closing.

Kees uses the permutations of the sestina form to dramatize a situation so hopeless it makes withdrawal prudent. Justice answers, using Kees's same six end-words, but to insist that matters can change, that Kees is wrong in his harsh self-judgment, and that he injures only himself with his conclusions. The end-words as Justice recycles them underscore the darkness in Kees's thoughts: others, voyage, silence, away (or a way), burden, and harm. To recycle them, to accept the burden of using just those end-words, is Justice's first act of sympathy, an act that places him alongside another's viewpoint. The poem that follows is not, however, a direct reply to Kees as much as a poem that unfolds in a time running parallel to Kees's own. Justice conceives what those others in Kees's poem might be thinking. And their thinking is directed toward the person who is, to them, one of the others, Kees himself. Justice's poem, that is, lends itself to being considered as the thoughts of those whom Kees had placed at the edge of his poem, at a distrustful arm's length. His poem, then, works to include Kees within it, as it explains how others might have seen Kees by generalizing about those who, like Kees, made themselves appear to be unapproachable, resisting conversation, or even abruptly turning away, ultimately to stand by themselves alongside the rail of the boat, not speaking. But Justice also understands how the Kees-surrogates that he has placed in his sestina are likely to be even further alienated by the awareness that they are being looked toward expectantly. Justice's poem not only reconstructs the scene of Kees's sestina, and even appears to speak from within it in the voice of those whom Kees saw from a distance as "the others," but it also offers to read with sympathy the figure of Kees, standing as the outsider to his own poem (but brought inside in Justice's poem).

The speaker in Justice's poem attains a breadth of understanding which allows for a moment of crystal clarity: "Each is alone, each with his burden. / To others, always, they are others. / And they can never break the silence" (*Summer* 14). These declarative sentences that produce home truths attain their haunting lucidity through their allusions to the circumstances of Kees and Justice, of one poet writing to another through the medium of the poem—an event that turns poignant once, as it turns out, one of these poets is most likely beyond any hearing. Of course others will always be other, each person will remain opaque to another person, and the silence cannot be broken. And yet for that silence to endure is too painful for Justice. His final lines extend themselves furthest to Kees, even as they are spoken with an awareness of how ideal they in truth are: "There is no way to ease the burden. / The voyage leads on from harm to harm, / A land of others and of silence" (15). The country that is "not like the others" is not to be found in this world. Justice's final half-strophe is not just a conclusive grouping of summary thoughts: it is his own anguished response to the reality that Kees has insisted upon. The poem closes on a land of distant others now silent, articulating with disturbing prescience the fate of Kees. How is it possible at this point not to think of all the poets who decided to cut short their lives, who became the "others" in the distance, and whose voices no longer speak?

Justice's use of the sestina, though rigorously obeying its formal rules, brandishes no message about discipline, self- or otherwise. Rather, it redefines the poetic tradition, presenting it as something other than an opportunity to display oneself as a competitor to other poets, all of whom are striving to outdo each other. Justice recognizes that the site of the sestina has become an area privileged by poets, colonized by them as a space in which they can speak with a freedom and even a sense of play not elsewhere sanctioned. But he then turns to redefine that space anew, taking advantage of the open line that it symbolizes to other poets, to speak directly about an issue of sensitivity that many poets will share. It is even possible to consider Justice's message a warning about the professional dangers of writing poetry—the anguish, the engagement, the isolation of the poet and the injuries that may follow. In any case, his poem may be a benchmark example of the sestina used as a medium by which poets pass messages that are special to themselves but that others might overhear.

The Sestina as Psychoanalytic Tool

Not all sestinas, however, understand their form to be so thoughtfully supportive. Leslie Fiedler, in an article well-placed for maximum visibility (it appeared in the *Kenyon Review* in 1956) maintained that the sestina's authority depended on its ability to extract from the poet submission to a design that is irrevocable. Fiedler scorned those poets who so misunderstood the opportune obligations of the sestina form that they sought to disguise the rigorous burden they carried. "It is only too easy to make the sestina an embodiment of ingenuity rather than necessity," he wrote, "to give the impression that the word at each line is sought and prepared for, a prize rather than a trap" (242). Such a turn toward the end-word as if it were the surprisingly apt choice produced verse writing that was no better than distraction. It was an attempt to ignore that "the sestina is presided over by a kind of cold mathematics that functions like fate" (241). For Fiedler, the poet of the sestina cannot elude that design but must submit:

> the successful sestina must make it seem that each monorhyme is seven times fled and seven times submitted to; that the poet is ridden by a passion which forces him back on the six obsessive words, turn and twist as he may. . . . Finally, in the *commiato,* there must be the sense (and this only Dante eminently maintained) that the key words have managed at last not merely to utter themselves once more, but to achieve their fated relationship, which the poet has desperately evaded through six stanzas. This means that the fulfillment of the *commiato* is likely to be a reversal, to stand in the same relationship to the rest of the poem, as the concluding couplet of a Shakespearean sonnet to the first twelve lines. (242)

Fiedler's intensely active version of the sestina holds out promise in its "reversal" of a temporary resolution or rest in the half-strophe of the envoy.

Certainly the sestina written during this time that has become most well known, Elizabeth Bishop's "Sestina" (first published in the *New Yorker* in 1956), accords with the warnings in Fiedler's essay, displaying the sestina not only as a form of discipline (Fiedler would approve) but as a deliberate example of the evasiveness that the form also encourages (as Fiedler notes with disapproval). Bishop's poem recalls a childhood moment in which she is drawing in a kitchen with her grandmother; the absence of her mother and father, while never openly remarked upon, is everywhere present. Or more accurately, the inability to address that absence, along with the weight it places upon a young child and that child's efforts to distract her-

self from the burden, are what the poem enacts through a form whose recurring end-words keep circling about a scene. One of a number of poems
about her childhood that Bishop began after *A Cold Spring* appeared in
1955, it was originally called "Early Sorrow," according to Brett C. Millier
(267), and "tears" is the notable end-word, Helen Vendler was first to remark, that is so unlike the others (house, grandmother, child, stove, almanac). The poem is about that unlikeness and its uneasy assimilation. Tears
in this poem can be found almost anywhere but on someone's face. The
rain beats "equinoctial tears" on the roof, the hot teakettle sputters and
"small hard tears / Dance like mad on the hot black stove," and Bishop as a
child draws a house and "Puts in a man with buttons like tears." While real
tears go unshed, their displacements emerge everywhere. It is not so much
that emotions are suppressed in this household as they are dispersed. Since
they appear in unexpected places, only a form like the sestina, which remorselessly resists the desire to move elsewhere, could so well depict what
is simultaneously covert and manifest. The very round-robin simplicity of
the form, its stubbornly mechanical trappings, is also associated with childhood—not childhood's simplicity as much as the child's inadequate ability to deal with stress except in ways that are intuitively wise. The sestina
can be a form whose immutable reprisals both dilute and intensify. Is the
power of Bishop's sestina, then, evident in the concluding half-strophe?
"*Time to plant tears,* says the almanac. / The grandmother sings to the marvelous stove / and the child draws another inscrutable house" (*Complete*
123). Hearing this ending, Vendler cried out in her essay that if anything
should *not* be inscrutable it is one's own house. "The voice speaking the last
three lines dispassionately records the coincident pressure of grief, song,
necessity and the marvelous; but in spite of the 'equal' placing of the last
three lines, the ultimate weight on inscrutability, even in the heart of the
domestic, draws this poem into the orbit of the strange" (98–99). Reading
Bishop's "First Death in Nova Scotia," Vendler saw Bishop undertaking a
similar move, structuring that poem through the eyes of the dazed child
trying to understand death: "The frightened child makes up three helpless
fictions, trying to unite the items of the scene into a gestalt" (96–97). An
element of the helpless and incomprehensible must remain as the defining
residue in both poems. The harrowing, heartbreaking quality of both stems
from witnessing the child's efforts to understand what no one can understand. Bishop's "Sestina" allows for that blankness to be inscribed directly
into the poem by according "inscrutable" so central a place in the concentrated moment of the half-strophe.

Addicts who seek to cure themselves, sociologist Jon Elster has noted, sometimes choose to "bind" or "pre-commit" themselves ahead of time to restrictions designed as curtailments, as Ulysses did by attaching himself to the mast when he knew he could not resist the sirens. When Bishop submits to the sestina she is in effect precommitting herself to a regimen that will deliver her back, and then back again and again for six times to revisit a scene that painfully portrays her own inadequate compensations for her absent parents. At the same time, however, it discloses that which she may not have seen so clearly as a child: the genuine (though helpless) love of her grandmother for her granddaughter. The scene that is reconstructed, then, is such an unlikely but inevitable mix of pain and joy that it seems plausible that it might have been delivered through some impersonal mechanism or system that checked interference with the flow of memory.

Bishop's sestina thus recalls John Ashbery's description of the form as one of those "devices for getting into remoter areas of consciousness": "The really bizarre requirements of a sestina I use as a probing tool rather than as a form in the traditional sense. I once told somebody that writing a sestina was rather like riding downhill on a bicycle and having the pedals push your feet. I wanted my feet to be pushed into places they wouldn't normally have taken" ("Craft" 124). As David Lehman has remarked, Ashbery's "analogy makes the whole procedure sound exhilarating, risky, and somewhat foolhardy, making it irresistible" (26) Ashbery, of course, is the last poet who needs encouragement to enter unexpected areas. But his formulation of the sestina as a device that propels the poet into territory from which, once committed, it is impossible to withdraw, radically recasts the form as a powerful hermeneutic in a way that James Merrill has honored. By positioning the sestina at a crucial turning point in *The Bait,* Merrill promotes it as a mechanism that can focus its speaker steadily on a task that he cannot escape from, even though he may wish to. Merrill's obedience, moreover, illustrates how the demands of the sestina, far from simply encouraging evasive tactics, can operate corrosively, as a crucial turning-point device that serves to focus its speaker steadily on a task that he cannot escape from, even though he may wish to. One of the play's central characters, Charles, has submitted to being dropped overboard attached to a fishing pole in a harness as if he were, for a moment, a kind of bait for the deep-sea monsters off the coast of Florida where he is fishing with his bored and indifferent wife and her arch and malicious brother. In the speech that represents Charles's thoughts as he is overboard and struggling to remain afloat, Merrill employs the sestina as a guarantee that this moment of self-reflection must play itself out. Duration, then, figures in Merrill's choice—to run through a sestina demands a certain amount of time, just as Charles submits to being overboard for a full ten minutes—but what Charles's long moment alone with himself is designed to produce is a sharply refocused perspective on his own life. It concludes:

> Innocent visions are those that proceed from self.
> Dolphin, medusa, hammerhead shark, starfish
> Shall look at me henceforth with Julie's eyes,
> Telling me ever and over to give my life
> Up to those eyes, sink, as I do through water,
> Towards the dark love children would call pain.
>
> Julie! This pain is sweet as loss of self.
> Draw me from water, leave me to the fish—
> You cannot save my life. I have seen your eyes. (*Bait* 92)

Merrill's choice of end-words (pain, self, water, fish, life, eyes) dictates a turn toward the reflective that will occur as a result of this test (water, fish) and be intensely personal (self, eyes) even as it promises disruption (life, pain). For Merrill, precommitting to a sestina with such an array of end-words is itself the equivalent of a rigorous test that will issue in new self-awareness. Without the sestina's forceful confrontations the equivalence of the descent into water with the descent into self would be an inanimate metaphor.

Merrill, of course, is always so much a master of disguises, of masks that reveal and conceal, of passages that lead only to whispered suggestions, that his uncollected sestinas like this one seem no more or less revelatory than any of his other texts. The self-awareness he dramatizes may just as well belong to someone else. But like the psychoanalysis to which he had just submitted before writing his play, as he explained in his 1993 autobiographical fragment *A Different Person,* the sestina that he envisions progressively strips away illusions by preventing its speaker from eluding concepts that are pivotal (252–53). A no less convincing example that a sestina equipped with trenchant end-words acquires a power of disclosure that can be profoundly disturbing is Isabella Gardner's "Sestina," a poem that she herself left uncollected until 1980 (when it was reprinted as "The Music Room" in her *New and Selected Poems*) even though it had appeared in the prestigious *Kenyon Review.* But the withholding of this poem from her collections is only the simplest of a series of denials and suppressions that the poem itself generates. In "Sestina" Gardner revisits a physical site, a location in her childhood home that is crisscrossed with negative memories. What those memories are, however, the poem refuses to disclose, even as it circles around them. After its six stanzas of describing the furniture in a music room with french doors and a cedar closet where a piano in a corner is set next to plants, she concludes her poem with this half-stanza: "Drained child, child still, you are buried in this room, / Embalmed like the plants, hanging in the closet, / Mute in hate as the piano, and deformed" ("Sestina" 613). It is by any standard an extraordinary ending. Although the poet is apparently speaking, she insists she is mute, and links her silencing to rage. She is more corpselike than living. She insists time has not elapsed meaningfully. She is a "Drained child, child still." That so much dissatisfaction surrounds the ending is in accord with Gardner's distinct unease throughout. As much is blocked in this poem as is manifest. Descriptive passages begin straightforwardly only to erupt into flourishes of rhetoric. By breaking into the elaborately figurative, syntax breaks down. Although the poem begins quite clearly, it soon burgeons into a thick tangle of virulent adjectives:

> You must never unlock the cedar closet;
> Nor open the white doors to the music room
> To be stared at by the french windows and drained
> Flabby by the sucking mouths of pastel plants
> Unseasonably bred, denatured, deformed.
> There in the corner crouches the piano
>
> That vibrates pianissimo piano
> And crescendos con amore in the closet
> of your mind . . . ("Sestina" 613)

The sixth line emerges into crisp focus, especially striking after the thicket of lines 4 and 5, but thereafter we tumble headlong into phrases that are outside English. The Italian phrases of course originate in musical instructions that are in one sense appropriate to the piece, but in another sense they are a group of sounds that purposely elude meaning. These shifts would seem to require some explanation, but the poem continues to circle around its subject in a descriptive rather than an explanatory mode. It soon loses even its fragile claim on the descriptive. At one point syntax breaks down entirely, in a shift that ends the third stanza in a hopeless tangle and begins the fourth stanza as a stark disjunction:

Only camphored clothing hangs in the closet
No souvenir, no clue to another room
Paper sealed the clothes are tidily deformed.

Go away. Do you think you can be deformed
Only once in the same way, that once drained
You cannot be drier? ("Sestina" 613)

To begin a new stanza with the stark injunction "Go away" only serves to confirm how little open exchange is occurring in this poem. Indeed, the question that follows becomes a prelude to language that remains at a shrill high pitch that is finally obfuscating: "O multiply impotent is he who plants / His target heel on these thresholds so deformed / By strangled battles" ("Sestina" 613). A single exception is that startling line: "Step back. There has been blood in the music room." Syntactically clear, it could not be more semantically uninformative. Whose blood? The blood of murder? Accident? Sexual trauma? And why pose such a question in the passive voice? Gardner's sestina, drawing her into forbidden territory, also serves as a protective cloak in a region that seems strikingly traumatized. Her reach is accommodated by the sestina's form even as she herself, commanding what context will be chosen for each end-word's appearance in every line, confutes full understanding, producing the fierce stalemate with which the half-strophe locks up the poem.

The Sestina as False Front

The disturbances that are uncovered in the sestinas by Gardner, Merrill, and Bishop result from uncommon applications of the sestina form. But the sestinas that are most prevalent in the 1950s are those whose content is, in one sense, utterly trivial. Far from uncovering disturbances, these sestinas proffer their form as a cover or front that erects a fire wall or barricade behind which the poet can act in a way that is blatantly autobiographical, personal, intimate, even a bit indulgent. Subject matter in these versions of the sestina has been chosen entirely for the poet's pleasure. "Difficulty" in these sestinas resides largely in the poet's compliance with the formal rules. Once those rules are met the poet has fulfilled all demands of responsibility and is entitled to write freely and openly about material that quite possibly has little likelihood of interesting others. Yet this suspension of the pressure on mainstream poets to be responsible figures of the community, otherwise so prevalent in the 1950s, may be that which most effectively explains the sestina's popularity. The sestina, obedient to one set of traditional formalist rules, earns an exemption from other rules whose transgression would have been unlikely in this era.

These versions of the sestina at first call our attention to their formal features, often in a title that simply announces "Sestina," then strive to divert us from identifying such features. This schizophrenic division of form from content appears with startling frequency (it was, of course, what Fiedler felt had "ruined" the form). While these poems flaunt their poet's decision to take up with a form that is rigorous and punishing, they will offset that burden by, first of all, producing a work in which the end-words seem to fall effortlessly into place as if they were the inevitable choice, and second, by evoking a subject matter that openly delights the poet. Any sense of the sestina as rigorous or punishing is thoroughly and transparently transcended; these are works, then, in which poets "effortlessly" display their sheer mastery of the medium. They possess it fully, manipulating language with such dexterity that the rigid sestina melts into what is in effect just a thirty-nine-line poem whose end-words almost coincidentally fall into a certain pattern.

Robert Francis, speaking of a sestina of his own and its thirty-nine end-words, has said: "If you drape thirty-nine iron chains over your arms and shoulders and then do a dance, the whole point of the dance will be to seem light and effortless" (47). His "Hallelujah: a Sestina" (from *The Orb Weaver*, 1960) is exemplary for transforming limitations into opportunities. To naturalize the recurrence of end-words, Francis multiplies repetition throughout, repeating his end-words more than the seven times that he must, but repeating other words as well, and also foregrounding these repetitions as sheer pleasures. In some remarks on his poem's origin, Francis explained that he first decided to attempt a sestina, and only after that did the subject of the poem—his father—enter into the work ("Commentary" 48). He began by choosing that "hallelujah" would be one end-word, and that led, as he says, "to another Hebrew word, Ebenezer," also his father's name (48). Out of that conjoining came the poem. Other end-words (praise, father, boy, hair) underscore how the poem is shot through with repetition, doublings, and equivalences. Marianne Shapiro has noted that end-words in a sestina "contract special relationships among themselves, generally forming into twos or threes" (23) and Francis's end-words pair off as surrogates for each other: "Ebenezer" is "father" for Francis, and "praise" is the same as "hallelujah." But then Francis's poem operates by unfolding repetitions until they seem to be found everywhere, not merely at the end of lines:

> Daniel, a country doctor, was his *father*
> And my *father* his tenth and final *boy.*
> A *baby,* and last, he had a *baby*'s praise:
> *Red* petticoat, *red* cheeks, and crow-black hair.
>
> A *boy* has *little* to say *about* his hair
> And *little about* a name like Ebenezer . . . (47, italics mine)

In a world like that of this poem which is all pleasure, recurrence becomes
sheer joy. By scattering end-words like "father" in additional placements
outside the end of their line, he embeds recurrence as the very foundation
of significance in the poem: "Could I ever praise / My father half enough
for being a father / Who let me be myself?" It is not only end-words that
recur in close proximity: "Preacher he was with a prophet's head of hair /
And what but a prophet's name was Ebenezer . . . ?" Syntax is also repeated:
"Stone of Help is the meaning of Ebenezer. / Stone of Help—what fitter
name for my father?" All sestinas recycle; in this, Francis lets that form
guide him back to old and cherished ground. The envoy is, not surprisingly,
reluctant to let the poem end. It resists closure by calling for the poem to
continue: "Such is the old drama of boy and father. / Praise from a grayhead
now with thinning hair. / Sing Ebenezer, Robert, sing Hallelujah!" (48).
Here the sestina is not an art of constraint but of surfeit. Instead of circum-
scribing the author, it encourages an art of embellishment. If its horizontal motion forward is limited, its vertical motion downward is endless. It
is a celebration of what endures, what persists through repetitions, and as
such it also celebrates itself. The form of the sestina, enduring over the centuries, is, in this variation, a form that is designed to inscribe itself within
itself. What counts, as a result, is less the individual example of the sestina
than the fact that the sestina, by producing another individual example of
itself, remains ongoing, a living tradition.

Francis's example of the sestina sanctions the display of an aspect of a
poet's personal world or inner life at its most intensely pleasurable, as a play
among words, in an orgy of language. Nowhere else in the 1950s was it so
permissible for the poet simply to indulge in such a display of emotion
toward the very stuff of language, toward words as if they could generate
the emotional attachments one had toward people. It is the payoff for accepting the sestina's unyielding form which, once accepted, at once becomes no longer demanding but a sensuous engine that sanctions the return of words, that promises that some words will, once stated, not then
vanish. In a time when the impersonal weighs heavily as a poetic value,
there is an element of genuine release afforded when the poet is allowed

to be freely excessive and even lavish with language. Jane Cooper's "Morning on the St. John's" is virtually unparalleled in the 1950s for the lushness of its descriptions; it revels in the dawn that gathers and intensifies into a morning from her Florida childhood alongside the St. John's River. As in Francis's poem, the more recurrence the sestina demands, the more it encourages Cooper to dwell on loving details. Here is the entire poem, with its voice rising into a higher and still higher pitch, employing the exclamation point eight times (and three times in one line).

Morning on the St. John's

This is a country where there are no mountains:
At dawn the water birds like lines of rain
Rise from the penciled grasses by the river
And slantwise creak across the growing light.
The sky lifts upward and the breath of flowers
Wakes with the shadows of the waking birds.

The shadows of the birds, the dancing birds!
With so much freedom who could ask for mountains?
The heron stands here ankle-deep in flowers,
Wet hyacinths that burn more blue with rain,
And waves of smaller wings hurl wide the light
All up and down the horizontal river.

And now the sun shakes blue locks in the river
And rises dripping-headed while the birds
Go wild in curves of praise at sudden light.
The fire that would flash instantly off mountains
Bathes this round world in dew as dark as rain
And then strikes green and gold among the flowers.

The dropping heads, the smooth and shaken flowers!
(Among the grasses, blue eyes by the river,
And in the garden, fires after rain.)
Under umbrella leaves the mockingbirds
Still nestle and trill quietly of mountains,
Then whistle Light!—cadenza—Light! and Light!

While higher and higher streams the opening light,
In bluish petals as of opening flowers,
More pure than snow at dawn among the mountains,
Paler than any flush along the river,
Beyond the reach of eyefall flight of birds,
It floods a sky swept innocent by rain.

The assault of sun, the long assault of rain—
Look how our darkness is made true by light!
Look how our silence is confirmed by birds!
The mind that pastured ankle-deep in flowers
Last night, must wake to sunrise on the river,
Graze wide and then grow vertical as mountains;

For even a glimpse of mountains fogged with rain
Or mirrored in a river brings delight
And shakes a man as dawn shakes birds and flowers. (*Weather* 13–14)

Exclamation points presume not just excitement but surprise. As control slips away, pronunciation rises in pitch. (This collected text differs from its 1957 *New Yorker* publication in a few alterations, one of which is that an exclamation point, originally in the ninth line from the end, has been replaced by a dash.) In one sense, the poem is nothing if not chaste, even pristine in its devotion to the natural world and its descriptions. But in another sense, the poem is astoundingly sensuous, its natural life interpenetrating itself effortlessly, delightfully. Bodies blend or fuse into a world that is itself all embodiment; light is felt with an intensity like that of touch. More than simple synesthesia is expressed in the excess of "whistle Light!—cadenza—Light! and Light!"—though this interplay in which sound is visual and the seen is heard helps explain why the poem can be at once densely interwoven and weightlessly evanescent. While such a line is obviously excessive, its repetitions minimize its extremity. As the words repeat themselves, it is as if the line is spilling over. What might have been excessive becomes, instead, an enactment of abundance.

Cooper's end-words seem to be surprising choices, they are so generalized and nominalized: mountains, rivers, rain, light, flower, bird. Their very generality, however, encourages a kind of comporting among themselves, as if they were comparable. Shapiro's observation that end-words pair off is true for this group, but they can be paired in a variety of ways. Mountains pair with rivers as opposites, but rivers and rain pair as cause and effect. Rain and light pair as opposites, but rain and flower pair as cause and effect. Here is one source, then, of the richness within Cooper's scenes, and another basis for the interplay that makes all so kinetic, even as the simplicity of the diction assures that the description of any particular moment will be thoroughly accessible. Of course the most important element in the poem, and the ground for its ability to be both powerfully emotional and remarkably pure is that it is a representation of the workings of memory. Returning in the mind to so cherished a site, the poet cannot resist circling about and around, invoking a dreamy and cyclic pool of phrases and words such as "dawn," "blue," "fire/fires," all of which recur three or more times. When this sestina is relocated as the opening poem to Cooper's 1968 sequence of family recollections, "The Weather of Six Mornings," its allegiance to a topography of memory is even further clarified, and its evocations clearly tilt toward richness.

Although few sestinas rise to the sumptuous and luxurious extravagance that Cooper sustains so remarkably, a surprising number aim in a similar direction. They are, that is, most interested in a display of expressiveness and the words that will return again and again are regarded as friendly aids to such a display. Richmond Lattimore's "Sestina for a Far-Off Summer" seeks to recall in lavish detail moments from a summer in his childhood. Fairfield Porter's "The Island in the Evening" is nothing more but nothing less than a remarkably placid description of children playing on paths near water as evening comes on. A companion sestina, "Great Spruce Head," is a lushly descriptive portrait of a Maine landscape. Here the sestina has become a miniature machine for generating poetic pleasure. If the poet has centered on a scene that longs to be dwelt upon, then the series of returns that are the requirements of the sestina are profoundly welcome. The end-words demand that the poet return again and again to this site of pleasure. And at the same time, the site of pleasure is essentially becoming no longer simply the landscape or moment recollected from memory: it is being supplanted by the recurrence of the words, by the pattern that is forming as language surrounds the poet, being knitted into an artifice that is at once sensual and personal.

Reading such deeply private recollections that form the core subject matter of so many sestinas also recalls that the conventions of 1950s poetry rarely encouraged and tacitly prohibited verse as an extended expression of pleasure; just as rare and no less controversial was the example of the poem as lavish memoir. For some poets, the sestina could become that corner where relief could be obtained from the relentless charge to produce texts that demonstrated civic competency. The sestina allowed the poet to have a life offstage and it opened that life to poetry. It also allowed the poet to acknowledge, and even to demonstrate, that the calling to the life of poetry had something to do with a love of language, with the sheer musicality that words always possess.

The troubling side to such an observation, to be sure, is that the sestina which places at its center the personal memoir or the lavish revery is also inclined to suppress the disjunction between the impersonality of its form and the sensuality of its content. What does it say about the circumstances under which this poetry has been produced when the poet of the sestina sets out to disguise the fact that the celebratory recollection or the revery on an intimate landscape is taking place only under rigorously controlled conditions? The form of the sestina is not supposed to intrude, it is supposed to be invisible, which is also why both Francis and Cooper include repeated phrases and words at various points in their text. As sestinas that pretend to be driven not by their form but by recollecting the poet's father or a river landscape from youth, their relationship to their readers is at some fundamental level deceptive, a matter of strategies of distraction and manipulation. All formal poetry, to be sure, gestures toward spontaneity, as if it sought to include within it even the reader's fresh surprise at its first unfolding. In one sense, the sestina is the ultimate test of how well a poet can write a formal poem whose formal features are not obtrusive. But the deception required for the sestina's form to be suppressed calls for measures most extreme. The willingness of poets to fall into complicity with such accommodations suggests there was a time when secrecy was not a disvalue but an acceptable procedure, especially if its end result could be justified by establishing an intimate space for the individual. Sestinas may flourish, then, in direct proportion to the unease poets feel when it comes to speaking freely about themselves in poetry that is personally meaningful to their private lives. Certainly the model of civic virtue in Ciardi's *Mid-Century American Poets* seems remote indeed from the secretive intricacies of these privately sheltering sestinas. Rather than representing a moment in the 1950s when a striking number of poets revealed their strong attachment to the discipline of working within a fixed form, the prevalence of the sestina may instead be the register of a deeper disturbance and a mark of a disjunction that exists not only between content and form but also between psyche and persona, between the individual self and the communal subject.

7 POEMS ABOUT THE BOMB: *NOIR* POETICS

*The whole country was lighted by a searing light with the intensity
many times that of the midday sun. It was golden, purple, violet,
gray and blue. It lighted every peak, crevasse and ridge of the
nearby mountain range with a clarity and beauty that cannot be
described but must be seen to be imagined. It was that beauty the
great poets dream about but describe most poorly and inadequately.*

—Brigadier General Thomas F. Farrell, witnessing the test
   of the first atomic bomb in 1945

*The supreme political fact of our lives is the atomic bomb. Am I
wrong? It is enormous; it occupies the whole world. It is not only
what it is but also the concentrated symbol of all hatred and injustice in every social and economic sphere. Speaking for myself, I have
lived in fear of it for fifteen years, fear it will go off, one way or another, and kill me and my family, or render our lives so intolerable
that we won't wish to go on. Maybe I am more timorous than most
people; I believe there are actually some Americans who never think
about the bomb. But poets? That would be incredible. No matter
how hard they try they cannot escape being included among
society's most percipient members. Yet if one were to judge by their
output one would have to believe poets are the least concerned
people in the world, not only on their own account but everyone's.*

—Hayden Carruth, "Poets without Prophecy" (1961)

Where *are* the poems about the Bomb that were written in its aftermath? In pursuit of an answer, Carruth set himself to read all the issues
published in 1961 of *Poetry: A Magazine of Verse* (335 poems by 139 poets).
He uncovered "two explicit references to the bomb, one a passing seriocomic remark" ("Poets without Prophecy" 356). His grim conclusion was

that contemporary poets could only be described as "hermits, lone wolves, acolytes—building poems in the wilderness for their own salvation" (356). Although Carruth did not mention it, he was himself briefly the editor of *Poetry* for ten issues between 1949 and 1950. During his tenure the magazine's track record was no more illustrious, publishing just two poems with "explicit references to the bomb," and just as in 1961, one of these was no more than a passing remark. In the June 1949 issue, H. L. Sutton began "News Item," a poem mourning a boy who had killed himself, with this allusion to modern times: "Deep in the third year of the Atomic Age / a boy has hanged himself for love— / An odd, archaic way for him to die" (143). "Atomic Age" here is simply shorthand for "advanced civilization," and there is only the barest hint that Sutton might be suggesting that the civilization has invented a way to commit suicide that is far more sophisticated than death by strangulation. Carruth in 1949 must have been more gratified by the second poem, John Berryman's contribution to the January 1950 issue, "The Wholly Fail," whose title pun on "holy grail" inaugurated a whole series of wordplays designed to grate irritatingly. In the text, a Parzival-like figure "Sir Partofall, our Best" undergoes a reductive transformation to become, by the end, "Partsusall," "transfigured, white with joy" who "Smiles thro' / the blast and fiery wind spreading out from zero—" (191). The quest for knowledge pursued by this Faustian figure has terrifying ramifications, summed up in the "zero" that is the poem's last word. Berryman's disgust and terror at what scientists (and perhaps Robert Oppenheimer in particular, the intellectual figure widely associated with the Manhattan Project) have wrought is unmistakable.

Carruth's possible pleasure at Berryman's contribution was, however, not matched by Berryman himself, who left the poem uncollected. For "The Wholly Fail" to be so restricted in its circulation is especially unfortunate—indeed, it remains an orphan still, absent from his 1989 *Collected Poems, 1937–1971*[1]—for, as Carruth complained in 1963, poems of any kind by anyone about the Bomb in the years following its invention are rare enough. Their scarcity has not gone unremarked. While tracing the commitments to various kinds of political issues through the writings of several recent poets in a 1985 anthology of critical essays entitled *Poetry and Politics* (which reprints Carruth's essay), editor Richard Jones pauses to remark that "what is truly curious" is that "poets have been largely silent on a crucial issue of the second half of the twentieth century: the bomb" (15). Only in the 1980s, Jones remarks, has the Bomb "made its way into a few poems"—a fact sharply underscored by John Bradley's 1995 anthology

Atomic Ghost: Poets Respond to the Nuclear Age, in which a majority of the poems were published since 1985.[2]

Of course the 1950s seem a most unlikely place to expect poems about the Bomb.[3] Poets have testified that their own habit in that decade was to exclude not only the political but even the historical from their work. Adrienne Rich, on the occasion of republishing her earlier books of poetry in 1993, viewed the first poem in *A Change of World* (1951) as a tissue of vacancies, a field of absences: "Nothing in the scene of this poem suggests that it was written in the early days of the Cold War, within a twenty year old's earshot of World War II, at the end of the decade of the Warsaw Ghetto and Auschwitz, Hiroshima and Nagasaki, in a climate of public fatalism about World War III" ("Introduction" xix–xx). The belief that poets of the 1950s consistently failed to address their moment in history was at the base of Donald Hall's influential 1959 critique "Ah, Love, Let Us Be True to One Another!" an essay in *American Scholar* in which he essentially repudiated the work of his own generation that he had recently helped to collect in the controversial anthology *New Poets of England and America* (1957). Rather than defending his contemporaries from disparaging reviews that accused them of slightness, he did an about-face and quite startlingly confessed: "I feel that I see a pattern among us of provinciality and evasion, which results in a reliance on the domestic at the expense of the historical" (311). To choose the domestic over the historical was to record small-time events in an American locale instead of enacting broad gestures within a vast expanse. It was to turn away from political and cultural responsibilities to withdraw into the pleasantries of a private world.

Hall's critique was a devastating blow that significantly weakened the reputation of the mainstream poets of his time and that helped prepare a positive reception for Donald M. Allen's 1960 counteranthology *The New American Poetry.* His remarks at once explained why there were no Bomb poems in the 1950s and no need to spend time looking for them. In his characterization of the poetry of his time, it would be foolish to expect any kind of involved and engaged awareness in an era which cherished the attention to local or intimate detail that the lyric could best deliver. If the lyric promoted intimacy as it gracefully unfolded within its own perfected space, it also blocked out the opportunity to include discordant voices. Intrusions were kept to a minimum in the neat, well-lighted little rooms that Hall sketched as the domestic poetry of the 1950s. What few exceptions there were could be explained away as rogue elements. Robert Frost predicted apocalypse in "Bursting Rapture" and he opened "U.S. 1946

King's X" with the provocative observation that America had "invented a new Holocaust" (both works were collected in 1947 in *Steeple Bush*), but Frost tucked both poems away in a section entitled "Editorials," among other verse whose belittlement of scientists and social planners and current foreign policy decision-makers permitted them to be bracketed as the off-shoot of the aged master at his most curmudgeonly. William Carlos Williams directly alluded to the Bomb in "Asphodel, That Greeny Flower" (first collected in his 1955 volume, *Journey to Love*):

> The bomb speaks,
> All suppressions,
> from the witchcraft trials at Salem
> to the latest
> book burnings
> are confessions
> that the bomb
> has entered our lives
> to destroy us . . . (*Breughel* 168)

But this was hardly the typical lyric of the 1950s, as Hall would have been first to point out. Williams at seventy was livelier than poets half his age. Why? Hall's answer might have been that Williams had the good fortune to mature in an era that encouraged experimentalism, thus giving him courage to undertake pioneering works like *In the American Grain,* a text that not only was decidedly historical but rethought the significance of American history. The example of Williams stood as a revealing judgment on present times. Typical of the 1950s was the fact that when a portion of "Asphodel" was excerpted for publication in the *Kenyon Review* in its Summer 1955 issue, it was book 3 that was published, in which there was no mention of the Bomb.

Just and Unjust Warfare: Civilians as Targets

Such caution was not typical of poets writing in an earlier era; it was not even typical, for that matter, of the years immediately following the Bomb's abrupt appearance. Especially quick to acknowledge its existence was the magazine *Poetry*. Jessica Nelson North's review of Ray Smith's *No Eclipse—War Poems* in the November 1945 issue began: "Written in the very dawning of the age of the atomic bomb, these poems reaffirm the spiritual values of human life" (160). This opening sentence itself reflects an awareness that the review was also written in that "very dawning," and its recognition of poetry as an art that could be timely was typical of *Poetry* in the mid-1940s. Along with Peter DeVries and Marion Strobel, North was one of an editorial committee of three who operated *Poetry* from 1942 on, after nominal editor George Dillon was drafted. The work of this group was not always appreciated (most of the female editors were displaced by males after 1945 and those who were left were summarily dismissed by Karl Shapiro when he was quickly named editor in 1950 after Carruth's termination).[4] But for the duration of the war they transformed *Poetry* into a journal proud of its ability to respond quickly to current events. Typically, titles of poems in these years linked the occasion of the poem with the progress of the war, as in Louis O. Coxe's love poem "For M.E.S. before D-Day" (September 1945 issue). Poems were laced with offhand references to sites that were known primarily from military campaigns. When Edwin Rolfe, in "Song" (December 1945 issue), mentions "the eagle view from Montserrat / west, the winding street behind the Tarragona cathedral," he addresses an audience that either knows the geography of the Spanish Civil War or understands the significance of these place-names. Randall Jarrell could count on readers to recognize the names of concentration camps when they appeared in the subtitle of "Protocols (Birkenau, Odessa)" in the June 1945 issue. Kenneth Koch's title, "Ladies for Dinner, Saipan" (October 1945 issue) contrasts the elegance of its first three words with the name of the remote military base from which the air war in the Pacific was being conducted. *Poetry*'s dedication, moreover, was not simply to chronicling wartime events. Works with a distinct political edge were also welcome. Not untypical was Winifred Cullen's "Defend Her in Time of Trouble" (July 1945 issue):

MacArthur gained—it's really odd
Four miles at Lingayen
We won at home with help of God
Four blocks against the colored men.

It's the skin that makes the difference
You are not beautiful
So we cannot ever love you
Or let you go to school.

In the Halls of Montezuma
You can do the tyrant harm
But at home the vigilantes
Will burn your daddy's barn. (195)

This depends upon a readership conditioned to recognize remote place-names even as it reveals how interest in the faraway may disguise an evasive swerve. (It also assumes a readership quick to recognize the clues that identify a voice that speaks for the African American.) At least during wartime, we are drawn into concern for "Four miles at Lingayen," though that area is fantastically remote, while we may be capable of ignoring injustice in the geography of our own locale. Cullen locates a homegrown tyranny against which no resources have been committed. Where is Lingayen and why are its four miles so important? Just where, come to think of it, *are* "the Halls of Montezuma"? In this poem, democracy's triumphs occur remotely.

Jessica Nelson North's ready engagement, then, with "the very dawning of the age of the atomic bomb" is not surprising, given a staff so willing to encourage poets to print work that conceived the poet as engaged with contemporary issues. Thus poems like Ruth Lechlitner's "Night in August" (published in the August 1946 issue but left uncollected in her 1948 volume, *A Way of Happening*) not only effortlessly invoked political concerns but proposed a contemporary emotional landscape in which the political could not be ignored. Her poem opens with a calm so profound we know it cannot last: "sitting quietly here on the green lawn last summer, / Waiting the first stars" (258). Indeed, what the "August" of her title means at the poem's opening has changed entirely by the poem's end. It is no longer a metonym for any summer; it has become a specific August, the August of 1945, forever imprinted in history. While the poem never leaves its backyard setting, and sustains an air of philosophical musing under the stars, it also steadily moves toward increasingly disturbing questions. When Lechlitner recalls the A-bomb, the tone of the poem shifts to its highest pitch: "the voice from a foreign shore / Where the grey bombers loose their metal thunder / And the split atom like a new dimension / Opens to hope— or death." After this passage, nothing in the poem remains the same. Though the poem concludes with the simplest of descriptions, not a moment escapes the oppressive weight of a new darkness that penetrates every instant. The Bomb is a "terrible mutation" that

> Moves equally in the mind, the heart, the substance and
>   the shadow;
> The hand, the chair, the meteor, the shadow—
> You in the room reading, the light a sun upon your head
> (the sun which is our life, our love, our future)
> And the child asleep upstairs in her small bed.
> And I in this August night, hear now one bird that calls
> From the black hemlock bough. And one star falls. (258)

Nothing could be simpler than this close, but as Lechlitner gathers to herself those whom she loves, it is as if she is driven to account for where they are, to enumerate with exactness their physical placement in relation to her, just because they are so endangered. They are safe, utterly safe within the walls of their home. But they are in danger as everyone now is in danger. What had once seemed permanent—the "you" sheltered in a room and surrounded by the soft light of a reading lamp (a reference that at once positions the current reader, likely to be in the same position, within the poem), the child asleep in a separate room in her own space—is now fragile, temporary, conditional, as fleeting as that bird's cry from the "black hemlock bough" or the plummet of a meteor. The sound and the sight with which the poem end have the status of a warning or omen. Both are lovely, as lovely as the portraits of her family, yet both are transient. How much else that we deem permanent is now only temporary? Lechlitner wants us to understand that the "terrible mutation" of the A-bomb refers not only to those who have suffered under its explosion but to the life around us which has permanently changed.[5]

The postwar *Poetry* was not the only forum for poems that sought to confront the new reality caused by the Bomb. Those attending the commencement ceremonies at Tufts University in Boston in 1946 would have heard, in the Phi Beta Kappa poem written and read by Dilys Bennett Laing, an extended piece in seven parts entitled "Not One Atoll" that directly confronted the Bomb. (Its title was a timely reference to the Bikini Atoll, which had just been evacuated as a site for a test explosion.) Moreover, Laing placed the ceremonial aspect of the occasion under question by writing not as a scholar or as a poet but as a woman and explicitly as a mother. Just as in Lechlitner's poem, where the extended reach of nuclear weaponry placed the family under siege, so in Laing's vision, children were set forward as the particularly helpless victims of atomic warfare. Indeed, her poem introduces the Bomb through a parental perspective:

> The atom is the smallest puppet spinning
> in the smallest slot machine. And children love
> the tale of the genii in the tiny flask
> who, once uncorked, is bigger than the world.
>
> So be it. Let them have their fairy tales.
> But when the fairy tale, blown up by Disney,
> steps off the screen and takes on weight and volume,
> and Donald Duck, the maniac, obeys
> his impulse in a world of three dimensions,

the audience leaves the seats and, running not walking,
batters itself to death against the exits.

Too late for counsel now. The nursery
Has hatched a Titan that could knock it cold. (40)[6]

What has been lost in the shifting of scenes from the Nursery to the Theater is that sense of overarching responsibility that has also been lost when the adult as caregiver yields to the politician, here impolitely configured in the cartoon version of an irresponsible hothead. This rapid transformation of the Nursery is typical of her concern. The dead at Hiroshima and Nagasaki to whom she would call attention were "Young children / blown into constellations, tiny worlds / too far and small for seeing" (41). In a later passage describing the rubble of a nuclear bomb, she envisaged survivors who would find stones and write upon them "with sharp smaller stones / poems and epitaphs and epigrams / for the dead lovers, for the murdered children, / the old people and the pets" (42). The dead to be commemorated in this next war are not soldiers but those who had formerly been regarded as "the civilian": young lovers, children, the elderly. This is in keeping with her stance throughout, which is to decry the Bomb's proliferation from a perspective established from within the family:

> This is the earth,
> my domicile, in whose domestic order
> I have a voice, small but authoritative.

> This is my father's and mother's home.
> Do it no harm. I love it. It is mine.
> I charge you not for any frivolous reason
> of curiosity or greed or fear
> to scar it anywhere. Do not hurt one island,
> no, not the littlest atoll, in the name
> of science or security. (43)

Laing's voice reverses expectations about responsibility. It is the scientists who are frivolous in their experiments, while those who can conceive earth's "domestic order" deserve to speak with authority.

Laing was not alone in her broad reaction against the Bomb. In 1945 anthologist and leftist poet Selden Rodman committed himself to writing what he would eventually call a "diary in verse." Published in 1947 as *The Amazing Year*, this group of 133 poems ranging in length from four lines to fifty-five lines was divided into four parts and covered the period from May 1, 1945, to April 30, 1946. When Rodman first learned of Hiroshima, he recorded his reaction in poems dated August 8, August 10, August 11, August 16, and August 31 that use sarcasm and irony to express outrage. They find an outlet for pain in anger, and they are sharply focused, like the entry from August 8, "Nobody Was Responsible":

> 150,000 workers with union cards filled vats in the dark.
> The voter and even the politician knew less than the curious lark.
> The brass-hats screamed at the scientists: "The long hairs have lost
> control!"
> And the scientists, being rational, left to God the concerns of the
> soul. (*Amazing Year* 28)

Underneath Rodman's scornful phrasing there remains bafflement at how so monstrous a device could have been conceived. Furthermore, the Bomb figured in one of the four photographic montages that Rodman assembled as part of his collection. Scattered through the volume, these were titled in the table of contents and linked with dates just like his poems.[7] The second of these pictorial texts, "Hearty Breakfast" (as in what the condemned man ate), is dated August 7, the day after Hiroshima. There, using words rather than pictures, Rodman evokes not only his anger but a deeper sense in which the existence of the Bomb eludes understanding. In his three other montages, visual images dominate. In one, hands hold watches and a clock is framed by bombers in silhouette hovering over a corpse, and in another, a man roughly embraces a woman who submits to him with her head held in pride. In another, entitled "Good Will toward Men" (dated December 25), Santa Clauses are multiplied indefinitely. But in the photomontage about the Bomb, "Hearty Breakfast," the visual dimension is not image-driven but centered on the verbal. In its middle are the words "Tribute" in large type followed by the phrase "to all those who helped in greatest scientific achievement of all time . . . the"—then in very large type— "ATOMIC BOMB." Withholding the visual from this one montage blocks comprehension. The words in large type substitute size and quantity for explanation. They also unfold in a steady horizontal line, unlike the odd vectors taken by all the other words, suggesting the absolute primacy of this one event. This is the new bedrock underlying experience. This reality unsettles all others, whether trivial ("Stork Visits Family of 9 in Coal Bin" reads one) or crucially important ("A United Europe" reads another). The only nonverbal sign is the dark figure looming in a corner, a cartoon entitled "Big Nations" holding a handful of cards, only one of which is show-ing: the ace of spades.

The importance that Rodman accorded the Bomb is emphasized not only here but in the final poem of the book, "Eadem Mutato Resurgo," in which his evidently affirmative ending is also darkly undercut by the cata-logue of obstacles the reader must proceed through to reach the final line. The last of four stanzas reads:

> End is mirage. Nothing that comes to birth
> Is ever lost, though hatred turn the lives
> Of flowers to poison in the boiling hives
> Along the orbit of this whirling earth.
> Babel; the rifle barrel; the bomber's torque;
> And Hiroshima in the heat of death—
> Wind back to shape in Time's revolving stalk.
> (*Amazing Year* 108)

Though "Nothing . . . Is ever lost," just how the "lost" is retrieved is left open to uncertainty: "Time's revolving stalk," after all, is nothing if not abstract. But this was a piece Rodman admired enough to choose as repre-sentative of his own work in the 1949 anthology he edited, *One Hundred Modern Poems,* an anthology whose third section ("The Age of Satire") he chose to conclude with Karl Shapiro's "The Progress of Faust," a narrative tracing the history of the paradigmatic scientist up to his most recent ap-pearance "In the American desert at war's end / Where, at his back, a dome of atoms rose" (168).

"Hiroshima," "Bikini"

One reason why poems about the Bomb could be written in the years im-mediately following the war was because poets had inherited from wartime a poetic discourse that validated engagement with current events. This also, however, explains why these poems could so easily be forgotten; they sig-naled their status as contingent speech, as words expressed in the heat of the moment, like Rodman's "diary in verse." As *Poetry* exemplified, World War II had been a chance to demonstrate that poetry did not sequester it-self in a time of crisis when strong and intense words were valued. From the earliest days of this war, from events in Spain in 1938, from the horror of the Warsaw Ghetto to the siege of Moscow, civilians were trapped in a conflict whose outcome they had no power to dispute. Poets were quick to design work that memorialized this outrage. And from there it was a short step to poetry about the Bomb for, as Laing had asserted, the Bomb expanded the scope of war beyond any reasonable boundary. In the numerous works in which poets recognized that the mark of an unjust war was the extent to which it involved the innocent a discursive foundation for anti-Bomb poetry was substantially in place.

Indeed, writers had on hand a single word, *Hiroshima,* the mere mention of which at once invoked war's tendency to victimize the innocent (as John Hershey, for one, was quick to recognize) but which could also be combined, for accusatory purposes, with other associations. This richly charged word could be used, for example, to indict inhabitants of a twenty-four-hour diner who lacked the ability or initiative to escape their shallow world. Midway through "The Iron Pastoral (All-Nite Lunchroom)" (published in *Poetry* in February 1947 and later that year in *The Iron Pastoral*) John Frederick Nims writes:

> Cullercrumb on bristles
> A bum eyes the waitress,
> Likes the plump seesaw
> Of her scooting hips;
> Lifts an awash teaspoon:
> In it curl drowsy
> Atoms that, rubbed wrong,
> Sprang Hiroshima. (262)

Nims is horrified by this temporary colony of bums and waitresses (and cops and truckers mentioned in other lines). They represent the shallow achievement of a civilization obsessed with management and control. Our wishes for a bright future have gone awry, as though a magic lamp had been mishandled, its genie unleashed not as ally but as monster. Nims hints at the vast gulf between the "drowsy / Atoms" in the teaspoon and the devastation of an entire city only to collapse them together, as if the intellectuals and scientists of our civilization were as heedless of long-term consequences as this shortsighted group in the diner, intent on making it through the night. Nims presents himself as if he were simply recording the chronicle of an "all-nite joint," a site readily conceded to others: "Here the cop and trucker, / Cap back, shoulder sloping, / At counter crouch, swimmers / Bent halfway on a raft" (262). But his story about the downcast and crestfallen runs disturbingly parallel with a story we can tell about our civilization. "In the all-nite joint," the poem ends, "Grins our shallow nature" (263).

Not everyone deployed "Hiroshima" with the novelty of Nims, but its power as a shock term was widely admired by poets. Leo Richards waited until almost the end before unleashing it in "Where Are Your Worshippers," in a special "All Negro" issue that Langston Hughes guest-edited for *Voices* (Winter 1950), the organ of the Poetry Society of America:

> The city—
> An abandoned cathedral of smoking altars
> Made of
> Bones, flesh, blood-dreams.
>
> Where are the worshipers?
> Where are the worshipers?
>
> The incense of human bodies rises,
> Nauseates:
> The priest—war, alone inhales
> And lives.
>
> Priest—
> Where are the worshipers?
> Where are the worshipers?
>
> Hiroshima—
> Where have your children gone?
> Where have your children gone? (21)

Richards uses "Hiroshima" to refocus his narrative. What had begun as a description of the ruins of any city abruptly centers on one city, and at the same time, when the vocative "Hiroshima—" replaces "Priest—" there is a corresponding shift from "Where are your worshipers?" to "Where are your children?" The entrance of Hiroshima starkly changes the terms. The civilian population singled out for destruction in this bombing were the innocent victims who represented a next generation, all of whom have been obliterated.

"Hiroshima," however, like all signifiers that draw their strength from their timeliness, exhausted a bit more of its capacity to unsettle each time it was invoked. By 1954 Murray Noss could even include a visit to the site as part of his general impressions of contemporary Japan in *Samurai and Serpent Poems* (1954). "I mount the little concrete bridge and see / the cross-like shadow burnt thereon / of the unknown little man" (84). This is to write as a tourist, albeit one who seems duly numbed. James Merrill responded in a similar way, though in prose not verse, in "The Beaten Path," excerpts from a 1956 diary of travel in Japan. He was overwhelmed not by the horror of the bomb but by the grotesque and inept attempt by the "Peace Museum" to record what had happened. "It is a favorite tourist spot," he concludes his one-paragraph sketch. "Busloads of Japanese tourists come, gape, and, as the brochures say, 'Realize the mistake of their militarism.' There is an Atomic Souvenir Shop where you can buy don't ask me what. . . ." (146, ellipses his). What causes Merrill to fall speechless, to let words trail off, is not the threat of the Bomb but the encroachment even here of tasteless consumer culture.

Four years later, the place-name had been so thoroughly emptied of its frightfulness that Robert Lowell, in a dazzling twist in "For the Union Dead" (composed in 1960), could exploit just that vacuity:

> There are no statues for the last war here;
> on Boylston Street, a commercial photograph
> shows Hiroshima boiling
> over a Mosler Safe, the "Rock of Ages"
> that survived the blast. (*Union* 72)

Its appearance in an advertisement assures us that its controversy has been mooted. No longer personally terrifying, "Hiroshima" is an incident in the past, to be commercially appropriated like a trademark. The mushroom cloud, so quickly recognizable, is exploited to up the recognizability quotient of the Mosler Safe. What was once a symbol of dread has become one more image in a lexicon of images. The mushroom cloud that is "boiling" has a kitchen-stove familiarity that signals a certain domestication of turbulence. Much as Saint-Gaudens's bas-relief (which acts as the crossroads for Lowell's meditation in the poem) has been redefined by the passage of time—it is no longer a raw marker of public protest but a high culture relic of a bygone age—so a similar historical forgetfulness, which Lowell deems inevitable, eviscerates the strong moral commitment that had energized Boston a century before.

For a short time, "Hiroshima" would have a rival in the word "Bikini," a term whose rapid reassignment by French fashion designer Louis Reard in July 1946 distracted from its suitability as a rallying cry even as its new designation retained, if furtively, an appropriate aura of danger. That this name would have all trace of public terror drained from it, being effectively reassigned to a sexual sphere, must count among the more astonishing linguistic transformations of modern times. It has been forgotten that the tests on Bikini were what brought disturbing new information about the Bomb that even the elaborate disinformation campaigns of the Truman administration, as detailed exhaustively by Robert Jay Lifton and Greg Mitchell in 1996, could no longer contain. "It was Bikini, rather than Hiroshima or Nagasaki," Paul Boyer explained, "that first brought the issue of radioactivity compellingly to the nation's consciousness" (90). Discussion of that issue, Boyer demonstrates, was by no means confined to the intellectual quarterlies. He details a special feature by *Life* on the first anniversary of the tests (August 11, 1947) plus articles from *Reader's Digest* (April 1947), *Collier's* (August 1947), and concludes with *No Place to Hide* (1948), a Book-of-the-Month selection written by David Bradley (a physician who had served with the radiological safety unit at Bikini) that spent ten weeks on the *New York Times* best-seller list and sold 250,000 copies. As a result of this publicity, the way in which the danger of the Bomb presented itself shifted most disturbingly. Radiation is invisible and inaudible except to special measuring devices. The previous scenario of danger had been based on the model of the civilian in a metropolitan area, and it involved a target and a delivery system. While this in itself was a troubling expansion of the theater of war from a front line to a home front, it was as nothing compared to a silent and invisible enemy that struck without warning and did irreparable damage.

Unlike poems which centered on Hiroshima, the poems that alluded to Bikini—in the few years in which it was possible to evoke the place-name without distraction—virtually all registered intense dismay at the sudden expansion of the Bomb's dangers. Dorothy Lee Richardson's recast fairy tale, "Modern Grimm," in the February 1949 issue of *Poetry,* starts with an innocent quotation: "'Nibble, nibble, little mouse, / Who is nibbling at my house?' / 'Only the wind. / Only the wind'" (275). But that wind has been sown by "clever children" who have colored it a "brilliant shade":

> A rich-red wind over Hiroshima,
> Darkly blowing, brightly glowing,
>   A red-black wind
>
> We have sown the wind. Its seed we found
> And dropped it lightly to the ground.
>   We have sown the wind.
>
> The small thing split. It branched to bear
> A thousand red-black fruits in air.
>   We have sown the wind.

We have sown the wind. It rises high
Till it beats the air and blinds the eye
And sweeps a hole in the crouching sky
    Where the whirlwind rushes in! (275–76)

Typical of the harsh reprisal in a Brothers Grimm tale, in this story these heedless children (these scientists and politicians) never considered the consequences of their actions. Is this a parable? In one sense, to have "sown the wind" is, in the case of radioactive fallout, not to speak metaphorically but with literalness. This is no ancient prophecy but precise description; or more accurately, what was once ancient prophecy has now come vividly alive.

Richardson never mentions Bikini by name, but her focus on the wind, the carrier of lethal radioactivity, suggests concerns aroused by recent experiments. In the same issue two pages earlier *Poetry* printed "Bombós," a poem by Morton Seif explicitly linked to radioactive tests. After the poem's final line, Seif signs off by adding the word "Bikini" in smaller size type and in italics, as an author might complete a preface by recording its place of composition. Such a gesture is highly unusual. For one thing, it rigidly localizes the text, vigorously associating it with a specific place. Yet this particular place Seif is unlikely to have visited. For another, it threatens whatever closure has been arrived at in the text proper by adding this extra word, this afterthought. Ultimately, however, the appearance of the defining term "Bikini" at the end almost escapes notice because it pales beside the outrageousness of a text violently disrupted by syntax garbled beyond repair:

How many nights, bright from the ocean floor
Did you begat the day your rubble rained
On hidden tombs of Asia and the shore
Heaved upwards for the joy the earth had gained

Down by the old mill stream in Mejico
When gold and pus ran from Krakatoa
You were the only girl in Jericho
And I was a swimming protozoa

The red thewed braves rise from their graves like grass
There on the muddied mesa sands, the fall
Of cities in Castile has come to pass
Before Juan Luis could see the dead grow tall

> O Hiroshima Nagasaki Japs
> Jews Admirals Wops and Heroes all,
> The birds are frightened by the thunderslaps—(272)

And on for seven more stanzas, each with its own splintered sentences that push incessantly forward, their heavy rhythms forestalling any hesitation. "Bombós" is a poem that foregrounds disorder. Its observations roam around the globe, pausing over sites where violence occurs. Explosions cause widespread disruption, not just fissures in geography but cultural disjoinings as well. The bombastic rhetoric of the first stanza ("the shore / Heaved upwards for the joy the earth had gained") collapses into corny pop-tune echoes in the second stanza: "You were the only girl in Jericho / And I was a swimming protozoa." The "only girl" does not find an "only boy" but a protozoa reduced to life below even the primitive. What we may suspect early on, that the poem reflects the instability of an age of nuclear weaponry, becomes evident by the seventh stanza where the Bomb itself is hailed: "To Thee, mon enfant terrible, whose bloom / Binoculars and delphic pigs attend / Belongs the stemless being the mushroom" (273). A bloom to be witnessed by binoculars only that ends in a "mushroom" that is "stemless" needs no further identification, but if there is any question, a later set of lines pointedly rewrite Chaucer for the nuclear age, invoking an August date coterminous with both the Hiroshima and Nagasaki bombs as well as the first tests on Bikini: "What that August with swift sureness smote / The droghte vertue engendred in is the flower / Inspired hath in all the dead the roote" (273). Seif also garbles other texts:

> I met a tall white man in the ship's hold
> Who spoke to me in splintered French and said
> "Bonejaw moanahme, illfate azuretree"
> Jalap pills, scorecards, Quetzalcoatl sold
> And petals of the caked anemone

This recalls Hart Crane's "Cutty Sark" which opens: "I met a man in South Street, tall" (and which goes on to cite phrases in various languages, including references to Quetzalcoatl), as well as his "Atlantis" with its salute to the Bridge as "Answerer of all,—Anemone,—" whose "petals spend the suns about us." But Seif's echoing of *The Bridge*—itself a text in elaborate conversation with other cultural critics, including Eliot and Williams as well as Waldo Frank and Allen Tate—is only to announce its undoing: Crane's project to unify the disparate features of the modern world is now evoked only to dramatize that such unification is hopelessly beyond us. Seif's opening words, "How many nights," deny the "How many dawns" with which *The Bridge* opens. What has so pervasively disjoined what poets had previously striven to unite? The answer is voiced, as it were, outside the text in the 5-point typeface and italics that mark a conclusion beyond the last lines of the poem: "Bikini." After Bikini, conditions change this drastically, begetting a new day that is dominated by "How many nights." So "Bikini" fittingly appears as the last word, virtually unwriting the poem, taking over the space where, under other conditions, an author's name might have been placed.

As bold as Seif's experimental text is, other poems emphasize just as radically how disruptive the presence of the Bomb has suddenly become. Indeed, Berryman's "The Wholly Fail," when viewed alongside a piece by a contemporary like Seif, appears not simply as a missing link between the poet's early and middle experiments with language but also as an appropriately violent portrayal of what Berryman considers an enormous rupture in the traditions of western civilization. Most important is the attention Berryman draws to the workings of chance. He is critical of Sir Partofall even though he is "our Best," one of the "Wizards of Oak Ridge and Los Alamos," because he has no idea of his experiments' outcome:

> Your questrist foxing up a drug that may
> Or may not, who knows . . . so (but not a word)
> 'A livens wife's and mother's and son's coffee
> His own, therefore one holy night' next day
> None descends, if the silence in the house
> Is unusual and complete, like a curtain
> He will know (or will not, will he) he has failed. (191)

As this excerpt suggests, the poem twists toward the mechanisms of an Elizabethan revenge tragedy, with its behind-the-scene poisonings that may or may not work, "who knows." We had been warned before, Berryman is reminding us, of the Faustian mind that is drawn to experiments whose outcomes are uncertain. But that experimenting now endangers us all. The Physicist speculates "To see what he can find / Useful for mankind, / Useful although uncertain." But "Partofall" becomes "Partsusall" at poem's end, "transfigured, white with joy," who "Smiles thro' the blast and fiery wind spreading out from zero—." His experiment ends successfully, confirming a higher law of physics, but a by-product of his research is the annihilation of the world. Berryman's distorted language faithfully records a rupture so violent that the old rules of understanding are insufficient for indicating how extensively conditions have altered. In shock, we are so disoriented that previous structures of thought have become proportionately disabled.

Poems like those by Berryman and Seif reveal that the very contours of poetic discourse must undergo striking shifts if the changes enacted by the Bomb are to be registered. That "Bikini" will not lend itself for utilization in a precise system of meaning as "Hiroshima" did so cooperatively but will instead mutate alarmingly into a concept with disturbingly furtive connections is consonant with the particular danger represented by the events at Bikini. As the dangers of the Bomb become more pervasive, so conceiving of the Bomb begins to fall outside manageable structures. At one time, the Bomb's danger could be signified precisely in the example of an enemy airplane delivering a missile of destruction to a civilian area behind the front lines. After the 1947 Bikini tests, the danger of the Bomb began to shift: as radioactivity, that danger would become an invisible menace that escaped even the control of those who might administer it against a national enemy. And as defining the Bomb grows ever more elusive, so fewer and fewer poems will be able to mount a straightforward attack on it. Poems that vilify the Bomb or the Bomb's inventors assemble a target that focuses our wrath. As opportunities to vent anger and outrage, these poems would have been hits. But to the extent that they satisfyingly offer a target that represents evil they also would misunderstand that the shock of Bikini emptied of significance the idea that an enemy could be singled out.

That awareness is one perception at the back of Richard Wilbur's "We" (first published in the November 1948 *Poetry* but not collected in a volume):

"We ought to drop the bomb at once before
Those Russians do. I'm sure you all agree?"
Of course we do; and hearing of a war
The Continentals rise in clouds of tea,
Attired in looks of conscious artistry,
Decorous rags, and decorative gore.

"I fear we're growing soft," says Mr. Fee,
A hardened gentleman of several score.
"Lemon?" inquires Miss Blood. "It seems to me
We mustn't shilly shally any more."
The Continentals quick-step out the door
And pivot off around the shrubbery.

How good to have the Russians to abhor:
It lets us dance the nation on our knee
Who haven't been quite certain since the war
Precisely what we meant by saying *we.*
The alien elements have come to be
Entirely too enormous to ignore.

The servant girl has spoken back to me.
My dividends are yearly getting lower.
The nights are full of fires and burglary.
The Jews have bought my cottage by the shore.
I feel at times like locking up the door
And never even going out to tea. ("We" 127–28)

Wilbur understands that the Bomb is a solution to nothing. As a weapon, it returns us to the past, and worse than the past, to an attitude of smugness and self-righteousness that depends upon an ability to identify and persecute "alien elements." With a tart defiance not always associated with his writing Wilbur reveals what lies behind the desire to name an enemy.

Those desires are now obsolete. The Bomb, in its new dimension of the radioactive, is everyone's threat. "You have to hand it to the experts / They've got it all figured out," wrote African American poet Frank Marshall Davis in the final poem of *47th Street* (1948), a title that marked a Chicago geographical boundary as significant as New York's 125th Street. Davis was noting the new confidence with which professionals could calculate exact military costs, including the death of an enemy. But none of their self-ascribed confidence survives Davis's concluding line, wiping out all progress in a single stroke: "They've got it all figured out / Safe in their Home Offices— / If they forget Hiroshima" (104–5). To speak of "targets" was absurd; no one, now, could *not* be a target. As Dilys Laing had understood in 1946, the Bomb expanded the theater of war beyond any previous boundaries. The threat of radioactivity ridiculed the notion that the ravages of war could be contained. There was no escaping the Bomb. Even the evocation of the term "Hiroshima" would have been, in a sense, inappropriately nostalgic: as an application of force that event had been carefully limited. What never-as-yet voiced words could be found to evoke the omnipresence, the sheer inescapableness of the Bomb?

The *California Quarterly* and *Noir* Poetics

After 1952, a further complication to the problem of the Bomb was how to design a new poetic discourse that, in the unforgiving atmosphere of HUAC and the McCarthy era, would be equipped to register political awareness and still withstand groundless accusations of disloyalty. Because suspicion about one's loyalty would, at this time, inevitably accompany any work that set out to critique government policy, no analysis could escape vulnerability unless it were also oblique. But it was not simply the fact that poets, like other writers and intellectuals, would have been vulnerable if they had spoken out directly (though this was surely true); poets also believed that too blunt a critique would fail to earn audience respect. It would fatally resemble an earlier "activist" discourse associated with the 1930s that, when not explicitly discredited, no longer enjoyed fashionable endorsement. In a time when many had learned to read poetry through New Critical filters, plain speaking just wouldn't do. Intricate imagery that demanded careful attention was a feature now anticipated by readers if a text was to be extended recognition as poetry.

Nowhere was this problem of a poetic discourse that could be correct both politically *and* aesthetically more on display than in the pages of the *California Quarterly,* the short-lived (1951–54) but distinguished outlet for writers on the left founded by blacklisted screenwriter Philip Stevenson and associates. It exemplified what can only be called the extraordinary range of discourse in which political matters had to be conducted in the opening years of the decade. From its inception, the journal specialized in statements that steered wide of an explicitly ideological vocabulary. Its credo, as articulated in its first issue, was so far from a clarion call that it required active interpretation if it was to be understood at all. It concluded: "We hope to encourage writing that faces up to its time—writers who recognize their responsibility to deal with reality in communicable terms. . . . If we have a claim to newness, it is this moderate position in an immoderate time" (Spingarn). Just what kind of position is staked out here is by no means obvious, but by laying claim to a "moderate position," the editors were not simply opting to be prudent: they were also fighting to keep a leftist position from being stigmatized as inhabited only by radicals and disgruntled outsiders. Nonetheless, statements that appear in an opening-issue credo are not often open to different meanings.

Just what constituted properly effective political discourse in poetry was not at all evident even to the editorial board. This was itself a topic of discussion within the journal. George Abbe developed a poetics of ferocity in an essay, "The Role of the Prophet," which included generous selections of his own verse. He believed that "The prophet-poet must summon the dispersed and frightened forces of humanity; he must identify himself with the crushed and despairing, the vast roving bands of ordinary men who, assembled, can storm the crumbling walls of the past. His speech must be a weapon, especially in these times when it is no longer a question of peril only, but of survival" (7). To illustrate, Abbe chose from his own work "To Jesus of Our Daily Bread," which opens:

> I do not see you on a cross,
> But with a hammer in your hand;
> Not the bowed head, the blood of loss;
> I see you raise your eyes, and stand—(8)

But in fact few examples of poetry like this appeared in the journal's pages. Readers were more likely to find "The Fifties," a villanelle by English poet Roy Fuller, which begins:

> The wretched summers start again
> With lies and armies ready for
> Advancing on the fast terrain.
>
> Like those of China, Poland, Spain,
> With twenty territories more,
> The wretched summer starts again. (54)

Poets, it was assumed, knew their way around difficult forms like the villanelle. Thomas McGrath (a member of the editorial board) printed in the final issue of 1954 "The Hunted Revolutionaries," a four-part extravaganza in which the central two poems exchange and repeat key lines. These key lines take on new significance when they reappear in their different contexts as four angels are summoned, each from one of the compass points, to defeat four demons. McGrath's elaborate repositionings are not only politically but technically correct: indeed, his tour de force out-villanelles the villanelle.

For such a politically astute yet technically adroit poetics, no recent writer proved as exemplary as Hart Crane, who had sought to construct in *The Bridge* a text that laid claim to a social agenda without yielding its value as an aesthetic object. In Lawrence Lipton's long poem *Rainbow at Midnight,* one-third of which (in what would be its early version) was published in twenty-six pages of the Spring 1953 issue, Lipton addresses Crane directly:

> And you, Hart Crane,
> Who would have rung what sounding changes on

> The verb to fly, surrendered to the sea,
> Torn, perhaps, by ship's propellor—an irony!
> The machine absorbs the poet—contrariwise. ("Excerpts" 22)

Unlike Crane's own invocation to Walt Whitman in "Cape Hatteras" ("But who has held the heights more sure than thou, / O Walt!"), Lipton's address to Crane emphasizes the interrupted aspect of Crane's project. For Crane, Whitman could intervene effectively, importing a celebratory and democratizing spirit that potentially redeemed the destructive edge of the machine. But for Lipton, Crane isn't there to provide the same helping hand to him. Yet if Crane fell as a victim—"The machine absorbs the poet," as Lipton exclaims—his example lives on as a lure to others. Now more than ever it is his absence that is felt and registered as a judgment on us. Henri Coulette, in the central passage of "The Problem of Creation" (a poem bearing a dedication to Thomas McGrath), recalls Crane's death:

> And south by the Gulf, where Crane's bones,
> Washed by salt water, stain that sea
> And take it, for have we not words where
> Others have marrow, or is bone
> Obedient to wild genesis, the source, the sea? (32)

This is not an elegiac strain, however, as much as an accusation leveled against the doubt that infects the present. In Coulette's bitter words, as Crane's project increases in importance, the likelihood that it will be written therefore recedes.

Although two examples of the extended multisequence cultural epic appeared in the pages of the *California Quarterly*—Lipton's excerpts from *The Rainbow at Midnight* had been preceded by the complete text, spread over two issues, of a youthful E. P. Thompson's "A Place Called Choice" (both texts reaffirming a standard in which neither the poetic nor the political outweighed one another)—Crane proves useful less by serving as a model than as a glaring absence. He was one more instance of lost leadership that helped explain why the times were in crisis. (To an editorial board familiar with blacklisting, the pathos of a career like Crane's interrupted just as it was underway would also have their quick recognition.) That a lineage had been broken with Crane's untimely suicide lent credence to defining the mid-century as a period of odd disjunctions and peculiar omissions and unsettling gaps. Moreover, the synthesizing tropes of Crane's own writing, monumentally unifying as they were, would have been awkward to synchronize with the shadowy, troubled 1950s. Crane had constructed his elaborate rhetoric in part as a nativist refutation of Eliot's fashionably international despair; its pertinence at the moment was unclear.

Eulogizing Crane while avoiding his enthusiasms, the *California Quarterly* consistently lent its support to verse that mounted a critique that was more or less surreptitious, depending on just who was reading it. A favorite disguise borrowed trappings from the thriller. This example had its own distinguished origin in W. H. Auden's cryptic, flat descriptions of cityscapes in the 1930s that ominously conveyed something dangerous but out of sight. "Wandering through cold streets tangled like old string," Auden began "Brussels in Winter," one of the sonnets collected in *Another Time* (1940), "Coming on fountains rigid in the frost, / Its formula escapes you; it has lost / The certainty that constitutes a thing" (*Collected Shorter Poems* 123). These hollowed-out European cities, with their shifting frontiers and double agents, went over with surprising ease into the American idiom of the *roman noir* with its long and vacant avenues more welcoming to automobiles than people, its blurry zones where officials and detectives sought a clue to a mystery whose exact dimensions kept shifting. The pages of the *California Quarterly* highlighted verse in which the format of the crime novel or detective story was not used for simple background detail but as a self-conscious heuristic device that could best articulate a crisis specific to this time. In this respect, too, the journal shows its regional roots: *noir,* as a politicized genre, was a product of postwar Hollywood. *Noir* films with their "contempt for a depraved business culture," as Mike Davis has reminded us, amounted to "a kind of Marxist *cinema manqué,* a shrewdly oblique strategy for an otherwise subversive realism" (41).

In earlier years, Weldon Kees had been first to reclaim Auden's perspective by drawing upon *noir* material in "Crime Club" and "Xantha Street," both of which appeared in *Poetry* in 1943 and were collected in *The Fall of the Magicians* (1947). Relocating to the West Coast in 1950 only enhanced Kees's drop-dead tone. In "Travels in North America," the travelogue-poem he completed soon after his cross-country drive (at 110 lines, the longest work in *Poems, 1947–1954*), the Bomb appears without fanfare in a middle segment:

> The land is terraced near Los Alamos: scrub cedars,
> Pinon pines and ruined pueblos, where a line
> Of tall young men in uniform keep watch upon

The University of California's atom bomb.
The sky is soiled and charitable
Behind barbed wire and the peaks of mountains—
Sangre de Christo, Blood of Christ, this "fitting portent
For the Capital of the Atomic Age." We meant
To stop, but one can only see so much. A mist
Came over us outside Tryuonyi caves, and a shattered cliff.
 (*Collected* 115)

Here as elsewhere Kees is incapable of being scandalized. Corruption is so integral a part of all he sees that mere description alone discloses truths so bitter they are best not pursued. Tagging the Bomb as the "University of California's" is enough to suggest that someday every university will have its own, just as they now boast their own sports teams. Within that laconic exaggeration lurks a darker anatomizing of the arms race as a competition between act-alike rivals. Characteristically, Kees stands as the witness who, having seen it all, has grown to expect nothing. To the *noir* sensibility, the other side of the tracks is everywhere. The plainest description discloses menacing portents. "An ancient gull," he writes in one signature passage, "Dropped down to shiver gravely in the steady rain." This ravishing blend of assonance and consonance produces an extravagantly sumptuous surface just heavy enough to arouse an immense distrust. What is being hidden? Why does that gull, so wise and ancient, knowingly shudder? About the "Sangre de Christo" mountains, then, there is little to add except to remark that nothing in these times can be shocking. After all, the irony of locating the site for the all-destructive bomb next to these mountains, named so long ago, has already been finessed in what Kees presents as the commercialized language of the travel brochure.

As adumbrated through a *noir* poetics, the crisis on display is especially distinguished by its resistance to display. Like a city that has fallen into the hands of gangsters, even legitimate matters have become indirectly tainted with corruption. Unlike a conventional mystery with a deceptive scheme to be unraveled and a villain to be brought to justice in a cathartic ending, *noir* withheld the possibility that all filaments of the mystery could ever be untangled. One aspect of corruption might be brought to light briefly after an enormous investment of time and energy, but such illuminations were arbitrary, not solutions so much as temporary failures by those in power to manage the strictest control. In such a world, the only moral position to inhabit is to be an interpreter of clues, one who reads against the surface of things.

To regard the world as composed of messages that were fragmentary and scrambled offered a rich format for critique, one that poets on the left were ready to develop. Clues were gathered not to be jigsaw-puzzled into a clear picture but for associational assemblage as a generalized valence of meaning. This quintessentially *noir* nuance Edwin Rolfe put on display in "Mystery" and "Mystery II," two poems that were linked when they appeared alongside each other in the *California Quarterly* (though they were printed separately when Thomas McGrath collected them posthumously in the 1955 volume *Permit Me Refuge*). Rolfe's leftist credentials were impeccable—a member of CPUSA since the 1920s, he had memorialized service in the Spanish Civil War both in his 1951 collection of poetry, *First Love and Other Poems,* and in a prose chronicle of the Abraham Lincoln Brigade—and he had co-authored *The Glass Room* with Lester Fuller, a *noir* optioned as a vehicle for Bogart and Bacall, reprinted as a Bantam softcover in 1948 and translated (as *Un vrai Chopin!*) for Gallimard's Black Cat series in 1951.[8] Unlike the mysteries in his prose thriller, however, the mysteries in Rolfe's verse were never meant to be solved. What is central to the first poem, in fact, is not its most Audenesque feature, its setting in a fragmentary cityscape, but the silencing that has effectively muted all the voices in the work. Silencing in this poem is almost complete. It opens: "The corpse is in the central square, in the spring sun. / The hilts of two jeweled daggers tremble on her breasts" (*Collected* 220). This is the defiled body of a young woman, further "silenced" in that it goes unnoticed by passersby, ostentatiously absorbed in their own matters. And an even further silencing occurs in that no one steps forward as an official investigator of her death. "Somewhere, it is assumed, an invisible detective / broods," Rolfe writes, but when the detective speaks, at the end of the poem, he says less than nothing:

"Sooner or later, mark my word, we'll identify the woman,
and from that to finding the killer is just a small step . . ."
Only the children stand silent, and stare, stare
at the broken body, the tragic face, the living opulent hair.
    (*Collected* 220)

And even a final silence surrounds the children, though their intent staring suggests that a younger generation will assuredly not forget the outrages perpetrated by an older one.

Rolfe's adjustment of *noir* conventions points to an era not just in which crimes go unpunished but which deliberately turns away from acknowledging a crime has occurred. If printed only by itself, the poem might qualify as an example of how even politically committed poets like Rolfe learned to protect themselves by extending a critique only to withdraw it simultaneously. But in the second of the two poems that the *California Quarterly* published together, Rolfe conspicuously shifts the terms, and as cautiously as he had once proceeded, remaining rigidly within *noir* conventions, so in his second poem he proceeds recklessly, acknowledging the extent to which his discourse has been a code. In effect, by having submitted to a *noir* poetics, by deciding to speak only in coded terms, Rolfe had silenced himself—and that act of self-censorship is what he wants understood, in his second poem, as outrageous. So he begins by insisting that this poem should not be confused with formula gimmicks:

> Unlike the denouement in the popular novel,
> the mystery is never adequately explained:
> why the lad with the brilliant I.Q. ended up in a hovel;
> why, when the lovers set out on their picnic, it brutally
>   rained.
>
> And the sold-out innocent can never understand
> how the Fates that conspired against him, that turned him
>   into a sot,
> were simply the normal doing of his best, his truest friend
> who, promising all things faithfully, quite naturally
>   forgot. (*Collected* 222)

Now indeed there are true mysteries that escape explanation, such as why a truest friend might betray oneself (Rolfe is thinking of the HUAC trials). Yet these matters cannot be spoken of except indirectly. But rather than avoiding such sheltering conventions, Rolfe goes on to foreground them even more outrageously:

> The final chapter, as usual, long-looked-forward-to,
> is strangely, mysteriously ripped from the overweight book—
> so what can we, dear frustrated readers, think or do
> who invariably feel the richest prize in the hands of the crook,
>
> the lovely virgin with the dazzling hair won by the diseased roué,
> and all our golden Tomorrows wrecked on the dunghill of
>   Today? (*Collected* 222)

No one could have imagined so ill-conceived a plot. We have fallen into a melodrama in which someone else is writing a script so ineptly, so corruptly, that everything is inside-out. The ending that would have been apt, that would have restored balance, has been discarded. At the last we hear Rolfe's clear and unmistakably bitter voice ringing out, exposing the outrageous manipulation in which injustice triumphs.

The fourteen lines of Rolfe's poem unfold within the rhyme scheme of a Shakespearean sonnet. This display of traditional poetic skill serves to distinguish Rolfe's labor-intensive text from a product designed to be rapidly consumed. This was a distinction that other poets who were highly suspicious of the trappings of mass culture like the detective novel wanted to emphasize. Howard Griffin's "The Detective Story" (collected in *Cry Cadence,* 1947), dramatically enumerated all the ways in which the genre confused our fears with our needs: "This is the pre-arranged pursuit, / The secret savagery of gun" (53). The experience was infantilizing: "We play the game that children play" (53). *California Quarterly* contributor Naomi Replansky, in "Whodunit?" (collected in *Ring Song,* 1952), wanted to see "why" replace the "who." For her, the formulaic writing too easily escorted the audience past issues of social justice. Thrillers also suggested that societal ills could be traced back to single villains:

Who coulda done this dreadful deed
If it wasn't me or you?
O cover the valley for a track
And comb it for a clue.

It wasn't me it wasn't you
It was the man we chase. (22)

In foregrounding melodramatic devices, Replansky suggested, the formula discouraged that self-reflexive understanding that might be the beginning of political consciousness.

Noir did not recommend itself to everyone as a means toward thoughtful critique. Anthony Hecht was another poet who viewed the genre as hopelessly formulaic, and he concluded "The Private Eye: Detective Story" (an uncollected poem first printed in 1948 in the *Kenyon Review*) with this portrait of an investigator in lordly aloofness, contemplating harsh truths:

The Private Eye reclines in isolation
As though in quarantine against the plague,
And to inspire his earthly meditation,
Drinks the elixir of the Brothers Haig:
    Knowing what it is possible to know,
    That the grass is dry, the wind continues to blow. (628)

To Hecht, the investigator's final perspective is not a privileged insight into dark modern realities but only dismaying evidence of his emotional poverty. Hecht's figure "holds allegiance only to that truth / Sustained by brazen stares, and called empirical . . . Sooner or later all of them shall die / By the steel logic of the Private Eye" (628). That "steel logic" prohibits the sympathetic understanding necessary for genuine art. What a more thoughtful writer might be able to portray as insoluble complexity the pulp novelist's investigator is bent upon simplifying into a solution: "Though motives be as tortuous as lace / The Private Eye shall make them as a string" (628). Hecht's version of the private eye differs so markedly from Rolfe's because his investigator believes that he is able to conceive of solutions—a luxury denied to Rolfe's.

This respectful disagreement over how to define the private eye is itself testimony to its richness as a cultural trope in this period. Formula conventions were cheap, brutal, and violent, and for some they proved to be disturbingly successful at defining the world in which we found ourselves. The sonnet that Rolfe employed in both his poems is, after all, not a form our culture instinctively embraces. "We are detective stories now," opened a poem by H. Phelps Putnam that the *California Quarterly* printed:

> We are the authors and we know
> The corpse, the villains, and the plot;
> We know the cause and the results;
> We can trace them backwards in the books,
> Which sell at second-hand rates.
> The stories work; and the slaughter
> Is intense and the villain jugged,
> Or by self-murder killed.
> We know the answers, so why wait?
> We have two hands which should
> Be severed from our wrists. (20–21)

The poem's title, "Authors Write Books," reproduces the vapid news headline that occurs when the literary meets the journalistic. But the story, Putnam insists, is one we know already, all of us. This scandalous genre really holds no surprises.

Don Gordon: Making the Covert Overt

Leftists in the 1950s were by no means united over the usefulness of mass culture. Many were inclined to distrust formula genres as writings whose obvious crudeness undermined the very possibility of subtle, complex interchange. In the Summer 1952 *California Quarterly,* producer Herbert J. Biberman related an anecdote from his jail time as a member of the Hollywood Ten. Upon learning that *Hamlet* had been scheduled for the weekend film, prisoners in his block set out angrily to boycott it, insisting on their right to be amused by lighter fare. In response, Biberman offered them a verbal preview of the play that in effect pitched Shakespeare to the inmates. His synopsis was cleverly designed to encourage the inmates to find positions for themselves within the play. For Biberman, great art *was* popular art. And this was a truth that was hidden from disenfranchised groups by those in power who had every reason to value the soporific platitudes of mass culture. Junk texts not only purveyed narratives that were designed to ratify current conditions but their formulaic crudity made it unlikely that their audience would ever pick up the sophisticated techniques of interpretation that would allow them to question with effectiveness the circumstances around them. The thriller or detective tale, however, was not quite so confining as other examples of formulaic writing. *Noir* conventions incorporated skepticism as foundational. For their readers they could be a first step toward actually cultivating the skills necessary for cultural critique. Because nothing was as it seemed, everything was open to interrogation. Indeed, taking things at their face value might actually be dangerous. *Noir* heroized scrutiny. When surfaces shimmer with anxious uncertainty, astute readers must proceed suspiciously, prepared to read against and around the apparent text.

To edit and write for a readership that could assume that poems would be elaborately encoded freed a few poets to address an issue that to them was urgent: the Bomb's astonishing assimilation to patterns of everyday life. Some poets felt that not to address that in one way or another carried the risk of inadvertently producing additional texts that helped further accomplish the normalization of the Bomb. Yet for the *California Quarterly* writers, engaged in a political poetics, the matter was unusually complicated. For them the Bomb was likely to seem one more symptom of a whole range of social ills that were deeply embedded in a thoroughly incorrect ideology. When Curtis Zahn lashes out at "fine young U.S. couples / Reluctantly engaged in the awful practice / Of blowing up the entire frigging universe" (42), he is mocking an ideal of good manners and proper behavior, and the Bomb is not even a secondary target—it is simply present to help exaggerate the scale of the young couple's devotion. The Bomb, though references to it are scattered throughout the pages of the *California Quarterly,* rarely warrants anyone's exclusive attention.[9] Thomas

McGrath included it at a key point in his seventy-two-line sequence entitled "In a Season of War," employing it in a question that delivers us from part 2 to part 3:

> Where are our dreamed and charming Magi then
> To point the star of peace across the world?
> Where our saviors to redeem the time
> Beyond frontiers of the atomic Rose?
>
> 3
> Only ourselves. (Upon the midnight street
> We meet the future but it wears no face.)
> Only ourselves. (Or at the factory gates
> The woman with the leaflet crying: Peace!) (37)

As prominently as the Bomb is positioned as a political question, however, it is equally enmeshed in the particulars of a poetic tradition. The phrase "atomic Rose" recalls T. S. Eliot's investment in religious tradition in *Four Quartets* even as it sets that over against Hart Crane's critique of the misbegotten quest in the "ATLANTIS ROSE drums weave the rose" passage from "Cutty Sark" in *The Bridge.* Here as elsewhere, McGrath sets out to divulge the common ground on which a literary tradition and an activist tradition could meet. For McGrath it was politically important that "In a Season of War"—composed in three segments of two equally apportioned stanzas, in a precise blank verse with occasional rhyme—could muster credentials that were prosodically impeccable. Yet the inclusion of the Bomb at this point yields results that are questionable. It represents the equivalent, on the political spectrum, of a device as standardized and widely accepted on the poetic spectrum as iambic pentameter. Its status as an example testifies to how thoroughly embedded it has become in current cultural consciousness, but the fact of its embeddedness is not what scandalizes McGrath.

Depicting as a scandal that sense in which the Bomb had become commonplace—in effect, foregrounding what has receded into the background—was a task for which some poets were unprepared. British poet Roy Fuller's "Images of Autumn" (from the Autumn 1953 issue) was a poem that explicitly addressed just what readers nowadays expect to find in a poem. Fuller understood that the poet had a "New interest in the world," an interest that failed to coincide with conventional autumn imagery. In citing examples of events that held the new poet's interest, he included "the predeflation plunge in Kaffirs, / And tests of tinier bombs to atomize / Troops in the field" (56). The equivalence suggested by Fuller's listing is significant. An alteration in the rate of currency exchange in a distant region provokes concern equal to that of testing more manageable bombs. The Bomb, in Fuller's carefully weighted words, is presented as an unspectacular instance of a crisis. As a result, the poem actually downplays how pervasive the Bomb has become. For one thing, by introducing the idea of a miniaturized Bomb Fuller localizes its capacity for destruction. The consequence, surely unintended, implies that a scaled-down Bomb can be restrained.

When poets in the *California Quarterly* quietly refer to the Bomb as one more of the outrages with which they are all too familiar, they risk becoming unwitting accomplices in the acclimatization of the Bomb. One poet who demonstrated it was possible to escape that dilemma was Don Gordon, though he was distinguished precisely by the outrageously casual way in which he invited the Bomb to figure in his work. It is so simply a part of the work, so effortlessly invoked, that it gathers to itself a particular terror:

> When the special and sacred explosive
>   was dropped,
> The cabinet explained: it was to save
>   the city.
> They have saved the city, he said,
>   but the people are dead. (19)[10]

This is not just satiric dismissal. Abruptly appearing in the middle of a longer work, its deadpan delivery mimics an official language that is already so profoundly compromised that it lacks the energy even to dissimulate. The outrageous contradiction (saving the city at the expense of its citizenry) parades its logic brazenly, as if it expects to go unquestioned by citizens who have been numbed into silence.

Gordon's work appeared in the *California Quarterly* with enough regularity (in the issues of Autumn 1952, Winter 1953, Spring 1954, and Summer 1954, often with several poems) that he must be counted as one of the voices that the editorial board most wanted to be heard. (He was a member of an informal writing group that included, among others, Rolfe and McGrath.) His poetry assumes that the Bomb is the single most important mechanism by which the cold war institutionalized itself throughout every level of society. Its omnipresence establishes a war mentality from which we cannot escape. It has arranged the continuation of World War II though with a shuffled set of opponents. When he brought together his poems in 1958 in a collection entitled *Displaced Persons,* he underscored just how thoroughly a post-Hiroshima landscape had become taken for granted, with all the moral compromises that included. The third poem in that collection, "The Kimono," describes a woman who had appeared in a newsreel with the imprint of her kimono burned on her back. What rivets Gordon's attention is the normalization of the Bomb's horror, the domestication of such images, and the accommodation we make to escape their blunt impact. "The Kimono" is a rarity among Gordon's poems, however, in that Hiroshima is overtly named. It can go unnamed elsewhere in the collection, perhaps, because its moral climate is everywhere. Rather than referring to the Bomb, Gordon is more likely to write (in "One Nine Five Three," a poem that first appeared in the *California Quarterly*) "As we try to dream / The rocket goes twice around the globe, / The warhead ticks in the bedroom" (*Displaced* 27). We are always being located within a morally barren landscape that has penetrated our innermost spaces, creating a bizarre no-man's-land that is both utterly alien and yet instantly recognizable. No explanation is ever proffered for the ominous twists and turns that are presented in such a deadpan tone. These are not prophetic images but glimpses of a new social reality that we had better accustom ourselves to.

"The landscape has been subtly shifted," Gordon observes. "It is out of focus or we are" (*Displaced* 51). The displacement acknowledged in the title of his collection pervades every line. Since no one ever mentions the threat of imminent extinction, we help displace ourselves, sustaining this cold war that transforms us all into refugees even as we believe we are at peace. Gordon's task is to render overtly the covert aspect of our denials. "Sunday Afternoon" begins drowsily enough, with its carefully paced words, as though we can at last appreciate our newly expanded capacity for leisure:

> Slow   blue   tepid
>
> time floats in the living room
> as innocent   as soft   as smoke.
> The afternoon bears a litter of musical moments:
> Promptly on the hour come in the dogged comedians:
> Brass knuckles fix the face of laughter
>   as the murder opens. (16)

Nothing soothes in what the radio brings. To look beyond the barrage of amusements insistently delivered to us for processing—a hodge-podge of Schubert piano pieces like the Opus 94 *Moments Musicaux* with tough-guy comix battling for laffs—is to realize that the design in all this material is to promote distraction. Why distract?

Luckily the hired killers strangle the afternoon:
The man might otherwise look at the woman
    or the woman at the man;
Someone might notice the mushroom of cigarette
    smoke, the scientific elf at the window. (16)

Our compulsions for avoidance are what Gordon would expose. His brusque allusion—the "mushroom" of cigarette smoke—testifies to the existence of a reality that we apparently deny even as we immediately recognize it. This other world of the censored is hidden because it is terrifying, yet as the suppressed it only terrorizes us further. Moreover, to deny that it concerns us only further substantiates its existence, a perception Gordon unpacks in his last stanza:

The man and the woman lock themselves in the room
    in the afternoon of an era.
Everyone else escapes.
All figures are caught in the act of living; everything
    is normal in Herculaneum
The instant before the ash. (16)

Crisscrossing paradoxes openly vex these lines. Those who retreat may live, those who escape are caught. Yet these outrages are what we manufacture for ourselves. Gordon's commitment is to a poetic narrative so blatantly in avoidance that it screams to his audience about the ways they have positioned themselves in postures of denial.

Moreover, he makes it clear how cooperative we have been in arranging our own demise. His poems portray a dystopic landscape in terms so laconically neutral, so bereft of any sign of protest, that they are among the most effective depictions of the silencing that had overwhelmed not only leftists but almost everyone in these years. If his lines seem at first surreal and nightmarish, a second glance reveals them to be disarmingly literal. This thoroughly unsettling mix is on display in the opening stanzas of "Consider the Meaning of Love" as originally published in the *California Quarterly* (it was collected in *Displaced Persons* as "The Destroyers" but without its opening stanza):

Consider the meaning of love in the time
    of the murderers;
Examine the heart as the brain goes blind
    with fear;

Observe the flower in particular when the house
    is burning.

They blew up the island like a fish in a hole
    in the killer Pacific:
That was the day the world embraced itself;
That was the day for lovers under the sign
    of the active cloud.

When in an hour of night the windows are lit
    in the famous buildings,
A cold wave crosses the frontier of the generation
    in its sleep,
The coyote howls, the vulture comes down
    from the sky.
It is the hour of fever, the hour to study
    the nature of love. (37)

No sooner than any one of these statements begins to sound awry, it turns into a statement that can be effortlessly decoded. Why should the "hour of fever" also be "the hour to study the nature of love"? The first line rides on an understanding that the air has been poisoned and that an antidote is desperately needed even as it avoids saying so. What is striking, though, is how plainly it avoids saying so. Gordon's verse is at once both hidden and disclosed, even as it is also more than just that relationship. It is true that no one reading the second stanza would be likely to doubt that the island in the "Pacific" was exploded as the result of a nuclear test, nor is there any room for questioning whether radioactivity might be present in the "active cloud." Yet it is equally true that nothing explicit in the lines is ready to concede the accuracy of such a reading. What is unusual and ultimately disturbing about the way Gordon's lines perform is not just this game of cat and mouse but that the game as he plays it is handled so openly. That hiding and disclosure must occur, that the most crucial matters can only be approached through a screen to be deciphered, is what this poetry is about. It is coded language that is, in one sense, never so subtle as it might be, even as it is, in another sense (and to the extent in which it always falls away from its own subtlety) extraordinarily subtle, recording with precision the reality of its own coding precisely to object to it.

What remains startling in Gordon's work is not that his every mention of a "cloud" is a reference to nuclear radioactivity—though that is indeed the case and a move he undertakes in several poems: "When the air is burning and the cloud signals unbearable change, / The dissenter is born alive on the edges of the weather" (*Displaced* 23). Nor is it shocking that an entire lexicon of code words exists, words that clearly mean one thing even as they appear to mean another. What is shocking is that everyone knows and no one objects. The scandal of Gordon's poetry is that it brings no news. Not only do we deny that which we know, we even know that we are denying that which we know. Believing there is no escape from what is inescapable only places a higher premium on such helter-skelter and jury-rigged escapes as we can helplessly muster. While such writing may have flowed effortlessly from a society of West Coast film writers whose appreciation for the subtleties of coded expression must have been honed to a fine edge by the realities of the blacklist, it is also writing that is remarkable on its own: it performs a little dance of its own silencing. Not until W. S. Merwin's *The Lice* (1967) would language that was so mute yet so delicately aware of its own muteness again be on display—and again for political reasons. Yet such gesturing was typical of Gordon's work from the 1950s, and that it was welcome in such a range of periodicals—the acknowledgments for *Displaced Persons* include *Harper's, Saturday Review, Poetry, American Scholar,* and the *Western Review,* among others—suggests that a public alert to appreciate the extent to which silencings, as well as the need to communicate in code, had now become deeply enmeshed, pervading not only the way texts were written but even the way texts were read.

8 POEMS ABOUT THE BOMB: NUCLEAR FAMILY

> *... at Pompeii*
>
> *The little dog lay curled and did not rise*
> *But slept the deeper as the ashes rose*
> *And found the people incomplete, and froze*
> *The random hands, the loose unready eyes*
> *Of men expecting yet another sun*
> *To do the shapely thing they had not done.*
>
> —Richard Wilbur, "At Year's End"

> *It is in the nature of our life today that a poem should seem to say*
> *one thing while actually intending its opposite. We live opposed.*
> *The extremes blind us with light or leave us sightless in darkness.*
>
> —Paul Engle, "Why Modern Poetry"

How pervasive was the denial that Don Gordon sought to foreground? How often was it true that at the very moment when the Bomb seemed absent it was urgently present? How likely was it that a passage in which someone alluded to "the atom" in the most general of terms was also a passage that lent itself to functioning like Gordon's willfully obtuse poetic surface, alerting a readership not to accept the denial but to take note of the act of denial implicit in the move? For writers on the left like Gordon, there can be clear-cut answers to such questions because the discourse within which such problems occur has itself been arranged suggestively to invite a level of audience input that is designed both to hold harmless the writer and to give play to the skepticism of the reader. And for poets as skillful as Richard Wilbur, whose "Year's End" allows readings that satisfy both an obtuse reader and an astute reader, the problem remains ingeniously suspended. But for others, decisions are not so simple.

By the early 1950s, poems that were attempting to send a message against the Bomb had to acquire a subtlety new to political writing in America. To register dismay at the Bomb's proliferation in a way that conveys just how thoroughly the Bomb has *already* instilled itself in our consciousness demanded a poetry capable of engaging its readers even as prudence dictated it should operate indirectly—a poetry that sought to arouse but had to forswear catchwords and slogans. Without access to a framework that assures a linguistic context, however, such poetry risked becoming so anomalous as to go unnoticed. It was not helpful that the magnitude of the terms in which the Bomb was discussed, when it was discussed at all, was enormous. John Hall Wheelock could write in 1956: "The atomic age dramatizes, and brings home to us, with almost blinding vividness, the fact of our mortality." And when he added "—not simply the mortality of the individual but of the race" (13), the effect was not to clarify the dilemma but magnify it beyond all manageable proportions.

Even recognizing whether certain poems might be *implicitly* about or against the Bomb proves difficult. It is possible for John Berryman to signal, through the elaborate codes to which he draws attention in the closing stanzas of "The Dispossessed" (the title poem of his 1948 collection), that he is narrating a story that is unspeakable, and therefore cannot be directly addressed:

> an evil sky (where the umbrella bloomed)
> twirled its mustaches, hissed, the ingenue fumed,
>
> poor virgin, and no hero rides. The race
> is done. Drifts through, between the cold black trunks,
> the peachblow glory of the perishing sun
>
> in empty houses where old things take place. (*Collected* 67)

When the responsibilities of historical engagement are reduced to the formulas of melodrama by a passive citizenry—the "dispossessed" of the title—then indeed the "race / is done," and the "perishing sun" may evoke a nuclear fireball (already embedded in the parenthetical reference to the "umbrella" that "bloomed"), and civilization and tradition amount to no more than "empty houses where old things take place." Berryman's elaborate allusions and counterreferences invite and repay skeptical interrogation. But an aura of unresolved suggestiveness hovers around poetry by others, inviting a disturbing sense of paranoia in the questioning reader. May Swenson ends "Any Object" (from her debut collection of 1954, *Another Animal*) with these e. e. cummings–like lines:

> then every New descends from me
>
> uncoiling into Motion I
> start a massive panoply
> the anamolecular atoms fly
>
> and spread through ether like a foam
> appropriating all the Dome
> of absoluteness for my home (163)

Up until these eighth and ninth stanzas, the poem had been a pleasantly engaging piece that took delight in such rhymed tercets as "any Hour can be the all / expanding like a cunning Ball / to a Vast from very small" (163). Experimental by 1950s standards (but a typical Swenson production, with its idiosyncratic capitalization and its lack of punctuation), it could appear as a charming exercise in the paradoxical: "any Single becomes the More / multiples sprout from alpha's core." And the ending, it is true, could still be taken in that spirit, as if Swenson were simply appropriating scientific terminology ("anamolecular," "ether") to continue expanding her visionary narrative. On the other hand, when atoms start to fly, surely readers in the 1950s would find their attention distracted from the linguistic realm. Moreover, Swenson has chosen words that, by 1954, had accumulated some dark overtones. "Dome" in particular comes heavily freighted, in use as an alternative description for the mushroom cloud as well as appearing in the "dome of atoms" reference that concluded Karl Shapiro's "The Progress of Faust," one of the earliest and most reprinted of Bomb poems. Nonetheless, nothing in Swenson's ending signals delivery of a "message." She might be drawing upon this vocabulary to demonstrate a scientific lexicon need not be alien to poetry.[1] But the effect is to allow a willing reader to extract a fragmentary narrative about the invention of the Bomb from a poem where it peers, Cheshire-cat-like, from now the foreground, now the background. How we gauge it remains a problem not to be solved. Is Swenson closing with an intimation of our proximity to apocalypse, evoking that cannily with oblique allusions? Or are her overtones virtually "unconscious," a trace of an anxiety so deeply assimilated that it is a background presence? Or was the poem designed to raise these very questions— or avoid them?—or "raise" them by "avoiding" them? The text invites the grounds for reading it paranoiacally.

With other poets, however, there is no question that their work was calculated to draw attention to the current inability to confront a nuclear presence that has become so embedded as to resist articulation. Helen Bevington's fifty-six-line "Report from the Carolinas" (printed in the *New Yorker* in 1952, collected in *A Change of Sky and Other Poems* in 1956) insinuates the Bomb into its narrative with such elegant seamlessness that it must be counted among the most powerful works that trace the subtle disruptions that have been visited upon everyday life. In Bevington's poem, the Bomb is there are at the precise moment we least expect it, yet its sudden presence has a retroactive authority that reveals how dominant it had been from the start. Her "Report" makes its way as that simplest of forms, the list. She begins:

> It's a debatable land. The winds are variable,
> Especially winds of doctrine, though the one
> Prevailing breeze is mild, we say, and southerly.
> We have a good deal of sun,
>
> And our peach trees bloom too early. The first light promise
> Is lightly kept in a Carolina spring
> (It blows both hot and cold). Yet by February
> There is the flowering
>
> Of yellow jasmine and sudden gold forsythia,
> And mockingbirds; at night the threat of snow.
> Northerners passing on their way to Florida
> Say it's not Florida, though,
>
> This in-between land. (72)

Bevington's opening tone, so leisurely, verges on the vacuous, even the scatterbrained. Fecklessly, line lengths wax and wane, and as if the poet was just rattling along, words gets repeated: "the winds are variable, / Especially winds of doctrine," "The first light promise / Is lightly kept." Contractions abound, a rarity in the diction of 1950s poetry, along with that slackest of verbs, the *to be* traditionally eschewed by poets. Early in the 1950s, Bevington's reputation rested upon two previous volumes, *Dr. Johnson's Waterfall* (1946) and *Nineteen Million Elephants* (1950), both of which were touted on their dust jackets as light verse. Her *New Yorker* readers, glancing at her name at the bottom of the poem in those days before the magazine deigned to list a table of contents, were ready for some quiet entertainment or another spoof, like those on the Lake Poets for which she had been celebrated, or her gentle rewrite of Wallace Stevens in "Six Ways of Looking at a Hummingbird." But if the "Report" spoofs anything, it is the readerly expectation of Bevington's audience looking forward to a lightweight experience. Masquerading as elegant chatter, the poem is well underway before ominous signs begin to emerge. Yet so unerringly frolicsome is Bevington's tone that such signs remain easy to deny. North Carolina's amiable winds turn out to be "winds of doctrine" (this also makes us reconsider the opening sentence). Night brings "the threat of snow" and vulnerable peach trees "bloom too early," as if the weather had been affected in some way. Bevington continues to drift with apparent aimlessness between signs of nature and markers of culture, summoning flowers and birds in neat verbal interchanges ("We have quail in the yard, and dogwood in the woodlands, / A skyful of buzzards"). Where will this pleasant ramble end? Bevington confesses: "The chances are one becomes a little provincial, / Too quick to see as a microcosm this / Mid-country" which she then describes in the final list of her poem:

> Where the apricots flower too soon and the mimosas
> Flower endlessly, where now, in the sun-strewn days,
> The H-bomb is to flower, in all the seasons—
> Another crop to raise.

> And nobody says, of the region down by Ellenton,
> That winds are gathering there, or that, on the whole,
> They threaten ill. Yet, in the imagination,
> Fear is another shoal. (74)

These thirteenth and fourteenth stanzas abruptly resituate everything. Indeed, every loopy observation, every pleasant bit of patter, now seems in retrospect to have been deliberately edged with an element of nervous denial. When later in the poem Bevington repeats her opening remark that "winds are variable," those winds now seem to carry the ominous burden of radioactive fallout. "We naturally view the weather with misgiving," she writes, and though she goes on to refer to crops, she also evokes other misgivings, since now the wind can deliver wide-scale disruptions. In a 1971 prose memoir recalling the era of the 1950s, *The House Was Quiet and the World Was Calm,* Bevington enumerated all the reasons people had to feel anxious at that time: "People feared the mushroom cloud of death from the sky, feared radioactive fallout, feared the possibility that the earth might shift on its axis or that a chain reaction might destroy the planet" (145–46). While her prose condemns these things, her poem reproduces the pervasive anxiety of the time with cunning elegance. The Bomb is by no means limited to "the region down by Ellenton." It pervades and corrupts the imagination; it is like one of those "dangerous shoals, outlying and inhospitable" that she also describes, that belie the calm of the sea.[2]

Bevington's conspicuously indirect approach to the Bomb foregrounds a dread that would otherwise escape foregrounding. On the one hand, the H-bomb is out of place in these lists of mockingbirds, cotton, and magnolias; on the other hand, so pervasive is the Bomb that what is now out of place is the old-fashioned notion that any havens exist that elude the Bomb's long reach. As Bevington understands, pleasant chitchat about the weather is no longer possible, for the winds now bear the threat of radioactivity. Thus Olga Cabral concluded "The Cloud on Yucca Flat," a sonnet from *Cities and Deserts* (1959), with words of dead-end simplicity: "we were the enemy" (37). Without directly mentioning radioactivity, she describes a weather cycle, the fall of "a thin dry dust / that never heaven shed before" which is not rain but "a rust / and rot of life that warned no sentinel." The syntax of her opening sentence is awkwardly awry: "The cloud on Yucca Flat on Rome was rained / this morning . . . " Placing the object before its verb clashes the New Mexico testing ground against Rome. But the gap formerly separating distant places has collapsed, and areas whose remoteness once guaranteed their impregnability now turn vulnerable. Not only does this silent and deadly "fearsome dust" fall without warning, but it falls where no one wants it to fall, not on marginal outposts but on centers of civilization. We are the enemy, then, not only because we have constructed such a monstrous chain of events but because we have managed to target ourselves. Our bombs are turned against us no less than against any enemy.

The Child as Quintessential Civilian

The sense that we have outsmarted ourselves, that we have bound ourselves within a series of nonnegotiable moves that actually lessen our survivability, may help explain why the child begins to figure so prominently in Bomb poems after 1950. To depict the child as a target of the Bomb was, to be sure, not a novel strategy, and in some respects it is a return to the poetic discourse that first surrounded the Bomb poems written so close to World War II. John Hershey ended *Hiroshima* (1946) with a ten-year-old child's testimony. Powerless, unarmed, appealing to adults for protection, the child is the civilian par excellence—as Randall Jarrell, among others, realized in his war poetry. When he depicted a concentration camp through a child's eyes it emphasized the barbarity of a system unable to distinguish between civilian and soldier. As victim of the Bomb, the child underscores the horror of a no less unreasonable system by which nations arm to decimate each other.

In Jarrell's poems of the 1940s, the child exemplified the civilian. But in the poems of the 1950s it is more the case that the civilian has been reduced to a child. When it comes to the threat of the Bomb, the civilian simply has no role to play, no opportunity to intervene except to fret on the sidelines, a figure with no power and no responsibility. Spencer Brown begins "Spinning Jacks" (in his 1956 collection *My Father's Business*) as a father picking up jacks that his children "left all strewn / Over the floor" after bedtime. What to the child appears as an innocent object strikes the adult in a different light, especially to one who has served in the military. These jacks resemble "twelve right-angled tank-traps." Twirling a number of them aimlessly, the father also spots their resemblance to an "electron system"—a system that at once is recast in a military scenario:

> But it is collision
> Not yawing age, that interrupts most orbits.
> Two barely kiss from planetary dance
> As by a bullet or an embolism
> Either or both resume crystalline stiffness.
> In the midst of life we become angular road-blocks. (124)

With chilling speed, Brown moves from toying with jacks to world's end. Yet that speed is not only justified, it is entirely realistic. In the midst of life, he begins, echoing the Book of Common Prayer only to twist it into a euphemism: "we become angular road-blocks." In the midst of life we are near death, or more pointedly, in the midst of our domestic setting, where we may believe we are safe with our family, we are never immune from a military "solution." As the state is to the citizen so the parent is to the child. But to live in the Atomic Age is to acknowledge that the citizen is as much a target as any military base. And once the lines that separate the military from the civilian have been compromised then the ability of a parent to shelter a child has been permanently disabled.

In "Children Are Game" (from her 1955 collection *Birthdays from the Ocean*), Isabella Gardner, walking through a winter forest, regards "shrill quick children skating on the pond / a safe and thousand miles from reef and shark" (21). So odd an observation as the last, concerning the child's safety, opens up the gulf that lurks, it seems, just the other side of many moments in the 1950s:

Children Are Game

I have come often to this forest,
home to these never not green trees.
Now, in a grove of auburn bones
the spindling skeletons of summer flowers,
I hear the soft snow hiss through fir and spruce,
the shrill quick children skating on the pond
a safe and thousand miles from reef and shark.
What wings will whistle down this resined bark,
what monstrous blooming blast belief?
Children should not come to grief.
I swore that even crows could sing
I thawed my winters thinking spring
And now am always cold, with reason,
for bombs can blossom in any season.
The pheasant's chicks scratch posted ground,
children are game the whole year round
skating the thin ice of the pond
gay and innocent and spruce:
while I in a grave of once-were flowers
and stiffer than their thready bones
forget these seen to be green trees
too mindful of the forest. (21)

Not just these children skate on thin ice. Gardner draws attention to her
own lack of control over her work. When bombs can "blossom any season,"
then chilling transpositions will occur, like the other, raw meaning of
"game" that slides into "children are game the whole year round."
Gardner's ending, even as it works through the type of "metaphysical"
changes that many poets in the 1950s presented as a mark of their professional skill (deploying a language of paradox and contrary imagery), also
critiques that convention as a series of desperate and helpless moves. In the
entanglement of the final lines we are told the forest is a graveyard, yet its
bones are feathery-fine, bones of flowers too frail to escape obliteration.
Rather than focusing on these bones, Gardner prefers to concentrate on
life: those trees that are "seen to be green" surely represent children still
young, still growing strong, unlike the "thready bones" of flowers. But a
contrary message overwhelms here. If she desires to assign the attributes
of the green trees to those children—that would make them into an emblem of strength—she finds she cannot. At this moment in history, children are not saplings with a long history before them but fragile flowers

that may not outlast a season. Even as Gardner moves to demonstrate her skill and authority (and form here is particularly subtle: the end-words of the last six lines are identical to, but reverse the sequence of, the end-words of the first six lines), she finds herself helpless. She would prefer to shelter the children; what she is left with instead is a set of rhetorical moves. When warfare has become so radically primitivized, no one can assure protection. We are all children now; we are all game. Without a way to shelter children, Gardner has no way to be an adult. The children remain in the same forest within which she is condemned to wander.

Muted so elaborately, Gardner's voice is also protesting its own silencings. Muzzled voices are an element in the Bomb poems of the mid-1950s, though not all present themselves subtly. In 1945 Iowa Writers' Workshop founder Paul Engle published sixty-four sonnets about his daughter's first ten years of life, calling it *American Child*. When he added thirty-six new sonnets and published a revised edition in 1956, he was newly recording (albeit gingerly) his own distress at events that had ensued in the subsequent decade. The first version of *American Child* had, of course, no inkling of the Bomb. But as early as sonnet 9 in the revised and updated edition, his daughter has overheard talk about the hydrogen bomb, and when she asks for an explanation of it, her father cannot provide her with an answer. Her question freezes the entire family into a rigid tableau that must eventually explode in emotion:

> She hears the voice say, Estimates go higher
> On millions dead from H-bombs. No defense.
> Then, as the curious wood says, What is fire?
> She asks, But what is *that?* And her intense
> Voice trembles as she adds, a bomb? The thought
> Shakes her like a dog an old felt hat.
> She lifts her head in trust and anguish, caught
> Between her love of us, and fear of *that.*
>
> Enduring our knowledge like a dread disease,
> We wait in silence. Then the whole room jars
> As she screams, I'll ask *her,* and with a wild
> Crying hugs her doll, while my arms seize
> The live, exploding element of child. (11)

Perhaps no sonnet sequence can entirely escape the dangers of gigantism. Engle's later additions to *American Child* were especially ambitious. It is quite plausible that he aimed in the sestet of sonnet 9 to reproduce mimetically the one narrative that the 1950s held most unthinkable: the tension of the cold war snapping at last, unleashing a "live, exploding element." More interesting, though, is the extent to which the mere mention of the H-bomb has devastated the family structure even before this melodramatic ending. For one thing, Engle's daughter learns of the Bomb from a source outside the family, a "voice" that emanates, to judge from its evident professionalization, from a radio or television. This harsh and cold display of the factual ("millions dead from H-bombs") is itself entirely opposite from the family's enclosing circle. In the preceding sonnet of the sequence, the daughter accompanied her family to a lake where she sported in "fish-furious waves," then safely fell asleep in her father's arms where she "smiles from her beach of dreaming / Narrow along the world's wide sea of dread" (*American Child* 10). But the beach of sonnet 8, narrow as it is, is entirely absent from sonnet 9. To the daughter's inquiry, the whole family falls mute, though her emphatic voice signals her distress. Moreover, this muteness persists through the next five lines of the poem, drawn out over the gap between octet and sestet, a muteness made striking by the daughter's increasing agitation. It can be no surprise, then, that her solution is to turn and grasp her doll. By holding her doll, she reconstitutes the family that mysteriously vanished at the mere mention of the Bomb. Her gesture, that is, is strikingly "adult" and responsible, a shaming contrast to the silence and inertia of the adults in the room.

From such a child an adult can learn; indeed, her father is galvanized into action at the end. Yet that action, Engle is careful to note, is fraught with helplessness. It is his "arms"—not an "I"—that "seize / The live, exploding element of child," as if his agency had already been stringently limited. And if this is an embrace, it is a violent one. It disturbingly echoes the suicidal gesture of one seizing an explosive grenade and absorbing the blast into one's own body. If the child has been thrust into adulthood, the adult has been infantilized. What is at stake, Engle's poem suggests, is not only an ability to communicate between generations but a faith in continuity. Does the current generation have anything of value to hand on to the next? If adults stammer like children while children struggle with matters that are beyond anyone's comprehension, then what is there to learn, finally, except one's own helplessness?

"A father's no shield / for his child," Robert Lowell wrote in "Fall 1961" (collected in 1965 in *For the Union Dead*), sometimes regarded as one of the earliest poems to protest the Bomb. But he might as well have been summing up a decade's worth of poetry that had slowly been discovering the same truth. Not only was a father an unlikely figure as a militant but that same father was unable to find a way to shelter his offspring from "the chafe and jar / of nuclear war" (*Union* 11).

Nuclear Family

Yet poets in the 1950s in fact often did write poems that set out to do precisely that which Lowell deemed to be the quintessential response to the Bomb—to be a shield for their child. That is, poets in surprising numbers wrote pieces in which their primary role was not to speak in the voice of the professional or the sober analyst or the civic-minded intellectual but in the voice of the parent or parent-surrogate whose very poem was being extended as an offering to a child as if it could be an act of sheltering. In none of these poems is the Bomb ever mentioned directly. But the extent to which a poem must include a direct reference to the Bomb in order to evoke its presence is always a problematic feature of poems about the Bomb. Consider Hyam Plutzik's six-line poem (probably composed in 1951 and collected in 1959 in *Apples from Shinar*), which accomplishes its task nicely without mentioning the Bomb:

> This star is only an augury of the morning,
> Gift-bearer of another day.
>
> A wind has brought the musk of thirty fields,
> Each like a coin of silver under that sky.
>
> Precious, the soundless breathing of wife and children
> In a house on a field lit by the morning star. (*Collected* 114)

This, which is the entire poem, could be mistaken for no more than a lyric appreciation of the morning light were it not for its title: "And in the 51st Year of That Century, While My Brother Cried in the Trench, While My Enemy Glared from the Cave." With its title restored, it is clear that the beauty of the moment is the last thing that holds Plutzik's interest. He wants to know why things that should be as universal as starlight, as the wind, as calm sleep, should now be deemed rare and precious gifts. How vulnerable everything is in this simple scene! What does it mean for Plutzik to waken by himself and commune with the morning star, with the wind? In effect he is saying that our fate is now in the hands of the stars, cast to the wind. Underneath a surface tone of awe Plutzik has inscribed a coruscating irony: the "coin of silver" is not just synonymous with glistening early morning light—it echoes with the thirty pieces of silver with which Judas was paid. Nonetheless, the feature crucial to the poem is not this fierce irony but Plutzik's longing to counteract it with a sheltering gesture. That longing goes unanswered, however, and the performative aspect of this poem—its inclusive gesturing—exists as little more than a helpless murmur, insufficient to counteract the nameless and unmentionable threat that stands at the horizon. As we read, the poem's circumstances grow increasingly desperate even as they remain disturbingly representative.

How large a step is it from a poem like this, in which it is not inappropriate to invoke the Bomb as an unstated presence, to a poetry which directly confronts anxieties that are linked in other poems to the Bomb? More precisely, when there exists a body of poetry that makes a case against the Bomb by objecting to the targeting of the family and its children, how can that fail to influence the reading of another body of work that turns upon actively intervening to shelter the child? Questions like these become especially pertinent by the midpoint of the decade when the number of poems that allude even indirectly to the Bomb sharply diminishes.[3] That this scarcity would occur is, in one sense, not surprising. By the mid-1950s the Eisenhower administration had greatly intensified the disinformation program that it had been developing to counter public concern over the hydrogen bomb, a program that was minute in its attention to detail. To take just one example, Joyce Nelson has described the 1952 television broadcast of the Yucca Flat, New Mexico, H-bomb test as a triumph of normalization. Sponsored by the U.S. Council of Advertisers (a meta-advertiser of sorts to represent all American commerce), the broadcast sought to dissolve the Bomb's aura of danger by surrounding it with gestures of everydayness such as the ubiquitous commercial. "The very popularity of this mass medium," Nelson writes, "with its pleasurable entertainment function in the home, could ideologically manage and contain the spectacle of bomb blasts imaged on its screen" (40). The hydrogen bomb required management on such a scale because its greater explosive power demonstrably increased the threat of radioactive fallout. "The most portentous event of 1954," wrote Richard M. Gordon in the preface to *The Unicorn Book of 1954,* the yearly update of the Funk & Wagnalls Encyclopedia, "was the death of a humble Japanese fisherman . . . the first victim of a hydrogen bomb." Although eighty miles away from the test blast site, "he was fatally burned by a fallout of radioactive ash carried by the soft sea breezes" (vi). That the nation which had provided first victims for the A-bomb was now performing a similar function for the H-bomb was an irony not lost on commentators.

The H-bomb offered no advance on security; if anything, it only under-scored the threat of silent and invisible radioactivity, an enemy against which there could be little defense. As the dangers of the Bomb grew ever more invisible even as the Bomb itself grew ever more pervasive, turning upon the essentially uncontrollable effects of radioactivity (which were, in that haunting phrase, "carried by the soft sea breezes"), might not the poetry that registered those dangers itself move underground, like its nem-esis becoming itself both pervasive and invisible?

Of course poets in the 1950s might have written numerous poems to and about children even if the Bomb had not been a constant in their lives. This prosperous generation, once its service in the military was complete, married young and quickly raised a family. Of that population who came of age during and after World War II, 96.4 percent of the women and 94.1 percent of the men were married—"the most marrying generation on record," in Elaine Tyler May's words: "most couples had two to four chil-dren, born sooner after marriage and spaced closer together than in previ-ous years" (*Homeward* 20). The number of children born each year rose from 3.6 million in 1946 to a peak of 4.3 million in 1957—"an average that year," J. Ronald Oakley calculated, "of one baby every 7 seconds" (119–20). Poets were not exempt from these demographics. Indeed, the academy's new willingness to extend support to poets meant a steady employment that guaranteed that an entire generation of poets had the time and the leisure to help raise their children and take pleasure in watching them grow. Inevitably, such surroundings would enter their writing. As F. W. Dupee observed, reviewing the *New Poets of England and America* anthol-ogy assembled by Donald Hall, Robert Pack, and Louis Simpson in 1957: "Marriage is obviously an attractive as well as advisable state for the young poets, and it provides them with a stock of poetic objects. Home, wife, children, parents, pets, gardens, summer resorts, travel *en famille* make up the unromantic romance of this poetry" (456).

Nonetheless, neither demographics nor economic circumstances en-tirely explain how one form of this domestic verse, the address to the young child, came to be practiced so widely. It was not, after all, sanctioned by any current literary tradition. Indeed, distinct impediments to it had to be over-come. If the mainstream poets of the 1950s looked back for guidance to the High Modernists (Eliot, Pound, Stevens, Crane, Moore) examples of the poem that celebrated the child within a family setting were simply non-existent. From that first generation of modernists one might justly con-clude that membership in a dysfunctional family was among the premier qualifications for being a poet. Not even among those poets who were, in Randall Jarrell's discrediting phrase in his "Fifty Years of American Poetry," members of the "tradition of feminine verse" (329)—he cited Elinor Wylie, Edna St. Vincent Millay, Louise Bogan, and Leonie Adams—could examples be found of a domestic verse that extended itself to children. Just how aberrant was such verse? That can be demonstrated best by enumerating the many precepts of the New Criticism violated when a poet wrote to his or her son or daughter.

To begin with, this new domestic verse was devoid of the ironic mask or of anything like a "persona." The poet who was acting within the poem and the poet who signed the poem were one and the same. Not only did this mean there was no opportunity to display the ironic mode, but the biographical fallacy cautioned against by W. K. Wimsatt and Monroe Beardsley in an essay that was a cornerstone of the New Criticism was being openly disrespected. When a setting or address was mentioned, when someone was named, that statement was to be taken as recording an actual name rather than conceiving a figurative one. The geography of Iowa City in the 1950s is precisely inscribed in W. D. Snodgrass's sequence of ten poems addressed to his daughter, "Heart's Needle" (1959), from the dismaying little zoo in the City Park with its fretful animals to the dusty exhibits of the taxidermist's art in the university's MacBride Hall. The same is true when Robert Lowell recalls settings from his own childhood in "91 Revere Street," the exact address where his parents resided. With such direct and conspicuous references, poets were asking their readers to set aside interpretive skills that they had been arduously cultivating. As Marjorie Perloff has demonstrated, it is metonymy not metaphor that dominates *Life Studies* (*Poetic Art* 80–130). When reading John Ciardi's "For My Son John" (in *I Marry You: A Sheaf of Love Poems,* 1958), there is no reason to assume that Ciardi's son's name is *not* John. Apart from the kinship it denotes, no other significance accrues to the name (as it would have had in a poem with an explicitly Christian setting). In a similar way, it would be absurd to link monetary values to the name of T. Weiss's daughter in "To Penny When She Comes of Reading Age" (in *The Catch,* 1949).

Another New Critical standard set aside by this poetry is the assumption that the central words in a poetic text must be ambiguous and polysignificant. These are poems of affectionate address that define the poem as an intimate space in which a loving interchange can unfold. Here poets take up actual names to dwell on them lovingly. "I love to say your name, the name I know," wrote James Wright in "A Call from the Front

Porch" (*Green Wall* 90). Indeed, poets often paid homage to the centrality of the child's name by locking it into the poem's title. Robert Penn Warren's poem about his daughter, "To a Little Girl, One Year Old, in a Ruined Fortress" (from *Promises: Poems 1954–1956*), is carefully subtitled "To Rosanna." While the most common situation is that of a parent addressing an offspring, the poet need not be the parent of a child and the child need not be the offspring of the speaker. Although Ciardi wrote one poem to John as well as others to his younger son Benn ("Two Poems for Benn" in *I Marry You*), he wrote other pieces to the children of friends. In these poems that address a child not the poet's own, the title is most often highly particularized. Robert Pack's "An Attempted Blessing (on the Birth of Emily Heilbrun)" appeared in *A Stranger's Privilege* (1959). Mona Van Duyn's three part poem "To My Godson, on His Christening" was collected in *Valentines to the Wide World* (1959), and Isabella Gardner included "Canzonetta (for a God-son Aged Five, Stewart Gardner")" in *The Looking Glass* (1961).

This desire to mark the poem as arising from a particular occasion, as unfolding within a specific moment, opposes the aspiration toward the universal and the ahistorical that some New Critics identified with the self-sufficient text. And insofar as this writing commemorates a transitional event, it performs rather than represents. "For Lori My Daughter on Her Second Birthday" appeared in Robert Dana's *My Glass Brother* (1957). Louis O. Coxe collected "For My Son's Birthday" in *The Wilderness* (1958). Birthday celebrations surround James Wright's "A Presentation of Two Birds to My Son" (*The Green Wall*), and Alan Swallow ends *The Nameless Sight (Poems, 1937–1956)* with "For My Daughter, Aged Five." As popular as birthday poems were, they may have been outnumbered by poems that greeted a specific child at his or her birth. Jane Cooper dates "For a Boy Born in Wartime" as written in 1949, for her retroactively published collection *Mercator's World, Poems, 1947–1951*. John Ciardi wrote "On the Birth of Jeffrey to William and Barbara Harding," including it in *As If: Poems New and Selected* (1955). Donald Justice addressed the newly born child of a friend in "To a Ten Months' Child" (scrupulously subtitled "to M.M." and collected in 1959 in *The Summer Anniversaries*). The age of these children made it impossible that they would understand the poet's words at the time they were being spoken. But what is important here is not just the moment but the link of one generation to another—that continuity is valued immensely. It is never too early to express that concern. At the midpoint of "Nine Poems (to an Unborn Child)," from Muriel Rukeyser's 1948 collection *The Green Wave,* a dramatic shift occurs when after the question "Who is there?" (77), Rukeyser begins to address a "you," a figure still so unknown as to lack even gender. (That child "will enter the world where death by war and explosion / Is waited.")

That so deviant a discourse could arise outside a regulatory mechanism as authoritative as the New Criticism in the 1950s is noteworthy. Only a most compelling circumstance could sanction writing diametrically opposed to so many widely accepted norms. A renegade poetry of such dimensions cannot be entirely explained by the fact that poets actually belonged to families and were deeply involved in raising their children. For this new domestic verse to flourish, some framework had to be at hand which would allow both practitioners and readers to align their texts. Heretical from a New Critical standpoint, these texts would need another framework from within which they would appear to be recognizable and orthodox. While it would be far too simplistic to say that the Bomb poems of the 1940s evolved into the new domestic verse of the 1950s, it nonetheless remains true that this domestic verse directly compensates for omissions that were identifying features of that discourse which enabled poetry about the Bomb. For example, when this domestic verse insists upon producing a moment of intense intimacy, it is at once displacing that leveling anonymity which, in poems about the Bomb, so distressingly eliminated the distinction between the civilian and the military. In addition, when this domestic verse turns performative and virtually enacts in gestures its moment of intensity, it is counteracting the passivity with which whole populations were being asked to accept their victimization. And when this domestic verse speaks from one generation to another, firmly intervening in history, registering its presence, it is denying the literal end of history that might be the product of the Bomb's detonation. In short, what is a rogue discourse from the New Critical perspective becomes, when considered as an interventionary counterpart to anti-Bomb verse, a compensatory discourse that is responsive to just those matters that poems about the Bomb had been identifying as under threat.

Other traits, too, link this domestic verse to anti-Bomb poetry—an edginess about the future, for example. When these writers stand alongside a crib they are unprepared to speak with the confidence of Yeats whose voice in 1919, in "A Prayer for My Daughter," rose firmly to counter the violence of the storm that seethed around his daughter's cradle. Yeats had answers that confronted difficulties even if they could not ultimately resolve them. The storm, by the end of his poem, had been quelled. These poets, however, falter as they speak; they are simply not sure their voices will be heard in the future—or that there will be a future in which voices can be heard:

> Taking down
> the little I overhear, I write
> this poem for you that you
> will perhaps read it
> when these days will be
> to you as you are now for us. (39)

What is striking about this passage toward the end of T. Weiss's "To Penny When She Comes of Reading Age," which otherwise consists of sketches of family moments, is that peculiarly ominous "perhaps." On the one hand, the world into which this child has entered is uncertain enough that she may never be in a position to read these words. On the other hand, if the poem is a record, it can also be an intervention, and the act of setting down these words forges a link, albeit one that is tenuous, between "these days" and later days. These poems are often crisscrossed with traces of doubt, and their messages can seem vitiated. "I cannot interpret for you this collocation / Of memories" (28), writes Robert Penn Warren in the fifth and final poem of his sequence "To a Little Girl, One Year Old, in a Ruined Fortress" (1956). His ending acknowledges the child's fundamental separateness: "You will live your own life, and contrive / The language of your own heart" (28), he continues. However platitudinously Warren proceeds, in a nuclear age such sentiments are tinged with darkness. The message these poems deliver is less than comforting. It often dwells disconcertingly on the limits of the adult's power. "Have I heart / To watch you range, and neither sight nor speech / Mark you even now beyond my reach?" (22) asks Louis O. Coxe in "For My Son's Birthday" (*The Wilderness* 1958).

And yet as much as these poems register uncertainty about the future, they also undertake an almost desperate effort to resist and defy anxiety. Raeburn Miller's address "For Megan Hall Merker, Newly Born," collected in Paul Engle's 1961 anthology of texts from the Iowa Writers' Workshop, *Midland,* shifts its perspective from stanza to stanza, playing short term off long term, alternating between a cribside morning scene in which the child's movements are pleasurably described ("I hadn't seen you cry / With such obvious delight in your own noise" [520]) and a late-night setting in which the poet broods darkly over loss and disappointment ("I know what it is like not to decide, / To wait at night for one trustworthy hint" [521]). The world of sorrow into which children fall in these poems is, for their adult writers, a given, and it arouses defensive instincts. Robert Huff's poem to his daughter "For Ursula," collected in 1959 in *Colonel Johnson's Ride,* is subtitled "who refuses to position herself for exit from her mother's pool and is torn midwinter from her sleep" (3). When John Berryman opened "A Sympathy, A Welcome" in *His Thoughts Made Pockets & The Plane Buckt* (1958), a poem to his son Paul—"Feel for your bad fall how could I fail, / poor Paul, who had it so good. / I can offer you only: this world like a knife" (*Collected* 157)—he was not acting the part of the skeptical intellectual in his mordant title but adapting the features of domestic verse for his own use, right down to the direct address in the second-person singular and the inclusion of his son's name.

If these poems falter, then, they also recover themselves, and that their poets have found a way to speak at all becomes in itself a positive trait. The silencing of the poet was, in many Bomb poems, implicit within the work. In them, the work could proceed at best awkwardly and surreptitiously, often by accommodating itself to an elaborate code. In striking contrast, the only time silencing surrounds poems written to children is when the poets turn toward a possible future. But in the present moment, as the poet stands by a crib or memorializes a christening or birthday or anniversary, these are works that not only clearly speak to another person but call attention to that speaking voice at its most intimate. This is almost the defining instance of this poetry, the source of its performative gifts, and it is why it finds so beneficial the form of direct address. As the voice in the poem sends each word out toward that particular child, it is as if a fold is opening in the poem, a temporary pocket within which the beloved can be sheltered. The enunciation sacralizes not just a name but the deep and abiding relationship in which generations are bound to one another. "My little son, I have cast you out / To hang heels upward, wailing over a world / With walls too wide" (110) begins Anne Ridler, writing on her son's christening in her 1952 poem, "Choosing a Name." On a similar occasion, Philip Murray opens "The Christening" with: "Child, you are about to be given a name" (203). Such apostrophes, especially when they are the opening words of the poem, sound a pitch that establishes a voice of deep reverence. These particularizing addresses appear throughout W. D. Snodgrass's "Heart's Needle" (the poems of which were first published between 1954 and 1957), composed as it is almost entirely in the second-person singular; at crucial moments, it particularizes its mode of address even more explicitly, as at the close of the sixth poem when the poet must admit to his daughter that he has remarried: "Child, I have another wife, / Another child. We try to choose our life" (*Heart's* 51). Snodgrass's ear for such movements must have been sensitized by the example of Berryman, one of his teachers at the University of Iowa, whose *Homage to Mistress Bradstreet* (1953) contained passages in Bradstreet's voice:

> Pioneering is not feeling well,
> not Indians, beasts.
> Not all their riddling can forestall
> One leaving. Sam, your uncle has had to
> go from us to live with God. "Then Aunt went too?"
> Dear, she does wait still.
> Stricken: "Oh. Then he takes   us one by one." My dear.
>   (*Collected* 138)

Berryman's use of direct address makes Bradstreet's concern for her children, so intensely in evidence in her own seventeenth-century poetry, sound all too contemporary. With more delicacy, in "Home after Three Months Away" from *Life Studies* (1959), Robert Lowell gently makes a space for his daughter, turning to chide her exactly as if what she had interrupted was this very poem:

> When
> we dress her in sky-blue corduroy,
> she changes to a boy,
> and floats my shaving brush
> and washcloth in the flush . . .
> Dearest, I cannot loiter here
> in lather like a polar bear
>   (*Life* 77, ellipses in original)

In this moment familiar to every parent, the child's need to be recognized takes precedent over all else, including the task at hand (shaving or writing a poem). Lowell's direct address opens a loving space within the poem for his daughter, a listener who has a singular status, whose importance compels the poet to override other social rules including those that might require silencing. Most of all, however, what we hear in such moments is the poet's voice at its most intimate—both hesitant and yearning, extending itself to another.

So startling is it in the 1950s to hear so intimate a voice that it has an outsize effect. If it is the case that to hover anxiously over a child is to wonder if there will be a future, any future at all, then perhaps it is also true that the task of the poem can be to project a future. Just that desire is implicated in the poet's intimate voice, shaping words that the child is not yet able to understand but that are being banked for comprehension at a distant time. This deep desire to make a future happen is not fanciful. Uncertainty about whether there will be a future needs to be counteracted through sheer acts of will. When poets turn their extraordinarily sensitive ears to the future, some hear nothing, a silence, the void. Hearing nothing they must fill it with words that will deny the void, that conceive possibility (the way conceiving a child enlists a future), however desperately and anxiously. Whether there will be a future at all rests for a moment upon these poems that, by figuratively projecting a future, seem virtually to construct it.

The "Fifties Poem"'s Contrary: Domestic Verse

In just these poems, a body of work exists that answers where the Bomb poems of the 1950s are to be found. With the only discourse that could encompass the Bomb of the mid-1950s a model that had to operate through covert designs, poets might consequently drift from that model to a more focused set of circumstances that promised direct relief from the psychological and emotional tensions that surrounded the issue. By writing a poetry that sheltered the child, the poets who practiced this domestic verse extended protection to those whom the Bomb had most conspicuously and unfairly targeted. Even if it was fictive, an intervention of some kind was being propounded in such work. The gesture alone would offer some temporary relief from anxiety. By locating the poem within domestic space, the poet shifted the terms of the discourse into a dimension that implied manageability. Just choosing to fix limits within a domestic setting would have served to distance the Bomb's threat. At the same time, even as these poems offered a solace otherwise unavailable, they appeared to understand how provisional their relief was. The sense that the act of writing, whatever its performative features, was only verbal—that it was more wishful than activist—was a part of the work.

If this cross-generational, interfamilial poetry of the 1950s is reconsidered in context, it forms a poetic discourse that stands as a counterweight to the period style so otherwise in fashion. It also makes Donald Hall's 1959 attack on the domestic, in a document central to the devaluation of the poetry of the 1950s, begin to seem more simplistic than sensitive. Hall marked the family as an area that was entirely private, whose configuration could have little to do with other social units or larger social issues. As a result, he could propose that the poets of his generation were flawed because they had turned away from the responsibilities of cultural concerns to withdraw into the pleasantries of a private world. For the bearings of his argument, Hall took direction from reviewers who had been negative toward the anthology that he had recently coedited with Robert Pack and Louis Simpson, *New Poets of England and America* (1957): James Dickey in the *Sewanee Review* and F. W. Dupee in the *Partisan Review*. Although the basis for Dickey's complaints was quite general—"The fault of most of this poetry," he wrote, "and perhaps of most poetry is that one simply doesn't believe it" ("Presence" 297)—he stressed that the scale of this poetry was inadequate. Speaking for himself as one more "new poet" under forty years of age (the criterion for inclusion in the anthology, though he himself had not been invited to appear), he wrote: "we have given a charming and deliberate smallness far more than its due" (289). Dupee's attack was even more pointed. In a review entitled "The Muse as House Guest," he depicted the poets as provincials whose interest in family life betrayed their status as amateurs. Such unintellectual behavior was a scandal. By evincing interest in the domestic, these poets had feminized themselves and thus let their whole generation down. In his 1959 essay, Hall shows he has digested these arguments and is ready to accept public rebuke. His tone throughout his essay is one of confession and quiet self-rectification. "I feel that I see a pattern among us of provinciality and evasion, which results in a reliance on the domestic at the expense of the historical" (311).

At an earlier point in the decade, however, the role of the domestic had been theorized quite differently. Philip Blair Rice, the associate editor of the *Kenyon Review*, noted in remarks delivered in 1954 that postwar writers had pressing reasons for sheltering and even overvaluing "what's common." He suggested that a generation "whose conscious and subconscious minds have been formed successively by depression, war of nerves, war, cold war, the little war, and again cold war" was apt to produce "a literature that cultivates the simplicities of daily life, as a relief from these things" (437). Rice poses the contrast as interestingly as possible, placing the small details of daily life against a vast and terrifying historical background. He reminds us that poetry which could resemble an apparent retreat may also be in dialogue, albeit obliquely, with large and disturbing issues.

Hall's repudiation of the domestic dismisses Rice's perspective by insisting that the "domestic" and the "historical" can only be construed as mutually opposed categories. For Hall's own poetry, it must be said, such a characterization would be accurate. When he took to writing about his family in the 1950s, he regarded it as one more opportunity to display a mastery of metaphysical wit. The poems he produced had little to do with actually observing a family and much to do with conforming to a style of presentation then in high fashion. The birth of his son prompted several poems in his first book, *Exiles and Marriages* (1956), but these were primarily occasions to display not affection toward his child but his own cleverness. "Epigenethlion: First Child" (which he chose for reprinting in his *New Poets* anthology) wittily developed what Hall defined as "The mortal paradox" (*Exiles* 106): the notion that the birth of a child initiates the mortality of its parents who now face their future demise because the life of the family has passed on to the firstborn. "My son, my executioner," Hall thus begins his poem, and although he takes his son in his arms in the next line, what the poem is about is not such expressions of tenderness but the display of wit occasioned by the unpacking of the paradox in his opening line. In "A Relic of the Sea," Hall investigates the question "Where do illusions come from?" and this leads him to revisit toys stored in an attic. All his observations are subjugated to the overarching inquiry into the origin of the illusory, so that when his son makes an appearance, he is at once enmeshed in a skein of paradoxes: "The daily loss created by the child, / Who wants to keep on growing, / makes new activity appear defiled" (*Exiles* 109). On still another occasion, in "Fathers and Sons," Hall finds himself standing over his son's bed just as his own father, he recalls, stood over his. Rather than delighting in this coincidence, he twists it into the basis for a theory of religion: "Over my bed / Last night there stood / The form I dread / Of father God." He concludes we are always to be ruled by an "over-shape" and that there is "no escape / From the fixed world" (*Exiles* 70). Hall evidently reveled in his marriage (he composed an epithalamion to his bride as well as a set of wedding speeches that he included in his collection). Every indication is that he delighted in the birth of his son and felt deep affection for his parents, dedicating his first collection "For Donald A. Hall, Sr., and Lucy Wells Hall, in love and gratitude." But it never occurred to him to register in his poetry the presence of any of these individuals. No wails ever emanate from his son. Do soiled diapers mark one of the limits of metaphysical transformation? Hall viewed his family as a pretext for composing intellectual meditations; for the purpose of his poetry, the members of his family were subjects to be incorporated into literary tradition.

Hall's aesthetics in 1956 were sharply defined by what he was convinced were the latest standards—or, more narrowly, what a well-educated Harvard graduate had been trained to consider as acceptable poetic discourse. But that view had an alternative, one that was developed with intensity and engagement by other poets, both men and women, who turned to children, whether their own or someone else's, to speak to them with an urgency, as though the simple act of sheltering as parent or adult had itself fallen under threat. There could be no firm or fast distinction between the domestic and the historical for most persons of concern and goodwill in the 1950s. More than the penetrating power of the Bomb is at issue when poets begin to record its presence invading the family. It is one thing for the poet who wishes to send a message to the government to be silenced; it is another thing when the poet who wishes only to extend care to a child finds that words are unavailable. For this kind of deep exchange to be silenced or even muted is to register a fear that generations can no longer continue. It is akin to a confession of despair. The gap that these poems acknowledge (and yearn to close) between adult and child is a particularly intense and deeply personalized way of representing the catastrophic teleology of the Bomb. If the Bomb signifies the end of history in a most literal sense, then the child who represents the next generation is a projection into the future that affirms what the Bomb threatens. Yet in the 1950s, it is just that simple continuity that is endangered. Deep within the shelter of the family a shadow falls that has no name. Its very lack of nomenclature associates it with that reality which everyone knows is unthinkable.

Epilogue: Domestic Verse, Confessional Verse

In 1952 *Poetry* magazine reacted in an unprecedented fashion to the record number of quality submissions it was receiving from (in editor Karl Shapiro's words) "colleges and universities and from the poetry workshops and summer writing conferences of America" (249). Shapiro indulged in his fondness for setting aside entire issues for one topic (May 1951 had been devoted to the Activists, July 1953 would be exclusively the poetry in translation of Juan Ramón Jiménez), and he turned over the February 1952 issue to two of the most successful and productive university poetry workshops, the Iowa workshop, under the direction of Paul Engle, and the University of Washington workshop, headed by Theodore Roethke. Space was apportioned equally between the two, and each director had a few pages in which to introduce his poets. Engle quickly made it understood how selective he had been able to be: "The poems from Iowa are not the selected best of a year or two, but those available this autumn. In the Spring of 1951 the best poems of the season were published in a booklet, *Poems from the Iowa Poetry Workshop* (The Prairie Press, Iowa City, Iowa, $1.00) and various others from the class have been eliminated by acceptance from *Poetry, The Kenyon Review* and other magazines" ("Poet and Professor" 270). The poems in this issue were simply the autumn crop plus a few choice selections that had already been culled by prestigious journals. Engle's proud message was clear: the Iowa workshop generated enough fine poetry to fill a half-issue of *Poetry*, plus a booklet, as well as numerous pages of highly selective quarterlies.

Of all these young poets, the one who would have had the most reason to be pleased by the final arrangement of the February 1952 issue was Robert Shelley, who had entered the Iowa Writers' Workshop after earning a B.A. in English from Washington University in St. Louis in 1949. Although considerations of space operated against featuring any single writer (one work per poet was the tacit rule, broken only when the Washington group led off with three poems by L. E. Hudgins), Shelley was positioned for display more nicely than any other. He came last, his Shakespearean sonnet "Harvest" the final word. Except not quite: unexpectedly, his work returned in the pages of the book review section where Brewster Ghiselin (director of one of the few other writing workshops that existed in those pioneer days, that of the University of Utah), was reviewing the very booklet that Paul Engle could not resist plugging in his introduction ("The Prairie Press, Iowa City, Iowa, $1.00"). In his review, not only did Ghiselin single out Shelley by name—"The best poems in the collections are by Peter Hald, Robert Shelley and James B. Hall" (288)—but he quoted in its entirety one of the two poems by Shelley that were included in the booklet, "Evening in the Park" (which had been accepted for publication in the Winter 1951 *Furioso*). As a result, Shelley's work was foregrounded twice, and in its second appearance, it was the subject of a commentary of some length. That commentary bears reproduction in full, as does the poem by Shelley that preceded it:

Evening in the Park

Paper boats soon sank in midlake
And *crackerjack* icons turned to tin;
Balloons went limp. At precisely what point
Desire atomized I do not know, but they
Were restless gathering the bowls and cups,
Had expected too much probably.

As colored lights went off one by one
Things lost fixity and the whole park
Seemed adrift on a darkened excursion
And they were ghosts in a sea of debris.
They hurried to waiting cars and could have slapped
Their children whose hands smelled of crushed fireflies
And shone with a greasy green light in the dark.

Something more might have been done [Ghiselin writes] to determine the meaning of the symbolic boats, icons and balloons. Yet the indeterminacy of these objects, beyond their easier significance of sustaining construct, nave, idol, tin god, and the like, is consistent with the

ignorance and pathetic carelessness of the defeated beings whose hopeless courage shapes the lilt of casual dismissal in their comment on their
losses, "Had expected too much probably." In the second section of the
poem the park itself becomes a boat washed on a journey brief and di-
gressive like a pleasure trip, in every sense "darkened"; and in the last
line the "sea of debris" shows to baffled ghosts a green light of passage
that suggests gravegleam and sea phosphorus. Though success of this
kind depends primarily upon insight, it is impossible without technical skill of the kind observable in Shelley's use of faintly echoing rime
substitutes (assonance in *lake, they,* a modified consonance or fading
ablaut rime in *tin, point*) devices which sustain and emphasize the the-
matic effects of slack integrity and imminent disintegration. (288–89)

Here is an occasion that is just the opposite of one we had seen earlier, that
in which William Arrowsmith's negative review bars the door fast against
Ashbery. In contrast, Ghiselin wants to greet Shelley warmly and invite him
over the threshold. And as Ghiselin presents that work, it merits such a
welcome because it demonstrates several things: a sensitivity to the sound
of language, an ability to describe a setting in such a way as to transform it
convincingly (from park into boat), and a sympathy for "defeated beings"
and their "hopeless courage." What is just as interesting, however, is what
Shelley apparently need *not* demonstrate—what gets bypassed in Ghiselin's
review: for example, an ability to write about the disappointments of a family or of family matters. The children who appear toward the end ("Their
children," as Shelley distinctly states) go entirely unmentioned by Ghiselin; indeed, Ghiselin seems to have transformed them into "baffled ghosts"—
or is it the entire family that has been so dematerialized? Judging from what
Ghiselin avoids, to write about the family may be a handicap. It is certainly
not a feature worth pointing out in a review designed to highlight strong
points.

Ghiselin has no eyes, it seems, for family. He promotes the poem as a
series of effective patterns that emerge from a challenging subject matter.
But then Shelley himself does not seem entirely confident of where his own
poem is going. When he startlingly blurts out: "At precisely what point /
Desire atomized I do not know," his odd locution is doubly transgressive,
especially in the context of the New Criticism and the high valuation it
placed on impersonality. Instead of remaining in the background, the poet
enters his poem in his own first-person singular voice, as a presence who
interrupts the events he is describing. Then, having caused that much of a
fuss, he proceeds to profess ignorance about those who are the characters

he is creating. On both accounts, he appears to have surrendered control of his poem. But that, of course, becomes one of the startling, unexpected strengths of this work. For his surrender is not simply a loss of control: it in effect signals a transfer of power from the poet to his subjects that abruptly invests them with a definite substantiality. They briefly attain an opacity that grants them a measure of dignity, even as such dignity as they have will be eroded in the downward spiral of the day's events that charts the course of the rest of the poem. The innovative edge in the poem stems from this shift of weight from poet to subject. The poet's subjects could have seemed insubstantial figures to be dismissed (as indeed Ghiselin proceeds to do), but Shelley's poem works against that, or perhaps better, hopes to work against it but is not quite sure how. In truth, the family is not all that "real"—their reality is intermixed with elements of insubstantiality, as if they were icons that could signify entire lives even as those lives remain artificial and commercialized, like the *crackerjack* icon which has lost any status except its identifiability as a trademark.

From Ghiselin's words of praise, however, no one would be quick to conclude that Shelley's poem centered on a family with children, or more accurately, began by observing examples of someone in the park, initially a "they" (a couple? a group?), who acquired, in the course of the poem, an identity as a family. It never matters to Ghiselin that the figures increase their presence as a family throughout the poem. Real poems, that is, are about something other than family matters—the metaphoric changes a poet orchestrates, perhaps, as he turns a park into a boat. Yet Shelley's poem ends so conspicuously that it seems impossible that Ghiselin could overlook the presence of those children's hands glowing with that "greasy light," indicating how this long day cannot easily be set aside: the dirt of its disappointment has its own staining imprint.

Shelley was not able to appreciate the welcome extended to him by Ghiselin (with whom, incidentally, he had studied during a summer at the University of Utah) nor did he live to develop the possibilities at which his poem hinted, not the least of which was the ambiguous relationship among the members of this group. Under circumstances that perhaps remain beyond clear explaining, he died in Iowa City on April 25, 1951, of a self-inflicted gunshot wound.[1] He was twenty-five years old. But he left a distinct impression on his classmates, on Donald Petersen, who composed a handsome tribute to his memory, a seven-poem sonnet sequence that appeared in *Poetry* in 1954, and on W. D. Snodgrass, who recalled him, in a 1986 interview, as a pioneer: "We had all been writing in a neo-Symbolist, neo-Metaphysical style," he remembered. "It is very strange to marry the Metaphysicals and the Symbolists, but that is what we were trying to do. And all of a sudden, Shelley wrote these very straightforward, quite lyrical, very lovely poems. . . . He only wrote about six or eight before he committed suicide" ("Interview" 26).[2]

Snodgrass's sequence about the young daughter from whom he was separated by divorce and remarriage, "Heart's Needle," entered literary history as a significant breakthrough when published as a volume in 1959 (it won the Pulitzer Prize). But its poems had been finding their way into print since early in the 1950s—as indeed the sequence itself records, with its daughter who was "born / When the new fallen soldiers froze / In Asia's deep ravines" (*Heart's* 42) and whose narrative unfolds through ten poems, each centered on a subsequent season, beginning in the winter of 1952–53. A number of them had been placed in *Botteghe Oscure* in 1954; others were accepted by the *Hudson Review*. On their strength, Snodgrass received a 1957 Ingram Merrill fellowship, and that same year, four poems of the ten were anthologized in the widely distributed *New Poets of England and America*. When these poems appeared as a volume in 1959, they were hailed as initiating a radical breakthrough that ushered in the frankness of the 1960s. But these works had circulated most successfully through the 1950s. Robert Lowell had been Snodgrass's instructor at Iowa in 1953, and he remembered them some years later when, frustrated at attempts to complete his prose autobiography, he began rearranging sentences into free verse lines to begin the sequence known as "Life Studies" that was published as part 4 of *Life Studies* in 1960. Is it possible that the newness imputed to *Life Studies* and *Heart's Needle* was overstated by M. L. Rosenthal's influential 1960 review of their writing as a new kind of verse, a "confessional" poetry that depends upon remorseless candor? Many of the attributes of that verse were first on display in poems that centered on the family, in the domestic verse of the 1950s.

Yet such poetry could have remained invisible for a considerable period. Domestic verse stood just outside the categories by which verse received its accreditation. Ghiselin's review offers an example of a family that can stand at the center of the poem yet still go unseen. But the family's invisibility was not just a function of symbol-hunting critics: the very poets who wrote domestic verse were just as quick to withhold legitimacy from their own works. No framework for valuing them existed. This generation of poets who had actually been blessed with the time to enjoy their family had been provided that time by a university that expected them to act as functioning professionals. Poets were rewarded who produced works in which they demonstrated that the language of poetry was a serious, responsible discourse. Works that centered on one's children or one's family were misusing an opportunity to promote civic welfare. The tender sentiments of the everyday—it was *assumed* that their existence was not open to question. Not surprisingly, then, when poets did write about their families, they rarely drew attention to these particular poems. Only with rare exceptions were these poems afforded a leadoff role in a volume. They were most likely to be found in the middle of a collection. They were unlikely candidates for showcasing in an anthology. And they were the poems consigned to oblivion the soonest—designated as work that need not be collected. None of Babette Deutsch's collections include "Solitudes," a poem tracing a child's growth; it first appeared in the *California Quarterly* in 1954. Isabella Gardner's "Sestina," her childhood recollection of a cloistered drawing room that was published by the *Kenyon Review* in 1953, was included only in her *Collected Poems,* never in any individual volumes. Muriel Rukeyser made an impassioned plea for poetry about the experience of childbirth in a review-article in *Poetry,* but Barbara Howes's "Delivery Room," a description of childbirth that *Poetry* published in 1956, never reappeared in her 1959 volume, *Light and Dark,* or in subsequent collections. Both W. S. Merwin and James Wright regularly published in journals far more poems than they ever collected in their volumes. Among Wright's poems written when he was at the University of Minnesota in 1957–59 are several that speak to his young son. Almost all were left out of subsequent volumes. In the sequence of poems about family that concluded *The Drunk in the Furnace* (1960), Merwin collected fewer than half of the poems he had written on his forebears, all of which had been published in journals as well-known as the *Paris Review,* the *Nation,* the *Atlantic,* and the *Hudson Review.* (Many of these Lowell found to be exceptionally helpful when he was struggling to make over his autobiographical prose into the free verse of *Life Studies.*)

In one sense, the invisibility of domestic verse was assured because its unabashed tilting toward the caring gesture placed it outside the New Critical terms by which mainstream poetry understood itself. But in another sense, it is the very absence of the grandiose that marks these poems as so completely invisible. The authority of this verse rested in the modesty of its gestures. In these poems in which an interchange was to occur between family members of two generations, between a parent and a child, poets were necessarily assembling a discourse in which the vernacular would dominate. Hyam Plutzik demonstrates in the opening lines of "To My Daughter" (from *Apples from Shinar* [1959]):

Seventy-seven betrayers will stand by the road,
And those who love you will be few but stronger.

Seventy-seven betrayers, skillful and various,
But do not fear them: they are unimportant. (*Collected* 89)

This poetic line takes its cue from features like parallelism and refrain. To give the appearance of writing directly to another is essential. What drives such poems are the rhetorical possibilities of the second-person singular, the "you" who is at the center of the poem. In "A Presentation of Two Birds to My Son" (collected in *The Green Wall* [1957]) James Wright begins by pondering his topic: "Chicken. How shall I tell you what it is, / And why it does not float with tanagers?" The poem stalls after its first word, then sets itself in motion. These lines do not pretend to be authoritative statements but are offered as backstage glimpses, conversational matters. Simplicity of speech, though, is not enough; the whole act of this writing signals intimacy by enabling one to address another. Few poets in the 1950s can resist this moment, this benediction that seems to sacralize the name as it is enunciated, as it is brought into print. Such apostrophes, when they are a poem's first words, sound a pitch that establishes a low hushed voice of reverence. As the poet's voice carefully pronounces that name by which the beloved is known, the effect is to open a fold in the poem, a temporary pocket within which the beloved can be housed. Even though the title of Peter Everwine's poem establishes a distance between speaker and subject— "On a Photograph of My Grandfather, Paolo Castelnuovo"—the opening address serves to overcome that remove (even as the hesitant sentence-fragments acknowledge it): "Grandfather, fortune's child is fair of face. / Watching you now, posed in the granite light / Of some Italian noon. I find no grace, / No radiance to warm this northern light" (452). Male poets who are approaching their fathers with tenderness tend to display their attitude at once, in the first word of the poem. "Father, since always now the death to come / Looks naked out from your eyes into mine" (*Summer* 21), Donald Justice begins "Sonnet to My Father" from his 1959 collection *The Summer Anniversaries*. Howard Moss's "Elegy for My Father" (from *The Toy Fair* [1954]) opens similarly: "Father, whom I murdered every night but one, / That one, when your death murdered me" (21) By their invitational constructions, these poems coax us into taking up subject positions within them; to read them is to become invested in them.

This domestic verse establishes new rules for readerly and writerly participation in which intimacy replaces distance and emotion replaces analysis. In some of these poems, the "you" who is addressed becomes an element in the poem, a listener included within it, even someone who contributes important lines. The poem, then, openly borrows features from other kinds of intimate communications like the memoir or the letter—or the valentine. In the first of her "Three Valentines to the Wide World" (the lead sequence in the July 1956 *Poetry,* collected in 1959 in *Valentines to the Wide World*), Mona Van Duyn records a question posed by an eight-year-old:

> "Mother, is love God's hobby?" At eight you don't even
> look up from your scab when you ask it. A kid's squeak,
> is that a fit instrument for such a question?
> Eight times the seasons turned and cold snow tricked
> the earth to death, and still she hasn't noticed. (3)

Van Duyn shifts casually back and forth between second-person and third-person, and at a later point in the poem, realizing that the child's question has gone unanswered, she even addresses her directly as if to apologize for this delay: "No one answers you. Such absurd / charity of the imagination has shamed us, Emily." Soon after, Van Duyn introduces the second-person singular again, only this time it pertains to her:

> I remember now. Legs shoved you up, you couldn't tell
> where the next tooth would fall out or grow in, or what
> your nose would look like next year. Anything was possible.
> Then it slowed down, and you had to keep what you got. (4)

Just as it signals that Emily will grow disjointedly and inhabit Van Duyn's perspective even as Van Duyn projects herself into Emily's, so we are caught up in this entire poem as a mix of inner musing, direct address, and recorded comments. Similarly, in James Wright's "Mutterings over the Crib of a Deaf Child" (first published in 1956, collected in 1957), two voices meet, a cautious voice that raises skeptical questions about the child's ability to survive and an animated voice that provides lyrical answers that defend the child's potential for adaptability:

> "How will he hear the bell at school
> Arrange the broken afternoon,
> And know to run across the cool
> Grasses where starlings cry,
> Or understand the day is gone?"

Well, someone lifting curious brows
Will take the measure of the clock.
And he will see the birchen boughs
Outside sagging dark from the sky,
And the shade crawling upon the rock. (68)

Both voices, finally, are loving addresses, though that is not at once obvious. One is an outer voice that deals with apparent problems, the other an inner voice that is the source of the strength that gets problems solved. But both are concerned for the child. If Wright sails too close to a dewy poetic diction ("the birchen boughs / Outside sagging dark from the sky") it is out of a desire to invoke locutions that are particularly visible (and free of the need for auditory stimulus), as well as powerful traditional images. But finally, this poem exists to proclaim the loving gesture as powerful not in spite of but because of its irrationality:

"Well, good enough. To serve his needs
All kinds of arrangements can be made.
But what will you do if his finger bleeds?
Or a bobwhite whistles invisibly
And flutes like an angel off in the shade?"

He will learn pain. And, as for the bird,
It is always darkening when that comes out.
I will putter as though I had not heard,
And lift him into my arms and sing
Whether he hears my song or not. (68–69)

Skeptical questions go on forever; real wisdom at some point draws a line and moves along. What might look like aimless puttering turns out to be a gesture of intricate protectiveness, including both child and speaker. With this closure, Wright ends with words both defiant and tender, powerful without yielding their vulnerability. In Wright's poem, as in others, we are given examples of works that are driven by deep necessity. Nothing about them is covert, and little in them seems to be guarded; in their emotional yearnings, in the helpless love they express for their children, they are urgent in their willingness to expose emotion.

Just such features from domestic verse stand behind the positions that were evolving in some of the earliest examples of confessional verse. Nonetheless, it is true that the version of the domestic that Snodgrass and Lowell and later Anne Sexton produced was centered on family situations that were deeply problematic. (In this respect, the work of Robert Shelley is even more prescient.) "Heart's Needle" depends on a writing in which actual individuals are not present to each other but are constrained by adverse circumstances. In this sequence, there are no problems that are easily soluble: "No one can tell you why / the season will not wait" (*Heart's* 46), Snodgrass begins one poem to his daughter. "I cannot fight / or let you go" (*Heart's* 60), he concludes another. When his daughter, walking between her parents, approaches a puddle and expects to be swung aloft, her parents instead "Stiffen and pull apart" (*Heart's* 44). The sequence keeps circling back to moments in which an offer of shelter is interrupted or ruined. The area in a yard is cordoned off for a garden, though with an ominous fragility: "Four slender sticks of lath stand guard / Uplifting their thin string" (*Heart's* 43). But once the garden is planted with its "mixed seeds" it is almost at once disturbed, as if its orderliness is a proposition that attracts chaos. Not only do "Strange dogs" and "moles tunneling" circle it as enemies, but his daughter is the "first to tamp it down." Snodgrass must end by telling his daughter: "You should try to look at them [the seedlings] every day / Because when they come to full flower / I will be away" (*Heart's* 43). The sequence is crisscrossed by such moments in which efforts at domestication simply fail; indeed, more than just failing, these efforts turn instead coercive or manipulative or evasive. What it means to offer shelter, for example, is complicated in these poems by the reappearance of so many creatures who are held in cages. Twice in separate poems father and daughter visit the small zoo in the local park; in the ninth poem, the stuffed animals in a natural history museum eye him warily from behind their glass. While the parklike settings of many poems are neat, tidy, and interrupted only by the memorable windstorm of a single day, such geography also underscores the curtailing of the expressive. No broad expanse in which open and free movement is possible ever endures for long in any of the poems. By always writing to his young daughter (who begins the sequence as a baby), Snodgrass assures that linguistically his range will be limited. To speak directly, then, becomes a nearly impossible achievement; indeed, to do so would seem to visit pain and disruption. As a result, the value of straightforward and simple speech is enormously enhanced. At the same time, just where and how and under what circumstances such direct addressing will occur in any sustained fashion is left hauntingly, distressingly problematic.

Lowell's ending to his sequence of family poems is no less dependent on an explicitly nonverbal gesture that is, as he says in a 1964 essay, an affirmation "both quixotic and barbarously absurd" ("On Robert Lowell's 'Skunk Hour'" 107). Yet the mother skunk in "Skunk Hour" who, "with her column of kittens swills the garbage pail" and "jabs her wedge-head in a cup / of sour cream, drops her ostrich tail, / and will not scare" (*Life* 84) delivers, on the one hand, a mock cornucopia. Now that site of refuse which Lowell had recalled his father policing so fastidiously—"out in the alley," he wrote in "91 Revere Street," "the sun shone irreverently on our three garbage cans lettered: R.T.S. LOWELL—U.S.N." (*Life* 43)—is opened as a feast. To have the top off that which had been shunted aside as trash is freeing. Lowell is only half-joking when he writes: "I stand on top / of our back steps and breathe the rich air." As outrageous as this ending is, it also presents the undeniable gift of a restored proportion, precisely because it evokes the animal self with its capacity for survival. When the skunk turns her back on him, she breaks the chain of self-absorption that has been building through the final poems of the sequence; her refusal to acknowledge his intensity releases him and grants closure to the poem and the sequence. Life will continue, whether studied or not. Lowell's high pitch of intense, "satanic" obsession, with its lines borrowed from Milton ("I myself am hell; nobody's here—") is punctured by the intrusion of the antiliterary creature, who brings relief. Those models that can most helpfully teach us how to endure, Lowell suggests, are not likely to present themselves under elegant auspices; but their appearance at utterly unexpected moments only validates their capacity for survival. In an earlier draft, reprinted in Stephen Axelrod's study of Lowell, Lowell's skunk lacked both a gender and a family:

> My headlights glare
> On a galvanized bucket crumpling up—
> A skunk glares in a garbage pail.
> It jabs its trowel-head in a cup
> Of sour cream, drops its ostrich tail,
> And cannot scare. (250)

This first-draft skunk is not domestic at all but Lowell's tortured double; without discernible gender, it angrily returns his agonizing glare. Antisocial, aggressive, "urban," it offers no outlet from Lowell's torment. Indeed, insofar as it acts like a rabid creature, it infects nature with Lowell's own madness. By contrast, the mother skunk of the final version, while "moonstruck," is eminently sane. She is buffeted by a "column of kittens" that is like a phalanx of troops which will lend her strong support; but rather than menacing Lowell, she provides an example of family solidarity. Her domesticity shelters him as well.

Lowell's inarticulate but eloquent scavenger mom—an unlikely cold war heroine—is a long way from the citizen-poet that Ciardi promoted as he approached mid-century. But the idea of a citizen-poet, even though it had the backing of a whole generation of writers who sought to redeem the sacrifices of World War II by projecting a future in which the individual could continue to be a witness to history, was in question almost at the moment it had been conceived. Not the least of the flaws that led to the undermining of Ciardi's project was the absence from it of those voices of those who still remained outsiders. Moreover, the linguistic frameworks within which the claims for a poetry of civic discourse operated were, though they were defined so as to uphold a specific degree of broadness, rigidly maintained. An insistence on maintaining standards for a mainstream style may have been driven by the uncertainties of those who were new arrivals and who wished to be as specific as possible about the guidelines necessary for successful membership. But the result was that alternate voices had no arena prepared in which they might register their difference: what might have seemed a broadening of the arena for poetry became, in effect, an area that had been sharply diminished. Only some citizens, as it were, had the capability to be citizen-poets. If poets like Richard Wilbur (or Ciardi as Italian American or Plutzik as Jewish American) could be acutely sensitive to class issues—largely because they were such beneficiaries of the postwar abundance that sustained the upward mobility from one class to another—that interest was inadvertently developed at the expense of questions of gender or race. More precisely, the emphasis on defining in a book review a set of linguistic attributes that would qualify as civic discourse may have been a positive proposal insofar as it prepared a neutral site that would welcome all to participate within it. But in the actual defining, poets proceeded by branding as minor those writings that did not suit qualifications of linguistic neutrality. The citizen-poet was white and male (and had usually graduated from Harvard). The rich inventiveness of Rosalie Moore, V. R. Lang, and Katherine Hoskins could have only a temporary impact, like a pleasing "ornament," while the positively demanding positions of Langston Hughes, Melvin B. Tolson, and Hyam Plutzik brought up concerns that—unlike Berryman's smoothly suburbanized topic—looked oddly out of fashion.

What was behind the slow change in poetic style that can be seen in the 1950s? It was not the exclusion of these alternate voices that troubled poets; those other voices, to the extent they circulated at all within the mainstream, were at best only tolerated. Instead, what change there was was driven by the slow and persistent collapse of the authority of the state. Although the prestige of the state was at an all-time high in the immediate postwar years, the confidence in the government that helped underwrite the project of the citizen-poet began to be undermined as early as the late 1940s, no doubt fueled by the defeat of Henry Wallace and a third party that could function as a viable alternative. What confidence in the state remained was squandered recklessly after 1952 with the lackluster performance of the Eisenhower regime, the panic engendered by McCarthyism, and, most of all, by the sheer inability to conceive of a manageable forum in which to discuss the possibility of a nuclear holocaust. The collective paranoia and schizophrenia that resulted not only mocked the concept of a poetics of civic responsibility but served to press poets into imagining ways in which their own anxiety and desperation could find some outlet. Turning deeply inward, then, was in one sense a direct response to outward pressures, to political and historical realities that were inescapable even as they resisted understanding.

A better version of the story of poetry in the 1950s, then, begins with the radiant possibility of a new poetics—writings by mature citizen-poets whose experience has been tempered by the depression and by World War II and who believe in the existence of a wisdom that can be collectively enhanced—but then recognizes not only the limits of that particular program (conceived too narrowly, sensitive to class over race and gender) but also how a disabled government eventually fostered a quite different kind of writing: a secretive, anxious poetics that valued intimacy almost to the point of withdrawing into it, even as it produced poetry that could be, on occasion, deeply and powerfully moving. The fundamental idea of repositioning the lyric to detail a domestic situation, to depict the relations between family members, and specifically to compose with a sharp awareness of the child and the child's role in the family, and even more specifically, to present that relationship as under some threat, as somehow clouded or problematized—that is no sudden breakthrough fostered by an individual genius like Snodgrass or Lowell but the particular subgenre that the 1950s had been driven to produce, even though the decade consistently rewarded its poets for doing almost anything but writing verse in that manner. Of course in one sense such a poetry was, by the standards that were being promoted, a failure. Domestic verse, for one thing, all too quickly suggested that poets were not the savvy heavyweights who were ready to take their place among the other professionals newly awarded disciplinary status within the university. Some of the poets who refused to turn inward—poets who, like Tolson and Plutzik and Moore and Lang and Hoskins, confronted larger issues—emerge from this era with a dignity that they did not win easily (and they still lack the reputations they deserve). But it is domestic verse, as redefined in all its complexity as an example that integrates elements of failure within it, as the obverse of the academic verse of the citizen-poet, that must be regarded as the strongest heritage of mainstream poetry in the 1950s. And when the mainstream poets were placed in a position to understand from their own writings that they were as much on the outside as others they had been quick to dismiss, then the circumstances were set for the explosion of the 1960s. To understand that is to begin restoring some proportion to this forgotten era in literary history.

Notes

Prologue

1. Although the mass culture panic of the 1950s has been examined from many different perspectives, no one to my knowledge has positioned mainstream poetry in relation to it. For discussion of the role of literary intellectuals (other than poets) and mass culture see Andrew Ross (*No Respect,* esp. chaps. 1 and 2), Stephen Whitfield (esp. chap. 3), and Neil Jumonville.

2. As an example of the alliance formed in the 1940s between these workshops and the cutting-edge discipline of the New Criticism, consider that it was the Iowa Writers' Workshop under the guidance of Paul Engle that brought Warren Carrier to the University of Iowa to teach a course in the New Criticism as well as courses in European modernists like Gide, Baudelaire, Mallarmé, and Lorca, as Carrier has explained in his memoir of those years (19). The poet-critic tradition of the first-generation New Critics (Tate, Winters, Blackmur, Empson) had a distinct appeal to new writing program graduates because it legitimated their own interest in current literature, a literature still kept at arm's length by most postwar English departments. Many second-generation New Critics, however, including those spokespersons as well known as Cleanth Brooks, Austin Warren, René Wellek, and Eliseo Vivas, were exclusively critics.

3. The vocabulary of the critique of mass culture borrowed heavily from the anticommunist polemic of the day. The manipulation of crowds by political leaders could be vividly evoked as a scare tactic. "Hollywood represents totalitarianism," concluded anthropologist Hortense Powdermaker in the final chapter of her 1950 study *Hollywood, the Dream Factory: an Anthropologist Looks at the Movie-Makers* (a section of which was featured in the October 14, 1950, issue of the *Saturday Review of Literature*): "More and more do people depend on what they read in their daily newspaper or what their radio commentator says, for their opinions. This means that man functions passively, taking over opinions,

ideas and prejudices ready-made from others. Rather than actively examining a number of choices and making up his own mind. In a totalitarian state all the mass communications are controlled by a ruling clique, and no choice is permitted the citizen. In the United States there is a choice, but relatively few people avail themselves of it" (322). Similar concerns were voiced in *Nonverbal Communication* (1956), the pioneering text in semiotics that Jurgen Ruesch co-produced with poet Weldon Kees to study "the communicative behavior of man." Pointing out that "Specialists in mass communication" had been "recruited largely from radio and television, advertising, propaganda, and the big circulation magazines," they concluded that these specialists "seem to gear their operations to a single end: capturing an audience and controlling its thought" (3).

4. The idea that the audience for mass culture can be strong, not weak—that is, that the audience can make distinct decisions as it selectively processes particular aspects of the mass culture object—is familiar to us, primarily through the work of John Fiske and Michel de Certeau. But it was just a glimmer on the intellectual horizon in the 1950s. Reuel Denney was a sociologist who was a co-author of the first edition of *The Lonely Crowd* (with David Riesman and Nathan Glazer) as well as a poet (*Connecticut River* appeared in 1939, *In Praise of Adam* in 1961). When he collected some of the essays he had been writing on the popular arts since 1948 as *The Astonished Muse* in 1957, he suggested in his Introduction that the methodological approach of sociologists had distorted their understanding of the active role of the mass culture audience: "Since the audience is very often studied as the object of a concerted effort to change minds and tastes (as the object of a campaign, one might say), it tends to be reflected in research as a passive entity. . . . There is rather less study of the way in which an audience or audience segment chooses among the media leisure alternatives. . . . The total effect of audience studies so far, then, is to understate the grasp by the audience, or by significant parts of the audience, of the formal and artistic conventions which mediate meanings for them" (18–19). It would be fifteen years before sociologist Herbert Gans would write in 1974 that the audience for popular culture "cannot be considered a mass" (32). Gans's research viewed audience members not as "isolated individuals hungering for and therefore slavishly accepting what the media offers them, but families, couples, and peer groups who use the media when and if the content is relevant to group goals and needs" (32).

5. *Discovery* differed from *New World Writing*. It had its own editor, novelist Vance Bourjaily, and it was priced aggressively at 35 cents (not the 50 cents of a Mentor Book). At one point in the 1950s, many paperback publishers were eager to have their intellectual review, and in every one, poetry was prominently displayed. (*New World Writing* often featured a poetry selection chosen by a well-known younger poet like Wilbur or Ciardi.) Avon Books began the *Avon Book of Modern Writing* in 1954 (edited by *Partisan Review* editors William

Phillips and Philip Rahv), and Doubleday introduced the *Anchor Review* in 1955 (edited by Melvin J. Lasky).

6. If one characteristic defines the mainstream poetry of academic modernism it is the prevalence of formalist devices. In the February 1952 *Poetry,* a by-invitation-only issue celebrating forty years of monthly publication, the preponderance of verse is formalist in one sense or another. Fifty poets were in that issue with one poem by each. Twenty-four poems employed rhyme-schemes in notable fashions (one used off-rhyme, another featured monorhyme). Thirty-five poems displayed a distinct rhythmic line, usually iambic tetrameter, and forty poems arranged themselves in stanzas. But the fifteen poems that ventured toward free verse never entirely unmoored themselves from the precepts of formalism. Seven broke their lines into separate and measured stanzas, and four assumed a rhythmic base that could be described as loose blank verse. Indeed, some of the most "radical" of the contributors revealed a deep admiration for formalist techniques. An excerpt from William Carlos Williams's *Paterson (Book V)* (here entitled "The River of Heaven" but an early version of "Asphodel, That Greeny Flower"), marches down the page in the three-line segments that Williams called the variable foot:

> Of asphodel, that greeny flower, the least,
>   that it is a simple flower
>   like a buttercup upon its
> branching stem . . . ("River" 89)

Of the two aggressively experimental contributions in the fortieth anniversary issue, one is a description in prose of a photograph by Atget as reconceived by Byron Vazakas, and the other is by Jose Garcia Villa. Villa's "Theseus" illustrates his trademark use of punctuation and capitalization; but it unfolds in a precise stanzaic form that requires its opening and closing lines to rhyme:

> Pythagor,Angel,rest,and,repeat.
> Rest,and,repeat.Till,
> With,the,gold-awaked,Verb,in,orience,lock,
> Taurus,of,Minos, in,His,brightverb,sleep:
>   —With,wreck,all,East,
>   The,Vertrical,complete. (82)

The double sonnet by Anthony Hecht and sonnets by John Berryman and Oscar Williams in this issue, all in iambic pentameter, may be placed at one extreme of the formalist spectrum, but texts that represent the other extreme cannot be said to represent a clean break from such conventionalizing poetic devices as traditional metrics, rhyme and strophic form.

7. Evan Carton and Gerald Graff further state that "both New Critical theory and method were ideally suited to the task of teaching a vastly expanded and demographically more diverse population of college students" (305). Graff noted that the beneficiaries of such a method were not just the "new, mass student body that could not be depended on to bring to the university any common cultural background" but also "the new professors as well, who might often be only marginally ahead of the students" (173).

8. Karal Ann Marling also discusses the New Look as an instance of a "postwar aesthetic" that "asserted the importance of deliberate artfulness" (14). That this artfulness was widely available to many women is evident in the inclusion by both Partington and Marling of family photographs of their mothers outfitted, circa the late 1940s, in the New Look.

Chapter 1: The Notorious Example of Richard Wilbur

1. For other examples of *Kenyon Review* fiction in which the central character is a professor and the setting is an academic institution, see stories by Elder (Autumn 1952), Jarrell (Winter 1953 and Winter 1954), Stern (Spring 1954), Curley (Autumn 1954), Macauley (Winter 1955), O'Connor (Autumn 1956), Wain (Spring 1957), and Logan (Summer 1958). Most of these do not offer attractive portraits of college life, especially in departments of English. "The character of the professor, even when in the hands of a professor, continues to be unsavory" (185), remarks John O. Lyons in his 1962 study of the college novel.

2. Statistical studies of postwar enrollment indicate that this population not only was predominantly male but was also very much interested in an education that would improve them not materially but culturally. Richard Cándida Smith cites information from a 1974 study by Keith W. Olson that indicated that between 1945 and 1956 there were 225 million veterans who attended college under the GI Bill. (Sixty-five thousand were women.) As early as 1947 enrollment in universities and colleges had increased by 75 percent over prewar levels. "Educators were surprised by the educational choices veterans made," writes Smith. "The assumption that their primary goal would be to learn practical skills was overturned when veterans who attended college-level institutions preferred liberal arts education over professional training" (80). In a 1946 UCLA study cited by Smith, 44 percent of veterans polled about their principal aim in attending college listed "self-improvement" (81).

3. "Comparing his early poems, let's say, to Richard Wilbur's," wrote William Matthews, "we see that Wright used traditional forms clumsily" (101). To Leonard Nathan, Wilbur also signified tradition: "For some—Richard Wilbur comes first to mind—the conventions hold their own powers" (168). Much like the "fifties poem" itself, Wilbur fits with ease into this role as a tossaway referent, an example that pops up in passing.

4. He is even in danger of losing his name altogether. When Dave Smith is explaining that James Wright's first book, influenced by Frost and Robinson, "was the kind of poetry that Wright has referred to as 'quietist'" he adds that "it did not entirely conform to Donald Hall's survivor's description of poetry in the 1950s: 'Here was the ability to shape an analogy, to perceive and develop comparisons, to display etymological wit, and to pun six ways at once. It appealed to the mind because it was intelligent, and to the sense of form because it was intricate and shapely. It did not appeal to the passions and did not pretend to.' Wright's was most unlike this paradigmatic poetry" (xiii). Within this quote from Hall are words describing Wilbur that Hall had originally reserved *exclusively* for Wilbur. Hall was offering a catalogue of what he considered the accomplishments in Wilbur's first book that only he had achieved in the 1950s. Smith's citation, then, takes words written as praise twenty years before and presents them as a characterization that is supposed to summarize the limitations of a particular time. Perhaps most strikingly, Smith never mentions Wilbur's name at all: Hall's quote is presented as if it were describing all "fifties" poetry. Of course Smith is a poet, not a scholar, and will be cavalier about his sources. Nevertheless, Wilbur's assimilation to the negativized field of the "fifties poem" could not be more complete.

5. For a markedly different reading, see John Gery, who views it as the earliest in a group of three antinuclear poems (including the late 1950s "Advice to a Prophet" and the late 1960s "In the Field"). While the two later poems are works of thoughtful dissent, "'A World'" occupies a different category. A late 1940s Wilbur poem that fulfills Gery's project is "Year's End," discussed below.

6. In another uncollected poem from the same year, "We," he underlined the class bias and anti-Semitism in upper-class fears of encroaching disaster: "The servant girl has spoken back to me. / My dividends are yearly getting lower. / The nights are full of fires and burglary. / The Jews have bought my cottage by the shore" ("We" 127–28).

7. "All" is, of course, a useful word to a poet evoking abundance in a constricted space. But it is very nearly a signature of a Wilbur poem. Since the word lends itself to many uses, its persistent recurrence is never particularly noticeable. Able to function as pronoun, adverb and adjective, the word enjoys a mobility few possess. Yet Wilbur employs it with a pervasiveness that borders on the obsessive. He uses it to universalize a moment in passing, as at the close of summer (in "Exeunt") when "All cries are thin and terse" (*New* 265). Or he uses it to allow a single example suddenly to multiply rapidly, as in with a sweeping gesture: "The sshh of sprays on all the little lawns" (*New* 329). Or he uses it to point casually to a loose collection of things, careful to preserve their ragtag edge, as figures in the wall fountain at Sciarra who seem "Happy in all that ragged, loose / Collapse of water" (*New* 272). These uses are by no means unnatural or excessive; Wilbur always employs the word casually, in passing, never as part of some

buried code. But employ it he does, to an extent nothing short of remarkable. More specifically, it appears at least once and sometimes more often in more than two-thirds of all the poems he has published over the course of fifteen years. Between 1947 and 1961, Wilbur published 143 poems (excluding translations), and at least once "all" appears in ninety-one. In forty-two poems it appears once, in twenty-eight twice, and in twelve three times. Eight poems use it four times and a remarkable two poems manage to find five places for it.

8. Paul Boyer places 1948 as the year in which the new administration of Harry Truman took the first steps toward maintaining what can only be called a major disinformation campaign in order to allay the nationwide anxiety about the threat of nuclear disaster: "the mood [of the nation] became one of dulled acquiescence" (291). Richard Gerstell's widely reprinted paperback *How to Survive an Atomic Bomb* was published in 1950, and various "authoritative" magazines like *U.S. News and World Report* featured articles entitled "You Can Live despite the A-Bomb."

9. Insofar as "things of this world" derives from Augustine's *Confessions,* it is a phrase that aims precisely at complicating the relation between the objective and the conceptual world, as in this passage: "I have learnt to love you late, Beauty at once so ancient and new! I have learnt to love you late! You were within me, and I was in the world outside myself. I searched for you outside myself and, disfigured as I was, I fell upon the lovely things of your creation. You were with me, but I was not with you. The beautiful things of this world kept me far from you and yet, if they had not been in you, they would have no being at all" (Book X, paragraph 27). Perloff's demand for thingliness, then, is so thoroughly at odds with Augustinian idealism that it in effect judges the poem from a position that is utterly alien to it—Altieri's strategy when "contrasting" Wilbur with Lowell.

10. Perloff also states that the poem's "meter is predominantly iambic pentameter . . . with some elegant variations, as when a line is divided into steps (see lines 4, 15, 18, 30) presumably to create a more natural look" ("'Step Away'" 84). In fact, the poem is a metrical rarity for Wilbur, a piece with extensive metrical substitutions. Nearly every line has at least one, sometimes two anapests, and several lines employ non-iambic substitutions in the metrically sensitive second foot (lines 1, 9, 10, 12–15, 17, 20, 22, 25, 29 and 30). Lines 21 and 24 seem only to have four beats, though they are not distributed as tetrameter. In short, this is one of Wilbur's most conversational and least metrically regulated texts. If Wilbur were aspiring to "timelessness and universality," he would surely have avoided such down-home ordinariness.

Chapter 2: Anthology Wars

1. Along with assembling a 1937 anthology of American and British poetry for the Modern Library (an edition that was expanded in 1946), Rodman had

also written a study of the contemporary African American painter Horace Pippin and had published in 1941 a three-act play in verse dramatizing Toussaint L'Ouverture's successful rebellion on Haiti. At the time of his 1949 anthology, he had also completed three books of his own verse, one of which, *The Amazing Year: May 1, 1945–April 30, 1946: A Diary in Verse,* adapted techniques drawn from the 1930s documentary.

2. Rodman's collection, however, has never occupied a central position in the discussion of American anthologies. Though it enjoyed an enviable level of mass-market penetration, it has gone unmentioned in recent examinations of the American poetry anthology by Alan Golding in 1995 and by Jed Rasula in 1996. Its absence from literary histories may be explained in part by the rise of the university as a vigorous institution in the postwar years. As mass-market paperback, it never earned the prestige of the anthology chosen as required reading in the classroom. To be sure, incorporating it into a scholarly discussion of postwar poetry also complicates the narrative developed by Golding and Rasula that argues that the fifties poetry scene was entirely depoliticized.

3. Four of these poets—Schwartz, Shapiro, Jarrell, and Lowell—were in the process of winning designation as representative figures: they had been singled out by F. O. Matthiessen as the most recent poets to be included in his 1950 revision of *The Oxford Book of American Verse.* But the eleven others, though they all had at least one book to their credit, were less well known. Those with one book to their credit were, the biographical notes explained, about to publish a second: these included (in 1949) Richard Wilbur, John Holmes, E. L. Mayo, and John Frederick Nims.

4. Wilbur's achievement as a poet lies precisely in his ability to sustain within the same poem readings that range from the rather simple to the wonderfully complex. Most poems are not constructed so intricately. It is important to recognize that his popularity rests on this ability to speak to both neophytes and initiates. Any one of the poems that Elliott chooses can be read transformatively, not as a simple celebration that valorizes Wilbur's own virtuoso language but as a work that interplays with truths we may not decide we want to hear. "Juggler," for example, while it could certainly encourage the idea that the artist's deft illusions are proposed as a norm for an audience that is willing to be entertained, is also shot through with passages that reserve the juggler's role as a desperate attempt to deny hard truths. "A ball will bounce, but less and less" is the sentence that opens the poem: "It's not / a lighthearted thing" (*New* 297). The feats of the juggler, then, are presented as temporary efforts that are doomed to fail. And Wilbur drops references throughout that darkly note not only the juggler's facility but the connection with other cultural beliefs: "a heaven is easier made of nothing at all / Than the earth regained."

Chapter 3: Policing the Mainstream/Curtailing Feminine Excess

1. Throughout his glossary Elton is surely drawing upon W. K. Wimsatt's "The Concrete Universal," published in *PMLA* in 1947 and one of the series of essays (the others include "The Intentional Fallacy" and "The Affective Fallacy") by which Wimsatt set out to codify the hands-on practical criticism of the first generation of New Critics by abstracting a set of underlying rules. Collected as *The Verbal Icon: Studies in the Meaning of Poetry* in 1954, Wimsatt's position papers were crucial reconfigurings of the tenets of the New Criticism so that they could apply to all literature, not just the poetry of the High Modernists, the Renaissance, and the Metaphysicals.

2. "Libra" is identified, in the contributor's note, as "the pseudonym of one of the better-known young American novelists." A likely candidate for authorship of the essay is Gore Vidal, whose name is absent from the discussion except in a passage where the conclusions of John Aldridge's *After the Lost Generation* (1951) are held up for ridicule. (Aldridge had been an unsympathetic reader of Vidal's work.) In *Palimpsest: A Memoir* (1995), Vidal assumes responsibility not only for the idea of the *New World Writing* series of the 1950s but also for the editing of the first issue where, he remarks, he appeared "under a cautious pseudonym" (248). No pseudonymous works appear in the first issue, however, where Vidal is openly represented by a short story, "Erlinda and Mr. Coffin." His memory of contributing pseudonymously may be accurate, but it may pertain to this essay in the fourth issue. (No other works appeared in *New World Writing* without proper identification except for a tribute to Dylan Thomas reprinted from the *Times Literary Supplement* in the fifth issue, and this appeared under the byline of "Anonymous" rather than under a pseudonym.)

3. Jerome's elaborate divagation may have been prudent, for in this era, even a brief mention of homosexuality in a distant country was enough to cause a scandal. John Ciardi's biographer Edward Cifelli explains that as poetry editor of the *Saturday Review,* Ciardi in 1957 accepted and published Harold Norse's "Victor Emmanuel Monument (Rome)" (collected in *The Dancing Beasts,* 1962) which somewhat irreverently described that monument, in the manner of Roman citizens, as a typewriter or wedding cake, guarded by "a squad of *bersaglieri* there, the hand-/ picked of all Italy." Norse got into trouble when he notably distinguished his tourist-poem from other verse of the time by ending with a frank description of the *bersaglieri* as "Any night by the white marble ploy / . . . in whispered assignations / picking up extra cash, from man and boy" (16). The ending shocked *Saturday Review* readers, and when editor-in-chief Norman Cousins asked Ciardi to defend his decision to publish the poem, Ciardi—on a fellowship that year in, of all places, Rome—offered a most inadequate explanation, insisting in an open letter to the readership that he had *meant* to reject the poem but then erroneously placed it in a pile of "accepted" works. *Saturday Review* was a large-circulation magazine and the scandal escalated—so rap-

idly that the Italian government took steps actually to deport Ciardi, who in fact left for America shortly thereafter.

4. Five years after the letter to Arrowsmith, Porter had a chance to say more directly what he valued in Ashbery's poetry when he reviewed his Tiber Press volume *The Poems* (with prints by Joan Mitchell) along with volumes by O'Hara, Kenneth Koch, and James Schuyler in a 1961 *Evergreen Review*. There he had the freedom to develop concepts he could only gingerly approximate in this letter, and he began by insisting that "Ashbery's language is opaque: you cannot see through it any more than you can look through a fresco" ("Poets" 224). The collaboration between Ashbery and Mitchell won his praise as superior to the others (all the volumes of poetry included contemporary prints) because "They are both abstract." Porter also felt compelled to describe Ashbery's lines as innocent: "He has retained the clear but incommunicable knowledge of the child who was surrounded by heaven in his infancy, when a sense of wonder precluded judgment" (225)—a description, by the way, that seems more in keeping with Porter's own poetry than Ashbery's.

5. Garrigue also provides an excellent example of the poet who is welcome to a journal as a contributor, then treated as a baffling and alien presence when that journal makes her the subject of a review. Few poets appeared as regularly as Garrigue in the pages of the *Kenyon Review*. Her poems, usually in groups of two or three, were included in the issues of Autumn 1942, Spring 1943, Winter 1944, Autumn 1945, Autumn 1946, Autumn 1952, Autumn 1957, Winter 1962, and Winter 1963. But when Geoffrey Hartman reviewed *A Winter Walk by the Villa d'Este* for that journal in 1960, he was quick to diagnose her as a poet with major problems: "She takes too much after the paradigm of water; one is never sure of the vessel, the total form of the poem. . . . A whole poem may be spun out of hers sense for movement" (695). One of the poems Hartman singled out for particular disapproval, "Soliloquy in the Cemetery of Pere LeChaise," won the Union League Civic and Arts Foundation Prize in 1956 after its appearance in the July 1956 *Poetry*.

6. For a penetrating examination of book reviews on Bishop early and late, a surprising majority of which withhold praise from her work, see Timothy Morris, who regards many of the reviewers as serving "as a model for the silencing of female writers in general: they can either write exactly what they see, scholars will argue, or they can write exactly what they feel; in either case, more complicated expressions escape them" (109). Male reviewers unabashedly regard her not as a poet but as a woman poet. Edwin Honig thus opens his 1956 *Partisan Review* piece: "Elizabeth Bishop's poetry aspires to a very high order of craft and sensibility—to a perch, say, which only Marianne Moore, among living women poets, precariously occupies" (115). Note that Honig's recasting of that "very high order" into the spatial metaphor of a precarious perch robs it of its superiority.

Chapter 4: Versions of the Feminine Baroque

1. Biographical notes on the back of *The Grasshopper's Man* explain that Moore earned her M.A. degree from the University of California and worked on newspapers writing book reviews for the San Francisco *Leader* and as a staff writer for the Oakland *Tribune* radio station. In 1941 she married a journalist, left her radio job, and joined the group of Activists led by Lawrence Hart. In 1948, she and her husband were living in what was then the rural backwaters of California's Mendocino County, seven miles from the lumber town of Willets, with two daughters (two and five years old), on an eighty-acre wooded tract with no electricity or phone.

2. In recent years, the Activist movement has begun to receive a small portion of the attention it richly deserves. Moore published a sequence of meditations, *Gutenberg at Strasbourg*, with Floating Island Press (California) in 1995. Jeanne McGahey, a poet whose work is often as interesting and as challenging as Moore's and who first appeared in a 1941 New Directions anthology (*Five Young American Poets*), had a 1989 selected poems, *Homecoming with Reflections*, included in the prestigious "Contemporary Poetry Series" sponsored by the *Quarterly Review of Literature*. The Woolson/Brotherston Press in the 1970s was firmly committed to publishing Activists in strikingly attractive editions, including McGahey (*Oregon Winter*, 1973), Lois Moyles (*I Prophesy Survivors*, 1971, and *Alleluia Chorus*, 1978), and Fred Ostrander (*The Hunchback and the Swan*, 1978), as well as Laurel Trivelpiece (*Legless in Flight*, 1978). Not all Activist writing is available in limited editions: the University of Pittsburgh Press included *The Climbers* (1978) in its Pitt Poetry Series, a selection of work by John Hart, son of Lawrence Hart and Jeanne McGahey. The basis for a deeper understanding of the Activist aesthetic is available in Patricia Nelson's "Rosalie Moore and the Activist Movement in Poetry" (M.A. thesis, New College of California, 1998) which also includes invaluable background material on the formation of the group.

3. O'Hara's biographer Brad Gooch tells the story of the misplaced Lang poem but he refers to it with the title "Words for Frank O'Hara's Angel" (149). There is a poem by Lang, "To Frank's Guardian Angel," with an ending identical to the ending that Gooch quotes in his biography of O'Hara, that appears in Lang's *Poems & Plays* (118). Presumably this is the misplaced poem that Gooch notes in his O'Hara biography. The textual accuracy of *Poems & Plays* is open to question, marred as it is by typographical errors and omissions. For example, line 1 in "Waiting and Peeking" should probably end: "nobody listens to the Norns," as it did when published in *Poetry* 84:2 (May 1954), 77. (The edition substitutes "Norms" for "Norns."). And left unaccountably uncollected from *Poems & Plays* is "Philosopher-King" from *Poetry* 74:2 (May 1949), 69.

4. Hoskins's papers on deposit at the University of Delaware have been cataloged with exemplary thoroughness. Among her manuscripts in the archives are listed other poems, short fiction, an incomplete novel and five plays (pro-

duced, but not published). An overview of the available material is on the internet: see <http://www.lib.udel.edu/ud/spec/findaids/hoskins1.htm>.

5. Jarrell's allusion in "Fifty Years of American Poetry" may seem all too brief: "I am sorry to have no space in which to write about such individual poets as Adrienne Rich and Katherine Hoskins" ("Fifty" 330). But Hoskins was not being relegated to a footnote when Jarrell sent regrets in this way. Even a mention in this talk was, from Jarrell's viewpoint, a sign of considerable achievement. Recalling her husband's preparations, Mary Jarrell counts the space allocated to individual writers as if Jarrell had once done the same: "To cover fifty years of American poetry in a one-hour speech, Jarrell singled out fifty-seven poets to mention. Who got the most space was significant and who placed at the finish line was significant. In his conclusion Jarrell gave Wilbur 230 words, Shapiro 250 and Lowell 700" (*Letters* 457). In this fifty-year overview, Jarrell's own name was conspicuous by its absence, although an attentive audience member, once over the puzzle of its absence and the shock of hearing the name Karl Shapiro sandwiched equally between Wilbur and Lowell, might have been inclined to murmur in response (especially after hearing Shapiro's work praised for its un-Shapiro-like but Jarrell-like qualities such as its "clear Rilke-like rhetoric" and "frankly Whitmanesque convolutions"): "Not Shapiro, no—Jarrell, Jarrell!"

Chapter 5: Epics True and False

1. To be sure, Berryman would not limit himself to just a portrayal of his former mistress. As a fantasy figure, Bradstreet can become any woman at all or a Superwoman. In a passage where Berryman-as-lover is agonizing over a dream in which several women had been murdered, Bradstreet moves quickly to assuage his doubts and fears. When Berryman says, "I wonder if / *I* killed them. Women serve my turn," Bradstreet replies: "—Dreams! You are good." To which Berryman answers "—No," provoking a further counter-response to soothe his anxiety (34:2–4). This particular exchange was one that Eileen Simpson, Berryman's wife in those years, remembered as having a "familiar ring." She also remarked that unlike Bradstreet, when she attempted to "reassure him" she had to speak "at great length and unpoetically" (227).

2. Berryman's unconventional upbringing could provide no source for these descriptions of a happy homemaker. His mother he eventually came to consider a suspect in his father's mysterious death when Berryman was twelve (the police ruled his death to be a suicide). No children had issued from his slowly collapsing marriage to the psychoanalyst Eileen Simpson. He was on the final section of the *Homage* when he gravitated toward the bustling household of Robert and Sally Fitzgerald (she was pregnant with her fifth child) in suburban Ridgefield, Connecticut—a journey that biographer Paul Mariani sees as calculated as a tactic to complete his poem.

3. All through the 1960s, Berryman was on record contrasting *Homage* with *The Waste Land,* as Golding himself has demonstrated. As Golding notes in his discussion of Berryman's oppositional relationship to Eliot (66–69), the uncoupling originated in a remark by Edmund Wilson ("the most distinguished long poem by an American since *The Waste Land*"), but Berryman always emphasized the unlikeness of the comparison.

4. Though completed by 1948, the manuscript was not published until 1951 because Knopf, Hughes's publisher at the time, declined it. *Montage* was rejected by other publishers until Henry Holt accepted it as part of a multi-book contract. Additional evidence for the "long poem" status of *Montage* is the fact that Hughes never broke up the individual poems in the text, either when offering the manuscript to other publishers or, most dramatically, when arranging his *Selected Poems:* there all the poems were reprinted in sequence in their entirety. And as Arnold Rampersad points out in his edition of the *Collected Poems* (1994), Hughes "clearly refers to the whole book as a 'poem' and stresses that the parts should be read in sequence" (672). Indeed, it is the single example of a set of texts by Hughes that Rampersad does not break down for republishing into chronological order of writing. Dramatic evidence for bebop's penetration of black popular culture may be heard in solos by the guitarist and bassist in the Nat "King" Cole Trio as featured in *Killer Diller* (1948), a film merchandised exclusively for a black audience. The evening of entertainment at the Apollo Theater includes tap-dance, comic monologues, sweet bands (Andy Kirk's Clouds of Joy) and Cole's jazz trio.

5. In *Ask Your Mama: 12 Moods for Jazz* (1961), a set of poems to be read within but against a melody identified at the start as "Hesitation Blues (Traditional)" Hughes also includes a "musical figurine" that he identifies as "the impudent little melody of the old break, 'Shave and a haircut, fifteen cents'" (*Collected* 475). The figurine, as Hughes develops it in *Montage,* is like a musical after-comment that is both minimal but recognizable; like a nod of the head, it acknowledges the message has been received. But like bebop or "be-bop" or "re-bop" or "de-dop" the term in *Montage* remains unsettled: in "What? So Soon!" it has been replaced by a *"Figurette"* that nonetheless clearly resembles the figurine: *"De-daddle-dy! / De-dop!"* (398). In addition, several poems in *Montage* end with a "Comment from a Stoop" or "Comment against a Lamppost" that offer closure by depicting an audience responding to what has been said. These small details serve the crucial function of situating the poem in a street-corner world of vernacular comments that portray a sharp communal audience quick on the uptake.

6. What may be most important about Hughes's strategy in such apparently throwaway fragments is that they retain the aura of their own invisibility. They seem entirely inconsequential—or at best, the kind of snappy patter that peppers a hard-boiled novel. When the African American prostitute in Raymond

Chandler's "Pickup on Noon Street" (1950) learns that Smiler is without funds, she snaps: "Keep your paws down, see! Tinhorns are dust to me. Dangle!" (1) Hughes's voices cannot speak with such dazzling ferocity (nor is he so ready to romanticize commercial sex). He intends that these voices should nearly elide themselves, that they carry within them the sense in which they seem to be both transgressive yet unimportant. For us to be able to recognize them, then, and bring them out of the obscurity becomes the crucial undertaking. Hughes stages auditory events that block easy dismissal.

7. Details of Liberia's history that were compressed in Tolson's poetry initially appeared in a prose summary on the inside dust jacket of the hardcover edition, providing invaluable stepping-stones for first-time readers. Specifically, the material presented poetically in "Mi," Sol" and "La" is summarized on the dust jacket, suggesting Tolson wrote the copy.

8. The italicized non-English phrases are, in order of appearance: "Victory to India" (Urdu), "Long live Pakistan" (also Urdu; these are patriotic slogans of two nations opposed to one another and separated by a quote from Rudyard Kipling's "Mandalay"), "We'll show the world" (Russian), "Mohammed the messenger of God" (Arabic), "the belly has shrunken" and "East wind rain" (both Japanese—this last phrase consists of the code words used in a telegram to indicate diplomatic breakdown between Japan and America in November 1941). Tolson's notes to his poem translate the phrase that is in Russian and the phrases in Japanese, but leave the rest as they are. An edition of the poem that is completely annotated—which is to say, an edition that annotates both Tolson's text *and* Tolson's footnotes to his text—appears in the *Oxford Book of Modern American Verse* (2000).

9. Jon Stanton Woodson, author of a pioneering dissertation on the *Libretto,* asserts in a 1986 essay that "Tolson makes things difficult for the reader in that he provides notes that do not help explicate the poem," notes that "mention books which in turn must be entirely read to get at Tolson's meaning" (35). Woodson argues that Tolson sought to embed his poem in knowledge that was specialist, arcane, exclusive—available only to the initiate, specifically the follower of the teachings of G. I. Gurdjieff (as had some of the members of the Harlem renaissance like Wallace Thurman and Jean Toomer). While traces of Gurdjieff's vocabulary remain in Tolson's work, it is important to recall how catholic were Tolson's reading tastes.

10. Tolson first developed the contrast between the ferris wheel and merry-go-round, as Robert Farnsworth has noted, in his weekly column for the *Washington* [D. C.] *Tribune,* where he wrote: "Racial superiority and class superiority produced the hellish contraption called the Ferris Wheel of history. Democracy will produce the Merry-Go-Round of history" (*Caviar* 92). In a footnote to line 619, Tolson identifies "the underlying unity of the past with the ferris wheel and the present with the merry-go-round" (*"Harlem"* 205). As part of his visionary

program, then, Tolson now sketches a world culture that has passed beyond a ferris wheel model that structures social status along a vertical dimension (high on top, low on bottom) to a model of a democratically or socially leveling merry-go-round which operates along a horizontal dimension and allows all to ride at the same speed as equals. The merry-go-round, as Langston Hughes understood, had an immediate significance for those living under the Jim Crow separatism laws. The "Colored child" who speaks Hughes's 1942 poem "Merry-go-round" could ask: "Where is the Jim Crow section / On this merry-go-round, / Mister, cause I want to ride?" . . . "On the bus we're put in the back—/ But there ain't no back / To a merry-go-round!" (240).

11. Not every footnote is loaded, however. On occasion, Tolson uses the footnote more or less conventionally. In a text peppered with languages other than English—some of them non-European—the footnote is an indispensable guide. Explaining that *"Karibu wee!"* (line 84) means "welcome" will be necessary to all but a few readers. Of course Tolson's confident annotation of foreign phrases (identifying snatches of Arabic, Greek, Latin, Urdu, Japanese, German, Russian, Spanish, Portuguese, Italian, and French) demonstrates the cultural competence that makes it difficult to dismiss his viewpoint. The footnotes help Tolson ground his poem in the literature of the western tradition (references abound to works by Shakespeare, Goethe, Dante, Petrarch, Ovid, Martial, Aeschylus, Sophocles, Milton, Shelley, and Hardy) and also allow him to display an impressive familiarity with early modern French poets, including Blaise Cendrars, Jean Cocteau, Andre Salmon, and Guillaume Apollinaire. But many references simply testify to a wide knowledge: Tolson calls upon the sociology of Gunnar Myrdal and Herbert Aptheker; the philosophy of Nietzsche and the activism of Camus; operatic arias by Monteverdi, Mendelssohn, and Bach; fragments from the pre-Socratic poet-philosopher Xenophanes; numerous passages from the Old and New Testaments; and works by a variety of historians, centered on a range of cultures around the globe, from a popular uprising in the south of Brazil to the battle with Portuguese monarchs for gold reserves along the Niger River to a Spanish scheme to encourage Kentucky to secede from the union.

12. Plutzik acknowledged, in the first edition, that "Parts of *Horatio* were written under Summer Faculty Fellowships granted to the author in 1954 and 1958 by the University of Rochester." Segments appeared infrequently through the decade, two in Elliott's 1956 anthology, others in the *Yale Review* and the *Transatlantic Review,* still others in Plutzik's second collection, *Apples from Shinar* (1959).

Chapter 6: The Lure of the Sestina

1. There were honorable examples of the double sestina, including a dialogue by Sidney that was reprinted in the *Viking Portable Medieval and Renaissance*

Poetry edited by W. H. Auden and Norman Holmes Pearson in 1950. This poem, moreover, Empson had quoted in its entirety and discussed with exceptional flair in *Some Versions of Pastoral* (second edition, 1948). But this was not a form that gained popularity in the 1950s. Only one instance comes to mind, Gene Derwood's "Double Sestine (A Fragment)," left unfinished at her death and posthumously published in 1955.

2. Robert Pack's "Sestina in Sleep" (Spring 1955 *Sewanee Review*) adds rhyme. Pack limits his choice of end-words to three sets that rhyme, and furthermore demands that each stanza must end with a syntactically similar line that acts like a refrain. Thus stanza 1 ends: "It is not time, not time for you to sleep," while stanza 2 closes with: "It is the act, it is the act that dies"; "It is their time, it is their time to play" closes the third stanza and so on.

3. To these titles Paul Fussell might have reacted with a brisk and dismissive nod. The problem of the sestina, he argued in his influential 1965 treatise on the mechanics of poetry, *Poetic Meter and Poetic Form,* was that it could never be more than a plaything, and thus it could never be more than an occasion for poets to pursue matters of interest only to them. He described the sestina as "a complicated Italian and French form of perhaps dubious structural expressiveness in English," and he ended with an explicit warning: "like many imported forms, the sestina, regardless of the way it is tailored, would seem to be one that gives more structural pleasure to the contriver than to the apprehender" (145). Unless we are prepared to become adepts and take delight in the game, the sestina will shut us out. Fussell is unprepared to consider the possibility that readers may take pleasure in being addressed as if they were peers of the poet.

4. As Justice explained in a 1995 interview, however, his sestina was formulated as a response to Kees's sestina, not to his disappearance. Kees vanished in the interim between Justice's writing of his sestina and its first publication in the *Hudson Review.* Yet so intimate did the address seem between Justice and Kees that the appearance of the poem prompted Kees's father to contact Justice in the hope that the six words in the poem could provide a clue to his son's whereabouts. In a memory that is still painful many years later, Justice recalled how difficult it had been to inform Kees's father that he had only been following a poetic convention ("Interview" 39).

Chapter 7: Poems about the Bomb: *Noir* Poetics

1. The *Collected Poems* only reprints the poetry from the volumes that Berryman assembled for publication in his own time. Poems that appeared exclusively in journals are omitted. Berryman's biographer John Haffenden associates "The Wholly Fail" with a project from 1948 to 1949 that was never completed and that had as its working title *The Black Book.* In a 1966 interview reported by Haffenden, Berryman described it as a "Mass for the Dead" in forty-

two sections whose subject was to be "the Nazi murderers of the Jews" (205–6). The individual sections, if this one is any indication, could have overlapped with other wartime issues. Three poems under the title "The Black Book" were collected by Berryman in *His Thoughts Made Pockets and The Plane Buckt* (1958).

2. An exception is Gregory Corso's "Bomb" which Bradley's *Atomic Ghost* anthology reprints from *The Happy Birthday of Death* (1960). But this poem in the shape of a mushroom cloud is, like other works by Corso, primarily a send-up of solemnity in art. Corso's voice is that of the Beat innocent whose simplicity permits an enjoyment of life that the Bomb irritatingly threatens. Similarly, Ginsberg's notorious lines from "America" (from *Howl*, 1956)—"America when will we end the human war? / Go fuck yourself with your atom bomb / I don't feel good don't bother me"—position the speaker as an individual who is harassed by the various demands made by his own country on him to act as a responsible citizen. Although these works may seem to protest, their light touch, like Reed Whittemore's humorous "Lines Composed upon Reading an Announcement by Civil Defense Authorities Recommending that I Build a Bomb-shelter in My Backyard" (from *An American Takes a Walk*, 1956), practically serve, I think (albeit inadvertently), to accustom their readers to the presence of the Bomb.

3. Readings of antinuclear poetry in two recent studies by Rob Wilson in 1991 and John Gery in 1996 focus almost exclusively on poems written from the late 1950s onward, thus implying that poets produced no antinuclear poetry in the 1940s and 1950s. The post-1960 antinuclear poetry that they describe was underwritten by a post-1960 poetic discourse that openly sanctioned dissent and that was fueled by protest against the Vietnam war and a deepening concern (and despair) over ecological issues. As a result, post-1960 poetry is based on a set of presentational strategies different from the pre-1960 antinuclear poetry discussed in this and the following chapter.

4. Shapiro's descriptions of these events occurs, without naming names, in Chapter 3 of his autobiography *Reports of My Death*.

5. Lechlitner's reference to the sun as "our life, our love, our future" may seem excessive, but the fact that she describes the sun in a parenthesis, as if in an aside to the reader, suggests she is alluding to the way the example of the sun was widely invoked to explain how the fusion in an atomic bomb could unleash so much energy. Truman's August 7, 1945, announcement of the Hiroshima bombing (twice quoted and once paraphrased so that it appears three times in different stories on the August 7 front page of the *New York Times*) explained that "The force from which the sun draws its power has been loosed against those who brought war to the east." The symbolism of the Japanese rising sun, in Truman's words, is dramatically counterpointed by the reality of the Allies' physical harnessing of the source of all natural energy. But Lechlitner's line,

sensitive to that usage, may have been heard by readers in 1946 as a defiant refusal to allow "the sun" to be co-opted as an ally. Thomas McGrath employed
a similar concept, though with his own punning twist, in the last lines of "The
Second Heresy of Parson Chance," first published in *discovery* (No. 2) in 1953:
"Man fixed the stars in compass courses, made trains run / On time everywhere,
split the atom and, / Having put out the Son, puts out the sun" ("Heresy" 147).

6. The reference to "Walt Disney" and "Donald Duck the maniac" seems
poetic if we consider "Donald Duck's Atom Bomb," written and drawn for the
Disney corporation by Carl Barks and distributed in 1947 as a premium from
Cheerios breakfast cereal. In Michael Barrier's 1981 synopsis, "Donald invents
an atom bomb that goes 'fut' instead of 'boom,' and two professors are summoned to inspect Donald's handiwork. One of them, Professor Sleezy, a foreign
expert, steals the bomb, and accidentally ignites it" (101) The story thus suggests that university intellectuals may be foreign agents. But Laing's objection
to the story would primarily turn on it as an attempt to normalize the bomb,
to render it inconsequential by associating it with readily identifiable cartoon
characters and by marketing it for children.

7. Rodman's photomontages have a complicated lineage that may be traced
back to the seven illustrations that Russian Futurist A. M. Rodchenko prepared
for printing among the poems in Vladimir Mayakovsky's 1923 long poem *About
This*. All seven of the photomontages are reproduced with the poem in *Mayakovsky* (170–213).

8. *The Glass Room* exemplifies how a formula genre can be adapted for use as
a vehicle of social commentary. It warns against right-wing fanatics who plan
to turn frustrated veterans into anti-Semites and red baiters. Its narrator and
hero Phil Norris, suspected of murdering his wife, to clear his name must go
underground in Los Angeles with the help of a glamorous companion who
becomes the heroine. In a climactic chapter, the villain is revealed as orches-
trating a mass rally in which a mob of veterans displays hostile feelings they
have been duped into believing. Who is responsible for the plight of the unem-
ployed veteran? "The whole audience rose to its feet, yelling its lungs out, shout-
ing, 'Rosenfeld! Morgenthau! The Jews! . . . The international bankers! . . . The
niggers and the Jews!'" (Rolfe and Fuller, *Glass* 224) Many deft touches center
on the postwar veteran. In the opening chapter, an out-of-work veterans prods
Phil into reluctantly purchasing the then-familiar red poppy that memorialized the veteran. At a party a few hours later, someone who is about to dismiss
Phil as inconsequential spots the poppy in his lapel and profusely apologizes:
"Forgive me, sir . . . I had you all wrong. You can never tell a book by its cover."
The shifting significance of the poppy reveals the culture's contradictory attitude toward the vet as someone it cannot decide whether to honor or try to
forget. The vet remains on the streets, begging for a livelihood, while the artifact that represents the veteran is a fetish with commanding authority in cer-

tain social circumstances. Rolfe was only one among many left-wing writers who turned to pulp-market *noir* in the 1940s and 1950s. For the names of other authors, see Wald (17–19).

9. One example of how cavalierly the *California Quarterly* editors could treat the Bomb as a "problem" can be glimpsed in the shortened version of Lawrence Lipton's *Rainbow at Midnight* excerpted for publication in the spring 1953 issue. In the final book version, published in 1955 by the leftist Golden Quill Press (and a selection of the Book Club for Poetry), the fourth poem "On Instruments," from Part One ("Night Flight") ends with an allusion to cities that "tremble / In the shadow of the Bomb" and wittily identifies rockets as "our homeopathic charm against / The Bomb," asking: "what shall save us from ourselves?" (18). But the excerpts from "Night Flight" that *CQ* published did not include this poem in their generous (twenty-seven page!) excerpts from the long work. However, this version may not have been available to the editors. The final version of *Rainbow at Midnight* differs in several respects from the magazine excerpts. Lipton omitted the long poem in nine three-stanza segments that originally served as an introduction in the magazine version, and in the book version he included lengthy dialogues in which a figure identified as "The New Man" fell into abstract conversation with a chorus of figures who represented different aspects of the community. The revised version printed as a book seems to have been reconstructed to be a dramatic performance. A prefatory note after the title page reports that "The first public oratorio performance of *Rainbow at Midnight* was presented at Beverly Hills, California, June 12, 1954, with a quartet of voices."

10. A peculiarity of Gordon's work are lines that wrap around early rather than take full advantage of the space to the right of the page. Although there is a typographical convention that reproduces the long poetic line by wrapping it around in the way Gordon's lines appear, it seems to be the case that Gordon wanted his lines split in precisely this manner. The split, that is, causes a double line-break, an internal interruption of the line's movement. Since Gordon's poetry is distinguished neither for its attractive diction nor for its intricate syntax nor compelling rhythm, it may therefore be important for the poetry to have this double line break as one of the few enriching features of the language that Gordon permits his work.

Chapter 8: Poems about the Bomb: Nuclear Family

1. Because a "scientific" vocabulary in itself may attract a poet's interest, the poet's choice of a scientific diction is not always a clear-cut pathway for determining when lines may covertly allude to the Bomb. Barbara Gibbs's "Sequence," a group of four sonnets collected in *The Green Chapel* in 1958, offers tantalizing clues, especially in its second sonnet, which opens with these prophetic tones: "Let all who at their own center rest / Ponder upon the atom's

potency, / How with a fragile equilibrium blest / It teeters on the brink of anar-chy" (74). While this sonnet concludes in a manner that lends itself to a certain apocalyptic reading—"Now is the chain begun that endeth never"—nonethe-less the overall trajectory of the four sonnets seems to resolve into a narrative that is "philosophical" in its speculative reach.

2. In a revised version of the poem published in 1971 as a preface to Bevington's prose memoir, *The House Was Quiet and the World Was Calm,* she allowed herself to be more explicit about "the region down by Ellenton," as she defined it in 1952, calling it now "the bomb site down by Ellenton" (*House* 4). Other 1971 revisions indicate a change in the political atmosphere: they opt for the sharpness of precision over a blurry suggestivity. "The hydrogen bomb is ours, in all the seasons," she writes in 1971, undoing the original 1952 line: "The H-bomb is to flower, in all the seasons." In 1971 she says bluntly: "Out there you find Cape Fear." Earlier she had observed a bit more casually: "One cape is called Cape Fear." Appropriate as these revisions may be for her prose memoir in which she angrily recounts the political decisions of the 1950s (on the Korean war she writes, "To meet Soviet aggression, we risked a full-scale nuclear war, the annihilation of mankind, and kingdom come" [*House* 145]), they are changes whose clarifications edge the poem away from its original effect.

3. Of course exceptions exist to this, and some are significant. Peter Kane Dufault's *Angel of Accidence* (1954) concluded with "The President Orders Con-struction of the Hydrogen Bomb" (75–76). At its close, the president is being interrogated by a reporter whose unvoiced questions are our own. The presi-dent's answers are inadequate:

One question? Well,
if it's off the record, shoot.
Old mule feels good today. . . .

What? Sir, decision fell
on me as Commander-in-Chief.
A matter of ordnance. Anyway,
You can't stop History.

Oh, I see.
Well, wouldn't it be a relief
to know how it all ends, eh?
And now, sir, if I may—
I'm due: my shower and rub.
Then, the Lions Club. (76)

While deriding the smug voice of unflappable authority (that nonetheless swerves to whatever answer is sufficient to silence the questioner), Dufault nicely insinuates the idea that the Bomb represents the end of History. But the poem, though collected in a volume published in 1954, was most likely written much earlier since it points to an earlier incident, either the decision by Truman to bomb Hiroshima or Truman's go-ahead to develop the H-bomb. *Angel of Accidence* gathers work from both the 1940s and the 1950s (the poem titled "Hill Walk, November 1948" is among its pieces).

Epilogue

1. According to the account in the Iowa City *Press-Citizen* the .22 caliber rifle shot was not immediately fatal. The press report states that he was found by his roommate, William Stuckey of St. Louis, at 3 P.M. and died at 11 P.M. that evening. (Forty-five years after the event, it was this lingering after the shot that Carl Hartman, with whom Shelley had worked as an editorial assistant on the *Western Review,* still recalled painfully.) The Johnson County coroner ruled the death "a suicide due to ill health," and the newspaper reported that Shelley had been a patient at the University of Iowa's Psychopathic hospital "for 30 days last year." Warren Carrier, in a memoir about the early years of the Iowa Writers' Workshop, sheds some further light on the incident. Carrier had been hired in 1949 to teach, among other subjects, a cutting-edge course in literary criticism; he was at Iowa for three years. "The student with whom I learned the most was Robert Shelley. My course in modern literary criticism often turned into a dialogue with Shelley as we explored the intricacies and limits of criticism. And Shelley, had he lived, would, I am convinced, have ranked with Justice and Snodgrass and Stafford as a poet. His inability to cope with reality and especially with his homosexuality led him to suicide, a sad event for which all of us who knew him felt guilty" (23).

2. It is not clear whether the poem in *Poetry* and the poem in *Poems from the Iowa City Workshop* are among these "six or eight." Both poems focus on domestic arrangements, and they employ a simple diction within a complicated syntax. Both seem to be different enough from Shelley's other publications, all of which would have been submitted to magazines well in advance of his death. He had published "Le Lac de Cygnes" and "The Homing Heart" in different issues of the *Western Review* in 1948, "Monologues: A Young Prince to the Dying King" in *New Directions in Prose and Poetry 12* (1950) and "Aspects of the Evergreen" in *Perspective* (1951). A review of a book of poetry by John Frederick Nims appeared in the *Western Review* (where Shelley was an assistant editor) in 1951. In addition, his application to the University of Iowa in 1949 mentions publications in small magazines plus reviews for his hometown newspaper, the *St. Louis Post-Dispatch.*

Works Cited

Abbe, George. "The Role of the Prophet." *California Quarterly* 2 (Spring 1953): 3–9.

Allen, Donald M. *The New American Poetry*. New York: Grove, 1960.

Altieri, Charles. *Enlarging the Temple: New Directions in American Poetry during the 1960s*. Lewisburg, Pa.: Bucknell University Press, 1979.

Alvarez, A. "Imagism and Poetesses." *Kenyon Review* 19 (Spring 1957): 321–28.

Ansen, Alan. "A Fit of Something against Something." In *Disorderly Houses*. Middletown: Wesleyan University Press, 1962. 41–42.

Arrowsmith, William. "Nine New Poets." *Hudson Review* 9 (Summer 1956): 289–97.

Ashbery, John. "The Compromise; or, The Queen of the Cariboo." In *Three Plays*. Calais, Vt.: Z Press, 1982. 31–120.

———. "Craft Interview with John Ashbery." In *The Craft of Poetry: Interviews from the New York Quarterly*. Ed. William Packard. Garden City: Doubleday, 1974. 111–28.

———. *Some Trees*. New Haven: Yale University Press, 1956.

———. "Two Scenes." *Kenyon Review* 18 (Spring 1956): 273–74.

Auden, W. H. *Collected Shorter Poems: 1927–1957*. New York: Random House, 1957.

———. "Foreword." *The Grasshopper's Man and Other Poems* by Rosalie Moore. New Haven: Yale University Press, 1949. 7–10.

———. "Foreword." *Some Trees* by John Ashbery. New Haven: Yale University Press, 1956. 11–16.

———. "Foreword." *The Green Wall* by James Wright. New Haven: Yale University Press, 1957. ix–xvi.

———. "Making, Knowing and Judging." In *The Dyer's Hand and Other Essays*. New York: Random House, 1962. 31–60.

Augustine. *Confessions*. Trans. R. S. Pine-Coffin. Harmondsworth: Penguin, 1961.

Axelrod, Stephen Gould. *Robert Lowell: Life and Art*. Princeton: Princeton University Press, 1978.

Barrett, William. "Declining Fortunes of the Literary Review." In *Anchor Review No. 2*. Ed. Melvin J. Lasky. New York: Anchor, 1957. 145–60.

Barrier, Michael. *Carl Barks and the Art of the Comic Book*. New York: Lilien, 1981.

Berryman, John. "The Art of Poetry: An Interview with Peter Stitt." 1972. Reprinted in *Berryman's Understanding: Reflections on the Poetry of John Berryman*. Ed. Harry Thomas. Boston: Northeastern University Press, 1988. 29.

———. *The Collected Poems: 1937–1971*. New York: Farrar, Straus & Giroux, 1985.

———. *Homage to Mistress Bradstreet*. New York: Farrar, Straus & Giroux, 1956.

———. "The Long Way to McDiarmid." *Poetry* 88 (Apr. 1956): 52–61.

———. "The Wholly Fail." *Poetry* 75 (Jan. 1950): 191.

Bérubé, Michael. *Marginal Forces/Cultural Centers: Tolson, Pynchon and the Politics of the Canon*. Ithaca: Cornell University Press, 1992.

Bevington, Helen. *The House Was Quiet and the World Was Calm*. New York: Harcourt, 1971.

———. "Report from the Carolinas." In *A Change of Sky and Other Poems*. Boston: Houghton Mifflin, 1956. 72–73.

Biberman, Herbert J. "Saturday Night with Hamlet." *California Quarterly* 1 (Summer 1952): 38–43.

Bishop, Elizabeth. *The Complete Poems, 1927–1979*. New York: Farrar, Straus & Giroux, 1983.

———. "The Fish." In *Mid-Century American Poets*. Ed. John Ciardi. New York: Twayne, 1950. 276–78.

———. "It All Depends." In *Mid-Century American Poets*. Ed. John Ciardi. New York: Twayne, 1950. 267.

———. *One Art: Letters*. Ed. Robert Giroux. New York: Farrar, Straus & Giroux, 1994.

Bogan, Louise. *Achievement in American Poetry*. Chicago: Regnery, 1951.

———. "Verse." *New Yorker* 35 (Nov. 28, 1959): 239–40.

Bogardus, Edgar. "In This Hotel There Are No Rooms." *Kenyon Review* 17 (Winter 1955): 114–15.

Boyer, Paul. *By the Bomb's Early Light: American Thought and Culture at the Dawn of the Atomic Age*. New York: Pantheon, 1985.

Bradley, John, ed. *Atomic Ghost: Poets Respond to the Nuclear Age*. Minneapolis: Coffee House Press, 1995.

Breslin, James E. B. *From Modern to Contemporary: American Poetry, 1945–1960*. Chicago: University of Chicago Press, 1984.

Brooks, Cleanth. "Milton and the New Criticism." *Sewanee Review* 59 (Winter 1951): 1–22.

Brown, Ashley. "The Poetry of Anthony Hecht." In *The Burdens of Formality: Essays on the Poetry of Anthony Hecht.* Ed. Sidney Lea. Athens: University of Georgia Press, 1989. 10–25.

Brown, Harry. *The Beast in His Hunger.* New York: Knopf, 1949.

Brown, Spencer. *My Father's Business and Other Poems.* In *Poets of Today,* vol. 3. New York: Scribner's, 1957.

Burden, Jean. "The Atomic Age—Pasadena, California." *Poetry* 70 (July 1947): 191–92.

Cabral, Olga. *Cities and Deserts.* New York: Roving Eye Press, 1959.

Carrier, Warren. "Some Recollections." In *A Community of Writers: Paul Engle and the Iowa Writers' Workshop.* Ed. Robert Dana. Iowa City: University of Iowa Press, 1999. 18–23.

Carton, Evan, and Gerald Graff. *Criticism since 1940.* Vol. 8 of *The Cambridge History of American Literature.* Ed. Sacvan Bercovitch. Cambridge: Cambridge University Press, 1996.

Carruth, Hayden. "Poetry Chronicle: Parnassus Stormed." *Partisan Review* 20 (Sept.–Oct. 1953): 577–80.

———. "Poets without Prophecy." *Nation* 196 (Apr. 27, 1963): 355–56.

———. "Three Poets." *Poetry* 95 (Nov. 1959): 116–18.

Chandler, Raymond. "Pickup on Noon Street." In *Pickup on Noon Street.* New York: Ballantine, 1972. 1–48.

Ciardi, John. "Elegy Just in Case." In *Mid-Century American Poets.* Ed. John Ciardi. New York: Twayne, 1950. 252–54.

———. "Our Most Melodious Poet." Reprinted in *Richard Wilbur's Creation.* Ed. Wendy Salinger. Ann Arbor: University of Michigan Press, 1982. 52–56.

———. "Recent Verse." *Nation* 178 (Feb. 27, 1954): 183–84.

———. *Selected Letters of John Ciardi.* Ed. Edward M. Cifelli. Fayetteville: University of Arkansas Press, 1991.

———. "Two Nuns and a Strolling Player." *Nation* 178 (May 22, 1954): 445–56.

———, ed. *Mid-Century American Poets.* New York: Twayne, 1950.

Cifelli, Edward. *John Ciardi: A Biography.* Fayetteville: University of Arkansas Press, 1997.

Cooper, Jane. "Morning on the St. John's." In *The Weather of Six Mornings.* New York: Macmillan, 1968. 13–14.

———. "Nothing Has Been Used in the Manufacture of This Poetry That Could Have Been Used in the Manufacture of Bread." In *Maps and Windows.* New York: Collier, 1974. 29–60.

Corso, Gregory. "Bomb." In *The Happy Birthday of Death.* New York: New Directions, 1960. 60.

Coulette, Henri. "The Problem of Creation (for Thomas McGrath)." *California Quarterly* 1 (Winter 1952): 32.

Coxe, Louis O. "For My Son's Birthday." In *The Wilderness.* Minneapolis: University of Minnesota Press, 1958. 40–41.

Cullen, Winifred. "Defend Her in Time of Trouble." *Poetry* 66 (July 1945): 195–96.

Culler, Jonathan. *Framing the Sign: Criticism and Its Institutions.* Norman: University of Oklahoma Press, 1988.

Curley, Daniel. "The Appointed Hour." *Kenyon Review* 17 (Autumn 1955): 543–74.

Davis, Frank Marshall. *47th Street.* Prairie City, Ill.: Decker Press, 1948.

Davis, Mike. *City of Quartz.* New York: Vintage, 1992.

Davison, Peter. *The Fading Smile: Poets in Boston from Robert Frost to Robert Lowell to Sylvia Plath, 1955–1960.* New York: Knopf, 1994.

de Certeau, Michel. *The Practice of Everyday Life.* Trans. Steven Rendall. Berkeley: University of California Press, 1984.

Denney, Reuel. *The Astonished Muse.* Chicago: University of Chicago Press, 1957.

Derwood, Gene. "Double Sestine (a Fragment)." In *The Poems of Gene Derwood.* New York: Clarke & Way, 1955. 62–64.

Deutsch, Babette. "Scenes Alive with Light." In *Richard Wilbur's Creation.* Ed. Wendy Salinger. Ann Arbor: University of Michigan Press, 1982. 12.

———. "Solitudes." *California Quarterly* 3 (Autumn 1954): 42.

———. "Waste Land of Harlem." *New York Times Book Review,* May 6, 1951. Reprinted in *Langston Hughes: Critical Perspectives Past and Present.* Ed. Henry Louis Gates Jr. and A. K. Appiah. New York: Amistad, 1993. 32.

Dickey, James. "From Babel to Byzantium." *Sewanee Review* 65 (Summer 1957): 508–30.

———. "In the Presence of Anthologies." *Sewanee Review* 66 (Spring 1958): 294–314.

Dufault, Peter Kane. "The President Orders Construction of the Hydrogen Bomb." In *Angel of Accidence.* New York: Macmillan, 1954. 75–76.

Dupee, F. W. "The Muse as House Guest." *Partisan Review* 25 (Summer 1958): 454–60.

Eberhart, Richard. "The Groundhog." In *Mid-Century American Poets.* Ed. John Ciardi. New York: Twayne, 1950. 234.

———. "On 'Love Calls Us to the Things of This World.'" In *The Contemporary Poet as Artist and Critic.* Ed. Anthony Ostroff. New York: Little-Brown, 1964. 4–5.

Elliott, George P., ed. *Fifteen Modern American Poets.* New York: Rinehart, 1956.

Elster, Jon. *Sour Grapes.* Cambridge: Cambridge University Press, 1988.

Elton, William. "A Glossary of the New Criticism." *Poetry* 73 (Dec. 1948): 153–62; 73 (Jan. 1949): 232–45; and 73 (Feb. 1949): 296–307.

Engle, Paul. *American Child: A Sonnet Sequence.* New York: Random House, 1945.

———. *American Child: Sonnets for My Daughters with Thirty-six New Poems.* New York: Dial, 1956.

———. "Poet and Professor Overture." *Poetry* 79 (Feb. 1952): 267–70.

————. "Why Modern Poetry." *College English* 15 (Oct. 1953): 7–11.

Everwine, Peter. "On a Photograph of My Grandfather, Paolo Castelnuovo." In *Midland: 25 Years of Fiction and Poetry Selected from the Writing Workshop of the State University of Iowa.* Ed. Paul Engle. New York: Random House, 1961. 452.

Farnsworth, Robert M. *Melvin B. Tolson, 1898–1966: Plain Talk and Poetic Prophecy.* Columbia: University of Missouri Press, 1984.

Farrell, Thomas F. Quoted in L. R. Groves, "Report on Alamagordo Atomic Bomb Test." Appendix P in Martin J. Sherwin, *A World Destroyed: The Atomic Bomb and the Grand Alliance.* New York: Vintage, 1977. 308–14.

Fiedler, Leslie. "Green Thoughts in a Green Shade." *Kenyon Review* 18 (Spring 1956): 238–58.

Fiske, John. *Reading the Popular.* Boston: Unwin Hyman, 1989.

Fitts, Dudley. "In Minute Particulars." *New Republic* 127 (Oct. 6, 1952): 27–28.

Fitzgerald, Robert. "Patter, Distraction in Poetry." *New Republic* 121 (Aug. 8, 1949): 17–19.

Ford, Karen. *Gender and the Poetics of Excess: Moments of Brocade.* Jackson: University Press of Mississippi, 1997.

Francis, Robert. "Commentary." In *Poet's Choice.* Ed. Paul Engle and Joseph Langland. New York: Dial, 1962. 48.

————. "Hallelujah: A Sestina." In *The Orb Weaver.* Middletown: Wesleyan University Press, 1960. 46–47.

Frost, Robert. "Bursting Rapture," "U.S. 1946 King's X." In *The Complete Poems of Robert Frost.* New York: Holt, Rinehart and Winston, 1964. 568, 569.

Fuller, Roy. "The Fifties," "Images of Autumn." *California Quarterly* 3 (Autumn 1953): 54, 56.

Fussell, Paul. *Poetic Meter and Poetic Form.* Rev. ed. New York: Random House, 1965.

Gans, Herbert. *Popular Culture and High Culture.* New York: Basic Books, 1974.

Gardner, Isabella. "Children Are Game." In *Birthdays for the Ocean.* Boston: Houghton Mifflin, 1955. 21.

————. "Sestina." *Kenyon Review* 14 (Autumn 1952): 613.

Garrett, George. "Against the Grain: Poets Writing Today." In *American Poetry.* Ed. Irvin Ehrenpreis. London: Edward Arnold, 1965. 221–40.

Garrigue, Jean. "'Dark Is a Way and Light Is a Place.'" *Poetry* 94 (May 1959): 112–14.

————. "For the Fountains and Fountaineers of Villa d'Este." In *Jean Garrigue: New and Selected Poems.* New York: Macmillan, 1967. 64–72.

————. "Setpiece for Albany." In *The Monument Rose.* New York: Macmillan, 1953. 51–52.

Gates, Henry Louis. *The Signifying Monkey: A Theory of African-American Literary Criticism.* New York: Oxford University Press, 1988.

Gery, John. *Nuclear Annihilation and Contemporary American Poetry.* Gainesville: University Press of Florida, 1996.

Ghiselin, Brewster. "Poets Learning." *Poetry* 79 (Feb. 1952): 284–89.

Gibbs, Barbara. "Sequence." In *The Green Chapel.* New York: Noonday, 1958. 73–77.

Ginsberg. *Howl and Other Poems.* Introduction by William Carlos Williams. San Francisco: City Lights Pocket Poets No. 4, 1956.

Golding, Alan. *From Outlaw to Classic: Canons in American Poetry.* Madison: University of Wisconsin Press, 1995.

Gooch, Brad. *City Poet: The Life and Times of Frank O'Hara.* New York: Knopf, 1993.

Gordon, Don. *Displaced Persons.* Denver: Alan Swallow, 1958.

Gordon, Richard. "Preface." *The Unicorn Book of 1954.* New York: Unicorn Books, 1955. vi.

Graff, Gerald. *Professing Literature: An Institutional History.* Chicago: University of Chicago Press, 1987.

Greenberg, Clement. "The Present Prospects of American Painting and Sculpture." In *Clement Greenberg: The Collected Essays and Criticism.* Ed. John O'Brian. Vol. 2: *Arrogant Purpose, 1945–1949.* Chicago: University of Chicago Press, 1986. 160–70.

Gregory, Horace. "The Postwar Generation in Arts and Letters: Poetry." *Saturday Review* 36 (Mar. 14, 1953): 13–14, 64–65.

Griffin, Howard. "The Detective Story." In *Cry Cadence.* New York: Farrar, Straus and Company, 1947. 53.

Gross, Harvey. *Sound and Form in Modern Poetry.* Ann Arbor: University of Michigan Press, 1965.

Gunn, Thom. "The Calm Style." *Poetry* 93 (Sept. 1958): 378–84.

———. "Excellence and Variety." *Yale Review* 49 (Winter 1959): 295–305.

———. "Voices of Their Own." *Yale Review* 49 (Winter 1960): 589–97.

Haffenden, John. *The Life of John Berryman.* Boston: Routledge & Kegan Paul, 1982.

Hall, Donald. "Ah, Love, Let Us Be True: Domesticity and History in Contemporary Poetry." *American Scholar* 28 (Mar. 1959): 310–19.

———. *Exiles and Marriages.* New York: Viking, 1956.

———. "The New Poetry: Notes on the Past Fifteen Years in American Poetry." In *New World Writing No. 7.* New York: Signet, 1955. 231–47.

———. "Oddities and Sestinas." *Saturday Review* 39 (June 16, 1956): 27.

———. "Sestina." *The Dark Houses.* New York: Viking, 1958. 47.

———, ed. *Contemporary American Poetry.* Baltimore: Penguin, 1962. 17–26.

Hart, Lawrence. "About the Activist Poets." *Poetry* 88 (May 1951): 99–105.

———. "Six California Poets." *Quarterly Review of Literature* 4 (1947): 4.

Hartman, Geoffrey H. *"Les Belles Dames Sans Merci."* *Kenyon Review* 22 (Autumn 1960): 691–700.

Hecht, Anthony. "La Condition Botanique." In *The Hard Hours.* New York: Atheneum, 1967. 72–73.

———. "Poetry Chronicle." *Hudson Review* 9 (Aug. 1956): 444–57.

———. "The Private Eye: A Detective Story." *Kenyon Review* 10 (Autumn 1948): 627–28.

Hemley, Cecil. "Within a Budding Grove." *Hudson Review* 13 (Winter 1960–61): 626–30.

Hess. Alan. *Googie: Fifties Coffee Shop Architecture.* San Francisco: Chronicle, 1985.

Hine, Daryl. "The Destruction of Sodom." In *The Devil's Picture Book.* London: Abelard-Schumann, 1960. 14–15.

Hodeir, Andre. *Jazz: Its Evolution and Essence.* New York: Grove, 1956.

Holden, Jonathan. *The Rhetoric of the Contemporary Lyric.* Bloomington: Indiana University Press, 1980.

Hollander, John. *Rhyme's Reason: A Guide for English Verse.* New Haven: Yale University Press, 1981.

———. "Winter in Indiana (for J. M. Zito)." In *A Crackling of Thorns.* New Haven: Yale University Press, 1958. 50–51.

Holman, C. Hugh. *A Handbook to Literature.* New York: Odyssey Press, 1960.

Holmes, John. "Metaphor for My Son." In *Mid-Century American Poets.* Ed. John Ciardi. New York: Twayne, 1950. 217–19.

Holmes, Theodore. "'. . . The Wine-Transfiguring Word.'" *Poetry* 96 (May 1960): 118.

Honig, Edwin. "Poetry Chronicle." *Partisan Review* 23 (Winter 1956): 115–20.

Hoskins, Katherine. "Conversation Pieces." *Hudson Review* 12 (Spring 1959): 82–91.

———. *Excursions: Poems New and Selected.* New York: Atheneum, 1967.

———. "Hoskins, Katherine (de Montelant)." In *Contemporary Poets.* Ed. James Vinson. 3d ed. London: Macmillan, 1980. 742–43.

———. *Out in the Open.* New York: Macmillan, 1959.

———. *Villa Narcisse: The Garden, the Statues and the Pool.* New York: Noonday, 1956.

Howard, Richard. "John Ashbery." In *Alone with America: Essays on the Art of Poetry in the United States since 1950.* New York: Atheneum, 1971. 18–37.

Huff, Robert. "For Ursula." In *Colonel Johnson's Ride.* Detroit: Wayne State University Press, 1959. 3–4.

Hughes, Langston. *The Collected Poems of Langston Hughes.* Ed. Arnold Rampersad and David Roessel. New York: Random House, 1994.

Humphries, Rolfe. "Verse Chronicle." *Nation* 170 (Mar. 11, 1950): 235.

Huyssen, Andreas. *After the Great Divide: Modernism, Mass Culture, Postmodernism.* Bloomington: Indiana University Press, 1986.

James, Clive. "When the Gloves Are Off." In *Richard Wilbur's Creation.* Ed. Wendy Salinger. Ann Arbor: University of Michigan Press, 1982. 106–18.

Jarrell, Randall. "Burning the Letters," "A Country Life." In *Mid-Century American Poets*. Ed. John Ciardi. New York: Twayne, 1950. 194–96, 197–98.

———. "Fifty Years of American Poetry." In *The Third Book of Criticism*. New York: Farrar, Straus & Giroux, 1971. 295–334.

———. "Poets," "Three Books." In *Poetry and the Age*. New York: Vintage, 1953. 200–214, 227–60.

———. *Randall Jarrell's Letters*. Ed. Mary Jarrell. Boston: Houghton Mifflin, 1985.

———. "The Refugees." In *The Complete Poems*. New York: Farrar, Straus & Giroux, 1969. 370–71.

———. "Verse Chronicle." *Nation* 166 (May 8, 1948): 512.

———. "The Year in Poetry," "Five Poets," "Recent Poetry," "Poets, Critics and Readers." In *Kipling, Auden and Co*. New York: Farrar, Straus & Giroux, 1982. 221–41, 242–47, 262–72, 305–18.

Jerome, Judson. "Poets of the Sixties." *Antioch Review* 4 (Summer 1959): 421–32.

Jones, Richard, ed. *Poetry and Politics: An Anthology of Essays*. New York: Morrow, 1984.

Jumonville, Neil. *Critical Crossings: The New York Intellectuals in Postwar America*. Berkeley: University of California Press, 1991.

Justice, Donald. "Interview with Dana Gioia." *American Poetry Review* 25 (Jan.–Feb. 1996): 37–46.

———. "Sestina on Six Words by Weldon Kees," "Sonnet to My Father." In *The Summer Anniversaries*. Middletown: Wesleyan University Press, 1959. 14–15, 21.

———, ed. *The Collected Poems of Weldon Kees*. Lincoln: University of Nebraska Press, 1960.

Kalaidjian, Walter. *American Culture between the Wars: Revisionary Modernism and Postmodern Critique*. New York: Columbia University Press, 1993.

Kees, Weldon. "Sestina: Travel Notes," "Crime Club," "Travels in North America," "Aspects of Robinson." In *The Collected Poems of Weldon Kees*. Ed. Donald Justice. Lincoln: University of Nebraska Press, 1960. 63–64, 71, 114–19, 129.

Keller, Lynn. "The Twentieth Century Long Poem." In *The Columbia History of American Poetry*. Ed. Jay Parini. New York: Columbia University Press, 1993. 534–63.

Kenner, Hugh. "The *Portrait* in Perspective." *Kenyon Review* 10 (Summer 1948): 361–81.

Koch, Kenneth. "Ladies for Dinner, Saipan." *Poetry* 67 (Oct. 1945): 80.

Kramer, Hilton. "The Abuse of the Terrible." In *Avon Book of Modern Writing No. 2*. Ed. William Phillips and Philip Rahv. New York: Avon, 1954. 152–62.

Krieger, Murray. *The New Apologists for Poetry*. Minneapolis: University of Minnesota Press, 1956.

Laing, Dilys B. "Not One Atoll." In *A Walk through Two Landscapes*. New York: Twayne, 1949. 36–44.

Lang, V. R. "The Elizabethans and Illusion," "The Suicide," "Already Ripening Barberries Are Red," "Anne, a Chorus Girl Quitting the Line, to Society," "A Lovely Song for Jackson." In *V. R. Lang: Poems & Plays*. Ed. with a memoir by Alison Lurie. New York: Random House, 1975. 76, 84, 86–88, 96, 107.

Lattimore, Richmond. "Sestina for a Far-off Summer." In *Sestina for a Far-Off Summer: Poems 1957–1962*. Ann Arbor: University of Michigan Press, 1963. 89–90.

Lears, Jackson. "A Matter of Taste: Corporate Cultural Hegemony in a Mass-Consumption Society." In *Recasting America: Culture and Politics in the Age of Cold War*. Ed. Larry May. Chicago: University of Chicago Press, 1989. 38–59.

Lechlitner, Ruth. "Night in August." *Poetry* 68 (Aug. 1946): 258–59.

Lehman, David. "Notes on Poetic Form." In *The Line Forms Here*. Ann Arbor: University of Michigan Press, 1992. 24–28.

"Libra" (pseudonym). "Ladders to Heaven: Novelists and Critics." *New World Writing No. 4*. New York: Signet, 1953. 303–16.

Lifton, Robert Jay, and Greg Mitchell. *Hiroshima in America: A Half Century of Denial*. New York: Avon, 1996.

Lipton, Lawrence. "Excerpts from *Rainbow at Midnight*." *California Quarterly* 2 (Spring 1953): 16–42.

———. *Rainbow at Midnight*. Francestown, N.H.: Golden Quill, 1955.

Lott, Eric. "Double-V, Double Time: Bebop's Politics of Style." Reprinted in *The Jazz Cadence of American Culture*. Ed. Robert G. O'Meally. New York: Columbia University Press, 1998. 457–68.

Lowell, Robert. "Caron, Non Ti Crucciere." In *A New Anthology of Modern Poetry*. Ed. Selden Rodman. New York: Modern Library, 1946. 416.

———. "A Conversation with Ian Hamilton." In *Collected Prose*. Ed. Robert Giroux. New York: Farrar, Straus & Giroux, 1987. 267–90.

———. "Current Poetry." *Sewanee Review* 54 (Winter 1946): 145–53.

———. "Fall 1961," "For the Union Dead." In *For the Union Dead*. New York: Farrar, Straus & Giroux, 1966. 11–12, 70–72.

———. "Home after Three Months Away," "Skunk Hour." In *Life Studies*. New York: Farrar, Straus & Giroux, 1959. 83–84.

———. "On Robert Lowell's 'Skunk Hour.'" In *The Contemporary Poet as Artist and Critic*. Ed. Anthony Ostroff. New York: Little-Brown, 1964. 107.

———. "The Quaker Graveyard in Nantucket." In *Mid-Century American Poets*. Ed. John Ciardi. New York: Twayne, 1950. 169–74.

Lyons, John O. *The College Novel in America*. Carbondale: Southern Illinois University Press, 1962.

MacDonald, Dwight. "A Theory of Mass Culture." In *Mass Culture: The Popular Arts in America*. Ed. Bernard Rosenberg and David Manning White. Glencoe, Ill.: Free Press, 1957. 59–73.

Marling, Karal Ann. *As Seen on TV: The Visual Culture of Everyday Life in the 1950s.* Cambridge: Harvard University Press, 1994.

Matthews, William. "The Continuity of James Wright's Poems." In *The Pure Clear Word: Essays on the Poetry of James Wright.* Ed. Dave Smith. Urbana: University of Illinois Press, 1982. 99–112.

May, Elaine Tyler. "Explosive Issues: Sex, Women and the Bomb." In *Recasting America: Culture and Politics in the Age of the Cold War.* Ed. Lary May. Chicago: University of Chicago Press, 1989. 154–70.

———. *Homeward Bound: American Families in the Cold War Era.* New York: Basic Books, 1988.

Mayakovsky, Vladimir. *Mayakovsky.* Ed. and trans. by Herbert Marshall. London: Dennis Dobson, 1965.

Mayo, E. L. "In the Web." In *Mid-Century American Poets.* Ed. John Ciardi. New York: Twayne, 1950. 152–53.

———. "Two Twayne Poets." *Poetry* 81 (Feb. 1953): 324–26.

McCall, Dan. "The Quicksilver Sparrow of M. B. Tolson." *American Quarterly* 18 (Fall 1966): 538–42.

McGrath, Thomas. "The Hunted Revolutionaries." *California Quarterly* 4 (1955): 10–11.

———. "In a Season of War." *California Quarterly* 1 (Winter 1952): 36–38.

———. "The Second Heresy of Parson Chance." In *Discovery No. 2.* Ed. Vance Bourjaily. New York: Pocket Books, 1953. 147.

Merrill, James. *The Bait. Quarterly Review of Literature* 8.2 (1955): 81–96.

———. "The Beaten Path." Reprinted from *Semi-Colon* 2.5–6 (1957). In *Recitative.* Ed. with an introduction by J. D. McClatchy. San Francisco: North Point, 1986. 143–51.

———. *A Different Person.* New York: Knopf, 1993.

———. "Perspectives of the Lonesome Eye." *Poetry* 67 (Mar. 1946): 296–97.

Michelson, Bruce. *Richard Wilbur's Poetry: Music in a Scattering Time.* Amherst: University of Massachusetts Press, 1991.

Miller, Raeburn. "For Megan Hall Merker, Newly Born." In *Midland: Twenty-five Years of Fiction and Poetry, Selected from the Writing Workshops of the State University of Iowa.* Ed. Paul Engle with Henri Coulette and Donald Justice. New York: Random House, 1961. 519–21.

Millier, Brett C. *Elizabeth Bishop: Life and the Memory of It.* Berkeley: University of California Press, 1993.

Moore, Marianne. "The Ford Correspondence." In *A Marianne Moore Reader.* New York: Viking, 1961. 215–24.

Moore, Rosalie. "Moving, by Roads Moved . . ." In *The Grasshopper's Man and Other Poems.* New Haven: Yale University Press, 1949. 29.

———. "Summer Camp: Wane." In *Of Singles and Doubles.* Andes, N.Y.: Woolmer/Brotherston, 1979. 10.

Morris, Timothy. *Becoming Canonical in American Poetry.* Urbana: University of Illinois Press, 1995.

Moss, Howard. "Elegy for My Father." In *The Toy Fair.* New York: Scribner's, 1954. 47–48.

Murray, Philip. "The Christening." *Poetry* 77 (Jan. 1951): 74.

Nathan, Leonard. "The Tradition of Sadness and the American Metaphysic: An Interpretation of the Poetry of James Wright." In *The Pure Clear Word: Essays on the Poetry of James Wright.* Ed. Dave Smith. Urbana: University of Illinois Press, 1982. 159–74.

Nelson, Joyce. *The Perfect Machine: TV and the Bomb.* Philadelphia: New Society, 1992.

Nemerov, Howard. "Seven Poets and the Language." *Sewannee Review* 62 (Apr.–June 1954): 312–20.

Nims, John Frederick. "The Iron Pastoral (All-Nite Luncheonette)." *Poetry* 69 (Feb. 1947): 262–63.

———. "Trainwrecked Soldiers." In *Mid-Century American Poets.* Ed. John Ciardi. New York: Twayne, 1950. 126, 133–34.

Norse, Harold. "Victor Emmanuel Monument (Rome)." In *The Dancing Beasts.* New York: Macmillan, 1962. 16.

North, Jessica Nelson. "The Secret Presence." *Poetry* 67 (Nov. 1945): 160–61.

Noss, Murray. "Hiroshima." In *Samurai and Serpent Poems.* In *Poets of Today,* vol. 1. New York: Scribner's 1954. 84.

Oakley, J. Ronald. *God's Country: America in the Fifties.* New York: Dembner, 1986.

O'Hara, Frank. "Rare Modern." *Poetry* 89 (Feb. 1957): 307–16.

Ohmann, Richard. "History and Literary History: The Case of Mass Culture." In *Modernity and Mass Culture.* Ed. James Naremore and Patrick Brantlinger. Bloomington: Indiana University Press, 1991. 24–41.

Olsen, Tillie. *Silences.* New York: Delacorte Press, 1978.

Ostriker, Alice Suskin. *Stealing the Language: The Emergence of Women's Poetry in America.* Boston: Beacon Press, 1986.

Ostroff, Anthony. *The Contemporary Poet as Artist and Critic: Eight Symposia.* Boston: Little, Brown, 1964.

Pack, Robert. "Sestina in Sleep." *Sewanee Review* 63 (Spring 1955): 249–50.

Palmer, Winthrop. "Ante Urbem," "Evensong," "Barbarians." In *The New Barbarian.* New York: Farrar, Straus & Young, 1951. 17, 19, 35.

Partington, Angela. "Popular Fashion and Working-Class Affluence." In *Chic Thrills: A Fashion Reader.* Ed. Juliet Ash and Elizabeth Wilson. Berkeley: University of California Press, 1993. 145–61.

Perkins, David. *A History of Modern Poetry: Modernism and After.* Cambridge: Harvard University Press, 1987.

———. *Is Literary History Possible?* Baltimore: Johns Hopkins University Press, 1992.

Perloff, Marjorie. *The Poetic Art of Robert Lowell*. Ithaca: Cornell University Press, 1973.

———. "'A Step Away from Them': Poetry 1956." In *Poetry On and Off the Page: Essays for Emergent Occasions*. Evanston, Ill.: Northwestern University Press, 1998. 83–115.

Petersen, Donald. "The Stages of Narcissus (to the Memory of Robert Shelley)." *Poetry* 83 (Dec. 1953): 141–44.

Plath, Sylvia. *The Journals of Sylvia Plath*. Ed. Frances McCullough and Ted Hughes. New York: Dial Press, 1982.

———. "Yadwigha, on a Red Couch, among Lilies (A Sestina for the Douanier)." In *Collected Poems*. New York: Harper & Row, 1981. 85–86.

Plutzik, Hyam. *The Collected Poems*. Brockport, N.Y.: BOA Editions, 1987.

Porter, Fairfield. "Great Spruce Head," "The Island in the Evening." *Poetry* 85 (Mar. 1955): 326–27.

———. "Poets and Painters in Collaboration." In *Art in Its Own Terms: Selected Criticism, 1935–1975*. Ed. Rackstraw Downes. New York: Taplinger, 1979. 220–25.

———. "To William Arrowsmith." July 23, 1956. *Boulevard* 6 (Fall 1991): 32–36.

Powdermaker, Hortense. *Hollywood, the Dream Factory: An Anthropologist Looks at the Movie-Makers*. Boston: Little, Brown, 1950.

Putnam, H. Phelps. "Authors Write Books." *California Quarterly* 3 (1955): 20–21.

Rago, Henry. "The Ungovernable Risk." *Poetry* 75 (Oct. 1949): 98–100.

Randall, Julia. "[Untitled review of Selwyn Schwartz and Rosemary Thomas.]" *Poetry* 76 (July 1950): 231–34.

Ransom, John Crowe. *Selected Poems*. New York: Knopf, 1963.

Rasula, Jed. *The American Poetry Wax Museum: Reality Effects, 1940–1960*. Urbana, Ill.: National Council of Teachers of English, 1996.

Replansky, Naomi. "Whodunit?" In *Ring Song*. New York: Scribner's, 1952. 22.

Rice, Philip Blair. "The Intellectual Quarterly in a Non-Intellectual Society." *Kenyon Review* 16 (Summer 1954): 420–39.

Rich, Adrienne. *Collected Earlier Poems*. New York: Norton, 1995. xix–xx.

Richards, Leo. "Where Are Your Worshippers." *Voices* No. 140 (Winter 1950): 21.

Richardson, Dorothy. "Modern Grimm." *Poetry* 73 (Feb. 1949): 275–276.

Ridler, Anne. "Choosing a Name." *Poetry* 81 (Nov. 1952): 110.

Riesman, David. *The Lonely Crowd: A Study of the Changing American Character*. With Reuel Denney and Nathan Glazer. New Haven: Yale University Press, 1950.

Rodman, Selden. *The Amazing Year: May 1, 1945–April 30, 1946: A Diary in Verse*. New York: Scribner's, 1947.

———, ed. *A New Anthology of Modern Poetry*. New York: Modern Library, 1936.

———, ed. *One Hundred Modern Poems*. 1949. Reprinted, New York: Mentor, 1950.

Roethke, Theodore. "The Shape of the Fire." In *Mid-Century American Poets*. Ed. John Ciardi. New York: Twayne, 1950. 78–81.

Rolfe, Edwin. "Elegia," "Song," "Mystery," "Mystery II." In *Edwin Rolfe: Collected Poems*. Ed. Cary Nelson and Jefferson Hendricks. Urbana: University of Illinois Press, 1993. 85–89, 166, 220, 222.

Rolfe, Edwin, and Lester Fuller. *The Glass Room*. New York: Rinehart, 1946.

Rosenberg, Bernard, and David Manning White. *Mass Culture: The Popular Arts in America*. Glencoe, Ill.: Free Press, [1957].

Rosenthal, M. L. "Fifteen in Transit: An Interim Anthology." *New Republic* 123 (Aug. 21, 1950): 18–19.

———. "Ladies' Day on Parnassus." *Nation* 184 (Mar. 16, 1957): 239–40.

———. "Lucidity—Six Variations." *New Republic* 128 (Jan. 5, 1953): 29–30.

———. *The Modern Poets: A Critical Introduction*. New York: Oxford University Press, 1960.

Roskolenko, Harry. "A Variety of Poets." *Poetry* 82 (Apr. 1953): 34–36.

Ross, Andrew. "New Age Technoculture." In *Cultural Studies*. Ed. Lawrence Grossberg, Cary Nelson, Paula Treichler. Routledge: New York, 1992. 531–55.

———. *No Respect: Intellectuals and Popular Culture*. New York: Routledge, 1989.

Ruesch, Jurgen, and Weldon Kees. *Nonverbal Communication: Notes on the Visual Perception of Human Relations*. Berkeley: University of California Press, 1956.

Rukeyser, Muriel. "Nine Poems (for an Unborn Child)." In *Out of Silence: Selected Poems*. Ed. Kate Daniels. Evanston, Ill.: Northwestern University Press, 1992. 75–78.

———. "Song," "Tenth Elegy: Elegy in Joy." In *Mid-Century American Poets*. Ed. John Ciardi. New York: Twayne, 1950. 66, 63–65.

Salinger, Wendy, ed. *Richard Wilbur's Creation*. Ann Arbor: University of Michigan Press, 1986.

Schevill, James. "The Coastguardsman in the Fog." In *Fifteen Modern American Poets*. Ed. George P. Elliott. New York: Rinehart, 1956. 195–99.

Schwartz, Delmore. "For the One Who Would Take Man's Life in His Hands," "Starlight like Intuition Pierced the Twelve." In *Mid-Century American Poets*. Ed. John Ciardi. New York: Twayne, 1950. 288, 298–99.

Scott, Winfield Townley. "Three American Women and a German Bayonet." In *Fifteen Modern American Poets*. Ed. George P. Elliott. New York: Rinehart, 1957. 232–33.

———. "The U.S. Sailor with the Japanese Skull." In *Mid-Century American Poets*. Ed. John Ciardi. New York: Twayne, 1950. 112–13.

Seif, Morton. "Bombós." *Poetry* 73 (Feb. 1949): 272–73.

Shapiro, Karl. "Editorial Note." *Poetry* 79 (Feb. 1952): 249.

———. "Elegy for a Dead Soldier." In *Mid-Century American Poets*. Ed. John Ciardi. New York: Twayne, 1950. 93–97.

———. "The Progress of Faust." In *One Hundred Modern Poems*. Ed. Selden Rodman. New York: New American Library, 1950. 167–68.

———. *Reports of My Death*. Chapel Hill, N.C.: Algonquin Books, 1990.

Shapiro, Marianne. *Hieroglyph of Time: The Petrarchan Sestina*. Minneapolis: University of Minnesota Press, 1980.

Shelley, Robert. "Evening in the Park." In *Poems from the Iowa Poetry Workshop*. Ed. Paul Engle. Iowa City: Prairie Press, 1952. 14, 15.

Sheridan, Edward Philip. "Review: *Handbook of Turtles*." *Furioso* 8 (Spring 1953): 53–56.

Simpson, Eileen. *Poets in Their Youth: A Memoir*. New York: Farrar, Straus & Giroux, 1982.

Smith, Dave, ed. *The Pure Clear Word: Essays on the Poetry of James Wright*. Urbana: University of Illinois Press, 1982.

Smith, Richard Cándida. *Utopia and Dissent: Art, Poetry and Politics in California*. Berkeley: University of California Press, 1995.

Snodgrass, W. D. "Four Gentlemen; Two Ladies." *Hudson Review* 13 (Spring 1960): 120–31.

———. "Heart's Needle." In *Heart's Needle*. New York: Knopf, 1959. 41–62.

———. "An Interview with Elizabeth Spires." *American Poetry Review* 15 (July–Aug. 1990): 38–46.

Solomon, J. Fisher. *Discourse and Reference in the Nuclear Age*. Norman: University of Oklahoma Press, 1988.

Southworth, James G. *More Modern American Poets*. Oxford: Blackwell, 1954.

Spingarn, Lawrence P., and Sonora Babb, Thomas McGrath, Wilma Shore, and Philip Stevenson. "[Untitled Opening Statement]." *California Quarterly* 1 (1952): frontispiece.

Stauffer, Donald B. *A Short History of American Poetry*. New York: Dutton, 1974.

Stitt, Peter. *The World's Hieroglyphic Beauty: Five American Poets*. Athens: University of Georgia Press, 1985.

Stock, Robert. "Disappearing Act: *The Collected Poems of Weldon Kees*." In *Weldon Kees: A Critical Introduction*. Ed. Jim Elledge. Metuchen, N.J.: Scarecrow Press, 1985. 185–91.

Stone, Ruth. "In an Iridescent Time." In *In an Iridescent Time*. New York: Harcourt, Brace, 1958. 7.

Sutton, H. L. "News Item." *Poetry* 74 (June 1949): 143.

Swenson, May. "Any Object." In *Another Animal*. In *Poets of Today*, vol. 1. New York: Scribner's 1954. 163.

Tate, Allen. "Introduction." *Modern Verse in English, 1900–1950*. Ed. David Cecil and Allen Tate. New York: Macmillan, 1958. 39–48.

———. "Preface." *Libretto for the Republic of Liberia* by Melvin B. Tolson. New York: Twayne, 1953.

Taylor, Henry. "Two Worlds Taken as They Come: Richard Wilbur's *Waking to*

Sleep." In *Richard Wilbur's Creation,* ed. Wendy Salinger. Ann Arbor: University of Michigan Press, 1983. 88–100.

Thompson, E. P. "A Place Called Choice." *California Quarterly* 1 (Fall 1951, Winter 1952): 12–24, 46–55.

Tolson, Melvin B. *Caviar and Cabbage: Selected Columns.* Columbia: University of Missouri Press, 1982.

———. *"Harlem Galley" and Other Poems by Melvin B. Tolson.* Ed. Raymond Nelson. Charlottesville: University of Virginia Press, 1999.

———. "Ti (from *Libretto for the Republic of Liberia*)." *Poetry* 76 (July 1950): 208–15.

Van Duyn, Mona. "Three Valentines for the Wide World," "Toward a Definition of Marriage." In *A Time of Bees.* Chapel Hill: University of North Carolina Press, 1964. 1–3, 13–15.

Vaughn, Robert. "A Sestina on Ezra Pound." *Western Review* 23 (Autumn 1958): 62.

Vendler, Helen. "Elizabeth Bishop." In *Part of Nature, Part of Us.* Cambridge: Harvard University Press, 1980. 97–110.

Vidal, Gore. *Palimpsest: A Memoir.* New York: Random House, 1995.

Vidich, Arthur J., and Joseph Bensman. *Small Town in Mass Society: Class, Power, and Religion in a Rural Community.* Princeton: Princeton University Press, 1958.

Viereck, Peter. "The Education of a Poet." *Atlantic* 187 (Mar. 1951): 75–77.

———. "*Vale* from Carthage." In *Mid-Century American Poets.* Ed. John Ciardi. New York: Twayne, 1950. 33–34.

Villa, José García. "Theseus." *Poetry* 81 (Oct. 1952): 82.

Vivas, Eliseo. "The Neo-Aristotleians of Chicago." *Sewanee Review* 61 (Winter 1953): 136–49.

Von Hallberg, Robert. *Poetry, Politics and Intellectuals.* Vol. 8 of *The Cambridge History of American Literature.* Ed. Sacvan Bercovitch. Cambridge: Cambridge University Press, 1996.

Wald, Alan M. "The 1930s Left in U.S. Literature Reconsidered." In *Radical Revisions: Rereading 1930s Culture.* Ed. Bill Mullen and Sherry Lee Linkon. Urbana: University of Illinois Press, 1996. 8–23.

Warren, Robert Penn. "To a Little Girl, One Year Old, in a Ruined Fortress (to Rosanna)." In *Promises: Poems, 1954–1956.* New York: Random House, 1957. 23–28.

Weiss, T. "To Penny When She Comes of Reading Age." In *The Catch.* New York: Twayne, 1951. 38–39.

Wheelock, John Hall. "The Poet in the Atomic Age." In *Poets of Today,* vol. 3. New York: Scriber's, 1957. 3–17.

Whitfield, Stephen J. *The Culture of the Cold War.* Baltimore: Johns Hopkins University Press, 1991.

Whittemore, Reed. "Four Men and Three Women." *Sewanee Review* 58 (Autumn 1950): 720–32.

———. "Lines Composed upon Reading an Announcement by Civil Defense Authorities Recommending That I Build a Bombshelter in My Backyard." In *An American Takes a Walk and Other Poems.* Minneapolis: University of Minnesota Press, 1956. 4.

———. "The 'Modern Idiom' of Poetry, and All That." *Yale Review* 46 (Mar. 1957): 357–71.

———. "Verse." *Furioso* 6 (Spring 1951): 80–82.

Wilbur, Richard. "An Interview with Richard Wilbur." By Philip Dacey. *Crazy Horse* 15 (Fall 1974): 37–44.

———. "Natural Song." *American Letters* 1.2 (1949): 76.

———. *New and Collected Poems.* San Diego: Harcourt Brace Jovanovich, 1988.

———. "Robert Graves's New Volume." *Poetry* 87 (Dec. 1955): 175–79.

———. "Tears for the Rich." *American Letters* 1 (Dec. 1948): 12.

———. "We," "Weather Bird." *Poetry* 73 (Nov. 1948): 127–28, 129–30.

Williams, William Carlos. "Asphodel, That Greeny Flower." In *Pictures for Breughel and Other Poems.* New York: New Directions, 1962. 153–82.

———. "Paterson Book V: The River of Heaven." *Poetry* 81 (Oct. 1952): 89–90.

Wilson, Rob. *American Sublime: The Genealogy of a Poetic Genre.* Madison: University of Wisconsin Press, 1991.

Wimsatt, W. K. "The Concrete Universal." *PMLA* 62 (Mar. 1947): 212–39.

Wimsatt, W. K., and Monroe Beardsley. "The Intentional Fallacy." In *The Verbal Icon: Studies in the Meaning of Poetry.* Lexington: University of Kentucky Press, 1954. 3–20.

Wollen, Peter. "Introduction." *Visual Display: Culture Beyond Appearances.* Ed. Lynne Cooke and Peter Wollen. Seattle: Bay Press, 1995. 9–13.

Woodson, Jon Stanton. "Melvin Tolson and the Art of Being Difficult." In *Black American Poets between Worlds, 1940–1960.* Ed. R. Baxter Miller. Knoxville: University of Tennessee Press, 1986. 19–42.

Wright, James. "A Presentation of Two Birds to My Son," "Mutterings over the Crib of a Deaf Child," "A Call from the Front Porch." In *The Green Wall.* New Haven: Yale University Press, 1957. 34–35, 68–69, 89–90.

Zahn, Curtis. "Officers, Gentlemen, Reluctant Violence." *California Quarterly* 1 (Autumn 1951): 41–42.

Index

Edward Brunner is professor of English at Southern Illinois University, Carbondale. He is the author of *Splendid Failure: Hart Crane and the Making of "The Bridge"* and *Poetry as Labor and Privilege: The Writings of W. S. Merwin,* also published by the University of Illinois Press.

Typeset in 9/13 ITC Stone Serif
with Stomper display
Designed by Paula Newcomb
Composed by Barbara Evans
at the University of Illinois Press
Manufactured by Thomson-Shore, Inc.

University of Illinois Press
1325 South Oak Street
Champaign, IL 61820-6903
www.press.uillinois.edu